KUDOS

Jerry Foster's volunteer support of the Sheriff's Office was invaluable, culminating in the success of many searches and rescues. Jerry spent much of his time working with youth inspiring them to be better citizens. Jerry's good work and volunteerism will be long remembered in Maricopa County.

Dick Godbehere - Maricopa County Sheriff, 1985-88

Hero or Hellion; Trailblazer or Hell-raiser, Jerry Foster lived life large. An early mistake and quest for redemption motivated an exhilarating life of energy, service and American spirit. Read this book.

Barbara Barrett - Former US Ambassador to Finland

Jerry is truly one of the most unique characters ever to hit television news - one of a kind. His passion and determination to be first with the best either drove you crazy or drove you to new heights of news coverage - it all depended on the day

Jim Willi - Principal & Senior VP of Multimedia
Innovation and former KPNX News Director

Jerry Foster and Sky 12 were one and the same. God help anyone in their way of getting the story. He defined television news in the Phoenix Valley, setting the bar for every other news operation in the United States.

Al Buch - Former KPNX News Director

Without question, Jerry's passion to serve, along with his unbelievable pilot abilities, saved the lives of many people during the time he assisted the Maricopa County Sheriff's Office. He was always there; ready, willing and more than capable of making a difference in so many search and rescue operations, it's hard to detail them all in a single book. As we became good friends through the years, I saw how deeply personally Jerry took each mission. He never gave up and was a driving force in his life … and ultimately in mine.

Larry Black - Former Deputy Chief, Maricopa County
Sheriff's Office

Jerry Foster's honesty in telling his story tugs at your heart. From his devastating lows to the euphoric highs, he has lived it all. An ordinary guy and an almost unwilling celebrity, Jerry lived his "both sides of the street" as only he could.

Fred Dees - Former Police Chief, Gilbert Arizona

As this book reveals the events that shaped his life, it soon becomes apparent that Jerry Foster's ego was tempered by the demons that chased him relentlessly. His actions made him a hero, his honesty makes him human.

Lana Swearingen - Author, We Were Army Wives

How to sum up flying six years, seven days a week with Jerry: "If you"re not good, stay home ..." When we took off we seldom knew what we would encounter or even if we would make it back. It was an inherently dangerous job, in an era with few limitations as to what we could do with a helicopter. Jerry did not just fly a helicopter, he strapped it on and became one with it. Absolutely an "A" game pilot who was at his best when the situations were most dangerous.

Bryan Neumeister - Certified Audio & Video
Forensic Expert and Former KPNX photographer

Whether or not you are one of the thousands of Jerry Foster fans, Earthbound Misfit is a book worth reading. It's about a life lived to its fullest. During his 20 years as a helicopter pilot and reporter in Phoenix, Foster participated in news, but more importantly, in countless rescues, spending over 20,000 hours in the air. You will read an honest portrayal of his aspirations, fears and accomplishments. He truly is a modern hero and fondly remembered by legions of people who followed his flights and heroic rescues.
Don Sorchych - Publisher & Editor, Sonoran News

Jerry foster is a true Arizona hero. I worked with Jerry in the early 1980s. In addition to our news gathering duties, Jerry and I were volunteer divers with the Sheriff's office and assisted with search and rescue activities on the lakes and rivers. I'd film it all, then we did live reports from the helicopter for "Action News" later. These are the scenes that make this book a must-read for a window into a time when helicopter news gathering was being established.
Chuck Emmert - Former KPNX photographer

After an incredible career laced with controversy, Jerry Foster flew off into the sunset, only to leave his fans wondering "what ever happened to ...." I am now thrilled to see that in *Earthbound Misfit*, Jerry personally takes the reader through his amazing journey from humble beginnings, to overcoming his mistakes, his rise to celebrity status, eventual fall from grace and the years that followed. It is an amazing story for not only those who recognize the name, but anyone who enjoys true stories of adventure. What makes this a real gem is how Jerry artfully turns his book into a life lesson on the importance of overcoming one's mistakes and including those closest to you in your struggles. *Earthbound Misfit* finally fills in the amazing story behind one of Arizona's most controversial, but best known and respected television personalities.
Dave Boehmer - Arizona native and Jerry Foster fan

EARTHBOUND
M I S F I T

JERRY FOSTER

with
DEE DEES

LifeGuides Press

ISBN: 978-0-9667829-5-0

Book design by Dee Dees
Cover design by Dave Boehmer
Website: www.sky12.tv by Andryea Foster

Published by
LifeGuides Press
Gilbert, AZ 85295
480 703-1244

Photo Credits:
Cover photo by Tom Story
Superstition Mountains - p. 448   Photo by Jeff Lewis
Lake Powell Moon - p. 509   Photo by Dave Boehmer

Printed in the United States of America

DEDICATION

For Linda who has stood by me,

Mom and Dad who were my heroes

*and Steve Ward, who contributed so much
and then left us too soon*

ACKNOWLEDGEMENTS

There is no doubt this book would not have been completed without the nudging and support of my family, especially my wife Linda, who patiently let me bounce ideas off her, and my daughter Andryea, who encouraged the idea of the book from the beginning.

I also thank my extended family; my Aunt Wanda Foster Ward, cousins Steve and Jane Ward, and ex-wife Dianna Conklin, for bringing back so many memories and helping me get the facts straight. Thanks to my good friend Buzz Stalcup for always being there.

I appreciate so much my former co-workers and partners, for their input and support; especially Susan Sorg and Bryan Neumeister. Also thanks to John Bass, Chuck Emmert, Bill and Bonnie Leverton, Al Buch, Jim Willi, Kent Dana and Ed Sharpe, for contributing their memories of our times together. Many of the photos in this book were taken by Bryan, Chuck or John.

Thanks go out to Dr. Jim Schamadan for his help with the AMES section, former DPS officers Clarence Forbey and Tom Armstrong, former MCSO deputies Larry Black and David Paul, former Police Chief Fred Dees, and pilot Len Clements for their contributions, and to Arizona Republic columnist E.J. Montini for the insightful quote from his column.

A special thanks also to Michael Goldwater for his proofreading expertise, and Ed Mell and Dave Boehmer for their assistance with the cover design.

I so appreciate Dee Dees, who stuck with me when the project became much bigger and took much longer than either of us anticipated. The book could not have been completed without her.

There are probably some I've missed, and if so, please know that I thank you all for your love, support and help throughout the process.

Jerry Foster

Thanks first to Jerry Foster for trusting me with his story. When I only knew him from his TV news days, I saw a hero because of his life-saving adventures. I saw a celebrity, because he was known throughout the state of Arizona. I saw a role model because our kids adored him and our son went on to become a helicopter pilot "just like Jerry." Through this process of working with Jerry and discovering the man behind the myth, none of those visions have diminished. However, I discovered that he is also a writer, as he actually wrote the stories, while my role was to help him turn them into a book. More importantly, I now know him as an ordinary guy who made mistakes along the way, owned up to them and accepted the consequences. I know a man who is more gentle and sensitive than the "hotshot" flyboy image the media labeled him. And I know a man I'm now proud to call a friend.

I also thank my husband Fred, who was immensely supportive and offered insight from a cop's point of view, and my kids, Joel and Jennifer, for being supportive of all my endeavors throughout the years.

Thanks to Lana Swearingen for her proofreading expertise, and to Bryan Neumeister for being patient when I struggled with the "techie" part of photographs.

And I add my thanks to all those mentioned by Jerry, who were so forthcoming with their stories and put up with my endless emails and questions.

Dee Dees

FOREWORD

Of those who could be called Arizona celebrities—Stevie Nicks, Linda Ronstadt, Mo Udall, Rose Mofford, and my own father, Barry Goldwater—there is a man you won't find on any national list, but who is well-known to anyone who lived in Phoenix during the 1970s and '80s: Jerry Foster.

For two decades Jerry flew around the state reporting the news, and often making the news as he plucked hikers from mountains and victims from raging waters. He was often a hero, and just as often a heretic, as he occasionally skirted FAA regulations.

Jerry was a reluctant celebrity, having come from a background of rough miners and poverty, yet he grew into the role and was able to comfortably hobnob with actors, musicians, politicians and others. One of his favorite anecdotes relates leaving a New Years Eve party at Dad's home, changing from his tux into jeans, and going on a late night ride with the Dirty Dozen motorcycle clan. As he puts it, he "walked both sides of the street."

I came to know Jerry in 1970 when he taught my dad, who already had licenses for a wide variety of aircraft, to fly a helicopter. From that point on the two became good friends and flying buddies. While Dad got a kick out of watching Jerry land the helicopter on the driveway in front of the house, Mom would often get annoyed at the noise and the dust being kicked up.

Jerry often flew Dad around Arizona on campaigns, or to take a break from politics and enjoy the quiet beauty of Lake Powell and the Indian reservations. I went along on one exciting flight where

Jerry flew low and fast over the desert, demonstrating how pilots flew missions in Vietnam.

Though his FAA issues would eventually contribute to his retirement, Jerry always had the best of intentions and never flew in a way that was a danger to himself or others. Dad flew with him for over 20 years and trusted Jerry with his life.

Jerry's story is one of overcoming his past, moving on to a bright future, and then doing it all over again. It's not just the story of a hero, it's also the story of an everyday guy who made mistakes and rose above them. I spoke with Dad one time about Jerry's problems with the military and he said, "...*that happened a long time ago and he was just a kid. I did the same thing when I was a kid, I just didn't get caught. He's a grown man now and I'm proud to call him a friend.*"

So am I.

Michael Goldwater

TABLE OF CONTENTS

PROLOGUE

October 21, 1959 - Camp Pendleton, California

0400 hours

Two hours until reveille. I was in a private room isolated from my barracks; a room reserved for guests and outcasts. I was not a guest. I had been living a nightmare for months, and was still in disbelief that this could be happening.

I had lain flat on my back for most of the night; not sleeping, barely moving, consumed by what was facing me in the morning. So many thoughts racing through my mind; so many questions.

What I had done was wrong—there was no denying that—and today the final justice would be carried out. Yesterday I had been released from the Marine Corps Brig at Camp Pendleton and transferred back to my company for discharge. They couldn't just give me a quiet sendoff; the Corp has a ceremony for everything. In a few hours I would be standing at attention in front of a company of my fellow Marines. Behind me would be two armed Marine MPs. To them it was a ceremony. To me it was an execution.

My thoughts went back to how I came to be here. As a toddler playing with toys, I was drawn to the ones having to do with the military. I marched my little toy soldiers through the living room and fought imaginary battles in my mind. World War II was in full swing and America's patriotism was at an all-time high. My dad was a decorated Marine hero who served in the South Pacific—not only with honor—but with distinction. He was my *hero*! My uncles and cousins were all serving and fighting in the military. I was raised and expected to become a Marine.

0550 hours

As I lay in that dark room, I could see, feel and hear the morning starting to come alive. Soon, bugles would blare, lights would come on, and the shuffling and grumbling of sleepy men would begin. The speaker system would loudly announce that a special formation would be held on the parade field at 0650 hours. More than a hundred Marines in their barracks would all be trying to do the same thing at the same time, and they would get it done. It's called teamwork. I had been separated from my unit for nearly six months. I was no longer a part of the team.

0557 hours

I watched the minutes ticking by like a death row inmate waiting for his execution; waiting, dreading and steeling myself for an experience I knew was going to be painfully humiliating. *Any minute now they'll come for me.* I had been transferred to this company specifically for discharge. I didn't know any of the men personally, but whether I knew them or not made no difference. This was a company of United States Marines, and I would soon be standing in front of them as an example of a "misfit." I was considered unfit to wear the uniform of a brother Marine. I closed my eyes and wanted so badly to be someone else, and anywhere else but here. How could I have let this happen? I thought back to five months ago.

May 11, 1959

Our company had just returned from a three-day combat march around the base, and we were all ready for some fun. It had been a good training exercise including a beach assault from a Navy landing craft. We were exhilarated, and emotions ran high in the company as we were dismissed for the weekend. I was on top of the world when I headed out the main gate with a carload of buddies, some of whom were hooking a ride to San Diego.

By Saturday evening our group had dwindled down to three soldiers and we had worked our way back to Oceanside. Late that night we still had plenty of party energy left, but had run out of beer and money. We discussed how to get more of either or both. We settled on a plan—one that would become the biggest mistake of my life.

It had seemed so simple: break into a tavern or bar, grab a case of beer and run. They'd never miss a case of beer. We found a little cocktail and dinner place that was closed for the evening. It was perfect.

I parked my car in the alley behind the restaurant and we looked for a way in. After several minutes of searching, we came across an unlocked skylight. I was the smallest, so was elected to go through the opening and unlock the door for the others. Once inside, the place was ours. We grabbed two cases of beer and the petty cash box with about 100 dollars in it. We loaded it all into my car and were gone. Laughing and joking as we raced away, we never gave a thought to consequences. As we continued partying through the weekend, I had no idea my life would be changed forever. Young, dumb and feeling invincible, we reported for duty Monday morning.

Several days later I was called to the Sergeant Major's office. "Private Foster, these two detectives from the Oceanside Police Department have a warrant for your arrest."

I felt like I had been kicked in the gut. It had never occurred to me that we would be caught.

"You're charged with second degree burglary, which is a felony," the detective said.

I was handcuffed and led out to a patrol car. The ride to Oceanside was a blur, as I was in disbelief that this was happening. The detective in the passenger seat turned around and hassled me during the drive.

"Somebody saw your car in the alley and thought it looked suspicious," he said. "He was concerned enough to write down the license number. Did you really think you would get away with it?"

I remained silent, but he wasn't giving up.

"Come on, Marine, you know we gotcha! Who helped you pull that off?"

"Sir, I acted alone," I replied. Marines don't rat on fellow Marines.

October 21 - 0600 hours

"Reveille! Reveille! All hands heave to and trice up. Hold a clean sweep down, fore and aft. Attention Headquarters Company! There will be a special formation on the parade field at 0645."

As far as I was concerned, the base speakers were blaring out my death sentence. I got off the bed and looked in the mirror, wondering if I'd ever see myself the same again. I dressed in a pair of jeans and a light sweater; the only clothes still in my possession. After I was arrested someone had been detailed to pack up my personal gear, which consisted of clothes and a shaving kit crammed into two cardboard boxes. My uniforms, insignias, any military gear, were all gone. I smirked, thinking, "at least they didn't get my dog tags."

Two sharp raps on the door were followed by the company Master Sergeant entering with a cup of coffee in his hand. He held it out to me with a smile and said, "Private Foster, we aren't even gonna feed you breakfast this morning. In a few minutes you'll be escorted in front of Headquarters Company for a release ceremony. Your personal gear will be loaded in the jeep. Good luck, son!"

With that terse comment, he was out the door. I still felt like I was heading for an execution.

Parade Grounds - 0655 hours

We made the short drive to the parade grounds in a military police jeep. I sat next to the driver and the Sergeant Major sat in the back seat with my two boxes of personal effects. The jeep came to a halt behind the company of Marines standing at attention. I was marched around to the front of the formation and halted front and center between the troops and the Captain.

"Sir, reporting with the prisoner as ordered," barked the Sergeant Major.

The Company Commander ordered, "Sergeant Major, you will escort your prisoner to the main gate, where you will hand him his separation papers and see that he departs this post. You will then report to me with his dog tags."

The Sergeant Major saluted as he replied, "Yes, Sir."

I was stunned! I didn't remember much after the 'dog tags' statement. I had thought I would be keeping those. I desperately wanted to hang on to some remembrance of my time in the Corp.

As the MP jeep pulled up behind us, the company of men stood at ease. I thought that was unusual, but the reason soon became clear.

Sergeant Major shouted, "Company ... Atten-SHUN! ABOUT FACE!"

The entire company turned their backs to me. We all stood there for at least a minute. It felt like hours. The message was clear as I looked at the backs of the formation. I was ashamed of myself then, and as I write this chapter today I am still ashamed and embarrassed.

While the Marine Company stood at rigid attention, I was stowed into the jeep and driven off the parade field. No one spoke a word during the 10-minute ride to the gate. This was the blackest day of my life, and I had no idea how my record might affect my future.

During that short drive, I looked back over the past six months. I had burglarized a bar, been arrested and convicted. I had pled guilty to the burglary and insisted I had acted alone. There was no trying to get away with it. I was sentenced to four months at a county work farm and five years probation. After receiving a month off for good behavior, I was released to the Marine Corps and brought back to Camp Pendleton. There I spent three weeks in the Marine Brig and working on a chain gang, while they decided what to do with me. Now it had been decided. In a few minutes, after almost six months of confinement, I would again be a free man. What I didn't know, was that I would never be free of the guilt and shame of my crime and discharge.

We arrived at the main gate and stopped behind the guard shack. I got out, unloaded my boxes and set them on the ground. I turned to face the Sergeant Major, who was holding his hand out, palm up. I had already anticipated this exchange. I returned his pleasant smile and said, "A Marine would tell you to take 'em if you can."

He just responded, "Jerry, you're not a Marine anymore, son."

He was firm but respectful, and didn't try to make me feel any worse than I did. A big, burly guy and a 30-year veteran, that Sergeant Major was the kind of man I had once hoped to become.

I was close to tears as I handed him my dog tags, but he was in the jeep and gone before my eyes could even cloud over.

A lost, lonely feeling came over me as I stared down at the two small cardboard boxes. Memories of all the manly things my Dad had taught me—shooting, fishing, fighting ... all that "never give up" stuff—surged back into my consciousness. What would he say now? My thoughts turned to my aunts, uncles and friends. I wondered how I could face them. Being a Marine was all I knew.

"I love you, sweetheart."

I was so engrossed in my own thoughts I hadn't even heard Mom walk up. I turned and gave her my bravest smile, and we hugged for a long time. Both of us were emotionally overcome by the events of the past months.

"I'm sorry Mom, I really blew it this time."

Nothing but my mother's love could have motivated me at such a low time in my life. Norma Ellen Foster was 33 years old and beautiful, which hadn't gone unnoticed by the guys in the guard shack. The red convertible she drove didn't hurt her image, either. What those Marines didn't know was, despite the image she portrayed, she had experienced her own hard knocks in life. She had been just 15 when I was born, and we'd had to grow up together.

We sat in her 1954 Oldsmobile for a while and talked over some options. We cried together, laughed together, and eventually came up with a plan. I promised her I would start all over, and she promised me we would see it through together.

As we drove out of the parking area, the guards smiled and waved, and for a brief moment, everything seemed normal. For just a moment, I felt hopeful that this ordeal could be put behind me and I could move on with my life.

I had no way of knowing I would *never* be able to put this painful memory in the past. In some ways I never left those parade grounds. I still carry the indelible memories of that brief period in my history; from the surreal images of the Marines turning their backs to me, to the sting of the Sergeant Major's words, to my vow to make a fresh start. The shame would lie dormant for a while, then return to haunt me time and time again. It would come to the forefront of my consciousness during a background check, in my nightmares, or in the constant fear that others would find out. In the end, it would contribute to my ultimate downfall.

But at that moment, I was safely tucked under the wing of love and security. Mom and I hit the road and headed for Phoenix.

1957

PART ONE

Chapter 1

Humble beginning

Mom and me

My mother, Norma Ellen Davis, had come from Monahans, Texas, born into a tribe of oil field workers who drifted around from one location to another in search of work. At some point the family switched to mining as a trade and continued the nomadic lifestyle. Mom was the third of four children born to John R. and Stella Davis. She was always close to her older siblings, Garlin and Lucille, and her younger brother, Phill. The family moved around so much that Mom only attended school to the third grade.

John Davis was a Baptist minister and Stella Davis was just a vague memory to Mom, since Stella and her last child both died as she was giving birth. When Norma's older brother Garlin went into the Army, the family split up. Fourteen-year-old Norma followed Garlin to Los Angeles where he was stationed.

Norma soon met Casmir "Swifty" Malin, a good-looking Polish fellow who rode a motorcycle. He left her with a large tattoo on her left arm and pregnant at fourteen. She didn't talk much about this time of her life, but I know she had much adversity to deal with at a time that wasn't so forgiving of such behavior. Yet a photo of her, with "Norma Malin" written on the back, shows a happy young girl.

I was born in 1940 in Los Angeles. Swifty had moved on, and Mom and I traveled with aunts and uncles to various mining camps for work. She was an excellent cook, and her engaging personality made it easy for her to make new friends wherever she went. She was also tough and overcame the challenges to make a comfortable life for us. We were gypsies, Mom and me.

I clearly remember one incident in the desert when Mom and I were caught in a flash flood. Mom got us out of the car and onto the roof. I clung to her, screaming "Don't drop me, Mommy!"

People were watching from both sides of the flooded road as she made her way through the swiftly moving water. I was terrified and still remember her calming words as she held me tightly, "Be brave Jerry. I won't drop you, baby."

I was about four years old when Mom left me with a minister and his wife in Oceanside, California. Brother and Sister Wilcox were pastors for a Pentecostal church. The "holy rollers" congregation scared me to death with all their yelling, singing, falling on the floor and speaking in tongues during services. The Wilcoxes were strict disciplinarians who baptized me and set out to save my soul with spiritual guidance. I remember yelling defiantly at them "I don't want to be a Christian; I want to be a Marine!" Even at that young age I was under the Marine influence. Mr. Wilcox worked at Camp Pendleton, and I loved seeing the men in their sharp uniforms.

Little Marine

I stayed with them for a year and my mother would visit when she could. I felt complete and utter loneliness between her visits. I had no idea who she was with or what she was doing during this time.

One glorious day, Mom came to get me. She said she had a new husband, I had a new dad, and we were all going to live together as a family. Bryan Pace Foster was wearing his Marine dress blues when I first shook his hand and called him "Dad." He went by his middle name, Pace, but his family called him Bryan. Throughout his life, Dad was a restless person; always looking for the next adventure, always wanting to move on.

Pace had to take on a lot of responsibility at an early age, his own father being a heavy drinker who would disappear for days at a time. He was the oldest of the kids, and his mother depended on him for everything. My Aunt Wanda remembers, "*He was just like a dad to me. He was nine years older and did the things a dad would have done. When I was five I broke my collarbone, and he carried me for a mile home to our mother. Then he had to go back to the ranch for a horse and ride to Duncan to find our father, wherever he was. Pace did things like that for me all my life. I just thought he was the greatest.*"

Born in Arkansas in 1913, Pace was still a child when his family moved to Virden, New Mexico, within spitting distance of the Arizona state line. They had a little farm, and his uncles were partners in the Day-Foster ranch. The Days were the parents of future Supreme Court Justice Sandra Day O'Connor.

According to Aunt Wanda, her brother could work like the devil, but just didn't want to be a farmer. Beginning at a young age, he had been doing his father's work for years. But when he was fourteen, he took off for California to work for his uncle at Shell Oil, and was driving a truck for them when he was sixteen. He'd go back and forth between California and New Mexico during his late teens.

During one of his stints in Arizona, when he was eighteen or nineteen, he worked as a cook in Florence and married a woman nine years older than himself. It was probably a marriage of convenience, because he had a house and she had a truck. It didn't last long, and he left her after a couple of years.

Pace continued moving around for several years, working in mines in Patagonia, AZ, during his mid-twenties. In 1937 he married a woman named Gladys in Phoenix and moved to Los Angeles. Almost immediately after the attack on Pearl Harbor, Pace applied to join the Marines and was in boot camp within two months. The following August, he was part of the campaign to capture the airfield on Guadalcanal. After a three-month R&R in New Zealand to recuperate from a broken arm, he rejoined his battalion and saw action at Tarawa and Iwo Jima.

While Pace was overseas, Gladys was living in Los Angeles. My aunt Wanda lived with her for a time, since her husband, Mack, was also in the service. During a period when the ship was back in San Diego, the two men made the three-hour drive up every two weeks to visit their wives. During one of those trips, Pace met my mom.

Aunt Wanda told me, *"He met your mother and really fell for her. He didn't even go visit Gladys anymore after that, and it seemed like their marriage was over. After he was shipped out again, he wrote my mother a letter and told her that "this was the one." He wrote 'I took Norma down to Mexico and told her I got a quick Mexican divorce, and I married her while we were there. I played a dirty trick on her; it's not legal, but she doesn't know it. I hope she's waiting for me when I get back.'*

"Well, when Norma found out that Pace married her without having a divorce she was furious and went off and married the first guy she met. You were about three or four at that time. When Pace came back and tried to go get her, he found out she'd married someone else. So he went back to Gladys, who'd had a baby by another man while he was gone. Pace got a job running a big farm in Xavier and hired his brother Chet to work for him. Pretty soon, once your mother realized he still wanted her, she divorced her husband and came up there to see him. That was it. He took off with her, turning his foreman job over to Chet."

Pace Foster was not only charming to the women, but he could convince anyone of just about anything. Years later he would convince a major construction company that he was a geologist, which would be the beginning of a new career for him.

From the time he came into my life when I was five, Pace Foster was always larger-than-life to me. He had the aura of a hero about him. He was a tough disciplinarian, but a good father, and I knew he loved me. I worshiped him and grew up

Bryan Pace Foster - my new Dad

with a strong desire to make him proud of me.

I was excited to have the holy-rollercoaster nightmare behind me, and to be with my family, especially now that it included a dad! We followed the work, and we lived in houses or trailer parks at mining camps. Anyone could be a miner in the 1940s; you only had to work hard, live a gypsy lifestyle and not be afraid of working underground.

We lived all over the western United States, following the mining jobs in Idaho, Oregon, California, Nevada, Arizona and New Mexico. I went to fourteen public schools and two private schools. We moved around so much that I couldn't reconstruct my childhood in terms of age and location without referring to old report cards and family letters my mother kept.

We lived paycheck-to-paycheck and Dad would sometimes have to get a loan from the mine owner. When we could afford it, the entire group of families would get together to see a movie, which was a huge treat. The miners were always welcoming and friendly, and people took care of each other back in those days. Dad was usually the manager or a laborer and Mom would work as a cook or waitress if the town was big enough for a café. Sometimes she was just a full-time mom. But money was always tight and she needed to work whenever she could. Uncle Phill and Uncle Garlin were always around, either living with us or somewhere nearby. The mining community was very close. There were many parties with family and friends, although we were never in one place long enough to make lasting friendships.

Besides the parties and good times, there was also a lot of drinking, arguing and fighting going on. Mom and Dad had some nasty, knock-down drag-outs when they'd had too much to drink. I'd often go to bed scared to death of the screaming and arguing, and the next morning one or the other of them may have had scratches and bruises. It took a lot to make Dad get physical, and Mom was capable of pushing those buttons. They tried hard to keep me out of it, but I always knew what was happening.

Dad and my uncles were tough guys, especially Uncle Phill, who was the youngest and toughest. There were always bar fights, drinking and hell-raising. I wanted to grow up just like them, but my biggest dream was to grow up to be a Marine.

Our nomadic lifestyle caused me to miss several semesters of school. Mom tried to home-school me, but struggled with it, having no more than a third-grade education herself. As a result, I did poorly in public school. I would later do better in military school because discipline was swift and strictly enforced. I paid attention to what I respected, and I had a healthy respect for the paddle.

I was always the new kid in school. The older I got, the more I had to defend myself against bullies wanting to make my life uncomfortable. The first time I came home crying from a beating, Dad said, "That's not what a Marine would do. You never turn and run, you stand and fight." He took me in the back yard and taught me how to fight. He bought boxing gloves and showed me how to use them. When my friends came over Dad taught us all how to fight.

It was important to him to be a good father, and he tried hard to do all the right things. But he was not affectionate; we never hugged and there was no demonstration of love. I often wished he could be more like my uncles Phill or Garlin. They always had time for me, and weren't afraid to show their love; especially Phill, who was always there when I needed him.

Sometimes, when one of my uncles showed me affection, I would feel the tension with my dad. He wanted to make me tough, and felt like they were making me soft. It was uncomfortable and I sometimes felt intimidated by him, but I also wanted to grow up to be just like him. Whenever Dad's war buddies came by, I listened to their stories of combat

With Uncle Phill

adventures in the South Pacific. Dad was a true warrior who had served in the First Marine Raider Battalion. His buddies showed him a lot of respect and when they left, it would be with a handshake and hug. I wanted the same.

My mother felt she had to protect me from Pace as much as she could. He had a fierce temper, but he wasn't abusive and seldom smacked me out of anger. Their opposing views on how to raise me was another point of contention between them, causing frequent arguments. Dad wanted me to grow up and be a man. Mom did her best to keep me safe and happy, and I always felt we were partners in this crazy world.

Fortunately, Dad's desire to be a good father expressed itself in other ways besides tough discipline, and we had many good times. There was a beautiful lake near one Idaho camp where we lived, and Dad took me fishing, teaching me how to catch two fish on a line. We hunted a lot, killing our prey only to eat. He had taught me how to shoot, and after I bested him one day during target practice, he said he was real proud of me for being a better shot than he was. That was an exciting day for me.

I started fourth grade in Wallace, Idaho. Then Dad got a job running a lumber camp so far back in the snowy mountains that I missed most of the school year. When we moved back to Wallace, Mom bought a little restaurant there called the "Banquet Café."

My parents fought a lot during this time and eventually I was sent to Marymount Military Academy, in Tacoma, Washington. I never really knew why, but I was eager to go. I didn't like all the fighting going on at home and wanted to get out of the middle of it. Dad told me how the military training would make me a better Marine. Mom wasn't crazy about the idea, but she could see the benefit, and let me go.

I attended Marymount Military Academy the second semester of the fifth grade, and my grades began improving right away. The school was owned by the Catholic Church and operated by an order of nuns. It didn't take long for me to catch on that the nuns' discipline was swift and stinging. Sister Mary Ralph was a teacher and my dormitory mother. Talk back to her and you were hauled to her office and bent over for the paddle. But she was also the first one to hold and soothe the loneliness of a homesick, young boy.

The only visitor I had that semester was Uncle Phill. He picked me up on a Sunday and we had a great day together. When the day was over, I couldn't stand the thought of him leaving. I broke down and wouldn't turn loose of his neck. "Please take me with you," I pleaded.

We went back to his car and had a good talk and a few hugs. He promised me that next year I could go back to school in Wallace, and we would all be together again. I had to stick it out for the rest of this school year and get my grades up.

I made it through the semester, but not without a tussle. One of my classmates from Virginia made a comment about how the "coal people" knew their place in the South, referring to my mining background. I hit him so hard he saw stars. We both got the paddle.

I wasn't raised as Catholic and it was difficult for me to get used to the format of the school routine, which leaned more toward religion than military. We were required to attend Mass in the morning and Chapel after dinner to recite the Rosary. That was hard for me because, though it was the same story of Jesus, it was told in a different way. My dislike was not of the religion, but of having it shoved down my throat every morning and evening. I wasn't hurt at all by the experience; I just had a strong dislike for the control they had over me.

We wore uniforms and marched around on the parade grounds. On Sunday evenings we paraded around for the parents who were dropping off their kids for another week. I liked marching and excelled to the point of being named Squad Leader. We had a commandant and a sergeant, both retired military, whom I liked and respected.

I left Marymount at the end of the school year and took away some good memories and average grades. I was ecstatic to get back to Wallace, and I spent that summer working with Dad at the lumber company. He cut the trees down with a chain saw and trimmed off the branches. I would use a pole to mark off the length of the logs so they could be cut into ten-foot lengths. It worked well until I stepped on a beehive from one of the fallen trees.

The bees swarmed all over me. I couldn't get away from them until Dad carried me away and beat them off with his shirt. I had several hundred stings all over my body. Dad had one. He took me to the camp medic who rubbed me down with a foul smelling goop. Two days later I was up and around, but our tree cutting days were over. We said goodbye to Idaho before the snow came.

Dad took a job in Telluride, Colorado, and I enrolled in school there, but it wouldn't be for long. Three months later we moved to Albuquerque, New Mexico, and said goodbye to the mines.

Trying something entirely new, Dad accepted a job managing a stockyard and auction. We lived just south of the Rio Grande River on South Iseletta Road, a predominately Hispanic area. I was the only white kid at Old Armijo School. At that time much of the teachers' instruction had to be in Spanish. I made friends and fit in as well as I could. One good friend was Bobby Cordova. Like me, he was from a rough neighborhood. We went to the local movie theater on Saturdays because it was a double feature with one movie in English. The rest of the week they were all in Spanish. A few years later Bobby and his family would have an unexpected impact on my life.

Our small, one-bedroom house was off the main road and next to a stockyard full of cows, pigs and goats that were to be put up for auction. Our back yard was adjacent to a roping arena used by the local cowboys day and night. Between the smells and the noise, it wasn't a good time for any of us and we were soon on the move again. Even though it was hard to say goodbye to Bobby, I couldn't wait to move on.

Part of my excitement was because my Uncle Tex and Aunt Johnny Maynard (my mother's aunt) were going with us to Umatilla, Oregon. During family get-togethers we shared some great times with them and my cousins. Wayne was my age and Patty was two years younger. The trip to Oregon would take at least a week, allowing Wayne and I to get in some trouble; but we sure had a great time.

Our convoy consisted of two old pickups and a 1949 DeSoto convertible we had bought new in Wallace. Aunt Johnny drove their Chevy sedan. One pickup had high plywood sides and carried two horses. The other truck was piled high with belongings from both families. We looked exactly like what we were: nomads.

The journey was interrupted regularly with breakdowns and flat tires. We had to stop and make camp early every afternoon to feed the horses and hobble them for the night. We spent most nights next to a river or stream, providing playtime for us kids after we did our part to help. Wayne and I took care of the horses, and Patty assisted with setting up our camp.

With cousins Patty and Wayne Maynard

Just before we got into Oregon, one of Dad's horses became sick and died. There was nothing we could do. Dad and Uncle Tex had to bury it just off the road. It was a very emotional loss for all of us. When we arrived in Pendleton, Dad sold the other horse and trailer, vowing never again to own a horse.

A dam was being built on the Columbia River near Umatilla, providing jobs that would be our source of income. The Maynards were going about a hundred miles farther downriver to work on another large dam being constructed near The Dalles, Oregon.

We moved into a trailer park operated by the dam contractor for their employees, but we didn't stay in Umatilla very long. Uncle Tex called Dad with an idea. He suggested the two of them start a construction company. Tex was a realtor, so Dad would build houses and Tex would sell them.

They were successful, and shortly after moving to The Dalles, our circumstances changed dramatically. We lived in a pleasant trailer park for a short time, then moved into our first home, which had been built by Dad. It was incredible: we had three bedrooms and a basement recreation room. The house was in a good location and had a view of the Columbia River from the back yard. The tension between Mom and Dad had almost disappeared, and they only drank on special occasions.

I liked the new life, but my report cards told a different story. I was getting mostly Ds, with one F in arithmetic. I had missed so much school and was so far behind, that it was almost humiliating. I wouldn't pay attention in class and became even more defensive. The principal, Alvin Unruh, was a very kind and patient man who did everything he could to help me, including meeting with my parents. But this only created a rift between me and Dad. I started talking back and acting out.

After one particularly bad time, I hopped a freight train and rode to the next town. A gas station attendant bought me a coke and a candy bar and called Mom, who came and picked me up. I wanted to make a point more than I actually wanted to run away.

At the end of the school year, Mr. Unruh said he would pass me if I learned my multiplication tables and promised to get a tutor to catch up. With Mom's help, I memorized the tables and we found a math tutor, a pretty, high school junior. We spent two days a week for two months going over math problems. As a fifteen-year-old, I was more interested in her than in learning two-pie-squared or whatever. But I did learn my tables, and in September I started back to school.

At first I did fairly well, and even earned a school letter in football. Then I got caught smoking pot with three friends, and the roof fell in. Principal Unruh had my parents come in with me and gave us a choice: I could be suspended for the semester, or withdraw and choose another school. If I chose the latter, he would make sure no record existed. My parents decided to pull me out of school and make other arrangements. Dad told me this was my last chance, and that I'd better either pull it together or find a job.

My last chance came in the form of San Marcos Military Academy in Austin, Texas. It was a five-star school owned by the Baptist Church. In January I entered the school as a cadet and had to toe the line. Here, the emphasis was on the military aspect, and the religion was optional.

At San Marcos

On my first day in Algebra 101, I realized I was in completely over my head, but my other classes and my behavior were satisfactory. San Marcos was a co-ed school with a small contingent of female cadets in the classrooms. We slept in semi-private rooms, stood inspections and marched around the parade grounds just like I had at Marymount. I didn't get into any trouble; at least, I didn't get caught. Except for failing math, my grades were satisfactory.

Dad had sold his business in Oregon and was now working as a mining engineer in Las Vegas. He formed a company with Uncle Garlin called Gar-Pac. Garlin had found properties in Arizona containing minerals in demand by the Defense Department. Titanium—a black mineral ore of iron—and Magnetite——a silvery metallic chemical—were both being used by the aerospace industry. These minerals were plainly visible in sandy washes between Phoenix and Tucson along Highway 87, and Dad and Garlin hoped to benefit from them.

Over Mom's objections, Dad sent me a bus ticket to join them in Las Vegas when the school year ended. As luck would have it, Mrs. Cordova, the mother of my friend Bobby in Albuquerque, was on the same bus. She had been visiting relatives in El Paso, and we sat together for the rest of the trip. By the time we reached Albuquerque, I had accepted her offer to spend some time with them in Truth or Consequences, New Mexico. I wasn't ready to go home, but I knew I was finished with school. I was only two years away from becoming a Marine, and that was all I cared about.

Mrs. Cordova called my Mom and asked her if it would be okay for me to stay with them for a while. Mom agreed it might do me some good. Bobby and I picked up right where we'd left off, and were best of friends once again. But Bobby had changed— for the better. He was now a straight A student and a football hero at Tor C High School.

My intended short visit turned into three months, and was the best summer I could remember. We didn't drink or smoke pot and didn't hang around with the kids who did. The Cordovas were an all-American family, and I grew to love them. The community was mostly Hispanic and I enjoyed the celebrations and family gatherings. With fall and the beginning of the school year approaching, Mrs. Cordova asked me if I would like to stay and go to school again. I was reluctant, but promised her and my mother that I would give it an honest try. I enrolled as a freshman and Bobby was a sophomore. There was nothing for me to prove here. Bobby was my mentor and very popular in school. Unlike the many other schools I had attended, there was no racism or bullying. We were just part of the community.

We all worked together and I gave it my best effort. But after a month it was the same thing all over again. I was in over my head and knew I couldn't catch up. I walked out of English class telling the teacher I was wasting my time, and that nouns and pronouns had nothing to do with being a Marine. It was the easy way out, and the Marines provided the only future I could see for myself. In another year I would be seventeen and planned to enlist anyway.

I stayed with the Cordovas a while longer and worked as a dishwasher at a small café. When I had saved enough money, I said an emotional goodbye to my surrogate family. The Cordovas had shown me a lot of love, and I would miss them and Bobby.

Las Vegas left me with few memories. There was constant bickering with my Dad at home. Looking back, I realize I was a smart aleck kid who had all the answers. I tried school again, but either flunked out or quit. My 1956 report card showed all classes graded "Unsatisfactory." I probably gave up and quit, since I was 16 now and able to work. I took a job as a busboy in the showroom of the Dunes Hotel. In the few months I worked there, I had quite a few celebrity sightings.

Liberace and some of his friends came in for the late show one evening and were seated in my section right next to the stage. The head waiter assigned me and three other waiters to the party, and we covered that table like flies on a cow-pie. I was thrilled to be that close to a celebrity, and the "Piano Man" was very kind and generous. When the evening was over he gave me a fifty-dollar casino chip and signed his name on my bus jacket, which I've kept all these years.

There was a great little deli on the strip called Foxy's. One of the few integrated restaurants in Vegas at the time, it was popular with many entertainers. Some of my co-workers and I occasionally stopped in for a late meal after our shift was done. One particular night as we were finishing our dinners, everyone's attention was diverted to one person: Elvis had entered the building! He was followed by Colonel Parker and three fine-looking ladies.

This was incredible! I could not keep my eyes off Elvis. Wearing a black suede jacket and pants with a red shirt, he looked exactly like all the pictures I'd seen. He was quite friendly; smiling and waving to everyone. We walked past his table as we were leaving, and I waved and smiled, saying, "See ya, Elvis."

To my astonishment, he looked up, smiled and waved and said, "See ya." I couldn't believe he looked right at me and actually spoke to me! It was the highlight of my time in Las Vegas.

In early 1957 we moved to Phoenix so Dad's business could be closer to the source of the minerals. Mom found us a little house on East Indian School Road near 24th Street, and Dad rented an office in a downtown hi-rise. They tried their best to get me back in school, but I would have no part of it and the tension between us continued to build.

A dramatic moment brought it all to an end. One night after dinner, Dad started in on me about going back to school. As we faced each other, I yelled in his face for him to leave me alone. He shoved me backwards, and I fell over the coffee table. As I was coming to my feet I lunged at him and took him to the floor. I had my fist doubled up to hit him, but he stopped fighting and just laid there. I knew he didn't want to hurt me. I just melted and started crying, telling him I was sorry. He opened his arms, and I fell into them.

Through sobs, I told him I loved him, I was sorry and I would never do that again. Laying on the floor together I said "All I want is to be a Marine just like you. I'll be a good one, Dad!"

From that day on I called him Dad instead of Papa. That night, I think we both felt for the first time we were really father and son.

Dad gave up trying to get me back in school. I got a job at a nearby Bayless grocery store, stocking shelves and carrying out groceries. My mother was happy being a housewife and life began to smooth out. One night Mom told me she had met the neighbors across the street, and I should meet their teenage daughter. A few days later I saw the girl out in her yard, so I walked over to say hello.

I liked Sandy Reed the first time I met her, and it was clear that she felt the same about me. Her parents, Mary Lou and Dave, were great people. I began spending more time with the Reeds than I did at home. I had never had a real girlfriend and until Sandy came along, I'd never really wanted one. She was fun and easy to be with. She was my buddy. We talked and laughed, went to movies and did those things teenagers do. We figured we would get married someday, but she let me know right away that while she was happy with a goodnight kiss, the other stuff would wait until we were married. I thought Sandy was the sweetest girl I would ever meet.

Sandy's dad tried to get me to go into a trade school and even offered to pay my way if I would just do it. I told him, "Dave, I was born to be a Marine."

They all understood. I had always planned to enlist on my 17th birthday, but when it rolled around that July, I didn't do it. Nobody said a word, probably hoping I'd forget about my dream. Sandy was now my first love, and I didn't want to leave her. I kept thinking about Dave's offer. I had never before considered going to a trade school, but as I thought about it, I realized there were several trades I might like to pursue. In the end, after a long talk with Sandy and both of our families, I decided to join the Marines.

On September 6, 1957, I took the oath at the recruiting office in downtown Phoenix, after which I was given a bus ticket and ordered to report to the Marine Corps Recruit Depot in San Diego, California. I had been waiting for this my whole life. Dad had prepared me well, and I knew about the strict discipline I was about to receive. I had heard all the horror stories about how the drill instructors screamed and carried on about everything.

Once I was there, my biggest surprise was how well prepared I was for the regimen. My two semesters at military school had certainly paid off; I knew how to march, how to shoulder arms, and most

Basic Training

importantly, how to keep my mouth shut. Dad told me, "All they want to hear is 'Yes, Sir' and 'No, Sir.' "

One of the first people I met was Jerry Feller from El Dorado, Kansas, who would become a lifelong friend. Since our last names both started with "F" we were listed next to each other, and we did nearly everything shoulder-to-shoulder. We had a lot in common, as most of his family were oil field workers, as mine had been. Jerry was quiet and smart. He helped me with the studies, and I helped him with the physical stuff.

It was a tough three months, but neither Jerry nor I had any trouble getting through it. Before graduation, we were each asked to fill out our request for a duty assignment. We both chose Sea School to start our careers. After we completed that school we would be assigned to a Navy ship as an Orderly to the Commanding Officer, or we could be assigned to Embassy duty. It was all spit and polish, and a very prestigious assignment. The form stated, in parentheses, "Only the good need apply."

Recruits were allowed visits on Sundays from 10 a.m until 2 p.m. Near the end of basic training Mom and Sandy drove over to see me. We could roam around the open areas of the base, go to a movie or just sit and talk. We opted for a grassy area next to the visitors center and snack bar. After having been on a strict, regimented diet for three months, I cannot tell you how good a candy bar tasted that day. The chocolate made my jaws ring, and the Coke burned all the way down.

Sandy was still my girl. She was excited that I had chosen Sea School and was doing well. Her mother sent along some homemade cookies and since sweets couldn't be taken into the barracks, I had to eat them all during the visit.

It was obvious something was bothering Mom, but I had to drag it out of her. She finally revealed that she and Dad were divorcing and that it had been coming for a long time. Dad had sold his business and was going to work in a different field. Mom had had enough of moving around and wanted to stay in one place. She told me how proud Dad was that I was doing well, and that he would keep in touch.

Mom assured me that the break up was amicable, but I still felt bad for her, knowing she would be alone. I was glad she and Sandy had become such good friends. Mom was smart, and I knew she was quite capable of making a better life, but I just could not imagine her and Dad apart.

Our four hours together went by too quickly, and at two o'clock I ate the last cookie and said goodbye to my two favorite ladies.

On December 22, 1957 I graduated from basic training and was honored as the High Shooter of my class. I had qualified as an Expert Marksman firing 222 out of 250 on the rifle range. My new duty assignment was at the Recruit Depot: Sea School. My buddy Jerry Feller was on the same list.

Following a short leave, we reported for duty at Sea School. It was all spit and polish, dress blues, marching, classes on everything from ships and how they operate to etiquette and serving General Officers. It wasn't an easy time, but Jerry and I breezed though and graduated as "Sea Going Marines." Based on my performance in Sea School, I was promoted to PFC (Private First Class) on March 25, 1958, and transferred to Camp Pendleton for a year, while awaiting assignment to a naval vessel.

It was a sweet beginning to a lifelong dream and desire to be a Marine. How could it have ended so badly? I should have heeded my Dad's advice: "Just keep your mouth shut, Son."

As I look back today, I see that I was on a long road to an incredible adventure that would be filled with ups and downs. Isn't that what life is really all about?

If I could change anything, would I? I don't know. Maybe when I've finished telling the story, I will be able to answer that question. Right now, I just don't know.

I do know that as Mom and I headed back to Phoenix on that dismal October day, I was ashamed of myself. I would never again show my face to the friends I had left there. It was years before I could contact Mary Lou, Dave or Sandy. I never again spoke with my friend Bobby Cordova. I just wanted to hide. It was the worst thing I could have done, but it was something I couldn't control. I had humiliated myself and caused much sorrow for my loved ones.

When I promised Mom I would change and make her proud, I meant it. I had no idea what was down that road.

Chapter 2

Our first home
612 N. 12th St

Mom and I rolled into Phoenix on an autumn night that still felt like summer. The top was down on the Olds that had faithfully brought us across a burning desert hell. We'd only had to deal with two flat tires and three water stops.

As a 19-year-old high school dropout with a felony conviction and an undesirable discharge from the Marines behind me, I was totally unprepared for the life we were settling into. Mom was freshly divorced, and we had no family or friends in Phoenix; no jobs, no place to live, and we were nearly broke. We had been life-long drifters, following my dad around and always looking for that pot of gold. This time Mom and I were on our own.

After I was arrested in May, Mom left the house where she and Dad had lived, and rented a small apartment in Oceanside to be near me while I went through the trial and spent time in the brig. Now we were starting over. We stayed in a motel on East Van Buren Street while we looked for a more permanent place to live. Mom scanned the want ads and found a little garage apartment near 12th Street and Roosevelt, for about sixty bucks a month. It didn't cost much because it wasn't much, but we had lived in worse. Mom had the bedroom, and I slept on the couch in the living room. The bathroom was about the size of a small closet and contained a shower, sink and toilet. There wasn't even a mirror for the prettiest gal in town. But this was nothing new and it worked for us.

We had moved often while I was growing up, as my dad chased one job after another all over the country. Mom became an expert in turning these old, often rundown, cheap rentals into comfortable places we called home. They renovated an old farmer's barn in Oregon, turning it into a cozy little home. I don't think we ever bought a home of our own except the one Dad had built in Oregon, which had been sold a few months later.

Within a few days of arriving in Phoenix, Mom had an interview at a "Guggy's" restaurant, located at Tower Plaza shopping center near 40th Street and Thomas. Guggy's was a local Arizona chain of coffee shops, with a fun family atmosphere.

The morning of the interview she rushed back home bursting with excitement. Not only had she been hired, but she was scheduled to start that very afternoon. She would work 4 p.m. to midnight; the best shift because dinner tips paid the most and we really needed the money. Mom looked gorgeous as she stood before me ready to leave for work. She wore a black skirt and blouse, a white apron and a little white hat perched on her long brown pageboy hairstyle. The fact that she had a figure like Sophia Loren added to her beauty. I told her she looked great, and saw the tears well up in her eyes. I jumped up off the couch and hugged her tightly for several minutes.

It hit us both at the same time: we were really on our own. Dad wasn't there to provide for us like he always had been. We both hugged and cried, and for the first time since leaving California we really felt the devastating loss of our leader for all those years.

Mom was set with a job, but it took me a little longer to start my new life. The transition from the military to jail bird to civilian was a difficult adjustment. All I'd ever wanted to do was become a Marine like my dad. Now what?

As a little boy I had listened in awe as Dad and his buddies told stories about their experiences. Dad was respected as a true American hero by everyone who knew him. I was old enough now to realize how special he was to have endured those battles in the South Pacific. He was some act to follow, but I wanted to try.

Dad had also expected that I would follow his career path. Like the son of a doctor would become a doctor; as the son of a Marine, I should be a Marine. In my heart and soul I could be nothing else. I had wanted to be a ground-pounding, trash-talking, rifleman; face down in the mud with bullets flying over my head. *HooRah!*

Now that dream was gone, and I was going to have to find another way to make Dad proud of me. I didn't know where to turn next. As Mom left our small apartment for her first day at work, I again vowed to someday make them both proud of their only son.

My mother's love was truly unconditional. Only 15 years apart in age, we grew up learning life's lessons together. We were both hot-tempered and stubborn, and had heated arguments that she would usually win. Mom was controlling and wanted to know everything I was doing; while I wanted to be independent, and rebelled against being treated like a child. Regardless of the problem or intensity of the argument, we were both quick to make up. I was always my mother's son.

We were a tight family, and Mom's brother, Phill Davis, was an important part of my early life. He always kept an eye on us, especially after Dad left, and made several trips to Phoenix to make sure we were alright. He would show up for a day or two and then head back to Nevada to continue prospecting for gold. Sometimes Mom would give him gas money, help him fill out papers or read important mail to him. He had never learned to read or write, but had trusted friends who helped him with official business. His lack of education didn't deter him from becoming successful in life. Uncle Phill had once lived a rowdy lifestyle, but seemed to have cut back and was settling down. We warned him about driving too fast and prospecting alone, but he was determined to find that pot of gold, and brushed off our worries. He was more concerned about our living situation and how I was coping with my discharge from the Marines.

Not so with Dad. I knew he was very disappointed that I had failed as a Marine. I wasn't sure how it affected our father-son relationship, but I knew from Mom he hadn't asked her for any details, and that told me a lot. I could say it didn't really matter because after all, I wasn't really his son, I was adopted. There's a difference, I told myself, though in my heart I knew there wasn't. He was my dad in every way that mattered, and I missed him. I was struck with the realization of just how important he had been in my life.

I had moped around long enough. It was time to get busy and find a job. I didn't have any real skills. I was okay at meeting people and I knew when to smile and when to shut up. It wasn't much in the way of qualifications. When I saw an ad for a delivery driver for Kelly's Cleaners at 2150 E. McDowell, I applied. All I had to do was pick up and deliver dry cleaning and laundry. I figured I could handle that.

It paid enough for me to be able to buy my own car, so I made my way to Sarawak Motors on Van Buren Street. I turned over 60 bucks and became the proud owner of my first car; an older model Hudson Hornet.

I stayed with Kelly's Cleaners a few months, then moved on. I knew the Phoenix area fairly well and had started making friends. Mom wasn't crazy about some of my acquaintances and cautioned me about them. One of her favorite quotations—which would become prophetic—was, "You are judged by the company you keep." I didn't think much about it at the time, but it later became significant.

Now that we were both working, Mom found another place for us to live. It was in a beautiful little trailer park on 48th Street, south of McDowell. We rented a 10x48 foot mobile home with two bedrooms and two bathrooms, and was as modern as anything I had ever seen. We had always had clean and adequate homes, but this was the fanciest place we had lived so far. The park had a swimming pool, laundromat and a clubhouse with pool tables. In our eyes, it was pure class. Instead of sleeping on a couch in the living room, I now had my own room. Living was good, and we were happy.

Mom was getting letters from Dad, who was doing very well. He asked about me, and Mom told him how I was doing and how much I missed him. I never knew why they had divorced, but I always hoped they would get back together. I also hoped and prayed that Dad would forgive my Marine debacle and our relationship would be the way it once was. I just didn't have a plan as to how I would make that happen.

We had been in the Valley of the Sun—the local's name for the Phoenix area—for almost a year and Mom was still working for Guggy's; now as head waitress. Guggy's management was opening a new restaurant near a downtown shopping mall and Mom had been asked to help get it up and running. She loved the company's management and seemed to have found a home with them. Within another year she would be promoted to manager of her first restaurant.

Guggy's was locally owned by the Guggisberg family of Phoenix and included several eateries similar to the modern day CoCo's, serving a good family menu and great pies. The operations manager was Jimmy Halverson, a very smart business man who would become a good friend and mentor for many years.

I was starting to feel better about life and to let myself have a good time. I had some friends and a girlfriend now and again. Since my discharge, I hadn't been able to face Sandy Reed or her family, so was on the loose again. I was working at a Union gas station at 48th Street and McDowell, just up the street from the trailer park. My shift was from 3 p.m. until we closing at midnight. I pumped gas, changed oil, and did some minor repairs. It was good experience and I learned a lot. However, there was one experience I could have done without.

One night I was in the process of closing the station and had just turned off the outside lights. I was bending down to put the cash in a floor safe when a car drove in with its headlights off and parked on the side of the office. I'd only had a quick glance at the driver, but it was enough to put me on high alert. I knew instinctively I was about to get robbed.

I picked up the phone, dialed the operator and told her my situation. I gave her the location and asked her to send the police right away. A few seconds after I hung up a man came through the office door with a gun pointed at my head. I was down on one knee getting ready to put a handful of cash in the floor safe. All the guy said was "gimme that money." I stood up and was about to hand him the cash when, through the glass behind him, I saw a Phoenix police car pull into the driveway with his lights off. When the robber turned to see what I was looking at, my instinct kicked in. I threw the cash in his face, grabbed the gun out of his hand, and took him to the floor as the officer came in. The robber went down with me right on top of him. By this time the cop was inside and took over the situation.

In another few seconds the driveway was full of cars with flashing red lights and more cops than I had ever seen in one place. Many of them shook my hand or slapped me on the back, telling me what a good job I had done. But when that robber saw the police car drive in, he pulled the hammer back on the .38, and I knew he was going to shoot somebody. I just reacted.

A reporter from the *Phoenix Gazette* showed up and interviewed me. The story in the paper the next day quoted me … "'I remembered my Marine training' said service station attendant Jerry Foster."

It had been a close call and Mom was nearly frantic. But she told me how proud she was and that was exactly what I needed to hear at that time in my life. Shortly afterward, I heard from Dad. My mom had sent him a copy of the newspaper article and, while he was impressed, he was also very concerned that I could have been killed. We talked about many things that day; even about the Marine Corps and how we all had to move on with our lives.

As the conversation was ending, Dad said "I'll be seeing you real soon."

"Okay Dad … I'll see ya!"

"I love you, Son"

"I love you too, Dad … "

I hung up the phone and cried like a baby. We had come a long way. Now, with my dad behind me again, life seemed a little brighter, although I wished for the millionth time that Mom and Dad would find a way to work things out.

Chapter 3

Reconnecting with Dad

Within another six months Mom was the manager of two Guggy's restaurants. She was really on a roll, and I wasn't doing too badly either. I was still working at the gas station and making new friends every day. The attempted robbery had given me a reputation as a guy not to be messed with. Now I didn't mind telling people that I was a former Marine, but I never mentioned my discharge status, and carefully avoided any in-depth Marine or military chatter.

I was getting restless, so when the service station changed owners, I decided to move on as well. I loved trucks and thought about driving big rigs. In the early 1960s, if you weren't in the Teamsters Union you didn't work as a trucker around the Valley. There was no option, so I joined the union as an apprentice. Every morning I signed in at the downtown union hall and waited for a local company to call in looking for a driver. I drove for a number of trucking companies and became a regular with Pacific Motor Trucking. Freight would arrive on trucks and trains overnight and be unloaded onto the docks, where it would be loaded onto my truck and delivered it to its destination. I drove a wide variety of trucks of every type and size imaginable, and I developed a love for them that would last a lifetime. I never had the chance to join the Teamsters Union as a full member, because my direction was about to change again.

A friend I'd met at the union hall told me about a good job in Northern Arizona. If I joined the Labor Union in Phoenix, they would send me up to Page, Arizona to work on the Glen Canyon Dam, which was being built on the Colorado River to provide hydroelectricity. Work had begun in 1956 and would continue for 10 years.

I jumped on the opportunity to do something different and it turned out to be a pretty good deal. I lived in the men's barracks, had great food at the mess hall, and was paid a good wage; all courtesy of the contractor. In return I worked my butt off digging ditches and doing all the petty little projects that were reserved for the new, lowlife laborers. It was all just part of the game, but I enjoyed the work and especially the people.

The town of Page was unusual in that it began as a construction camp in 1957 to house workers and their families while the dam was being built. The town was named after John C. Page, a former commissioner of the Bureau of Reclamation. As more construction workers continued to arrive with families, streets were laid out and scores of trailers were lined up in rows. Businesses started arriving and metal structures became stores. Babbitt Brothers Trading Company was the first supermarket.

Always aware of opportunities, my dad's sister Wanda and her husband, Mac, arrived in Page and opened a Rexall drug store. Having family in town kept me from being lonely and provided a diversion. At that time Page had no television, poor radio reception, and not much to do. People created their own entertainment with dances, barbecues and gatherings. I spent much of my off time with my aunt, uncle and cousins; Steve, JoEllen, Jane and Phil.

I was learning that getting along with people and doing a job well generally paid off. Before I left I was given the chance to do one of the more thrilling—and dangerous—jobs; reinforcing the canyon walls with steel rebar. Working in teams of two, we were suspended from long cables attached to windlasses,and dropped over the 700-foot walls with a jackhammer. While one man held the bit against the wall, the other man swung out and stood on the hammer to give it enough weight to drill into the wall. We drilled holes from 45 to 75 feet into the Navajo sandstone, inserted the bolts with expansion anchors, then forced concrete grout around them to secure them within the walls.

I had heard stories about accidents in the past, but I thought this was exciting stuff, and enjoyed it, until a few weeks later when an experienced high-scaler on the midnight shift died because of a faulty tie-off. That was enough for me. I quit while I could and headed back to Phoenix.

It was 1961 and I had only been home a few weeks when my Dad called and offered me a job. In the last few years, he had gone from being a hard-rock miner to a mining engineer. He had extensive knowledge of explosives: big bangs, little bangs … he could do it all.

When I was a kid, Dad would create little noisemakers out of whatever was on hand, just for the fun of it. But there was one instance while we lived in Umatilla, Oregon when he used his knowledge to make a statement.

A neighbor of ours lived in a filthy, rundown house next to a vacant lot where his rusted out piece-of-junk pickup truck sat. He was always at war with all the neighbors and the feeling was mutual. My aunt Ceil thought he looked like a pervert.

The neighbor yelled at my mom because our dog crapped in his already crappy yard. One night, after a few beers out on the front porch, my dad and an old Marine buddy, along with my Uncle Phill, made a night recon and blew that old truck to smithereens. The sheriff and fire department showed up and questioned everyone. The deputy knew who did it, but no one ever confessed. The result was that our neighbor became neater and friendlier.

Now Dad's expertise with explosives had netted him a contract to oversee a very large government defense project in Montana. The two contractors in charge, Del E. Webb from the Phoenix area, and the George A. Fuller Corporation out of

Chicago, wanted Dad to supervise the mining operation digging silos for a group of ballistic missiles. The miners would work around the clock and have their part done in less than a year.

Dad was doing well and I looked forward to seeing him. I was excited that he wanted me to work with him, though he didn't offer many details. I was on the road the next day, at the job site two days later, and working the next.

I drove a pickup truck and hauled the dynamite and blasting caps from Great Falls to all the work sites scattered around the state. As a warning to other would-be careless drivers, the truck had the word "EXPLOSIVES" painted in foot-high letters on every side. I enjoyed the freedom of driving through this beautiful Montana country and getting paid for it.

The company truck was a new Chevy with a two-way radio. I left the warehouse in Great Falls every morning and kept the silos supplied with powder, caps and fuses. I learned a lot about mining and even more about miners. They are hardworking men who spend eight hours a day with a pick and shovel. They loaded buckets, blasted, and loaded more buckets. Tough work breeds tough guys and good guys. I enjoyed pulling up to a site and watching the interaction as these men went about their business. After a while I was able to join in and be one of the boys. It didn't hurt that my dad was the boss. I felt a real camaraderie here, just as I had in the Corps. Now there was a difference, since no one here knew my past.

They all knew I just got out of the Marines, but not one thing more. I didn't talk about it and tried my best to completely avoid the subject. My story was that I served my enlistment and got out. It wasn't for me and that was the end of it. I still feared someone would find out my dirty little secret and expose me.

When I filled out the application for this job, Dad told me to put down my military history showing a three-year enlistment and honorable discharge. He assured me it wouldn't be checked. That was the first employment application I ever filled out falsely. Sadly, there would be many more.

During one of my drives to a worksite, I was pulled over by a Montana Highway Patrolman and ticketed for speeding. I forgot to go to court for it, which was a huge mistake. Several weeks later, on the Friday afternoon before Labor Day weekend, the same patrolman stopped me again for speeding. He knew I had the previous warrant out and took me to jail. I spent the entire Labor Day weekend there, until I could see the judge and pay the fine on Tuesday morning. I learned from that incident to always smile when stopped by an officer of the law.

Spending a few days in lockup was an interesting experience. The Lewistown jail was located on the second story of the police department. There were nine prisoners being held that weekend; mostly drunks and petty criminals. The jail had six cells and a large recreation room that served as the eating space and lounge. The cells were open all day and everyone played double-deck pinochle. It didn't take me long to learn the game, and I played for the whole holiday weekend. The food was excellent, and I confess to having had a great time, even though there was always that dread that one of the jailers would announce he knew about my criminal past. I was still on probation for the felony, but nothing was ever mentioned.

Other than getting speeding tickets, I was doing a good job and my dad seemed happy with me. He was always busy, so I didn't see much of him. The project was huge and spread over many miles. I listened to the two-way radio chatter on the company radio and kept up with who was doing what, and what was going on. One day I heard my dad's voice on the radio, with a strange rumbling sound in the background. I learned that the noise was the roar of a helicopter engine. Dad was heading to the same silo I was, so I stepped on it. I had never seen a helicopter up close before. When I got to the site and saw that little Bell sitting there, I knew I wanted to fly one.

I had my first helicopter ride that day. The pilot showed me how it could go straight up, straight down, and in a straight line while spinning circles. I figured I could never be as good as that pilot was, but I knew I could fly. I also knew it was financially out of the question.

Eight months after I started work there, the mining portion of the missile project was finished. Most of the crews were heading to the next job. The crew seemed like one big family of mobile miners; following construction the same way my family had followed gold and silver. I sure liked the money, and I really liked these guys. I had made friends and had fun. Goodbyes were hard, especially to Dad, who was already lined up for another big job out of the country. Besides, hauling explosives was dangerous. I needed something a little less hazardous. Like flying, maybe.

Chapter 4

Flying Lessons - 1962 - 63

I was back in Phoenix with Mom, and I wasted no time getting to Sky Harbor Airport and checking out the flight schools. I was stunned at the cost. No wonder none of my friends had ever considered being a pilot. It wasn't an idea that would have been discussed among my friends. Getting a pilot's license was for the upper crust; where I came from it was out of the question. Even in the Navy and Marines, only college graduates became officers and went to flight school. So becoming a pilot was never on my short list of dreams. Helicopters were fairly new to my generation and totally out of reach for me.

Still, not one to give up easily, I shopped around and found a little place called Davis Flying School. It was an old hangar and office that advertised flight instruction. Cliff Davis was as ancient as the musty old hangar. He was a frazzled old ex-crop duster; white-haired and skinny as a stick. He was a sight, dressed in a farmer's shirt and jeans; not what I expected a pilot to look like.

But all that mattered to me was that he had an airplane and could teach me how to fly it. He charged two dollars less an hour than the other schools I had checked, and his airplane looked safe enough. It was a high-wing single-engine Aeronca 7ac. It carried two passengers—a student in front and instructor in the rear—and it was equipped with a two-way VHF radio and an Omni receiver. Just the bare necessities.

Aeronca 7ac

Cliff told me they called it a tail dragger because of its two main wheels plus a wheel on the tail. He said, "When you learn how to fly this plane, you'll be able to fly anything."

I was sure eager to try. I had been making good money in Montana and saved almost $200 from my wages. I now had enough money in the bank to at least get through the solo phase. After that I would have to just fly when I could accumulate more cash.

Lack of money is always a setback in making dreams come true, and flying takes money … lots of money. At that time—the early 1960s—qualifying for the FAA private pilot certificate required about 45 hours of instruction and solo flight time. The cost was $9.00 per hour to solo and $18.00 dollars an hour with an instructor. It would cost me a minimum of $750 to get that private pilot's certificate and the necessary study materials: books, maps, plotters and other items. In 1962 that was a whole lot of money; nearly four times as much as I had in the bank.

Old Cliff was a good instructor, but he had a couple of habits that really irritated me. During the flight he would reach up and smack me on the back of the head to make a point. And when it was quiet I could hear his false teeth clicking in my headset, which just about drove me crazy.

I could do the flying part with no problem, but from the start I was worried about the "study" part of this new adventure. I'd have to take a written test from the school before my solo flight and another one prior to taking my first cross-country flight. There was a written test for everything, culminating in the big final exam given by the FAA. This was the one required for a private certificate from the FAA, and it involved an enormous amount of study.

Unfortunately, studying had always been my downfall in school and I had dropped out rather than deal with the frustration. Since I always knew I would be a Marine, I felt I didn't really need to finish high school anyway. Study was for those who needed it, I thought. Yep, I was one of those smart aleck kids who knew it all.

I was determined to do this though, so I learned all about the little Aeronca and breezed right through the written pre-solo test. I was ready to solo. Cliff and I took off from Sky Harbor and went to a little dirt runway about 10 miles north of Scottsdale. We made a couple of touch-and-go landings. After the third one Cliff told me to taxi to the end of the runway and shut the engine down.

I knew what was coming and I was stoked! Cliff went through the procedure with me. I was to take off and come back around and land. It seemed simple enough. As the old man walked away, I started the engine. I taxied back to the runway, made a clearing turn to check for other traffic, and pulled onto the dirt strip. This was it! I lined up and pushed the throttle wide open. The acceleration surprised me and I was off the ground before I was ready.

With Cliff out and only me on board the little Aeronca was much lighter, more agile and peppy. I felt the thrill of being the only one in the cockpit. When that realization set in, I got that gut-wrenching message from my brain that I was alone up here … and Cliff was down there. There was no one to help and it was up to me to get back down safely. I had to straighten up and put my training into practice.

I turned crosswind at the end of the runway, then downwind as I had been trained. Once downwind opposite the end of the runway, I pulled the throttle back and started my glide. I was nervous, but forced myself to settle down. It was all going according to plan when I turned onto final approach. As I crossed the end of the runway I leveled off and let the airplane settle toward the tarmac. As I went past Cliff, I thought it strange to see him waving his arms and jumping up and down.

About half way down the dirt strip I knew something was not right. I should have touched down by now, and the end of the strip was coming up fast. For some reason, I couldn't get the plane on the ground, so I pushed the throttle forward to make a go-around. With my heart pounding, I turned crosswind and then downwind just like before. As I came around and lined up again I could see Cliff making an exaggerated cutting motion across his throat with one hand. I wondered what he was trying to tell me. I closed the throttle and realized right away what I had done wrong the first time. I hadn't completely closed the throttle, causing the little airplane to stay above stall speed and unable to settle onto the ground. This time though, it all came together and I made a good three-point landing. I had soloed. What a thrill!

The old man approached and climbed in the back seat without a word. After he was strapped in and ready, he smacked me on the back of the head, saying, "Back to Sky Harbor. Did you learn anything?"

"Yes sir" I said, and we headed for home.

I flew a few more hours with old Cliff, until one day he didn't show up for a lesson. I was told by the bookkeeper that he was sick and might be off for a while. I never saw Cliff again, but I still smile when I think of him and my first solo flight.

I went back to work at the service station. Gas station attendants didn't make much money, so my flying had decreased to one or two flights a month. I found a new school at Sky Harbor that seemed to fit my needs. Saguaro Aviation was very well organized compared to Cliff's place. Les Taylor, the chief pilot and part owner, was a good guy who always seemed to need a haircut.

He usually wore baggy pants that seemed as though they might fall down any minute—long before it was the fashionable look.

The school was new, clean and very professional, and Les ran it well. He had a complete line of Cessnas; from the little 150 up to the 210, which had retractable landing gear and a constant-speed propeller. He also had a twin-engine Piper Aztec that was used for multi-engine training. The flight line at Saguaro was very impressive and so was the hangar.

After a flight with Les one day, he asked me to hang around and answer the phone while he took another student for an hour-long flight. I jumped at the chance, overwhelmed that Les had chosen me to guard all this and answer the phone.

It was a Sunday afternoon and no one else was around, so when they had taken off I wandered through the building and out into the adjoining hangar. The floor was painted a silvery-gray and was highly polished. Special tools hung on walls. Red "Snap-on" tool boxes on rollers sat around the big hangar next to work benches and painted trash cans. I was used to the disarray found in gas stations and mining shops, so the cleanliness and orderliness of this hangar was mind-boggling.

The instant I walked in the hangar door I noticed the little helicopter sitting off to one side. But like a kid saving the biggest, brightest Christmas present to open last, I avoided it until I had seen everything else. I could hardly contain my excitement as I walked over for a closer look. It was a Bell G-2, a two-passenger machine used for flight instruction. I had seen it before but tried to ignore it, knowing it was too far out of reach for a gas station attendant. But at this moment I was in charge of the place and was going to check it out.

I walked slowly around that little Bell, scrutinizing every inch of it. I sat in the seat and daydreamed about flying it until I heard Les pulling up outside. It had been a bittersweet hour. *If only ...,* I thought, as I quickly walked back into the office.

I knew then aviation was where I wanted to be. I was getting close to accruing the required hours for the private pilot's certificate. Then I'd have the written test given at the FAA office, and a flight test given by an FAA inspector or a designated examiner.

I kept on with the lessons while working at the gas station. I had switched to Blakely, a locally owned company with stations all around Arizona. Gas was 22 cents a gallon and it was only five bucks for an oil change and lube job.

Part of my job was going to the warehouse to pick up tires and other supplies. I had fun driving that Blakely pickup around town. It was fire-engine red, with spotlights, running lights, lots of chrome, and red, white and blue flags mounted on the fenders and body. I was living large when I drove by the home of a friend or girlfriend.

Chapter 5

Scottsdale Marshal's Office

While speeding through Scottsdale one afternoon, I was pulled over and given a ticket. The officer who stopped me was a customer at the service station and knew the manager. He gave me a good lecture and from then on I was more careful.

Another night I was served a warrant for not paying a ticket. Sergeant Richard Kendall took me to jail to post bond. We quickly became good friends, and he helped me out on more than one occasion.

I was working, flying whenever I could afford to, and spending most of my free time with my new friend, Dick Kendall. While hanging out with him around the Scottsdale Marshal's Office, I came to know most of the personnel there. One of the officers, Don Skousen, sold me his Pontiac convertible. I had that car a long time, and many years later we would still hassle each other over which of us got the worst end of the deal. In spite of that, I'm glad to say we're still friends today.

I also came to the attention of the Police Chief, Harry Wojokowski. Harry was a friendly guy and seemed to like me. After a while I worked my way into a reserve officer status. Scottsdale was a small city in 1962 and the department only had three patrol cars and one sergeant's car. I was allowed to take a patrol car and cruise the city neighborhoods to show a police presence, and I could assist the regular officers on calls and accidents. I was in heaven, and felt this would be a great way to redeem myself.

Scottsdale Marshal

I was good at the job and it wasn't long before I was hired as a full time deputy marshal. When filling out the application, I left out any mention of military service, and when I came to the dreaded question "Have you ever been convicted of a felony?" I wrote "No."

I knew it was wrong, but I needed a chance to redeem myself. I did remember my mom's saying: "Jerry, there is no right way to do a wrong thing." But when the chief offered me the job, I couldn't turn it down. I became a cop.

My first assignment was as a radio dispatcher. I wanted more activity, though, so I worked my eight-hour shift in the radio room worked another eight hours in a patrol car to build up my experience. My fellow officers liked me and so did the chief. I had completely changed my lifestyle and habits. I no longer associated with my old friends; those who did things that cops don't do. I was determined to be a straight arrow.

On March 8, 1963, shortly after I started working at the police department, Dick Kendall and I drove to Florence Prison to witness a 5:00 a.m. execution. The early winter morning was dark and still as we arrived at the prison. We were escorted through the gates, along the prison wall, past cellblock three toward the death house. The footsteps of the witnesses provided the only sound.

I had a sense of dread, knowing what was about to happen. We had been told only 12 witnesses would be permitted, but there were at least 30 of us. The silence was eerie, though we knew that everyone in the cellblocks was wide awake. We walked through the door of the death house into a brightly lit room with rows of chairs facing a wall of curtains. There was about a minute of sliding chairs and shuffling feet, and then silence again as we all stared at the curtains. No one said a word.

I thought my heart would pound out of my chest. The curtains opened, revealing the gas chamber. A huge man was strapped into the metal chair with his back toward us. The condemned man, Patrick M. McGee, had been tried, convicted, and sentenced to death for murder. Now he wore nothing but a pair of underwear. Warden Frank Eyman said something, but the words escape me. I was only conscious of the man in the chair.

The next sound was the clink of the cyanide dropping into a bucket below the chair. A few seconds later a vapor rose up in the chamber. McGee bent his head forward, took a deep breath and suddenly banged his head backward against the high-backed chair. The blood vessels were bursting under his skin. In another minute the execution had been carried out. That vision has remained with me all of my life. An eye for an eye and all that, but it was the most horrible experience of my young life to that point. How could I know that this event would pale in comparison to the tragedies that I was yet to witness?

I kept up with flight lessons and got my required hours logged. Now I just needed to pass the written test. Les Taylor set me up with a tutor and during my time off we pored over the study material. To pay for the tutor, I worked around the school cleaning up and answering the phone. When my tutor said I was ready, I went to the FAA office and took the written exam. I failed it the first time, but didn't get discouraged. I studied more and nailed it the second time with a perfect score.

On August 30, 1963, I took my flight test with a designated examiner and passed. I was now a private pilot, which meant I could carry passengers.

A few months after I went full time, Chief Wojokowski decided to retire. Rumors ran wild in the department about who would take over. Most of us were pulling for our assistant chief and he seemed to be in line for the job. The city leaders thought differently though, and hired an outsider. Walter C. Nemitz had recently retired as chief of the Los Angeles Police Department, and his appointment came as a shock to the department.

Speculation ran wild throughout the department, as we all wondered who else he might bring in? Who might he let go? What changes would he make?

Unfortunately, one change he made was me. It didn't take the new chief long to determine that the department had been a little casual with hiring practices. Nemitz ordered a background check on all the existing personnel, and I was the first to go.

I had been summoned and reluctantly made my way to his office, knowing what was coming. Not a day went by that I didn't worry about being found out. Surprisingly, Chief Nemitz was very professional and kind when he told me I was being terminated. "You're a good guy who made a mistake," he said. "But there's no place in police work for anyone convicted of a felony." He took my badge and gun, and I walked out the back door of the department, the weight of the world again on my shoulders.

The hardest thing I had to do was tell my good friend Dick Kendall the truth. He was hurt that I hadn't told him about it before being fired, but he remained my friend.

I was completely despondent and just wanted to be alone for a while. I felt like no one wanted me around, and I needed to hide. I was 23 years old and failing at everything I tried. I believed that Mom was the only person in the world who still loved me unconditionally, so I went home.

Once again I was humiliated and embarrassed and once again I had no one to blame but myself. Somehow I had known this was coming. I wished I'd had a clean record, because I loved being a cop, and I really liked Chief Nemitz.

Ironically, when I worked for the news stations later in my career, I was sent to interview him about news stories, and I saw and interacted with him at groundbreakings and social events. To his credit, he showed me respect every time we met. He was always cordial and never once brought up my past. I think he liked me; at least I hoped so, because I liked and respected him.

Even so, I never knew who else the Scottsdale Marshal's Office might have shared my file with, and the fear of exposure never completely left me. I still felt extremely vulnerable. After going home to Mom's, I laid around and moped for a while. None of my old friends called and neither did my new friends in law enforcement. I felt very much alone and on my own. My mind was clouded and I had no clue what I would do next. Uncle Phill came down twice from Nevada just to try to pep me up. On his second trip he was on his way to see someone in Albuquerque, New Mexico, and invited me along. I had nowhere else to be, but declined his invitation, thank you very much. One scowl from Uncle Phill, and I reluctantly reconsidered.

I was actually glad he was there, and now I was glad to be on the road with him. I needed the change and companionship Uncle Phill brought. By the time we reached Flagstaff we were back to the old routine and enjoying each other. The grins turned into laughs and the jabs on the arm turned into playful banter. He was not judging me, and I didn't need to be judged right now. During the long drive we had the chance to talk about many things. The trip turned into a soothing rekindling of what was and what might yet be. I was beginning to hope again.

It's amazing what a heart-to-heart talk with someone you love and trust can do for your outlook on life. Maybe this trip was a good idea after all. We pulled into Albuquerque late at night, got a little motel room, had a pleasant dinner, and then we both got a good night's sleep. Surprisingly, it was a great day.

After breakfast we headed toward the downtown area. Uncle Phill had been closed-mouth about who he was seeing. He would only tell me it was "a lady." When he turned into the driveway of a cemetery, I realized we were visiting the grave of my grandmother Stella. I had been here several times before with my mother.

Grandmother Stella died in 1941 while giving birth to a son. I was just a year old, and Uncle Phill was only 12 at the time. We didn't speak as we walked up to her gravesite. We just stood there looking at it and then I heard a sniffle. I froze when I saw the toughest guy I ever knew with tears in his eyes. He was from the neighborhood where men don't cry. When I realized why he was crying, I let my own tears flow. He said, "I'd give anything if my mother was still alive. Be thankful for what you have." Those words touched me very deeply. I vowed to keep the promise I had made to Mom; to make her happy and proud of me again.

On the trip home I began to come back up out of a very thick fog. There really was no choice. The visit was a turning point in my life, and I had learned a valuable lesson that day: I would rather have *my* sorrow and failures than Uncle Phill's sorrow and loss. I still had options; I still had hope; I still had life … and I still had my Mom.

Grandma Stella's gravesite

CHAPTER 6

A New Direction

 While I had been working as a cop, my Marine buddy Jerry Feller had finished his stint in the Marine Corps. He came for a visit and stayed with us while looking for work. He was soon hired as a guard at the Arizona State Prison in Florence, and he moved to Coolidge, just 15 miles from the prison.

Jerry stopped by for a visit one day about two months after I left the police department.

He suggested I go talk to the warden about a prison guard job, saying Warden Frank Eyman was a feisty old-timer who believed in second chances.

Eyman was once quoted as saying he had never rehabilitated anyone in his life. "They have to rehabilitate themselves. I've tried to re-educate and retrain them." He held on to that philosophy during his entire 17 years as head of Florence prison, and it served him well while dealing with the inmates.

Jerry told me about one inmate who—after his second escape attempt—was marched through the prison yard by the warden to an isolation cell and welded in. Eyman had given him a second chance and he blew it.

On the other hand, one of his guards was arrested for drunk driving and assault on a police officer. The warden gave him a second chance, and the guard made good and was now a Captain.

Eyman was tough, but also compassionate. Asked if he thought too many convicts were being paroled, his response was, "You never know whether a man is going to make it until you give him an opportunity."

"So," Jerry reasoned, "why not at least tell him your story?"
And so I did.

I sat in Warden Eyman's office at the Arizona State Prison, and told him the whole story of my background. He never took his eyes off me. I was nervous and intimidated just being in his presence. Eyman was a legendary lawman; a little guy who wore a big hat and was tough as nails. His office was like a museum of the old West. He may have looked like a little old man, complete with a layer of dust on his Levis and boots, but he was very much in command of everything around him. When the phone interrupted us several times, Eyman would listen, issue an order, and hang up. There was no indecisiveness about him.

When I finished my story, he got right to the point. He said, "Son, you're a jackass for lying to the marshal's office, but I believe in you. Pick up an application and return it to my secretary." He then pointed his finger straight at me and said, "Don't let me down, kid."

"Thanks, Warden, I won't." I released a lung full of breath I didn't know I'd been holding. He was going to give me a chance! The world looked brighter as I left his office.

Two weeks later I was a prison guard. At that time there was no formal training for the job. I was paired up with a more experienced man and followed him around while I watched, listened and learned. A couple of weeks later I was ready to go it alone.

I moved in with Jerry Feller, and we shared a little trailer in Coolidge; a small town made up of migrant farm help, cotton farmers and prison workers. The trailer had a bedroom in back, and a couch in front. I got the couch, and it felt just like home. It was a good place to live and the prison turned out to be a good place to work; actually one of the better jobs I'd had. The pay wasn't great, but working around prisoners was an inspiration to stay honest and play it straight.

I worked in cell block three, which also housed the death row inmates on the third floor. It brought back memories of the execution I had witnessed less than a year earlier. I never thought of it as a dangerous place, nor did I ever feel threatened by the inmates. There was a clear line between guards and inmates, and that line was never crossed during my experience. We escorted the inmates to showers, doctor visits, hearings, or any of a hundred different things. We served meals to the condemned men in their cells, since they weren't allowed to eat with the general population. In essence, I was a gopher for inmates who needed a lot of attention, as well as for superiors up my chain of command. I was respectful to those who respected me, and tolerant of those who did not, because I had now been on both sides of the fence, so to speak. While interacting with the inmates, I often thought, *There but for the Grace of God, go I!*

I counted my blessings.

Chapter 7

A Hearing and A Crash - January 1964

I had stayed in touch with Dick Kendall, my friend from the marshal's office. He was now a detective, and he kept me up to date on all the changes Chief Nemitz was making. The motorcycles were gone and so was the folksy name of the department. It was now the Scottsdale Police Department, which sounded a little more official. It was also better suited to the city that Scottsdale was becoming, even though it was still known as *The West's Most Western Town.*

Kendall put me in touch with a captain from the Arizona National Guard. He believed this captain could help me get a hearing that might lead to reinstatement in the Marines, or at least a change of disposition. I was excited about this possibility, and it now became my top priority.

It took several months for me to complete all the paperwork for my hearing. We didn't have a typewriter available, so Mom neatly printed all the information on the forms. I was granted a hearing before a Marine board in Washington D.C.; a board that would have the power to grant me a General Discharge or order me back to duty. I was hoping for the "back to duty" verdict, because in spite of everything, I still wanted to be a Marine. National news headlines made it clear that we were headed for hard times in places like Lebanon, Israel and possibly Vietnam. The Marine Corps just might need me.

Dick Kendall and Jerry Feller agreed to be my witnesses at the hearing. Mom came up with the money for all three of us to go. When I asked where she got the money, she said it was none of my business, but I assumed Dad and Uncle Phill helped out. I promised to repay her. We checked all the airlines for the best prices, but it was going to be expensive. It occurred to me that renting a single-engine airplane would cost less than three of us taking a commercial flight, plus it had the added advantage of letting me build up my flight time.

I called all the fixed-base operators who rented single-engine airplanes and found the best price on a Mooney Mark 21. It was a sleek little four-passenger, low-wing airplane with retractable landing gear, and could do 180 miles per hour at altitude. It was the most sophisticated airplane I had ever flown, and I was stoked. But Mom had a bad feeling about this trip; one of those motherly intuitions, I guess. I wondered if she was just disappointed because she wasn't going with us. She really wanted to go, but the Marine officer representing me suggested no family members should appear. My two witnesses were adequate.

I allowed one full day to get to Washington, two full days in there, and another full day to get home. All three of us had jobs and needed to take off as little time as possible.

We lifted off at four o'clock in the morning. Dick Kendall had a good knowledge of navigation from a stint in the Air Force, so I was the pilot, Kendall the navigator, and Jerry was responsible for handing up snacks and maps from the back. The flight took a lot longer than I had anticipated. We made little detours, stopped a few times, and got lost once or twice, but we had fun. By the time we hit the airport in D.C., we were bleary-eyed and ready for bed. We found a motel and crashed.

We were on a serious mission, but thought we should also have some fun and do some sightseeing while in our nation's capitol. We visited Arlington National Cemetery and some of the monuments around the city. Then we met with my hearing representative, Captain Jim Dunning, and were given a briefing on what to expect the following day. Captain Dunning was not optimistic about my chances, saying applicants normally waited five years or more before requesting a hearing. But he promised to do his best. We each briefed him on ourselves, and he told us the order of appearance. We would meet him outside the building at 1:45 p.m. and the board would meet at two o'clock sharp. He advised that it shouldn't take long.

Dick said, "Don't worry, you've got a good case, and you've got us to back you up. You'll be back at Camp Pendleton next month, face down in a mud hole."

He made it sound like a punishment, but I wanted that more than anything.

Jerry laughed and said, "Yeah, and then you'll be wishing you were back in the cushy job at the prison!"

I doubted that and hoped Kendall was right.

I imagined the hearing would be held at the Pentagon. Instead, we were in a four-story building in downtown Washington, not far from the Capitol. At exactly 1:45 p.m., Captain Dunning stepped out of the building and escorted us to a waiting room on the third floor. The board was hearing another case, so we waited a few more minutes, before the door opened. Three men from the earlier case emerged. One was about our age and in uniform. None of the three looked happy.

A few minutes later Captain Dunning and I were sitting at a long table, and the board members filed in and sat down. Captain Dunning did a good job outlining my case and all the circumstances surrounding our petition for a change in status of my eligibility to return to duty. The board was made up of two Marine Corps Officers and two Master Sergeants. They looked the part, and they were an impressive and intimidating sight. I had to reach deep down inside myself and suck it up, because I was nervous. But in the presence of other Marines, you'd better show no fear.

When Captain Dunning finished his presentation, the senior officer—a full Colonel—started the questions by asking me for the details of the burglary that night outside Camp Pendleton. I gave him a full and honest answer, starting and ending with the word "Sir." A Master Sargent asked, "Why do you want to come to the Corps?"

I replied that I had grown up wanting to be Marine, that my father had served with distinction, and I had always wanted to be like my dad … my hero. My mouth was dry as sand, and I'd have given anything for a mint or some water. I got through my answer though, and I felt good about it. Captain Dunning and I finished our testimony, and former Marine PFC Gerald K. Feller was asked to go in. He wasn't in there more than five minutes and came out with a blank look on his face.

He said, "All the Colonel wanted to know was why I was there. So I told him, 'because a Marine shipmate of mine was in trouble and needed my help.' "

I felt we had scored big on that response. Next they called Detective Sergeant Richard Kendall from the Scottsdale Police Department. At this rate, I thought, we would be off the ground before dark. Fifteen minutes went by, and Kendall was still in there. We wondered what was going on. Another 15 minutes passed before Dick Kendall and Captain Dunning emerged, smiling.

"Talk to me," I said. "How did it go?"

The Captain said it was the best and most positive hearing he had been a part of. Sergeant Kendall agreed and relayed all the questions. He felt the board was most impressed with the volunteer work I had done with Scottsdale PD before being hired.

For the first time since this procedure had started, I felt positive about the hearing. The military has its ways and protocols, and doesn't often bend, so I knew it was a long shot. *Still,* I thought, *this is my best shot and my last; and it just might work out!*

An hour later a young Marine stepped out and announced that the board had made its decision. We went back in, and Kendall and Feller took the seats at the table. Captain Dunning and I remained standing. The Colonel began by complimenting our presentation, especially having a former Marine shipmate and a Detective Sergeant to stand up for me. But the board felt that too little time had passed. My petition was denied. It was so ordered, and that was that.

I felt numb, unable to think. We went through the polite motions of thanking everyone, especially Captain Dunning who had done a marvelous job, as had my two friends.

By the time we got to a café and ordered a meal, it was close to 4:30. We still had plenty of daylight to get to the airport and be on our way. By the time we checked the aircraft, filed a flight plan, and got off the ground it would be getting dark.

Dick Kendall said "Jerry, you've had a hard day and we'll leave the decision up to you. Do you feel like you can safely fly for a few hours and get us out of here, so we don't have so far to go tomorrow?"

"Oh yeah, no problem," I replied.

I will forever regret my answer to that question. I have often thought back and wondered where our lives would be today if I had said no. But I didn't.

We went to the flight service station and got a weather briefing. There was bad weather out there and it was moving in. The person who briefed me did a good job of laying it out for us. We all agreed that by flying farther to the south, we could avoid a snow storm. Elkins, Virginia was forecast for 8500-foot ceilings with scattered clouds, and things were improving west of there.

I filed a flight plan and around 6 p.m. we said goodbye to Washington, D.C. Dick was in the right seat as navigator and Jerry climbed in the back and fell asleep. We were no more than an hour out when the trouble started. Those clear skies to the south were filling with clouds and they were dropping down fast. Our flight was VFR (Visual Flight Rules) because I wasn't rated for instrument flying. Flying VFR in bad weather, with low clouds, is not only a bad idea, it's against FAA regulations.

A few minutes later we were in the clouds and I thought it was raining. Then I realized it was snowing, and it was snowing hard! I knew I had used bad judgement in taking off in the first place, and I should have turned back right then.

We were in touch with the flight service station in Staunton, Virginia and tracking inbound on their VOR radial, being directed by radio signals from their station. We were at 8500 feet in the clouds and estimated we were about 60 miles northeast and would be descending to 6500 feet to get out of the clouds. With that, I eased the throttle back and started a slow descent. It was spooky for all of us, and Dick and Jerry were on ground watch. We knew there were mountains in the area, but figured they would be way below us when we broke out of the clouds. We flew a few more minutes with still no ground in sight. Elkins radio was still reporting broken clouds at 8500 feet.

Something is not right, went through my mind, just before I saw a light straight ahead. As we passed over the light, I spotted a building and a long open pasture.

I yelled, "We're going to land in that field!" That was the last I remembered as we slammed into the trees.

I wasn't unconscious very long before the frigid air woke me up. It took me a few minutes to figure things out, as a stream of thoughts crossed my mind: *I'm alive; I hear breathing and groaning from both guys; I hear running water; I'm upside down and trapped; I smell gas!*

The odor of gas got my attention. I knew I had to get out and get my friends out. I thought I was trapped until I realized my seat belt and shoulder harness were holding me in. Forgetting about being upside down, I hit the release and fell two feet onto my head. Dick was in and out of consciousness, and Jerry was making groaning noises. I kept talking to them, as I crawled out of the broken plane. I was relieved that there was no fire. By now the wreckage was getting cold and so were we. Snow was falling, and I knew we had to have help soon.

I had seen a building and a bright light as we were coming down, so I knew something or someone was out there. The light reflected off the clouds, providing slightly more visibility. I sat there, drifting in and out of focus, and getting sleepy. That realization woke me up, because I knew that sleepiness was the first sign of hypothermia. Next would be freezing to death. I yelled to my friends that I was going to find help.

Trees had cushioned our landing some, probably saving our lives. We had flipped over, with one wing straddling a small creek, which explained the trickle of water I heard. When I stood up and took a few steps, I tumbled down a 10-to-15 foot bank onto a dirt road.

I was only wearing a white sweater, a long-sleeved shirt and black trousers. Both of my loafers had come off during the crash. My ribs were tender and painful and the blood pouring down my face told me my head was cut open. I lay on that dirt road for a time, trying to get the energy to move again. When that panicky feeling of being warm and sleepy returned, I knew I had to get moving whether I felt like it or not. Now that I was out of the trees I could better see the light, along with several buildings about a quarter of a mile away.

My right leg was in terrible pain and I knew it was broken, but I set out toward the buildings. After what seemed like forever, I was in the middle of a road with a little general store on one side and a small house on the other. The big, bright street light had guided me to Headwaters, Virginia; just a crossroads in a very rural area. I spotted a pay telephone on the porch of the store and decided to try it. I struggled up the six wooden steps to the porch; each one agony for me. It was a slow process, as I was getting weaker from the cold. The pay phone required a dime to get a dial tone or operator and, too late, I realized I had no coins on me.

I made my way back down the steps and across the road to the little house, desperate to get help for my friends. After I pounded on the door for a while, an old woman finally cracked it open as she turned on her porch light. In my bloodied condition, I must have been a sight to her. She was a welcome sight to me.

"I'm freezing," I told her through chattering teeth. I could hardly talk, I was dirty and bloody, and obviously in need of help. The woman quickly opened the door to let me in. The last thing I told her was that my friends were still trapped in the airplane and needed aid right away. She helped me lie down on a rug, and tucked a white pillow under my head. I was out within seconds.

When 90-year-old Mrs. McCray called for help she must have thought I had been in a bigger airplane. Soon people were coming from miles around to help.

I came to with a large uniformed man wearing high-top black boots standing over me. He also wore a fur-lined cap with ear muffs and a badge on the front. Virginia State Trooper D. D. Kelley was asking me where the airplane was. All I could tell him was to follow my tracks. He left to go search, and I was out again. I didn't realize that the blood from my head wounds had frozen, and there was no trail to follow from the house. His search finally revealed the bloodied and scuffed area where I had fallen down the bank onto the dirt road, and from there he was able to find the plane. Dick and Jerry were carefully removed from the wreckage and within an hour we were all taken to Kings Daughters' Hospital in Staunton.

I was unconscious for almost two days, and by the time I came around, my mom was there. The first thing I asked was how Dick and Jerry were doing. She assured me that my friends had survived and would be okay. Jerry was being treated for cuts and bruises and a broken wrist. Dick had broken bones, cuts and bruises and a badly broken pelvis. I had a nasty skull fracture, caused by the fall on my head, that had taken more than 100 stitches to close. I also had several broken ribs and a broken shoulder, which I likely suffered when I fell down the 12-foot embankment. Ironically, the crash itself hadn't done me much harm; it was my movements afterward that did the damage. It was going to take some time, but we all would recover.

Captain Dunning had heard about the accident on the news and drove all the way to Staunton to see us. He told us that after we left Washington, he had talked to the colonel who was the senior officer at my hearing. Evidently, the board was impressed with our case and suggested we try again in 12 to 18 months. Encouraged by this, I assured him I would do so.

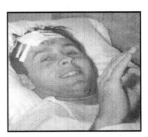

Recovering in the hospital

During our hospital stay, the people of Staunton and Headwaters rallied round in support. Policemen, pilots, ministers and local citizens visited and sent cards. Sunday school classes took donations for candy and flowers. Their kindness was overwhelming. Sometime later, after I had recovered, I wrote a letter to the newspaper thanking everyone for their kindness.

After nearly a week in the hospital, the doctors felt we could be flown home. Our transport required an air ambulance with a nurse on board to administer medications. Mom arranged everything, hiring Mike and Martha Mitchell who owned Sky Harbor Air Service out of Phoenix. We were all understandably a little leery of getting back into a small twin-engine plane. The flight was uneventful though, and after one refueling stop, we arrived safely in Phoenix. (A few years later, I flew that yellow and white Twin Beech part-time with Mike, and years after that it was enshrined in the Air and Space Museum in Washington D.C.)

The three of us spent a couple more weeks recovering at St. Joseph Hospital in central Phoenix. For a while it was thought that I might need brain surgery at the Neurological Center. Thankfully, that turned out to be unnecessary.

Kendall's injuries were the most serious, but we all eventually recovered—at least physically—though the terror of that ordeal will be with us the rest of our lives.

I'll always be grateful to my friends for going to bat for me at the hearing, and I'll always be sorry for causing so much pain and expense to them and my family. The guilt of being at fault is still with me today. I lost touch with my two friends over the years, but I think about them often. They were both what I was trying to be.

It wasn't long before I received a registered letter from the FAA, informing me that they were taking action against me for flying in instrument conditions without an instrument rating. The penalty would be a six-month suspension of my private pilot certificate. At that point, I didn't care. I had no plans to ever fly again.

I was called down to the Flight Standards Office of the FAA at Sky Harbor Airport for a hearing on the suspension. The hearing officer was Myles Ruggenberg. I already knew of this inspector through the airport grapevine. He had a reputation for being tough and a stickler for rules, and all the students feared drawing him for a flight test. I had no doubt that he would throw the book at me.

Ruggenberg took his time reading my file. His facial expressions conveyed all I needed to know about his opinion of the circumstances. He would look up at me and shake his head then look back down at the report.

"Mr. Foster," he finally said, "You screwed up. Do you want to request a formal hearing or will you accept a six month suspension?"

That was a no-brainer for me. I turned in my certificate and went home. I had no desire to ever fly again or see him again. But as often happens, we don't always get what we want in the moment. I would fly again, and more interestingly, Myles Ruggenberg would later become a close friend and mentor, and godfather to my daughter Andryea.

The next six months saw a barrage of legal wrangling and posturing by attorneys trying to collect money from me. I had medical debts, insurance claims and the owners of the downed airplane breathing down my neck. I was deep in debt and the future wasn't looking all that warm and fuzzy. I felt guilty and knew I was responsible, but I had no money. My family had already done all they could, flying back and forth to Virginia, paying for the air ambulance, and more. It seemed so hopeless. Advice from every corner of my world pointed in only one direction: bankruptcy. I had no choice.

I was a 23-year-old high school dropout with a bad discharge, a felony conviction, a suspended pilot's certificate, and was now bankrupt. I had failed at everything I had tried or wanted to be. Life was looking bleak.

Chapter 8

Phoenix 1964

I was starting all over with no idea what to do next. I had dreamed of being a Marine since I was old enough to salute. The recent hearing had squelched that dream again. Law enforcement work was also out. My short time as a Scottsdale cop brought the pain and realization that I could never do that again. I had failed. I was weak.

I was still recovering from the plane crash and taking some time to think about my life and where to go from here. Mom had me work for her at Guggy's for a couple of months, bussing tables and filling in as a breakfast cook. One of the regular customers was looking for help in his small saw-sharpening business, and was willing to train me if I was interested. *Why not*, I thought? I desperately needed a new career and the pay wasn't bad, so I signed on with Precision Saw Works at 56th Street and Indian School Road. I learned how to sharpen saws, knives, shears and all kinds of things that needed to be honed. It was a good job and kept me from dwelling on my troubles. I worked six days a week and began to find my way out of that terrible depression.

I met new friends; among them a very special girl named Charmaine. We were young and dumb and thought we were in love. After a whirlwind courtship, and despite objections from her folks and mine, we headed to Las Vegas and were married. Nine months later I was Dad to Kari Jill, the prettiest little girl I had ever seen.

Charmaine's father was a manager at Motorola and wanted to get me hired on there. The money and benefits were better than I was getting at Precision, and I wanted to do right by my new little family, so I applied. I was honest about my background, and with my father-in-law's recommendation, I was hired to work on the assembly line.

I tried hard to make it work, because I really *needed* it to work. I learned how to solder wires together and how to assemble a wiring harness for something. I never knew what. Every day was the same thing: coffee breaks and lunch in the cafeteria at the same time, usually in the same seat, next to the same person. The people were great, but factory life just wasn't for me.

My thoughts kept going back to Montana, and my ride in that little machine that could fly forward, sideways, backwards, straight up and straight down. Flying helicopters still seemed out of reach, but I was determined to at least get my instrument rating, and was once again taking lessons with Les Taylor at Saguaro Aviation.

Unfortunately, Charmaine thought my flying was taking money that should be going for baby clothes. It seemed we had fallen out of love just as quickly as we had fallen in. To no one's surprise, we separated soon after Kari was born and were divorced after just two years of marriage. Little Kari Jill and Charmaine moved in with her parents and I was off to Mom's again. The divorce was amicable and I officially became a weekend dad.

I figured my future at Motorola had probably shortened considerably with the loss of my father-in-law's backing, so I started looking again. Jobs weren't hard to find for someone willing to work.

I was reading the help-wanted ads in the newspaper when I spotted something interesting: "Apprentice embalmer wanted. No experience required. Will train." I called the number and talked with the funeral director, who went by the name of "Colonel Parker."

He explained he was looking for a helper who could assist with funerals and visitations. He needed an experienced driver for the hearse and limousines and he stressed that the work uniform was a white shirt and tie on the job, except for funerals, which required a black suit. "No problem," I said, looking down at my dirty white tennis shoes, blue jeans, and red t-shirt.

Then he said he would also teach me the art of "preparing" a body for burial. That made me a little nervous. When he and his wife were out of town I would be asked to stay in a small apartment in the back of the mortuary. The thought of being there alone at night made my heart beat a lot faster and I almost hung up. But he sounded like a nice man and I really needed to find a career and earn a living. I made an appointment for the next day.

The next morning, dressed in a newly purchased white shirt, tie and black trousers, I pulled up to M. L. Gibbons Funeral Home. It was located on the Apache Trail—or US 60—which was the main highway running east and west through the Phoenix valley. The mortuary itself was new and modern, with a home in the rear where the Parkers lived. They didn't have any neighbors and the place looked fairly isolated.

I had a problem with dead people, even though I had only actually seen one up close at a funeral. But I was apprehensive even walking by that casket. I was paying a price for the movies I had grown up with and still watched: *Phantom of the Rue Morgue*, *The House of Wax* and *Frankenstein*. As silly as that sounds, those movies had instilled in me a fear of dead people and the supernatural that took me years to get over.

Even as I walked in the door I was spooked. I met the Colonel and Mrs. Parker in the office. He did the prep work and she did the paperwork. They were very friendly and I had a good interview. There were other employees who worked part-time when things got busy, but it would mainly be the three of us handling the day-to-day duties.

Then it was time for the colonel to give me a tour of the "home" as he called it. I had been dreading this, but it was something I resolved to do. At this point in my life I was desperate for some direction. So far I had failed at everything I had tried. Desperate people don't make the best decisions.

We started with the chapel, toured the two viewing rooms, and went down the hall to the casket selection room. A display of a dozen or so options ranged from a cremation box to the expensive bronze and hardwood sealers models. They all had to be dusted daily, and the chapel and viewing rooms had to be dusted and vacuumed at the end of the day. So far it was going better than I had thought it would, until we walked through the double doors marked "Employees Only," where we entered into a hallway with two more sets of double doors and one regular door.

One set of double doors led to the apartment that would be used by the overnight on-call guy. That would be me. It was a small efficiency with kitchen and bed plus bath and shower. The colonel told me that I was welcome to bring extra clothes and personal gear and that I could use the refrigerator in the prep room for perishables. *Yeah, right,* I thought, *I'll just put my midnight snack in there!*

The second set of double doors took us into the prep room, as they called it in the biz. Today everyone knows what the prep room looks like because of shows like CSI that detail exactly what goes on in there; but in my day there were few public glances into a house of death.

At this time most of the mortuaries also provided ambulances for the community and police departments. I liked driving the ambulance, but picking up the dead and caring for the bodies just wasn't for me. The first time I had to stay on-call overnight was also my last. Strange noises bothered me all night long. By morning I was looking for a new career.

I worked various jobs, mostly at service stations, because that was something I knew. I was living at home and could afford to buy a car. I had a long way to go, however, and still needed to convince the Marine Corps to give me another chance.

By now our troops were being sent into Vietnam and some of my friends were there. I felt I was missing out as I watched the news reports and film of helicopters carrying out their missions. More than anything, I wanted to be a part of the action.

The news media were saying our troops were in a war they couldn't win. *What the hell did the news jerks know?* I wondered. I formed a very negative attitude toward the media. I would gladly have traded places with any of the soldiers flying those beautiful machines, but I was helpless to do anything about it.

In spite of everything I had been through, I had accomplished a couple of things I was proud of. I had made a promise to my folks to earn my GED and after months of study, and a little help from my friends, I passed the test given by the state of Arizona. I was now a High School Graduate. The second achievement was earning my private pilot's certificate. I was on a roll; Mom and Dad were happy, and I felt it was a new start.

Shortly after I moved back home, my father blew in for one of his quickie visits. It was good to see Mom and Dad together again and as always, I wished it would last. We had a great time and talked about a lot of things—mostly me and what to do with my life. We all agreed that flying could offer a good future, but it would take time and money. It would also require that I study hard, which had never been one of my strengths.

"Well," I joked, "I've got plenty of time, but how long will Vietnam last?" I still wanted to be there as a Marine and fight the battle, and I often told Dad so.

"Let it go," he cautioned. But he and I knew that there are some painful things that can never be let go. Dad was a distinguished Marine and combat veteran, and I had been kicked out. Every time I looked at him I felt shame and embarrassment. He had been a wonderful and loving role model to me, and no matter what else I ever achieved, I would always feel I'd let him down. I believed the only thing that would make it up to him would be to get back in the Corps.

Several days after Dad left, I got a call to meet Mom at the restaurant for dinner. We sat in a booth near the back and had a serious talk. I had no way of knowing that my life was about to change again.

"Jerry," she said "I went to Saguaro Aviation today, and put enough money in your account for you to get your Commercial Certificate and Instrument Rating. It'll take constant study and a commitment to do this. But if you do it, you might even get your Flight Instructor Rating. Are you willing to put in the work?"

Was I willing? "You bet," I answered. "But where did the money come from?"

All she would say was, "Pennies from Heaven."

It would be nearly fifty years before I found out where those pennies fell from. I promised Mom that I would make her proud—and I went to work to make it happen.

Chapter 9

Early Flying Days

Without a doubt 1965 would be the hardest year of my life so far. I had always had a difficult time learning, but I had never before had a reason to *want* to learn about anything other than being a Marine. Now I was faced with *having* to learn, and I would have to either step up to the plate or fail. It was that simple. I knew I couldn't—and wouldn't—fail, because too many people believed in me and were willing to help.

Still, it had taken a couple of tries to get through the private pilot written exam; and that was simple compared to the commercial exam. The instrument exam might as well have been rocket science as far as my brain was concerned. To say I had to buckle down and study hard is an understatement.

I continued working, but could now fly on a regular schedule. The flying was a breeze for me, and I sailed through the air work with the greatest of ease. There were a number of different flight instructors teaching me, but I did all my check flights with Les Taylor. I learned something from every flight and was an eager student. I completed all the ground school requirements and took the commercial written FAA exam. I failed with a 68 the first time, but studied for another week and passed with a 70 the next time.

On October 8, 1965, I passed the commercial flight test, and three days later I took the flight instructor test and passed on the first try. In December I passed the instrument exam and flight test. I was now licensed by the FAA to carry passengers for hire in a multi-engine aircraft on instrument conditions day and night, and I was licensed to instruct in single and multi-engine airplanes.

As 1965 was winding down, my future was looking better. Having earned all my pilot certifications was truly the greatest accomplishment of my life. My confidence soared, and I felt like things were beginning to turn around for me.

I had resumes out with all the airlines and fixed-base operators in the state, but I still needed to build more flight time. The more experience, the better the job. Same old wine in a brand new bottle, but I wasn't deterred one bit. I would take whatever came along.

The opportunity for my first real flying job came from a flight school at Deer Valley Airport north of Phoenix. I'd been hanging out at Saguaro Aviation for a couple of months, filling in for the more experienced instructors and taking every flight that was thrown my way; charter flights to other cities and airports, or sometimes as a safety pilot for a customer-owned twin-engine airplane. When you're a low-time pilot you fly whatever, whenever, and hopefully, forever!

In late October I got a call from Larry Young at Sawyer Aviation. His boss, Darrel Sawyer, had just landed a contract with Trans World Airlines to train their flight engineers as qualified pilots so they could help in the event of an emergency. Sawyer was a first-class operation and this would be a good learning experience for me.

It has been said that "learning something is easier if you teach it," and for the next few months I found that very true. I had to really study aircraft manuals and learn my stuff because these flight engineers were sharp guys. It was a good job for a new instructor, and I appreciated getting a start at Sawyer. I probably learned as much as I taught.

While waiting for a student one day, I watched a helicopter land out on the ramp for fuel. The pilot, Bill Hall, had been traveling around the country teaching people to fly in an old Bell 47. He was a real character with his shaved and polished head and an oil-stained, orange flight suit. He was a true helicopter pioneer and entrepreneur—like the barnstormers in the early days of fixed-wing aircraft—just looking to make a buck.

The Bell 47 was old and slow, but at only 100 dollars an hour, it was cheap to fly. Solo flights were only 80 dollars an hour. I only needed eight hours of instruction and four hours solo to qualify for my helicopter rating. Then Bill made me an offer I couldn't refuse.

For a mere twelve hundred dollars cash he would guarantee me a helicopter rating in two weeks. Within a couple of days, Mom helped me come up with the cash from a bank loan, and I was on my way to becoming a heavily-in-debt helicopter pilot.

For the next two weeks I taught the TWA guys to fly airplanes and Bill Hall taught me to fly helicopters. The old machine was just like that one up in Montana. I was stoked! I still wonder how I managed to fly and learn in that Bell. The battery was usually dead, requiring a jump-start every time we went out. It burned about two quarts of oil every hour and the old wooden rotor blades were out of balance, causing serious vibrations and noises. It was equipped with only a two-way radio and a compass for navigation. In spite of all that, flight time built up quickly and I was ready for my test in record time.

FAA inspector Gene Olson was the examiner. Truth be known, he didn't have much more experience with helicopters than I did. He was a brand new FAA-trained rookie just like I was. In the 1960s helicopters were a novelty and you didn't see many around. The technology was nowhere near what it is today, and this particular bird had its own unique problems.

There was a light rain that February morning as we walked toward the helicopter pad, but visibility was good, so we elected to go ahead with the flight. I performed a textbook preflight inspection, and we climbed into our seats. There were no headsets, so after the engine started we had to yell back and forth.

The start-up was normal and I picked us up to a hover and made a 360-degree clearing turn. Seeing no other traffic in the area, I lifted up and headed north. The field was uncontrolled and the old Bell lacked a radio, so it was everyone for themselves. We flew about a mile to where an old tire had been painted white and thrown into the desert to mark a helicopter pad. There was still a light drizzle and the machine began to shake more than usual.

As I made my approach to the tire, the shaking became stronger. Gene and I looked at each other in wide-eyed amazement. He pointed toward the airport and hollered at the top of his lungs for me to head back. By the time we were on short final to the airport pad, the vertical vibration was nearly uncontrollable, and we were both hanging on to the controls.

I didn't even settle into a hover: I just let that old Bell land itself, and while it wasn't pretty, it *was* a safe landing. Bill Hall realized there had been a problem and was right there with a ready story. He explained that wooden blades have a tendency to soak up water, and one blade might absorb more than the other, making it heavier and throwing the track of the two rotors out of balance. The longer you fly, the worse the vibration, he said. I thought it might have been considerate of him to tell us that *before* letting us take off in the rain.

On this day, two rookies barely made it back before the Bell would have shaken itself apart and killed us both. Gene gave me a passing grade on the flight test, saying "If you can fly that thing … you can fly *anything!*" As he stalked off the field, he made it clear to my instructor that he would never fly in that old machine again.

I had earned my certification and was now a helicopter pilot. Since I had a few hours of flight time left on my account, Bill told me I should go ahead and schedule a check ride for my helicopter instructor rating. Even though I was low on flight time, I met all the requirements. We scheduled a ride for the following week and I studied every night after work. I had to know everything there was to know about that helicopter because this time, my ride was with the FAA Chief Inspector, Myles Ruggenberg. Yep, the same guy who had suspended my certificate following the Virginia plane crash. He was known as tough and at this point, I was known as scared. I hoped he wouldn't recognize me.

The morning was bright and sunny when Myles arrived. The helicopter was fueled, oiled and ready to go. After checking my paperwork, he asked me to do a weight and balance, figuring his weight at 180 pounds and that we would be flying to Tucson. He asked me how much fuel we would have when we got there. I knew that we would not actually be flying to Tucson, this was just a test to see if I could figure it correctly.

Bill Hall knew from previous students what the inspector would ask, so I was prepared. I already had a weight and balance on my clipboard, but I said, "Yes sir," and sat down at a table. While Bill made small talk with the inspector I pretended to be going through the flight manual and doing the math.

After a few minutes, I said to Mr. Ruggenberg, "Sir, here is my weight and balance. We are within limits and should have approximately 30 minutes of fuel left at Tucson."

He took the paperwork and said, "Okay, let's go fly."

Several minutes later we were in the old Bell heading north. The machine was running like a Swiss watch and I was feeling confident and in control. I did a few landings and takeoffs followed by a simulated forced landing, all the while explaining what I would be telling a student. When we were finished, Myles said, "Okay, I have the helicopter, and I'll take us back to the airport."

I passed the flight test, and as Myles was filling out my temporary pilot certificate, he looked at me and said, "I see you got your instrument rating since I last saw you. And by the way, nice job today." He *had* remembered me.

In mid-January of 1966 I had an offer to move to Cutter Aviation, the Beechcraft dealer at Sky Harbor Airport. Owner Bill Cutter had just bought a Hughes 269A for flight training. Cutter had all the latest in single- and twin-engine airplanes, and Bill needed a dual-rated pilot who could fly both the chopper and fixed wing. Bill Sawyer recommended me and we parted as friends.

I was excited, but that old fear of being found out was still in the back of my mind. Once again I marked "No" to the felony question on the employment application. I wanted so badly to tell Bill Cutter the truth, but couldn't risk it. He was a nice guy, but would he be understanding and forgiving? I didn't want to lose this opportunity for a new career, so I kept my mouth shut.

This was the perfect job for a new pilot needing to build flight time and gain experience. I flew nearly all the Beechcraft models, including the single engine Bonanza and the twin engine Baron. Weekends were for charter flights, taking customers all over the country. During the week, however, I flew the helicopter for a local radio station, with a reporter along to broadcast the morning and evening traffic reports. This was my introduction to the Hughes 269A. It was a two-passenger machine that resembled a little grasshopper, and wasn't nearly as stable or forgiving as the Bell. Some pilots say it was hard to fly, but I didn't think so. I loved it from the very beginning.

One hot spring day during a traffic flight, the reporter was on the air describing an accident when the engine started coughing and sputtering. The reporter stopped talking in mid-sentence and looked at me. I immediately lowered the collective pitch and set up an autorotation—an emergency procedure that allows the machine to glide to the ground. I picked out a place to land and set the little chopper down in a dry river bed. There was silence between us as the rotor blades coasted to a stop. The reporter looked over at me and said, "I wet my pants."

I was happy to have avoided that embarrassment, until I unfastened my seat belt, stepped out onto the ground ... and promptly threw up.

As a pilot, you always wonder if you would make a successful landing in an emergency. I did, and learned a very valuable lesson: training, experience, and luck are paramount to a successful flying career. I was elated to have survived *and* saved the chopper. And Bill Cutter was happy. The problem was found to be a simple engine malfunction when the left magneto failed. It was easily fixed, and I was back flying the next day, but with a different reporter.

In Vietnam the fighting was becoming more intense and it looked like we might be heading for war. I was very happy at Cutter, and getting valuable experience, but something was still missing. That old fear of discovery was still haunting me, and I wondered if the FAA could stop me from flying if my past were known. I worried about what Bill Cutter would do if he found out. I was afraid of losing everything I had worked so hard to accomplish. I felt I needed to make a change of some kind, but didn't know what. The answer soon found me.

Chapter 10

Ft. Wolters, Texas - April, 1966

I met Pete Cronk while I was taking helicopter training with Bill Hall at Saguaro Aviation. Pete's family owned "Mag's Ham Bun," a small sandwich shop in Scottsdale renowned for the best ham sandwiches you'll find anywhere. "Mag's" had been a fixture and common meeting place in Scottsdale for years.

Pete had also taken lessons with Bill Hall and wanted to be a helicopter pilot. He didn't have enough time built up to get a flying job, and was stuck making ham sandwiches. He stopped by Cutter one day to visit with me and said he had applied for a job as a helicopter pilot instructor in Mineral Wells, Texas. The Army desperately needed instructors to train pilots for the war in Vietnam. Southern Airways had a contract to provide the Army with qualified pilots who would be trained as instructors. All we had to do was fudge our helicopter flying time a little and we would be hired. It sounded too good to be true.

I called Southern Airways, requested an application, and mailed it back. Ten days later I received a reply saying I had been accepted and asking when I could start. I called Pete and we agreed I should give Cutter at least two weeks notice. I had only been with them a few months.

Bill Cutter understood and wished me luck, then gave me a little advice: "Don't go down there and get patriotic and join the Army."

"No, that never entered my mind," I told him. We parted as friends, and I was off again.

A couple of weeks later Pete and I were heading for Fort Wolters, Texas in my Pontiac convertible. I was excited, knowing how desperately the military needed pilots. Pete didn't know my whole backstory, only that I served a short hitch in the Marines and it wasn't for me.

The U.S. Army Primary Helicopter School at Ft. Wolters had been training helicopter pilots since 1956. Its first graduating class in 1957 numbered only 35 pilots. Now—through its contract with Southern Airways—the school provided helicopter training to all branches of the service as well as to students from around the world. Because of the Vietnam conflict the vast majority of current students were Army. There had been over 3600 students in the class of 1966. We had no idea what were getting ourselves into.

When we arrived at the base we were taken to security to be logged in. The guard asked for identification, vehicle ID, and our letter from Southern Airways confirming that we were new hires. Then the dreaded question: "Do you have a criminal record?"

I replied in the negative, while my heart pounded loudly in my chest. Poe's "Telltale Heart" had nothing on what mine was doing!

I will never forget that moment. It suddenly hit me where I was and who I was messing with. This was a U.S. Army base owned by the U.S. Government, and I was here under false pretenses. I felt that at any moment my heart would explode. The moment passed with my heart still intact, and Pete and I were on our way to check in at another area; this time with a security pass on my front windshield. I made it through that one, I thought, but I felt certain the "day of reckoning" was imminent.

In spite of my fears, we completed all the paperwork and were assigned to a training flight that would begin in two days. We were told that living accommodations were better in Weatherford, a small town just a few miles to the east. We were on the payroll and headed toward a new home and life. At least I hoped so.

I made up my mind right then that since I was already on the horse, I might as well enjoy the ride. I was in too deep to back out now. I had come here knowing the chances were better than 50-50 that I would be turned down. If I fell now, it was going to be a very long fall.

We found a fully furnished apartment in Weatherford and entered into the world of helicopter instructors. Our school lasted 14 days, during which we flew with experienced instructors in the mornings and spent afternoons in the classroom. By the time we graduated we felt comfortable doing our job. Choppers were just coming of age, and this was the finest helicopter training available in the world. I always believed it was this training that helped me survive the very risky business of my later career.

We were now qualified instructors and ready to go to work. The primary course lasted 16 weeks, with the first eight weeks devoted to learning the basic flight maneuvers on a "stage field"— a small airport just for helicopters. During the final eight weeks the students learned to apply those basic maneuvers to unimproved or less-than-desirable landing areas.

Each instructor was assigned three students, and there were 30 students in a flight. A "flight," in this context was similar to a platoon. I never knew how many flights there were, but when Pete and I first saw the main heliport, we were amazed at the number of helicopters out there.

The school had started with 125 helicopters in 1956, and would peak at more than 1300 by 1969, so there were probably over 1,000 during the period of 1966-67 when we were there. We saw hundreds of the little machines on concrete pads surrounded by hundreds of acres of black top. Hangars were lined up in neat rows and they were a beehive of activity. The noise was incredible, with helicopters coming and going, hovering to and from the takeoff area, or being towed by jeeps to their hangars.

It seemed just as chaotic in the air, with helicopters coming and going in all directions, but we soon learned that the Army had a method and everything was under control. Military Police were everywhere and were all friendly, so far.

There would eventually be three heliports and 25 stage fields. Many of the fields were named for cities in Vietnam, so the students could become familiar with the odd-sounding names like Bien Hoa, Chu Lai, Vung Tau, My Tho and An Khe. They were spaced around Mineral Wells and could accommodate up to 30 helicopters. Each was equipped with a control tower, toilet facilities and training rooms. Traffic patterns included approach and departure lanes and areas to make full touchdown autorotations.

The job was great and I loved instructing. We taught in three types of helicopters: Bell, Hughes, and Hiller. I was assigned to a Hiller flight and Pete went to a Bell flight. Every week the flights alternated morning and afternoons, so that night flying could be worked in for all flights. In the beginning, Pete worked mornings and I worked afternoons.

Instructor at Ft. Wolters

While Pete and I loved the flying and teaching, we enjoyed our time off as well. We shared an apartment, were both single, making a good living, and having fun. Living in Weatherford was a wonderful experience for me. It was a happy little town, similar to all the small mining towns I had grown up in. Instead of miners, these locals were mostly farmers, with some military families in the mix.

The main highway ran right through the middle of town and the town square, which held many of the city's businesses and shops. The focal point of the square was the big white county court house, the pride of the town. Traffic had to slow to 25 miles an hour and crawl through the town square, because of the many pedestrians. Pete was caught zooming through that 25 mph zone at 45 miles an hour. After paying a 25 dollar fine, he learned the lesson: "Don't Mess with Texas."

The local hangout was the Dairy Queen. Pete and I ate many of our meals there and found our entertainment in the form of girls. Early on, we would sometimes double date, and it didn't take long for me to fall in love—a few times—with Texas. It was a great few months.

Change was in the air for both of us, though. Pete told me that he and Nancy, his hometown girlfriend, were getting married. It was no big surprise to me, but it marked a change in both our lives. In the short time we had known each other and shared the apartment, we'd had a blast and figured we'd be friends forever.

For the next couple of months I was living well; enjoying my job and watching Pete and Nancy get set up. I found another place to live nearby, but I didn't move until a few days after they returned from their honeymoon. After all, I wanted to be there for that very first breakfast.

Nancy was a nervous wreck, trying so hard to do everything just right. She was barely 18, and an absolute "10" on the male scale, except for her cooking. The bacon and eggs were overcooked and undercooked, respectively. The final straw for the new little bride was when she filled Pete's coffee cup with hot water from a brand new pot.

He looked up at her, and with his New Jersey accent and deadpan expression, said "Nancy, you forgot the coffee! Duh!"

For a few seconds we all looked at each other, and then burst out laughing. Then we headed to the Dairy Queen for breakfast. We loved Nancy. She was a welcome addition, and we had bonded for life

By the time my first students graduated I was feeling very comfortable with being an instructor.   I loved the job and the students were a pleasure to work with, although I had difficulty adjusting to them calling me "Sir." Whenever I walked up to our study table the soldiers would snap to attention until I told them "Carry on." I was loving it.

We all wore the same flight suits and baseball-style caps, except that the instructors wore black caps and students wore blue ones. I felt at home here and had no trouble making friends. The camaraderie among the instructors was similar to what I had experienced in the Marine Corps, and I needed that to feel fulfilled and secure. I still couldn't get past the nagging feeling that this was all going to end badly, just like the Scottsdale Police job, and the Marines.

I would get mad at myself for not enjoying the present, but having once experienced humiliation and disgrace, I never wanted to go through that again. The memory was always there, lingering in the back of my mind. If someone I didn't know left me a phone message, my first thought was of my "status." The stress was always there.

I sometimes wondered what my good friend Pete would think of me if he found out. I wanted so badly to just let it ride … to stay with this great job and play the odds. But I also wanted to be in the Army and go to Vietnam as an officer. I had given up on the Marines and had been thinking about flying for the Army. That was the reason I became a helicopter pilot in the first place; the reason I took those lessons at Deer Valley Airport less than a year ago. Now I felt I had some things going for me that might influence the Army.

I didn't want to talk to anyone at the base, but I had met a recruiting officer from Fort Worth at a social event and I gave him a call. We got together one Saturday morning and I laid out the whole story to Sergeant Randy Rogers, telling him about my desperate desire to join the Army.

He said, "Jerry, I'll look into it for you. I really think that with your helicopter experience, you'd have a good chance of getting in the Warrant Officer Candidate School."

I was very familiar with WOCS, since it was the program most of our students at Ft. Wolters were in. He said the Army was indeed "looking for a few good men." He believed in me, and that meant the world to me.

I headed back to Weatherford feeling like a million bucks. This bad dream I had been living was about to end. *Who knows*, I thought, *by this time next month I might be an instructor for the Army. I may even have a direct commission, and head straight to Vietnam!* I drove down the road singing, "I've got the world on a string, sittin' on a rainbow." When I returned to Ft. Wolters, I submitted the paperwork and waited. I had been told it would take about 60 days to get a decision. It would be a long 60 days for me.

My respect for the helicopter became a passion. I really had no idea what these little whirly-birds could do or not do until coming to Ft. Wolters. Helicopters are very complicated and fragile, much like a hummingbird. They need love, understanding and luck. Mistakes usually amounted to, at the very least, total destruction of the machine. A student can only learn that while in flight. You might only have a few seconds to initiate an emergency procedure that, if not done properly, could kill you instantly. The Army school not only taught students how to fly these machines, they also taught them the aerodynamics and theory of flight.

Our students and instructors did make mistakes of all kinds; some resulting in death and injuries. It wasn't always the pilot who was at fault, however, because the helicopter was still being refined into what it is today. There are so many moving parts and so many actions to be taken—all depending on the other to function properly—that it was imperative that a pilot learn what the machine was capable of doing. His life depended on knowing everything about it, and we were still learning the things it would *not* do.

The majority of pilot students were around 20 years old, and in a few short months they would be expected to fly the much bigger and faster machines of war. I give the Army credit: these pilot training courses were not a slam dunk for students. Everything was taught by the book. Maneuvers like the airport traffic pattern were expected to be carried out exactly as the book instructed or the student failed the flight. After three unsatisfactory rides, a student changed instructors. If another three rides were failed, it was adios; the student was out of there. It was a fair system, and as instructors, we were proud of our efforts.

Accident statistics were not kind to the Army's school nor to our pilots in Vietnam. The helicopter industry was new and struggling as the various machines were manufactured at a record pace. They were still learning. I know I was.

Life, as we all know, changes by the day or—in this case—by the phone call. Sergeant Randy Rogers called me the day before my second three students graduated. We were preparing for a military graduation ceremony followed by a formal dinner, with coat and tie being mandatory. This phone call brought the wires together in my brain that signaled a storm was a-comin'.

My friend Randy told me he had gone up his command and received a negative response to my request to join the Army. His superiors felt it would send a wrong signal to other offenders of the law, and they were uncomfortable because I had been discharged for "conduct not becoming a Marine."

Randy also told me to keep my eyes and ears open. He had feared from the beginning that once my background was out there, the higher-ranking officers might be concerned about a guy with my credentials working in such a sensitive position during war time. That had been the worst of my fears since the day I checked in. I could keep working and wait to see if the hammer was going to fall, but I didn't have a good feeling about the future.

I resigned two weeks later. I couldn't stand the thought of being fired again. When I lost the Scottsdale Police job it was almost unbearable and I didn't want to go through that horrible shame and embarrassment yet again; this time in front of my fellow instructors and students.

It was time to go. I told my Flight Commander, Don Wolgamott, that I had a family problem back home. He understood without asking. He knew I loved my job, but I had a higher calling that needed to be taken care of. After watching my second set of students receive their hard-earned Aviator Wings, I was ready to move on. I had completed my last contribution to the war effort.

I had been happy at Ft. Wolters, and loved the challenge of taking a student who had never flown a helicopter from ground zero to pilot status. Training was fulfilling for me and so was the camaraderie with other instructors. This was the best job I'd ever had and probably ever would have; and I had just walked away from it. Yet there was no doubt in my mind that I was doing the right thing. By getting away from the military base, I hoped that anyone up the chain of command who was worried about my record, would learn that I had quit and let it drop.

I told Pete and Nancy there was a problem that needed my attention and playfully told them to mind their own business. I reluctantly left Weatherford, telling myself I just couldn't take a chance on being fired or arrested; or even worse, escorted to the main gate with my personal belongings in a bag. I had lived that nightmare on my last day in the Marines. Never again.

Chapter 11

Petroleum Helicopters: June 1966

By now the helicopter market was hurting for pilots. Between the military and commercial needs, choppers of all sizes and types were in great demand. The high accident rate was causing insurance companies to require experienced pilots with more and better training. This situation seemed to be in my favor, so I headed southeast for Louisiana: Cajun country and land of the Rebels.

Petroleum Helicopters, Inc. (PHI) was the largest helicopter company in the world at that time, operating machines to and from oil platforms in the Gulf of Mexico. Their main offices and training school were located in Lafayette, Louisiana, just a short flight from the Gulf shore. Most of their choppers were the smaller Bells and larger Sikorskys; their purpose being to haul men, equipment and supplies to the huge fields of oil platforms out in the Gulf. Some helicopters were based on the platforms, while others stayed ashore at night.

Insurance companies required a minimum of 1,000 hours of helicopter flight time as "pilot in command," and the application asked if that was the case. I handled it the same way I handled "Have you ever been convicted of a felony?" I lied about the felony, and I produced a padded logbook that clearly showed more than 1500 hours to satisfy the flight time requirement. I was confident in my ability to do the job, I just wasn't confident that my past would let me keep it.

I was excited about this new adventure, as I've always loved the ocean and ships. Arizonans don't see many seagulls. Everything was different: the weather, the landscape, even the people. It was a bit like visiting a foreign country. Some of the locals spoke a dialect that was familiar, yet different. I now know they were probably Cajun, but at the time I had never heard that term. The first time I stopped at a roadside café and ordered coffee, it almost knocked me off the stool. When I asked where it was from, the waitress walked over and gave me a piercing look, and asked, "Boy, where *you* from? You one of those Yankees?"

"Yankee?" I asked. "You mean like Civil War Yankee?" That was what she meant all right, and Louisiana folks were proud Rebels. I drank my coffee and left.

My job entailed flying a three-passenger Bell 47G-5 from Morgan City, Louisiana out into the Gulf of Mexico to the oil platforms. The company required a six-day training class plus some flying to learn how to handle helicopters over water, and to become familiar with emergency procedures. An instructor was assigned to me and the company provided a motel room for the duration of my training.

Because we flew over water, all the 'copters were equipped with large airbags mounted on each side of the aircraft to keep it afloat in calmer waters. I quickly realized that flying here would be totally different from anything I had done before, and I really needed to pay attention. I was going to fly these little whirlygigs 50 or 60 miles over the ocean and then land on a 60-foot round platform, with nothing except a compass and a two-way radio to guide me. To complicate things, it could get a little dicey when visibility was low. I was definitely going to pay attention.

My instructor was Billy Frasier, an ex-army pilot who had been with PHI for about 10 years. Billy was a Tennessee boy, blond and slim, about 40 years old, and he loved to talk. The important thing though, was that he had several thousand hours of chopper time.

The little Bell helicopter looked much like the ones seen in the old M*A*S*H TV show. Three passengers could fit inside the huge bubble front, along with cargo racks mounted on each side. Fully loaded, the chopper could carry 1200 to 1500 pounds of people, cargo and aviation fuel.

It could cruise along for about three and a half hours at 80 mph. That may seem slow for an aircraft, but it wasn't a rocket, it was a reliable workhorse. It was also a helicopter, which meant it was temperamental. It liked 3100 rpm on the engine and nothing less was acceptable.

During training we did all the standard maneuvers. Landing and taking off on the water was a different experience. When the helicopter was sitting on the water you could taxi in any direction with the cyclic, control the speed with the collective, and control the heading with the tail rotor.

It was a strange feeling to be sitting in the water and trying to hover in one spot. The rotors stirred up the water, challenging the pilot's peripheral vision. Staying in one spot required concentrated practice.

I learned more about the oil fields and what my job required. I would transport people and supplies to a set of platforms about 30 miles south of the coastline. There were backup plans in case of bad weather and hurricanes. Every day would be something different, and I was looking forward to it.

We made several training trips out into the gulf and it was thrilling to make an approach to the steel helipads, some of which were 50 to 75 feet above the water. The size of the platforms was awesome, and some had helipads large enough for two or more machines.

On the sixth day of training Billy said I was ready for my check ride. I took a short evaluation flight with the PHI check pilot and was pronounced ready for work. I headed for Morgan City to report for duty.

Morgan City, Louisiana is about 50 miles southeast of the company's headquarters in Lafayette, and just a few miles from the waterline of the Gulf Coast. It's also surrounded by swamps. I'll admit to being a bit intimidated by all that swamp land. I had seen the movies and heard the stories about swamp critters. They didn't just bite; they ate you, boots and all. I wondered, *What's an Arizona boy doing in a place like this?*

The terrain wasn't the only difference: Arizona seldom gets rain, while near the gulf coast it rained regularly. Even when it wasn't raining, the skies remained overcast and dreary; nothing like the bright, sunny days back home. There were also creepy looking bugs, some of which seemed to be nearly as big as birds— at least to my eyes.

When I drove by the PHI Heliport in Morgan City, I had the same reaction I'd had at Ft. Wolters … *Wow!* There were at least 50 helicopters—large and small—sitting on the ramp. It was stunning and very impressive.

I located the office and checked in. The employees were pleasant and very helpful. The bulletin board had a list of nearby rooming houses and I found one that was cheap enough. I was told the meals were good and the place was clean, so I took it.

Once the paperwork was out of the way, I was sent to flight operations and assigned a Bell 47 G-5. I was briefed on the heliport procedures and traffic patterns, and I asked a lot of questions. When I finally ran out of questions, I was told to report at 6 a.m. for a seven o'clock flight. I felt ready to go, but still a little intimidated. Everything was so new, including Louisiana.

I reported the next morning after a hearty breakfast at the boarding house, which was just as I had been told; clean room, friendly people and great food. I checked in with operations and learned that I would be ferrying two engineers out to C-16 platform. The weather report indicated it was going to be a good day, with possibly some low clouds burning off later in the morning and winds less than 20 knots out of the southwest.

Couldn't be better, I thought. I looked over the wall map of oil field locations and found my platform. I planned my course, grabbed a cup of coffee and headed for the flight line. My ship was topped off with fuel and after a lengthy pre-flight check, I determined we were ready to go.

I was excited to be taking my first flight out as an employee. My two passengers arrived, we saddled up, and the flight was on. The area was easy to get out of, and as the sun rose, so did we, on a course of 247 degrees. Since I had a headwind, I figured I should be good on heading and arrive at the oil field in about 40 minutes.

I discovered that what they called "clear" in Louisiana, we consider "hazy" in Arizona. Outside the city, the terrain turned to swamp. Little patches of fog were spotted all along our route, but weren't a problem; they just looked spooky. Every now and then we noticed a disturbance in the water. One of the engineers looked at me and said, "Big 'gators down there, and they's hungry!" This was way more info than I needed.

I had leveled off at 500 feet and we crossed the beach 12 minutes later. The procedure was to stay in contact with the company dispatcher and report in when I crossed the beach to give my estimated time of arrival (ETA) at my destination.

"Dispatch, flight 233 crossing the beach, platform Charlie 16 in 20 minutes."

"Flight 233, dispatch, copy. Report landing."

"Roger, dispatch. Out"

I settled back and watched my heading faithfully, keeping it at 247 degrees. I didn't want anything to go wrong, and I wasn't comfortable with the visibility at all. It looked like I was flying into a thicker haze. Reassuring thoughts flitted through my mind: *After all it is my first flight; sure I'm going to be a bit nervous. It's only been five minutes since I crossed the beach and I still have 15 minutes until I should be at the platform.*

I still wasn't completely reassured. I could only see water and sky; nothing else. I was a little spooked to say the least.

Ten more minutes passed with no platforms in sight. My only navigation tool was a magnetic compass, so I just held 500 feet and a 247 degree heading. In another three minutes, there it was; Platform 16. It took another couple of minutes to approach and land. I looked over at my passengers, expecting to get a "nice job" or at least a smile, but they had dozed off. I'd been sweating bullets and they were sleeping like babies.

"Dispatch. Flight 233 landing on Charlie 16 "

"Roger, 233, dispatch, have a good day!"

My day *was* good, and I made several more flights that day to other oil rigs. I carried men to different platforms and hauled equipment back and forth from platform to shore. The next days and weeks were pretty much the same. I had no serious difficulties and even found myself bored at times. I missed the activity at Ft. Wolters and wished for the millionth time that I could have stayed there.

The work and living arrangements here were unusual. Pilots were on duty for 10 days straight and off for seven. I lived in the boarding house when I was off, but during my ten-day shifts, I lived on an oil platform.

The drilling platforms were like little cities, with different levels for sleeping quarters, bathrooms and various work stations. The little two-man rooms we slept in were nice enough, and we had TV, movies and excellent food. Drilling went on 24 hours a day on the upper deck. When the drilling was completed in one area, the platform was moved to a new location and a pumping platform replaced the drill rig. Work never stopped unless a hurricane was imminent.

I initially thought I'd really like the working schedule of 10 days on and seven days off. A whole week off at a time sounded great until the first time I experienced it. I was alone in a place where I didn't fit in, and I had no friends nearby. For seven days I just moped around the boarding house, took in a couple of movies, or laid around my room and read. By the time the week was over I was thankful to get back to work.

By the end of my second ten-day shift, I was comfortable with the work and familiar with the oil field. We were only 20 minutes offshore, and most times I could see the platforms shortly after I crossed the beach. The work was easy enough and I loved the old Bell helicopters. I just didn't care for my surroundings.

I was already missing Ft. Wolters. I felt like I had come so close to becoming an Army aviator. *If only ...*, I thought, for about the hundredth time. I knew I needed to give this place a chance; maybe meet some people or go to a singles club. I was at a loss as to how to fill my time. I was lonely, depressed, and homesick—not for Arizona, but for Texas.

I was in constant touch with Mom and Dad, and let them know how I was doing and what I was feeling. They didn't like the sound of Louisiana either, but they respected my fears and were supportive of everything I had going on. They were to me what fuel is to an engine: They kept me going. I so badly wanted to make this career work, and more than anything, I wanted to make them proud of me.

A month went by in the Gulf with no negative encounters or close calls of any kind. The job was easy, but not busy enough. Many times I would fly workers out to a platform and stay all day, getting only about two hours of flying time that day. Then there were some days I barely stopped at all. I would land, refuel, eat, and take off again. But those days were rare.

After several boring, non-eventful weeks, I was about to have a bad day. It was the last day of one of my 10-day shifts. I had made two runs that morning and was just back from lunch when dispatch called for another run.

"Jerry I need you to run a part out to the Bluewater platform."

"Okay," I said. "Where's Bluewater?"

He pointed to a map behind him. "It's 60 miles straight south, you can't miss it. On an overcast day like today, you'll see it 20 miles away. It's big and has lots of lights; looks like a big ship."

"Okay, I'm off. Where's the part?"

"It's on the way," he said, "they'll meet you at the helicopter."

Two hours later, a guy finally showed up with the important part that just had to be delivered right away. He handed me a small box containing an O ring for a drill bit, and said they needed it immediately.

As I left the heliport I noticed the wind gusting strongly from the southwest.

When I crossed the beach twelve minutes later, I still couldn't see the platforms, even though the forecast called for clear skies and light winds. There was nothing on the horizon but water, sky and haze. I was starting to get a bad feeling. My compass heading was correct at 240 degrees, altitude 500 feet, and airspeed 75 mph, so I figured I should be on the pad at the Bluewater drilling rig in 45 minutes.

There are times when the machine you're flying just doesn't seem to be acting the way your mind tells you it should. This was one of those times. The nose of the aircraft seemed higher than usual.

My imagination? I wondered. Maybe. I worried about it for a few minutes, and then it hit me. I had never flown the Bell 47 without a passenger. With no one but me inside, the ship was tail heavy.

That's all it is. Relax, Jerry! Then I thought I detected a miss in the engine, and was that compass swinging the right way? I thought I noticed a drop in the oil pressure, but a closer look told me it was right where it should be.

What's going on? I wondered again.

The mind plays strange tricks on you when you let it, and that's just what was happening now. Forty-five minutes later there was still no pad, and no Bluewater drill rig anywhere in sight. I went on for another five agonizing minutes. I was sure I had missed it.

"Dispatch this is flight 188. I am five minutes past my ETA to Bluewater and there's nothing in sight out here but haze. What is Bluewater reporting for weather, and what do you suggest I do?"

"Jerry, Bluewater says it's a little hazy and overcast, but winds and visibility are as forecast. They also say they just found their missing part, so you can come on back. How is your fuel?"

"I have two hours remaining on the fuel and I'm heading home." I was so relieved! It was going to take about an hour and 15 minutes back to the beach and another 12 minutes to Morgan City. I should still have 30 minutes of reserve fuel when I landed. No problem.

Over the company radio I heard other inbound flights complaining about the visibility and asking about weather changes. A few minutes later, dispatch advised all units to stand by for a weather briefing, and reported that a change was coming.

zzZZAAAPPP! And that was the last of the radio. It was the kind of "zap" that spoke for itself. There was no point in checking volume and squelch. This radio was dead! I sat in stunned disbelief as wisps of cloud and condensation moved toward my aircraft. The ceiling was dropping and I was now down to less than 300 feet over the ocean, and the whitecaps were getting bigger.

At times like this you wish you were anywhere other than where you are. All I could do was hold my heading and stay below the clouds. There was no question in my mind that this was some kind of pop-up storm, and I should be out of it any second.

I saw what appeared to be land ahead and now I was less than 100 feet above water. I crossed from the ocean over a small berm into the swampland south of what I hoped was Morgan City. Clouds intermingled with trees ahead, and it was time to land. I began circling and found a small patch of dry land with barely enough room for the helicopter to touch down. Even then, the tail hung out over the water. A light rain began to fall as I sat there at idle with the engine still running. If the clouds didn't lift in the next few minutes, I'd be here until morning. I didn't want to think about that.

As the minutes ticked by, the rain pelted harder and the clouds got thicker. I was here for the night, without even a radio to let dispatch know I was safe. I shut the engine down and made sure all switches were off. Several minutes later, the rotor blades coasted to a stop. I was very alone and way out of my comfort zone.

I stepped out of the ship onto the little patch of ground. It was a good enough spot and didn't appear to have been under water recently, so maybe I was okay. I got back in the helicopter and surveyed what I had with me. The first-aid kit included a thermal blanket, flares, flashlight and a snakebite kit. *But where's the "alligator bite" kit?* I thought, with a wry smile.

In my map case I also carried an emergency ration kit from the U.S. Army. C-rations were not that bad, and I had a choice of spaghetti and meatballs or beans and franks. I chose the latter and by the time I had finished and polished off a pound cake from a small can, it was dark and still raining. I had plenty of water and was thankful the FAA required us to carry survival gear. I could stretch out along the three seats and build a comfortable little nest. Now all I had to do was lay back and get some sleep, and hope the weather cleared by morning.

I slept well for a couple of hours before my eyes suddenly opened and I was wide awake. I had heard something. I lay quietly for a few more minutes and heard it again. It was a splash. A *big* splash! *Who or what would be splashing around in a swamp in the middle of the night,* I wondered, although I so badly didn't want to know. Movies had really messed with my mind. Scenes from *The Creature from the Black Lagoon* were already playing in my head. Oh yeah, it was gonna be a long night!

The splashing was sporadic and I knew it had to be alligators or *The Creature*. For the rest of the night I never even considered closing my eyes except to blink, and I barely did that. I knew at any second a huge *something* would crash through the bubble, and I would be eaten alive. I laid there waiting and listening. I tried not to move a muscle, for fear I would give away my position to whatever was out there.

Morning eventually came, but it was the longest night of my life. I swore that if I made it out of there alive, this Arizona boy would never again sleep in a swamp. Daylight began to seep through the chopper bubble, but moisture on the glass kept me from being able to see through it. I would have to get outside and wipe the glass off before I started the engine. I was eager to get going, but leery about stepping out into the unknown. I opened the sliding window and couldn't see anything dangerous; but isn't it always that way in the movies? You don't see it until you're got!

When I stepped out and stood next to my ship, I started feeling better about my chances of getting away in one piece. The weather was much better, with just an occasional drizzle, and no low clouds. I wiped down the bubble with a rag and was climbing back in when I heard the rotors of another helicopter.

I stood and watched as a Bell made its way toward me. The pilot came down low and hovered about 30 feet away. I gave the OK sign, pointed to my ears and shook my head "no." They understood that I had no radio, and motioned me to start up and follow them. They didn't have to tell me twice. As I lifted up out of that swamp and headed for base, I threw those alligators a one-fingered salute just to let 'em know they didn't scare me anymore.

It was a short 15-minute flight back to base. I had almost made it home the night before. They called it a pop-up storm. I later learned that several other ships had been stranded just as I had, but everyone else also made it back safely.

I went home and began my seven days off with mixed emotions about what to do now. I called my folks, and they agreed that Louisiana was no place for a guy who couldn't sleep with alligators. I knew my gulf flying days were numbered, because I just wasn't happy in Louisiana. It wasn't the company, the people, or even the state; it was me. I had found something at Ft. Wolters I loved doing, and would be damned if I just walked away from it.

I gave notice to Petroleum Helicopters, and headed back to Texas. I figured I could hang out with Pete and Nancy while I tried to get my old job back. I'd only been back a few days, when I ran into my old Flight Commander, Don Wolgomott. Pete had told him I went to Louisiana for better pay. I wondered what else Pete had told.

Well, so what, I thought.

I realized that anywhere I went, if I had to lie on the application, I'd be worried about my past catching up with me. That was the reality of it. I might as well be doing something I loved while I worried.

Wolgomott seemed really glad to see me, and didn't seem to mind that I'd left for more money. I asked, "What are my chances of coming back to work for you?"

"No reason why not," he said. "When can you start?"

"Three days," I said. And that was that.

Yes, I would give that U.S. Army School my best effort. If they fired me, it wouldn't have anything to do with my performance.

By mid-August my rehire paperwork was completed, and I was assigned to the same flight I had been with previously. It was good to be instructing again. The time that followed was one of the best of my life. I was doing what I loved and was spending time with Pete and Nancy. I had my own little apartment, friends and a great social life.

I called Mom, Dad and Uncle Phill often, and life was good for all of us. I had done everything I could to get back into the military, but it just wasn't going to happen. That dream was dead, but I was beginning to put it behind me and make new dreams.

One of those dreams arrived in the form of Dianna Kay Turner. I had been back at Ft. Wolters for several months when Mom called and said she had hired a waitress I had to meet. I was due some time off, and I went to Phoenix to check her out.

Mom told me when Dianna would be working, so I walked into Guggy's during her shift.

Dianna remembers, *"When Jerry came in, I didn't know who he was. He headed for a closed section and I told him he couldn't sit there. He told me 'I'll sit wherever the hell I want.' I tried again to tell him that section was closed and there was no waitress assigned to it. He walked past me into the kitchen, and came back out with Norma, who said, 'Dianna, I'd like you to meet my son, Jerry.' I thought I had just lost my job! But he gave me that great smile, and we hit it off."*

She was gorgeous, and I liked her right away. We went out several times that week, and before I returned to Ft. Wolters I proposed to her. We had only known each other a week, so I was surprised that she accepted! But as she said, *"I was very protected and didn't date much. So when a very attractive, worldly man comes into your life, what's a girl to do? I came alive when I met Jerry."*

Since things had already moved so quickly, we didn't see the point in a long engagement, especially with the distance between us. We married six weeks later, on May 15, 1967. After a small church wedding in Tempe, my new bride and I went back to Ft. Wolters. Mom always teased me that she got to pick out my wife. Mom had good taste; what can I say?

Shortly before Dianna and I were married I had told her dad my whole story. Pete was ex-Navy and only knew I had been a Marine. We had done a lot of kidding back and forth because I thought he looked like a typical swabby, with arms covered in tattoos, blond crew cut and a million-dollar smile. When I told him everything, his reaction was simple enough. He said, "You're the only one worried about it, so get over it; we're proud to have you in our family."

By the following autumn, I had been back at Ft. Wolters over a year, and Dianna had been with me the last few months of it. I now had enough flight time to qualify for other flying jobs, and I was dual-rated, allowing me to fly both airplanes and helicopters for pay. Everything was going great, but I was always open for new opportunities.

PART TWO

Chapter 12

Madison Aviation - December 1967

Madison Aviation

We were still living in Texas when I received a call from Madison Aviation offering me a job, and I was ready to consider it. Bruce Madison needed someone to start a flight school in Mesa, Arizona. I would instruct, manage helicopter contracts, and run charter flights.

I learned that my good friend Myles Ruggenberg had recommended me for the job, and I was honored that he thought so highly of me. Dianna and I were beginning to get homesick for Arizona, and she was missing her family, so we decided to take advantage of this opportunity and head back home. I filled out the paperwork and kept my fingers crossed. Nothing negative came back, so I guessed they didn't run a background check.

Dianna and I settled into a little one-bedroom apartment in Mesa, a few miles east of Phoenix. It was close to both our parents' homes, which was great, as we were both very family-oriented.

I had most weekends off and we went to Guggy's often to eat with my Mom. We also enjoyed hanging out with Dianna's family. She had two younger brothers, Steven and Keven; and a sister, Karen, all in their teens. Her mom and dad, Dorothy and Pete, were great folks; they all got along and seemed to be the all-American family. I liked them immediately, and the feeling was mutual, since they made me an honorary member of the clan. I still love them to this day.

Pete was the King Pin of the family, and like a second dad to me. He was tall, muscular and blond with a crew cut; a 1960s version of Arnold Schwarzenegger without the accent. Pete loved motorcycles and we rode together for years on our black Harleys. The entire family played together with dirt bikes and spent many days and nights out in the desert. Without a doubt, this was the happiest I would ever be with family and friends.

The only thing missing was my dad. He was in South America doing "something for somebody." He was very secretive about it, and that's about all he would ever tell us about that period. Mom and I both missed him.

I knew right away that returning to Phoenix was a good move. We were back where things were more familiar and I felt more secure. Sure; scorpions and rattlesnakes could ruin your day, but alligators in the Louisiana swamps were not to be messed with.

My job at Madison Aviation was a gift. Bruce Madison was a great employer and the crew was top-notch. The facility included a huge hangar where three twin-engine airplanes fit side-by-side with room left over for three helicopters. The boss's split-level office overlooked the hangar and flight ramp, and the ground floor contained a lounge with a little kitchen, restroom and shower. Everything was showcase clean, right down to the highly polished green floor. In good weather the huge hangar doors were kept open so we could watch airport traffic coming and going.

The crew consisted of four pilots, three mechanics and one bookkeeper. We all liked each other, and it was a great working environment.

Our fixed-wing aircraft included a seven-passenger twin Beech and a single engine Bonanza. The three helicopters consisted of a three-passenger turbocharged Bell 47G3B1; a four Pax Bell J2; and a Hughes 269a.

I was trained and qualified in all the company aircraft as time permitted, but first I would act as the company's helicopter instructor and manage the flight school operations.

Due to my instructor background with the Army, Mr. Madison considered me the authority on training. I liked the sound of that, and was ready to handle it.

Getting the flight school up and running was a different matter. Setting up the training syllabus and getting all the necessary approvals from the Federal Aviation Administration was a huge job that required a ton of paperwork and patience. The local office in Phoenix was a big help; especially my friend, Chief Inspector Myles Ruggenberg. He made sure all the required documents were in order and he flew with me in the helicopter.

Myles and the other inspectors were still learning about helicopters and only he and one other were rated to give flight examinations in them. Both inspectors were busy with other duties besides helicopter testing and needed some help. Myles asked me if I'd be willing to become a designated examiner for the FAA for fixed-wing and helicopter flight examinations. The same guy who suspended my license after the Virginia plane crash a few short years ago was now authorizing me to give flight tests and issue pilot certificates to qualified applicants. We both recognized the irony.

I was honored to be a pilot examiner for the FAA. I was now authorized to test students for private and commercial airplane and multi-engine certificates, including helicopters. I was moving in the right direction; as long as the Federal Government didn't check me out too thoroughly. I had come a long way and now had an even longer way to fall. I always kept in mind that this wonderful lifestyle could change in a heartbeat. It was a constant blemish I could never shake. I often wished I could sit down and talk to Mr. Madison about it, but I was afraid I could lose it all if he fired me. The "what if?" was always there.

Over the next few months business continued improving enough to require another instructor. Bruce Madison left the hiring up to me, and I chose Jim Elder, an ex-Army pilot. Jim took over the student training, allowing me to start working and flying in other areas.

One afternoon in late December, I was assigned to fly two

workers to a site near Mt. Ord; about 50 miles northeast of Phoenix. The men needed to check equipment at a mine they operated in a mountainous area that was covered with an unusual amount of snow.

Snow is not a friend to helicopters, and there are a number of ways to get in trouble with it. Landing can be tricky because the powerful downblast from the rotors can cause a "whiteout" as you land, reducing visibility to zero. The pilot loses contact with the ground in the swirling snow, resulting in a loss of control and a dangerous situation.

To make sure I didn't break through frozen deep snow, our mechanics put snow shoes on the Bell. These were long, wide boards that would—ideally—keep the machine sitting on top of the snow pack.

We departed Madison Aviation about 2 p.m. for the 40-minute flight to the mine. It was a beautiful clear day with calm winds and temperatures in the low fifties. When we reached the area the temp had dropped to near freezing. I found a good landing spot in a flat meadow about 100 yards from the mine at about 5000 feet elevation. The hard-packed snow hardly blew at all and the snow shoes held us with no problems. The workers said they would need about an hour, and we should be off the ground well before sunset.

I stayed in the helicopter reading the flight manual and was cozy and warm until approaching clouds hid the sun and the temperature began to drop. Nearly two hours later I saw the men coming down the hill. They were cold and wet and ready to go home. We loaded their stuff into the metal baskets on each side of the chopper, strapped ourselves in and prepared to launch.

I went down the checklist:

Rotor blade untied
Controls frictioned down
Battery on
Mixture rich
Magnetos on
Depress starter …

That's when the big engine should have roared to life, but there was not a sound. I pressed the starter a second time and the silence was deafening. I knew right away we were in for a long and miserable night. By now it was almost dark. The miners wore coveralls, boots and light jackets. My own jacket was abysmally thin and I was wearing street shoes. I was still learning.

There was no way to call for help and before long we were all shivering. Nearby was a small camp trailer that had been junked years before, but we looked at it as a possible shelter. The roof was partially caved in, and we were able to use the scraps to build a little cave-type structure we could huddle in. We found an empty bucket from the mine and used a five-gallon can of diesel fuel to start a fire inside the bucket. We burned raw diesel inside it all night long, until the bucket burned up. We burned everything that was loose, including an old couch and chair that had been in the camp trailer.

During the night it started snowing again. By morning more than 12 inches had fallen and it was still coming down. Somehow we managed to keep the fire going and survive the cold winter night, but we were a sight. Our faces and hands were black from burning the diesel inside our enclosure. Only our eyes and lips were showing. The rest of our bodies and clothes were covered with thick black soot. But we were alive and conscious, so we could still laugh and make fun of each other. The fire was making a big dent in our fuel supply.

About mid-morning we finally heard the glorious sounds of a helicopter in the distance and knew someone was looking for us. By noon the clouds thinned out and a rescue helicopter made it to our location. It was my co-worker and friend, Jerry Mullen, flying our Bell J2A, and he had brought a mechanic along. As I motioned for him to land behind my machine, I noticed he didn't have snow shoes clamped to the skids. He was settling onto the snow, when the skids broke through and he started to tip over backwards. Jerry was able to recover quickly to 100 percent and then to a hover. *That* was a close call!

As Jerry hovered, mechanic Glen Means opened the right

side door and tossed out two long, skinny GI-type gas cans. Then Glen jumped out from three feet above ground and nearly disappeared into the deep snow. While the chopper continued to hover, we placed one gas can under each skid to act as snow shoes and support the weight of the machine. The rotor wash caused zero visibility at times, but we achieved our goal.

Jerry reduced rpm to flight idle, and Glen and I moved away from the machine while the engine cooled down. As we stood talking, the helicopter slipped off the left gas can, rocked backwards and hit the tail hard on the snow pack. From that point it was total chaos. The main rotor blades smacked into the tail boom and for the next 15 seconds the helicopter literally tore itself to pieces.

Glen, the two workers and I hit the ground amid all the flying debris. None of us were hit, and when we finally looked up, Jerry was still sitting in the pilot seat unscathed. All that was left of the 'copter was the frame. We were all very lucky, and thankful that we hadn't been hurt.

Glen came up with the only solution that would enable us to fly out of this mess. We could take the battery out of the crashed ship and use it to start mine. An hour into that operation we were finally ready to try a start.

I went through the check list again, hoping and praying that this time it would start. I tried several times to no avail. The engine would turn over, but not kick in. After several attempts, the battery was drained and we were still marooned. Glen explained that this engine wasn't going to start because it got "cold soaked" overnight. "So did we," I told him.

Our only option now was to walk out. It was about two miles to the Beeline Highway on foot. The snow was deep, and we would have to cross two canyons, then follow a stream down to the road. It was either that or spend another night out here—and none of us liked that option. Who was going to rescue us now? We were all out of helicopters at Madison Aviation, and no one would know that our rescuer needed rescuing as well.

It was 2 p.m. when we started the long hike. The two

workers and Glen had boots on while Jerry and I were wearing street shoes. "Cold" doesn't even begin to describe what we were feeling. We trekked up and down ridges and finally hit the stream that would take us to safety. We kept moving out of fear that if we stopped, we wouldn't be able to start again. It was slow, miserable and freezing. We helped each other over fallen trees, slippery rocks and a partially frozen, knee-deep stream. We were walking popsicles. Thankfully, we were all young, healthy, strong and able to keep moving.

We made it out to the highway just before dark and flagged down a snowplow. The driver told us there was a search party about a mile up the road getting ready to hike to the mine looking for us. He alerted the highway patrol and within a few minutes help arrived. I will never forget the hot coffee one of the patrolmen had in a thermos. It's amazing how important little things can become in dire situations.

I was off for my second ride in an ambulance to a hospital, remembering another time I had been rescued from snowy conditions. I hoped this wouldn't become a pattern. Jerry and Glen were released right away, but the two miners and I, who had been out there longer, remained for two days until our body temperatures returned to normal.

Bruce Madison was a complete gentleman through this entire ordeal. He kept our families informed and made sure we had the very best of care in the hospital. His attitude about possibly losing the helicopter was very positive. He felt that since no one was hurt, we had all learned a valuable lesson or two.

We certainly had, and made sure we always carried rations and water for flights to remote areas. We had been stranded in the winter, but it's even more important to have water in the hot and dry Arizona summers, where temperatures soar well above 100 degrees. I learned something new about flying every single day.

A week after our ordeal, Jerry Mullen flew another helicopter back to Mt. Ord with two mechanics. My machine was repaired and flown out, and the other one was lifted with a sling onto a flatbed trailer and hauled out. Three months later it had been rebuilt and was flying again.

In the mid-1960s there were very few resources for downed or stranded pilots. A few precautions and some common sense went a long way in the helicopter industry back then.

Our little flight school was keeping Jim Elder and me busy, and I was starting to do other work: charter flights in the Bonanza, or hauling people around in one of the helicopters. Every day brought something new, interesting and exciting.

On days when we didn't have a flight, I enjoyed the interaction with the other employees. It was a small company where everyone was friendly and cared about each other. I felt so lucky to have found this job.

Chapter 13

Sequoia and Kings Canyon National Park

As summer of 1968 approached, Bruce Madison announced that he had successfully negotiated a contract with the U.S. National Park Service at Sequoia and Kings Canyon. The aircraft fleet consisted of one Bell 47G3B1, and one fixed wing aircraft, a Cessna 180. Both would be based at the park and used for firefighting, patrolling, and search and rescue operations. The contract ran from June through mid-August.

Three people were assigned to carry out the contract. I would fly the Cessna 180, Don Sides would fly the Bell with me as his backup, and mechanic Butch Button would take care of the maintenance.

This was a huge break for me. I would learn how to fly helicopters in the thin air of some of the highest mountain peaks in the United States, and I'd learn from the very best. Don Sides was very experienced in the mountains, and was well liked and trusted by the Park Service personnel. He had flown the same contract in past years and when he vouched for me, I was in.

I had a cute little cabin in the town of Three Rivers, California just outside the Sequoia National Park entrance, and I was looking forward to an exciting summer. Dianna had just started a new job with Wells Fargo Bank in Mesa, so wouldn't be able to go with me. But she did visit me once during that summer, and we set about creating our first daughter.

By the end of May, we were settled in with aircraft and ready to get started. The park personnel were easy to work with and made us feel right at home. True to his word, Don Sides was very generous with my mountain training, and I was soon quite comfortable jumping back and forth from chopper to fixed-wing. I liked both types of aircraft and enjoyed learning how to fly that Cessna 180. I flew in and out of some tricky areas; whether a high altitude dirt strip or the middle of a pasture.

There were a number of places to land the airplane in the back country; from large and small meadows, to rocky or dirt strips. One such landing field in the mountains was called Pickle Meadows. It was in a stand of trees at the 8500-foot level, and was about a quarter mile long and maybe 200 yards wide. The grade of the landing strip was so steep that heading uphill was the only way to land, and takeoffs had to be downhill regardless of the wind. Because of the high altitude, the normally aspirated, non-supercharged engine produced

Cessna at Pickle Meadows

considerably less power in the thin air. Pilot technique and a gentle hand were necessary. The single engine, four-passenger Cessna had a tail wheel instead of a nose wheel and was superbly efficient at hauling men and equipment into tight spots.

Once a week we would fly the helicopter to the summit of Mt. Whitney, the highest point in the contiguous United States at 14,495 feet above sea level. There was a small, level spot no more than eight feet square right on the summit. A windsock had been placed nearby and we were required to make approaches and departures into the wind. The approach had to be slow, yet fast enough to remain in translational lift until the bird settled onto the landing pad. The engine was supercharged and had plenty of power, which was necessary to keep the big, heavy rotor blades turning at 3200. If the rpm dropped too low, we had to abort landing and try again. But if the winds were gusting and variable, we might as well go back home or end up a casualty. I was a willing student and soaked up the techniques that would keep me alive and my passengers safe in the years to come. I made several landings

Mt. Whitney in background

on Mt. Whitney that year. At nearly 15,000 feet above sea level, I was breathing heavy and so was my mechanical hummingbird. In those days we didn't carry or use oxygen, so we didn't stay long. For man and machine, that was truly operating on the edge.

Don taught me so many valuable skills. His number one priority for landing was true: "Always land your tail rotor safely and the rest comes easy." Touching the tail rotor to anything was a sure way to die. When we attached any kind of cargo to the racks on the outside, we had to be very careful that nothing flew into it.

The tail rotor is turning over 600 feet per second and is the most fragile item on the machine when the engine is running. It's also nearly invisible while spinning and has caused many deaths and injuries from unwary victims walking into it. From the moment the engine starts, the tail rotor is the pilot's main priority when close to the ground or other objects.

Just as I had hoped, I learned to fly in the high, thin mountain air under Don's tutelage. I always look back on my experiences in the High Sierras and as an instructor for the Army, as reasons for my having survived so many tricky situations. There is no substitute for experience. Period.

Most of my missions were flown with Richard McLaren, the District Ranger for Sequoia and Kings Canyon. Rangers were interested in everything that went on in their areas, and Richard knew the park like the back of his hand. I liked the patrol work, and it didn't take long for me to get oriented to the park.

Sequoia and Kings Canyon National Parks cover more than 1,000 square miles of rugged mountains and deep canyons. During the summer, campgrounds were jammed with families on vacation, and highways to and from the Parks were always packed. I seldom saw that part. My primary job was to fly a daily recon around the park with a ranger. We were most concerned about fires started by lightning or careless hikers in the rugged back country. After thunderstorms passed through at night, little wisps of smoke were clearly visible the next morning. Depending on the location and conditions, firefighters were dispatched by ground or by helicopter. I averaged about two hours of flight time each day in either the 'copter or plane, depending on what was needed.

The Park Service was happy to have us there and it showed. Just a few years earlier the only way into the back country was by horse or mule. That meant that fires spotted by towers or airplanes could be fought only if firefighters could get to them. The blazes often burned a long time before rangers could reach them, or they just burned themselves out. With helicopters, men and equipment could be shuttled in and out in a fraction of the time it took before the 1960s. I hauled quite a few firefighters and loads of equipment throughout the summer.

Many times the chief ranger and I would be in the air circling a fire and directing aerial tanker drops over hot spots. This was one of the first years tankers were used. We also guided Don Sides into different locations with a water bucket hanging below his helicopter. During the fire season we were open for business daylight to dark and sometimes after dark for searches or medical flights.

Fires were just one part of the patrols. During the late summer, I made several high altitude rescues and recoveries. We kept a close eye on the hiking and climbing areas, searching for the lost or injured. I flew several medi-vac flights where Don made it clear that I was the pilot and he was the helper. In the late 1960s, patients were still transported in a litter attached to the skid on either side, just like in the M*A*S*H television series.

One night about 10 p.m. we were called out to rescue two hikers who had fallen into a ravine. When we landed, we found both men in bad shape with broken arms and legs as well as internal injuries. The men had fallen the previous day and, as luck would have it, a park ranger on horseback had found them just before dark.

The area was covered with rocks and boulders. We spotted the ranger's flare and flashlights and were able to land about 50 feet away. The area wasn't level so I had to sit there and hold power to keep the ship from sliding over on the smaller rocks.

Don and the ranger spent the next 15 minutes loading the two men into litters, then tying the litters inside the cargo racks. It was a tough job because of the uneven terrain and loose rock.

When they finished, Don put his head inside the cabin and hollered, "You take them to the park headquarters and an ambulance will be waiting. Come back and get me in the morning. These are big guys and we can't both go. You need the experience. Be careful!"

I started to protest, but Don was gone. I felt a moment of panic and fright, but just like the day I soloed, I was on my own.

This time, however, I had an injured man strapped to each side of the helicopter, and it was dark. I had no choice. I settled in and started my takeoff.

At 7,000 feet I slowly brought in the power, and I was using it all as we left the ground. I pointed the nose down into the ravine, built up some airspeed and headed for home. I felt bad for the two men strapped to the side. They were both conscious and were probably a lot more stressed than I was. The 20-minute flight to the landing pad felt much longer, and I thought we would never get there.

I saw the flashing red light long before I saw the pad. As soon as I touched down, there were rangers on both sides getting the victims ready for the ambulance. The hospitals close by didn't have landing pads as yet and this was the only way to do it. Thankfully, both of our victims lived to hike another day.

The next morning I flew in and picked up Don, taking along a thermos of hot, black coffee. He and the ranger had moved down the mountain and set up a camp. With the hikers' gear, they had a comfortable night.

That was my first experience with a medical evacuation in the mountains at night. I told Don about the panic and fear I had felt and he responded, "Get used to it, because if you're not afraid, you're not careful." Good advice!

I loved the thrill of not knowing what the next day held. Whether it was flying enforcement rangers on searches for poachers and marijuana entrepreneurs; or counting animals and hauling the occasional injured wildlife, I looked forward to whatever the day would bring.

The summer went by quickly and soon it was time to pack up and go home. We had done a good job for the Park Service. The personnel liked us and the feeling was mutual. We took home letters of praise from organizations such as the Sierra Madre Search and Rescue Organization, the American Mountain Rescue Association and of course, the U.S. National Park Service.

I had rescued or helped people in need, and that was a good feeling. It was a happy time in my life and I hoped I could make a flying career work. The one thing I always kept in mind was that I was literally flying my job. Every time I lifted one of these machines into the air, I was flying someone's huge investment, and it could become junk in a matter of careless seconds. Doing that twice—or even once—could be detrimental to a flying career, *if* you happen to survive such a mistake.

I was in a good place at Madison Aviation. The overall atmosphere was friendly and fun. We had a chief pilot, chief mechanic, bookkeeper, and a considerate boss. We didn't have the competitive attitude often found in the workplace. Everyone seemed confident in themselves and loved their jobs. I sure did.

Dianna and I bought our first home about five miles from Falcon Field Airport in Mesa. It was close to my mom and Dianna's family; meaning I could go riding on the weekends in the desert with Pete, Steve and Keven. We rode "tote goats," which were two-wheeled motor scooters with a Briggs-Stratton motor. Our favorite area was out by Red Mountain, about 20 miles northeast of Mesa. There were trails and old canals where we would race around all day having a great time. Just before dark we would load up the machines and head to Guggy's for a good dinner. Mom always pointed us to the restrooms to wash up before seating us in the back next to the kitchen door. She would joke that we looked and smelled like we had just swum across the Rio Grande River.

This was my first feeling of being part of a family since Mom and Dad were together. The Turners all liked me and I fit right in. Dorothy was the perfect working mother. She was a secretary and Pete was an engineer for Motorola. They lived in a Tempe tri-level that included a large shop where Pete built the tote goats and kept his beautiful, black Harley Davidson. I had owned a couple of bikes in my life, but nothing like Pete's; at least not yet. It wasn't long before I had one just like his, with lots of chrome. We rode all over the state; sometimes with wives, sometimes without. When we took off from intersections, I would follow Pete's lead and we would shift through the gears together, side-by-side, our Harleys making the kind of racket that was music to my ears.

Madison Aviation was busy with flight students that winter. A rated fixed-wing pilot could get a helicopter rating attached to his pilot certificate with about eight to ten hours of training. If the instructor signed off, a pilot could take the check ride and—Presto!—a new helicopter pilot came into being. Insurance companies would later set higher hourly minimums; such as 1,000 hours total time plus a minimum of 250 hours in helicopters, plus 50 hours in type for pilots with commercial certificates.

Helicopters had already proven they were here to stay with the military, but were still somewhat rare in the civilian market. However, new and valuable uses for the private sector were being found every day.

The accident rate was alarming in the 1960s and '70s, but most were a result of pilot error, not machine malfunctions. The pressure was on everyone in the helicopter industry to make it safer and fly it better. It was a booming time for aviation in America, and flying jobs were abundant for experienced pilots.

One day during lunch with my FAA friend, Myles Ruggenberg, he mentioned a local man who was planning to expand his business. The man was looking for dual-rated pilots for here and around the world. He already had a contract with USAID (United States Agency for International Development) in Nepal to fly an Allouette 11 and a STOL aircraft known as a Pilatus Porter.

This company had also just landed the contract to operate the new airport north of Scottsdale. Myles said he had recommended me to the boss during a luncheon with the City of Scottsdale. He said I should give some serious thought to joining a growing company that could use my expertise. I can honestly say I grinned from ear to ear when he referred to my "expertise." I never heard it put like that, and I will never forget it.

I talked it over with everyone in my family and decided to see what Bruce Madison thought. He had given me my first real chance and I would always appreciate his kindness. He told me to go for it and we're still friends to this day. Madison Aviation was a fine organization, and Bruce is a class act.

Chapter 14

Arizona Helicopters

Arizona Helicopters

The Scottsdale Airport began as a training facility for World War II Army Air Corp pilots. In 1953 the Arizona Conference of Seventh Day Adventists purchased it to establish Thunderbird Academy, a vocational school. The airfield became a training field for missionary pilots. In 1966 the City of Scottsdale bought the airfield portion of the property, and by April, 1967 had contracted with Arizona Helicopters Inc. to operate the airport.

Work on the airport was just beginning when I signed on with them in late 1968. Crews were paving the runway and building a terminal and a maintenance hangar. I felt right at home as soon as I arrived, because this was the same strip where I had soloed just a few years ago.

I was hired by Jack Holefelder, vice president of operations for Arizona Helicopters Inc., of Chandler, Arizona. The company was taking on the airport operation in addition to creating two new aviation companies that would be doing business at the airport. Scottsdale Aviation, Inc. would be a flight school with its own aircraft for training and rental. Southwest Airlines, Inc., would be a charter company using Cessna single- and multi-engine aircraft. The large maintenance hangar would house a Cessna-approved shop on one side and a Bell Helicopter-approved shop on the other. A parts department would also be onsite. It was an ambitious project and exactly what I wanted.

The owner and big boss was Robert M. "Tug" Wachs. He had been in the crop-spraying business at the nearby Chandler airport for years and was taking a huge financial jump into helicopter operation. This was a gamble because anything to do with aviation meant big bucks. I wasn't too worried about my future at this point; I was only concerned about whether there would be enough flying opportunities. Jack assured me there would.

I would be working with the five company-owned helicopters: three 47G3b-1's; one J-2A; and a G model that was used for training. It was going to take some time getting all the airport construction done, but that wasn't my problem. Jack had helicopter work for me, and he kept me busy. I did the usual stuff; flying people around for all kinds of reasons, and to look at all kinds of things. Most involved construction work such as hauling telephone poles, stringing wire, setting air conditioning units and transportation into rural areas.

Most of my flying was around the Phoenix area, as Jack kept me close to help out with student instruction. We were doing a pretty fair business with helicopter students, many of whom qualified for training under the G.I. Bill. Most had been to Vietnam and had lots of helicopter time, but they needed enough flight time to transition back to the civilian way of doing things. I heard plenty of war stories and hung on every word. I had missed out on something that would never come my way again.

That spring our daughter Andryea was born. She was a cutie who quickly developed a bubbly personality. I loved playing with her and enjoyed being a full-time dad. I wasn't home as much as I wish I could've been, because my job was keeping me hopping.

As we headed into the summer of 1969 our flying business started to pick up. We had been awarded several contracts with the U.S. Forest Service for the upcoming summer fire season, so all of the B-1s would be busy in Arizona and California this year. I asked Jack which area I would be sent to, and was told that I would cover the flight school and whatever flying came up here. Jack said, "The reason we hired you full-time was so you can cover all our bases here at home, since you're dual-rated."

I wasn't happy to hear this. My talent was flying the helicopter, but as an instructor, someone else always has the controls. "I don't like it," I said.

"Just do it," he said.

So I did.

I sure missed that family feeling I'd had at Madison Aviation. This was a different environment; a company run by a businessman who was interested in making money; and from what I could see, it was working.

As summer approached, three JetRangers and two B-1s were sent out on contracts for the Forest Service divisions in California and Arizona. When the temperatures climbed in the Southwest, our helicopter business took off, while our fixed-wing traffic died. Climbing into an aircraft with no air conditioning was like sitting in an oven, and the machine had to climb to several thousand feet for cooler air.

The first summer was a learning experience from a different perspective. There were four helicopters in the field; meaning four pilots and four mechanics in different locations who all needed time off, parts, money or whatever. I was busy all the time.

I was disappointed about not going out on contract with a helicopter, but I stayed busy with the overflow work on the fixed-wing side. Occasionally I would fly a mechanic and parts to one of the helicopters on contract, but mostly I shuttled firefighters around the Pacific Northwest to various hot spots in a Cessna 402 and a Twin Beech. Each aircraft could carry seven firefighters and their gear, plus just enough fuel to get there. I was always conscious of how to lighten the load whenever possible. Heavy flights were the kind that would cause me to mumble nervously to the airplane all through the takeoff and up to a safe altitude. But I also said a little prayer that I had put on *enough* fuel.

Flights into the night and early hours of the morning have a way of suddenly turning from boring to unsettling and spooky. The engines can seem to be running smoothly, but my experience and vivid imagination could change all of that quickly. All it took was an engine out of synch or the flicker of an amp gauge or oil pressure, and I was concerned. Ever since my forced landing of the Bonanza on a Texas interstate with Peter Cronk, I pay close attention to terrain as I fly over it. You never know when you might need a landing spot in a hurry.

One of my assignments that summer proved to be a highlight of my career. It was July 1969, and the big news was of the upcoming moon landing. Walter Cronkite came to Arizona to see the area around Meteor Crater where the NASA astronauts had trained for the Apollo moon mission. I flew him from Phoenix to the crater, and then around the area so he could do aerial photography of the training grounds. I was impressed to note that Cronkite did most of the filming himself. He was a great guy and a true gentleman

With Walter Cronkite

A job came in with the Mountain Bell telephone company to set poles and string the wire in Superior, Arizona. I was the only pilot at home base, so I took the call. I had no previous pole setting experience, but had done a lot of sling work, which involved hauling large pieces of equipment under the helicopter. Superior is sixty miles east of Scottsdale in a rugged area of hills, ravines and large boulders; terrain too rough for ground vehicles. Jack briefed me on the dangers and pitfalls of stringing wire across poles. "Thanks Jack," I said "it sounds exciting." I was off.

Holes had already been dug and it took a little over a day for me to set all seventy poles in them. I would pick up a pole on a 50-foot cable, lean outside the left door so I could see the load, and set it in the right hole. *Piece of cake*, I thought. A fuel truck followed along so we wouldn't have to return to base for fuel every four hours.

Stringing the wire required a large truck with a huge round cylinder of telephone wire to be reeled out. The wire was attached to the helicopter, pulled across the poles and secured by men on the ground.

I enjoyed this at first, but the farther I got from the truck, the heavier the line was. Jack had warned that if for some reason the cylinder froze up, the helicopter could crash to the ground. The only way to avoid disaster was to hit the quick release to let go of the line.

Stringing wire

Late that afternoon I was over a small ravine, flying sideways to keep the line out of the tail rotor and pulling about 50 yards of line when the cylinder suddenly froze. The helicopter violently nosed over, and I was looking straight at the ground. I hit the quick release, dumped the wire and managed to gain control in a matter of seconds. I was done with stringing wire and swore I would never do that again as long as I lived.

I was relieved to find Tug and Jack still at the airport when I returned. I told Tug what had happened and was completely honest when I said I wouldn't be finishing the job the next day. He called Jack in, and to my surprise he told Jack what happened and asked him if he would go out and finish the job. Jack laughed and pointed his finger at me and said, "I told you, didn't I?"

"Yes, Sir," I choked.

Instead of being unhappy, Tug told me I had done the right thing and, most importantly, I had brought my machine home in one piece. It truly scared me and taught me that it's a good thing to know your limits. No matter how competent you think you are, there is always someone who can do it better. We had a great summer and despite a few incidents, we did not lose any machines or pilots.

My home life changed a lot that summer, because I wasn't there very much. My hours were long and I had very few days off. When I left home in the morning Dianna had no idea when she would see me again. She was very understanding, while taking good care of little Andy and virtually every aspect of our home.

We missed the weekend trips to the desert; and the newest toy in our garage—Mr. Harley—would just have to wait until things were slower. Then it seemed like it was summer one day and autumn the next, and by late September all the contracts were finished.

The maintenance building had been completed during the summer and it was very impressive. Helicopters were lined in a row on one side and airplanes on the other. Everything was brand new and office tenants were already moving into the terminal building. Most of the employees had been hired. It was like starting up a new little city. We even had a front desk "manned" by smiling ladies to greet passengers and schedule flights, rentals and tours.

Arizona Helicopters was growing, along with an industry still in its infancy. Licensed, experienced pilots had their pick of jobs and could easily find work for power line patrol, photography, crop spraying, heavy-lift operations, firefighting, stringing lines and telephone pole placement.

However, there were problems early in the industry. Too many accidents caused insurance rates to soar. Military priority made parts difficult to get. Maintenance costs were unbelievable. Tug was an expert in the art of borrowing money, filling out reams of government paperwork and everything necessary to keep his helicopters in the air. He was a stickler for detail, and when I made mistakes he let me know about it behind closed doors. Learning helicopter operations from him was the equivalent of learning scuba diving from Jacque Cousteau.

Now I began wondering how I was going to fit in, because all the seasonal pilots were gone and I was the only one left. I had not realized I was the *only* full-time helicopter pilot. Jack said he had several part-time guys on call if work came up, but in the winter things were slow. He was confident I could handle it, and if I did need help, he would fly and so would the boss.

An assignment came up to fly a helicopter to Casper, Wyoming on a two-week construction job for a mining company. I'd be hauling men and supplies into a rural mountain area to stake claims. The work had to be completed by the first of the year, and an early winter storm had left the area blanketed in heavy snow. They needed the helicopter as quickly as we could get there.

I left for Wyoming the first week of November and planned to be home before Thanksgiving. I had never before flown a helicopter on a long cross-country trip alone, and was looking forward to the journey. I took off from Scottsdale early in the morning and flew north to Flagstaff, following the highway at 50 to 100 feet above the ground. The B-1, with its big plastic bubble, provided an incredible view for the pilot. Flying at low levels allowed me to navigate as though I were in a car, following the road signs. It was an amazing adventure!

As I sailed over the expansive mesas and plateaus just north of Black Canyon City, I spotted a large herd of antelope. They also spotted me and began running from the *whop-whop* of the rotor blades. It was a beautiful sight to see those powerful animals running in a loose formation. I snapped a picture and flew on north to Camp Verde. Once I had crossed the Verde River I could clearly see the San Francisco Peaks another forty miles ahead. I stayed low and skimmed over the trees like a happy little bird.

This was my idea of complete freedom. I would make a steep, climbing 360-degree turn and come to a gentle hover, then go into another slow 360 turn. The machine was comfortable at 3100 rpm and would sail along in level flight at about 75 miles per hour. There were a few times when I had a strong headwind that cars were passing *me*. That's a bit depressing to a pilot who might be in a hurry, but I was in no rush and was enjoying the scenery. At that speed you view everything from a different perspective. It's surprising how much more you can see just above the tree tops. A whole new world comes alive.

Beyond Flagstaff and past the mountains, the whole landscape changes to the incredible high Indian desert. My flight took me over the White Arch, a natural hole in the sandstone big enough for the chopper to zip right through. I felt like I was flying through the earth. I was in Navajo country, with its majestic and timeless outcroppings of sandstone rocks, carved by wind and rain into fascinating formations. This was my first time seeing it from the air.

I was in awe as I climbed over a red ridge glowing from the late afternoon sun, and watched Lake Powell come into view. There was the Glen Canyon Dam I had helped build several years ago. Up ahead was the little airport, and as I got closer to the town of Page, I could see my Uncle Mac's house and drugstore.

I called the airport on my radio. "Page Airport this is Helicopter 75 Bravo about 10 miles south, landing Page and requesting fuel and a phone call, over."

"Helicopter 75 Bravo, Roger … and the phone number?"

"Please call Uncle Mac at the Rexall drugstore and tell him I'll be landing soon. I called him when I left Scottsdale, so he's expecting the call."

Then I happened to see Aunt Wanda and Uncle Mac standing out near the strip, waiting for me. In my most professional voice, and hoping not to mess up the landing, I said "I will be landing from the south. Any traffic in the area?"

"No reported traffic, land at your own discretion; wind northeast at about five to ten knots."

Aunt Wanda was my dad's sister. She and Uncle Mac and my cousins were a happy family, and I loved visiting with them. They had a little houseboat on Lake Powell, and someday I hoped to have one as well. As a kid I had always loved coming to Page with Mom and Dad, and over the years the Lake Powell area would become my favorite getaway place.

My cousins were in school, so I wouldn't see them on this trip, but my aunt and uncle and I had a nice visit there on the ramp. Aunt Wanda had brought along a little snack pack of goodies, and now that I had provisions, I was looking forward to spending the night lakeside. I was on company time and was authorized to get a motel, but for me … camping on the lake was way better than any hotel room; and a treat I couldn't pass up.

We talked for a while, then I gave them a tour of the helicopter, paid for the fuel and was off. The late afternoon sun was at my back as I headed north from Page over Lake Powell. I skimmed over the lake, amazed to see such a large body of water; among the largest man-made reservoirs in the country. I had seen pictures that showed a variety of big and little canyons jutting off the main lake, and I was headed for one of those remote spots. I would know what I was looking for when I saw it.

When I spotted a beautiful set of sandstone rocks jutting up from the water in smooth shapes, forming a private pool with a nice sandy beach, that was where I wanted to be! I had found my own little island, with just enough room for the tail boom to hang over the rock formation. I still had another hour before sunset, so I took out my sleeping bag, spread it under the tail boom and arranged things to make a comfortable nest. I had sandwiches from Dianna with a note that I would read later, and a bag of goodies from Aunt Wanda. I was set.

I grabbed a sandwich and a Coke and found a good-sized boulder to sit on while I ate. I had a 360-degree view of what can only be described as "vintage" Navajo Country. I ate my sandwich, read the loving note my thoughtful Dianna had tucked in, and marveled at the beauty as the sun finally set and disappeared from the surrounding canyon walls.

It was getting chilly and would likely be cold in the morning. I arranged everything to make it easier to get up and go quickly, like a little bird. Before I crawled into my sleeping bag, I checked the cockpit to make sure the battery switch was off. A careless mistake could be very bad for a pilot's career.

I crawled into my sleeping bag and lay there for a long while; my happy face turned toward the beautiful night sky with billions of stars staring back. Just before I drifted off to sleep, I was thankful there was no such thing as fresh water alligators. I love you, Arizona.

I had nestled deep into the sleeping bag for warmth. When I first awoke to the day, only a little wisp of light touched my left eye. There was not a sound. Nothing. I have never heard such silence. It was almost eerie. I poked my head out of the sleeping bag to see a clear blue sky and the surrounding cliffs dappled in sunshine. Breakfast was a Coke and some chocolate chip cookies, while I sat enjoying the sight of the water and canyon walls. I wouldn't have traded my stay here for any five-star luxury hotel. This was probably the first time I truly appreciated the beauty of Mother Nature. I

Lake Powell moon

had only just begun my journey into this area that some call one of the most beautiful places on earth. I quickly rounded up all my gear and stowed it, did a thorough pre-flight and strapped myself in for a start. With a little nervous anticipation—I did *not* want to be stranded here—I reached the point on my check list to "engage starter." On the first turn that big engine fired up with a roar, engaging the rotor system to start spinning. It was going to be a great day. Cleared for take-off to the north.

My flight path would take me up the Colorado River to Moab, Utah and Grand Junction, Colorado, then to Rawlins, Wyoming and finally, Casper. I didn't fly a compass heading, I just kept the big compass "N" in sight and strayed right and left as I explored the unbelievable landscape. Adding to the serene beauty of this untouched land, was a changing sunlight from those big, white, puffy clouds.

When I landed in Casper, I was met at the airport by Ken Warner, president of the Lucky Bird Mining Company. He was a pleasant, middle-aged man with salt and pepper hair, and he was all about business.

Ken explained there were several square miles of terrain that required mining claims staked out before the first of the year. Some areas were only accessible by chopper.

The job was simple enough. I would haul equipment and

supplies to various locations in a rugged mountainous area where only a helicopter could do the job. The heavy snow had come early and caught everyone off guard. They were afraid if they waited until spring, one of their competitors would rush in to stake the mines. There was apparently a lot of money and prestige behind this venture, because we were going to work long days until the job was done.

I had snow shoes on the helicopter skids and was given a pair of small snow shoes for myself. The experience on Mt. Ord when the J-2 sank into the snow and beat itself to death was a lesson learned. There would be a six-man crew, none of whom had ever seen a helicopter. The first thing I did was give a ground school, covering the helicopter safety basics. My crew chief was a young Native American man named Roland, who I called Tonto, while he called me Birdman. He did a little ceremony, danced and sang to the "hummingbird god" for safe guidance. I almost laughed at first, then realized he was quite serious. I don't know that I believed it would work, but we didn't have any accidents. I'm just sayin' ... .

I liked every one of those guys, but never saw any of them after my time there was done. One of the perks of the job was being around so many genuine and friendly people. "Tonto" had served a three-year hitch in the Navy, and I told him I was a Marine. Even around friends, I felt inferior and guarded, thanks to my former missteps. I could not shake the guilt and was always worried about my past turning up.

Our camp was about sixty miles northeast of Casper and two miles off the main highway. The camp consisted of a large maintenance building and a bunkhouse that also housed the small office. As long as the highway was open, the workers could get in and out of town. On heavy snow days, we just wouldn't fly.

A room was booked for me in a single-story motel outside the city. Every morning and night I landed right outside the door of my room. It was a large unit that went unused in the winter, but sure was cozy for me and my Bell sidekick. When the snow kept me down, a steady stream of locals stopped by to have a look at the helicopter. Most of them had never seen a real working chopper up close. I was a bit of a celebrity, and the friendly folks made the depressing weather more bearable.

Parking at the motel

For the first two days I didn't do much except fly Roland and Ken around to survey the area to be staked. Everyone involved in the job got a short ride around the city and then it was down to business.

A flatbed truck was loaded with hundreds of wooden stakes that would be used to mark the mining claims. Each stake was four feet long, two inches square and pointed at the end so they could be driven into the snow every hundred yards. When summer finally came, these men would come back and drive the stakes fully into the ground to keep the claims on file. I never understood why the urgent rush and neither did the other guys. Ken would only smile and tell us it was business. As long as I could fly, it didn't matter to me.

I told my mom and dad how exciting it was, and also how ironic. My family had been chasing gold mines all over the Northwest for more than 100 years, and now I was flying miners around.

Our first two days were very productive. Using sling loads, Roland and I positioned stakes and gasoline in different locations, so the snow machines wouldn't have to return to the base camp every time they ran out of either.

On the third day we were grounded by heavy snowfall. Sometimes it came down so thick I couldn't see the little café across the highway from the motel. It was totally miserable. Just before that big storm hit, we put the helicopter inside a large hangar at the airport. After three days in a row of not seeing the sun, this Arizona boy was homesick for daylight and warmer temperatures; at least somewhere above freezing.

After four days on the ground we were finally turned loose. The only way into base camp now was by air. Snow plows would take another couple days to reach some of the rural roads. The conditions didn't slow us down. Each one of us was grateful to see the sun and to be working outside. Our six-man team was divided into three pairs. Two men would drive a snow cat pulling a flat trailer carrying tools and stakes. Another pair would follow behind on snowmobiles, driving the stakes into the snow. Roland and I would be in the helicopter dropping stakes in those areas that the ground machines couldn't access.

Hanging in the snow

The helicopter had baskets on the side that held about thirty stakes, depending on fuel load, wind and altitude, which generally ranged between 5,000 and 7,000 feet. The Bell had plenty of muscle to do the job. We rigged up a seat belt that would allow Roland to sit on the floor of his side and toss the stakes out. I would fly along just above the trees and every 300 feet or so, Roland dropped a pole. Most of them disappeared into the heavy snow, but they would be easily found when summer came.

It took about a week to complete the job from the air. Roland and the boys still had a lot of work to do, but the helicopter work was done. I had been there twelve days and was ready to get back home. But the next morning brought another snow storm, delaying my departure by two days.

When it was finally clear enough, I flew toward Arizona the same way I came; however this time I had weather to circumnavigate. I ended up flying south through Denver and Albuquerque. Regardless of the conditions, there is no feeling better than coming home from a successful mission in a trusty helicopter that starts and runs like a Swiss watch.

Chapter 15

Change in the Air

Andryea

I had been gone nearly three weeks and it was good to be home. Andryea had grown in that short time and was cute as a button. Dianna was happy to have me back, and of course she had a "honey do" list of chores waiting for me. "Tomorrow," I promised. I was supposed to have a week off, so there was plenty of time to work on that list. We had dinner at Guggy's that evening with my mom and Dianna's family, and I told them all about my adventure in Wyoming and the beautiful flight up and back. Pete and I planned a motorcycle ride the next day, since it was Saturday, and maybe Sunday we would take the whole family riding in the desert on our tote goats.

"What about the lawn and the other stuff you were going to do?" Dianna asked.

"I'll still have five days left," I told her.

The next day Pete and I rode our Harleys to Tortilla Flats, a tourist trading post and café near Apache Lake and the Superstition Mountains, about fifty miles east of Mesa. It was a great ride, and I was happy to be in the warmer Arizona outdoors.

On Sunday we all went to the desert and rode our machines until dark. We cooked burgers over a bonfire and joked about who rode the fastest, jumped the highest and fell the most. The Turners and I were one big, happy family. Other than my mother's devotion, I had never known this kind of love. I remember thinking about that terrible day in my past, which I still relived from time to time. I always hoped and prayed it would never come up again, especially during the good times in my life. Now I had a family and a job I loved. But I knew it could all end in a heartbeat. No matter how hard I tried, I couldn't let go of the past. We got home late that night, worn out. Just before we went to sleep I told Dianna that I would start on that list first thing in the morning.

After breakfast and some playtime with my little Princess, I headed for the garage to get the lawnmower. I finally found it after a bit, and then tried for the next hour to get it started. I was just about to throw it out the door when Dianna came out and said I was wanted on the phone by my boss, Jack Holefelder.

"Hey, Jerry have you had a good vacation?"

"It is good to be home," I said.

"Well, Mr. Wachs would like to see you after lunch in his office. Make it one o'clock. Don't be late."

"Jack, wait ... ," I started, but all I heard was a dial tone.

I glanced at Dianna, thinking, *This can't be good.* I knew immediately what it was about. Dianna came right over to me and took my hand. "What's the matter?" she asked.

I told her all I knew and the first thing out of her mouth was, "Do you think he knows?"

I realized she was living this nightmare with me. I had never seen that fear in her eyes until this moment. I showered and dressed, and decided to leave early. As I backed my car out of the driveway, my right wheel ran over the lawnmower. This was not how I had pictured my day off.

I hadn't had much interaction with the owner, but I knew a little about him from my FAA friend, Myles Ruggenberg. Robert M. "Tug" Wachs had been a B-17 pilot in the "big" war. When it was over he returned to Phoenix and settled in Chandler in 1947. He managed a crop duster company and flew a Stearman, spraying chemicals on farmlands to kill the crop-destroying pests. Tug worked long days, sometimes laying under a wing for a short nap with the rank smell of gas, oil and DDT in his nostrils. It was hard and dangerous work. By 1951 Tug had saved enough money to buy the small company he had been managing. He continued

134

his labor of love, and in 1960 he bought his first helicopter, a Bell G-2 that was outfitted to spray crops.

Tug believed the chopper was far superior to an airplane when it came to crop dusting. He said he could cover more acreage faster with the Bell than with the Stearman, and he also thought the downwash of the rotor blades would beat the chemical into the crops rather than just spraying it on. His competitors were delighted with his new toy, figuring that he would soon go broke. They believed helicopters were expensive and dangerous. But year after year, Tug kept on and proved them wrong.

As helicopters began to catch on in other areas, Tug took a gamble and bought more for other jobs. As his business grew, Tug formed Arizona Helicopters, Inc. in 1960. His next gamble was winning a contract with the Federal Government in 1966 to supply two turbocharged Bell 47G3Bls to USAID personnel in Kathmandu, Nepal. The machines would be operated in the rugged Himalayan mountains at altitudes of up to fifteen thousand feet. It was a risky contract, but it was working. Myles Ruggenberg said Tug had become an expert at filling out government paperwork, but his real talent was in borrowing money and financing projects.

Rumors circulated that Tug was going bankrupt. But to the surprise of everyone in the aviation industry, he landed the big one. He convinced the Scottsdale city fathers to give him a ten-year contract to build a fixed-base operation at their new municipal airport.

I thought about all of this during my drive to meet with Tug, which seemed to take forever. As I pulled into the airport I was convinced that I was about to lose my job. I had arrived early, but sat in my car until 12:55, then walked into the terminal and back to the offices. Tug's secretary, Florine Morgan, gave me a big smile and signaled me to go right in, saying Tug and Jack were expecting me. I shook hands with both men, declined a cup of coffee, and sat down beside Jack in front of Tug's desk.

Tug told me about the Nepal operation and how well it was

going. The pilot running the operation, Jim Burrell, had been with Tug a long time. Tug said Jim was going to be in Nepal for at least another year to 18 months, and then would be brought home as the company's chief pilot and vice president of flight operations. When that time came, Tug wanted me to take Jim's place in Nepal.

The enormous weight I had been carrying had lightened considerably. I was stunned! Not only was I *not* being fired, I was being offered a great opportunity. At that moment Florine came in and said Tug's wife was on the phone and needed to speak with him. I excused myself to go the bathroom. Behind closed doors I cried like a baby, I was so relieved. I washed my face and went back into the office.

Then Tug hit me with another stunner: he wanted me to work as the chief pilot and run flight operations until Jim came back. Jack had been pulling double duty and was needed for bids and contracts. Myles Ruggenberg had recommended me for the job. Was I interested?

"Yes, Sir," I said in my squeakiest voice.

We spent another hour talking about things to come. I would need to hire at least four helicopter pilots for contracts that had already been won. The jet age was approaching with the new turbine-powered Bell JetRangers. Four were on order and due to be delivered the following month. I would take the new pilots to the Bell factory school for transition training in Ft. Worth, Texas, after which we would bring the new JetRangers home. There was much work to be done before summer. I was still in shock, but elated.

"When do I start?" I asked.

"You're here, so get to work," he answered.

The minute I got out of the meeting I called Dianna and told her the incredible story. She was ecstatic, and the next question she asked floored me, because I didn't have an answer. "Did you get a big raise?"

All I could say was, "Duhhh."

I hadn't even asked Tug about pay. It didn't matter at that point, because I had come in fully expecting to go home that day with my final check.

On the way home that night I stopped and bought a lawnmower. Pete came over the next day and mowed the grass, because I had to leave early for work. Working for Tug meant a dawn-to-dusk schedule—often even longer.

I did receive a good raise and was now responsible for the flight school, the charter operation, refueling, and the line service that would greet and fuel the aircraft. I had an office in the terminal building near the main entrance with a view of the flight line. We had a front desk where customers could pay for tie-down and hangar services, and where students and charter flights were scheduled.

Our inventory consisted of a full line of single- and multi-engine Cessna aircraft, plus two Aero Commanders for charter. We were also a service center for Bell Helicopters and had three turbocharged B-1s and a G-model trainer.

For the past year Tug, Jack and Florine had been setting up an aviation operation; including permits, FAA certification and the miles of bureaucratic red tape required to make it work. All I had to do was step in, keep my ears open and my mouth shut, and learn how to be a manager.

My first priority was to hire four experienced helicopter pilots. I only had six weeks before the journey to the Ft. Worth Bell school to pick up the new helicopters. Florine gave me a stack of applications to review. Pilots were returning from Vietnam and looking for flying jobs, and most of them had more flight time than I did

Myles Ruggenberg was our assigned inspector and watchdog for the FAA. Tug hired Leonard Kilgore, a promotional expert, to bring in new business. Leonard was good at his job and the student and charter business began pouring in. He also created tours of Arizona, particularly around Sedona and the Grand Canyon. Tug made it clear to me that I was now a manager and should fly only when pilots were not available. There were times when Jack and I had to step in and fly and there were times of famine, as with any start-up business.

Within three weeks I had interviewed and hired four pilots for Bell school. Each was a veteran fresh from Vietnam and each was eager to relearn civilian ways.

Every day was unique and provided a learning opportunity. I was assigning flights to pilots, giving flight tests and doing a ton of paperwork. I had never been good at keeping track of things, probably because I'd never had this much responsibility. Under the watchful eyes of Tug, Jack and Florine, I managed to avoid making any big mistakes, and I felt like part of the team. I met with Tug and Jack daily and wasn't afraid to ask about things I didn't understand. I quickly learned from Tug that the bottom line was money and we never had quite enough. Tug was in debt up to his eyeballs and made no secret about it to anyone.

Tug was a pilot, a gambler and a very compassionate man. He gave me the chance of a lifetime and I admired and respected him. But I still could not bring myself to tell him my shameful history. I had already come so far in my flying career and I was afraid to lose everything I had worked so hard to accomplish.

The Bell Helicopter School lasted five days and was worth every bit of the time and cost we invested. The daily schedule was simple: classroom in the morning and flight training in the afternoon. The Bell 206A was a five-passenger machine powered by an Allison Turbine engine C-18 that developed 317 horsepower. We all transitioned to it with no problems. What an incredible machine! It was my first exposure to the jet age and the very latest in helicopter technology. By the time we flew the JetRangers home, we were all comfortable with them and ready to go to work.

Tug promoted me to Vice President of Flight Operations, even though he was still worried about the health of his business. He had taken an enormous risk in expanding, and his critics already had him pegged to belly up any day now.

I didn't know what Tug's balance sheet was like, but I was having the time of my life running flight operations for him. As my boss, he was all over me about a lot of things, and usually, rightfully so. I had a lot to learn about being a leader. But my fellow employees and I all wanted this company to be successful, and we all worked hard to make that happen. I could feel the tension and strain Tug, Jack and Florine were under, but the storms always seemed to give way to sunny skies.

I stayed busy and flew every day. I learned an enormous amount from maintenance test flights, as I would have the mechanic brief me before and after each one. I learned to recognize different signals the machine sends when something is not right. Knowing what to listen for and watch gives you the opportunity to correct a problem, particularly in fragile and special helicopters.

At this point in my career, I was finally content. I had the opportunity to not only fly all these magnificent machines, but to manage the operations and the crews. Arizona Helicopters was a great place to work, but a big responsibility and not always a happy place to be. Complaints flew and tempers flared; the usual ups and downs of a business.

In retrospect, I realize I did not have the temperament to be a good manager. I've always had to work at controlling my temper, and too often I'd go ballistic over the simplest things. I was quick to apologize when it was over, but those kinds of outbursts stay with people and make you look weak. I didn't see it then, but I realize now that it was caused by stress; something I never understood until I retired from the business. During my time at Arizona Helicopters I only fired one pilot, and to this day I feel bad about it. As much as I hated stringing wire, I liked managing others even less.

I made many friends, but rarely socialized, other than with family. I enjoyed being at home with Dianna and Andryea whenever I could, which wasn't often. I worked long hours, but Dianna took it in stride. I knew she was getting tired of making plans and then having to cancel them because of my unpredictable work schedule. On those holidays when families normally gathered, Dianna and little Andy usually went to the Turners' home alone. To her credit, she seldom complained, and we were very happy together. I was living the American dream.

Meanwhile, in Nepal, Jim Burrell was keeping his helicopters in the air and USAID had added a fixed-wing aircraft to the contract; a turbine powered Helio Courier designed for high altitude operations. According to Tug, Jim Burrell and the Nepal contract were keeping our companies going. It was a reminder that my days in Arizona were numbered.

Dianna and I were not looking forward to going to Kathmandu, Nepal. We both loved Arizona, and more importantly, we had our baby daughter to consider. I dreaded the thought of applying for a passport, for obvious reasons. What if I was turned down? Right now I was making the most of what I had and loving it.

Chapter 16

Death in the Desert

I had been assigned to KTAR-TV, Channel 12, to fly a reporter around who would do traffic reports from the helicopter. At that time, I had no idea this would later become my life for nearly two decades. Right now, I was just a pilot doing another contract job.

During this time I met Duane Brady, the news director and anchorman for KTAR. I liked him and we had developed a mutual respect for each other and stayed in touch occasionally. He would later become a good mentor to me.

One August morning Duane called me with a request. He said a grandmother and three young children were stranded in the desert somewhere near Carefree. Their car had gotten stuck in the sand and after a full day of trying to get it out, the grandfather left to go find help. None of them had any food or water.

The grandfather was found late the next day just outside

Carefree by a deputy sheriff. The old man was unable to make any sense and could only mumble that he left his wife and grandkids in the desert, but couldn't remember where they had been when they became stranded. The sheriff's office started a search by rolling available units to the area. As darkness closed in, all they could do was start checking roads and hope for the best. The news media picked up the story and things started to happen. The next morning Duane Brady called me for help. He met me at the hangar at 10 a.m. and we rolled out the Bell G model used for training. Duane asked if we could donate the time, and I quickly agreed. How could I not?

It was only a 15-minute flight to the area a mile east of Carefree. The landscape, though beautiful, consists of rugged, cactus-covered hills and ravines, criss-crossed with washed-out dirt roads and trails. In the late 1960s there was nothing there but wide open spaces. Death was a common reality in the desert for those who wandered in unprepared. This story shocked everyone. The grandmother and three little kids had been without food or water for nearly two days and time was now critical.

After landing and being briefed by the deputies, we got back in the air and started our search. We spotted the car within the first few minutes. My heart pounded as we ran up to it and found it empty. The deputy had given Duane a portable radio and he called in the location and circumstances. Tracks in the sand showed where the four had departed down the sandy wash. Duane guessed they were trying to follow the wash to the Verde River or perhaps to Bartlett Lake.

We were back in the air and within another few minutes we found the first victim; a six-year-old boy. We could see where he had been trying to dig into the sand with his little fingers for water. A Cholla cactus was stuck to his right cheek. His entire body was bruised and scraped from falling and dragging himself along. I had never seen anything like this in my life, and Duane and I were totally overcome with emotion. It had been a horrible and painful death.

I turned away, dropped to my knees and sobbed. I didn't want to, and tried not to, but it wiped me out. It took me a while to regain my composure. When Duane offered me a drink from our thermos I lost it again. Holding that thermos of ice water near that little boy's body was just too much. The veteran newsman had seen tragedy throughout his career and, though this affected him too, he handled it better than I did. I had never experienced anything like this before, and Duane helped me get back in control.

When the first deputy arrived we got back into the air. Five minutes later we spotted the grandmother and directed a deputy in a jeep to her location. We moved on and found the other grandchild a short distance away. The third child, a friend who had gone with the family, was found some time later under a bush where she crawled to get out of the scorching sun.

The entire country was shocked. Duane later produced a half-hour special report for KTAR, entitled "Death in the Desert." It was my first television interview. The program stressed that those deaths could have been avoided if the grandparents had taken a few precautions before setting out for a day in the desert.

That family also would certainly have had a much better chance of survival if some kind of air rescue program had been in place at the time. The Arizona National Guard had helicopters, but they weren't allowed to fly civilian search missions. They did, however, send a Bell Huey out after the three bodies were found. There were no city, county or state helicopters that could be called. Everyone agreed something had to be done—and now.

This experience provided my first inkling into the potential of helicopters working the news; as well as the potential and value of an on-call emergency helicopter.

Duane Brady shared the same dream, and he and I discussed approaching my boss about such a project. But Tug was having his own issues in keeping Arizona Helicopters going.

As happens with any tragedy though, it wasn't long before other stories hit the news, and the outrage of these lost lives faded away. It would be a while before a system was put into place that could help—but not completely cure—the problem.

That was another one of those tragic days I will carry with me my entire life. I felt so much pity for that grandfather. Unfortunately, that event would not be the last tragedy I would be involved in.

Chapter 17

Senator Barry Goldwater

With Senator Goldwater

In June 1969 we got a call to fly Senators Dennis DeConcini and Barry Goldwater to Gila Bend. I had flown Senators DeConcini and Paul Fannin in the past, and liked them, but Senator Goldwater was new to me, and I wasn't sure what to expect. Barry Goldwater had been the 1964 Republican nominee for President of the United States and had a reputation as a tough, tell-it-like-it-is kind of guy. He had just been re-elected to the Senate the previous November.

I went out to do my pre-flight in the 100-degree temperature. Both senators would have their aides with them, and the Cessna 402 would be hot until we got high enough to cool off. At least it would only be a short hop to Gila Bend, just 70 miles southwest of Phoenix.

Once the pre-flight was completed I went back to the terminal for a cool drink to soothe my parched throat. It was nearly time for them to arrive, and I was understandably nervous as I waited in the terminal. I thumbed through the flight manual just in case Senator Goldwater—a noted pilot himself—asked me questions.

This esteemed senator had retired from the U.S. Air Force Reserve as a Major General in 1967 and had flown nearly every type of jet fighter and bomber in the inventory. He was credited with helping make the Air Force what it is today—so I felt a huge amount of pressure to make a great impression.

A few minutes later they walked through the door. As I moved toward the two senators to greet them, I had to remind myself to stay calm. Senator DeConcini held out his hand first. "Hi Jerry," he said, as we shook hands, "have you met Senator Goldwater?"

"No, Sir," I said, as I reached out and took his hand.

"Hi Jerry," Senator Goldwater said with a smile. "Where's the john?"

"Who, Sir?" I squeaked.

"I need to pee," he said.

"Oh, yes Sir," I pointed to a hallway, "second door on the right."

Still smiling, he turned around and walked towards the restroom. I nearly passed out. I had already blown the first exchange and felt like an idiot. I wondered what the rest of the trip would be like.

As we walked out to the flight line, Goldwater pointed to a Twin Bonanza, telling me that he and his co-pilot, Ruth Rhinehold, had flown an aircraft just like it all over the U.S., and in all kinds of weather. Here was a guy who would pick up any mistake I might make. A great idea came to me.

"Senator," I said "would you like to fly left seat?"

"Thank you, I would like that," he said as we started boarding.

From that point on I learned why Senator Goldwater had been around for so long, flying a wide variety of airplanes. It must have been 180 degrees in the cockpit, but he was cool and calm as he began the preflight check.

"OK," said the senator, "read the check list."

Slowly and carefully, I called off every item on the list. Prior to take-off we made a 360-degree turn at the end of the taxiway to check for traffic at the then uncontrolled airfield. We seemed to be ready to go.

"Did I miss anything?" the senator asked.

"No, Sir," I responded, and we were underway.

Shortly after take-off, the senator called for the after take-off and cruising checklist. "We are going to 10,500 feet," he said. "Check the flight manual and see what our power settings should be."

Okay, I thought to myself, *it just so happens I did that back at the airport.* I thumbed through the manual for a couple of minutes, then confidently called out, "Senator, that will be 27 inches and 2,350 rpm."

With a slight smile, he looked over and said, "That's what I thought."

To my surprise, the power levelers and propellers had already been set correctly. The flight went smoothly and had just reached 10,500 feet when it was time to start the descent.

By the time we finished the checklists we were on downwind at the uncontrolled Gila Bend airport. We heard other aircraft in the pattern and radioed the gas shack that we were downwind and would be landing behind a single-engine Cessna. As we were on a short final approach to the runway in use, the office asked, "Is this the Goldwater party?"

I replied that it was, and they said, "We have a spot saved for you right in front of the office."

The landing checklist was complete and Goldwater smartly called off, "Check list complete, mixtures are full rich, props full forward and flaps and landing gear are down. Check list complete."

Yep, he has done this before, I thought, as the main gear gently touched the ground and he lowered the nose onto the runway. He called for flaps up, asked for the after-landing check list, parked the plane and shut down the engines. It had been a great flight.

That trip to Gila Bend was the first of many I would take with Barry Goldwater; many for business and many just for fun. I had no way of knowing then that we would also become great friends.

Barry had flown just about every kind of aircraft that existed except helicopters. This just would not do for an aviation buff like himself, and so he asked me to instruct him on this final frontier.

We began flight lessons around September 1970. His schedule was always busy and we had to work in a class whenever he was in Phoenix for a day or two. That November he soloed in a Bell Helicopter at Scottsdale Airport.

Since everything the senator did was news, a photo of him soloing was printed in the *Arizona Republic*. Barry sent me a copy of the clipping, on which he had written, *"To Jerry who had the GUTS to make this happen. Thanks - Barry."*

That clipping has been very special to me, as have the many other ways he showed his friendship over the years.

"You're doin' great, Senator!"

Chapter 18

AMES Project

AMES helicopter and crew

The AMES (Air Medical Evacuation System) project couldn't have come along at a better time for me. It provided the opportunity to put into play the experience I had built up over the years. I was also pleased to be working with the Arizona Highway Patrol, a group I highly respected.

AMES was a test program jointly funded by the U.S. Government and Arizona State University, to determine the feasibility of using helicopters as air ambulances for rural emergencies, highway accidents and rescues. It was based on the concept used by the Army in Vietnam that a wounded soldier had a better chance of survival if medical help was available within an hour. The AMES mandate was to prove that helicopters could do the same job in Arizona they were doing in Vietnam, and get an injured person medical help within that "golden" hour. AMES focused on treating people while on board, rather than waiting until they were in the hospital. This program would bring a new age to the medical profession, law enforcement and helicopters.

Arizona was chosen for the test grounds and the Arizona Highway Patrol was awarded the contract. They furnished six patrolmen (Sgt. Richard Sandheger, Duane Lynn, J. Martin, W.M. Blake, G. Schultz, and Robert J. Davis.) and we furnished two helicopters and five pilots (myself as Chief Pilot, Chad L. Haring,

Lyman Jantzen, Ellery Kramer, and Lance Stewart.) The AMES crew all wore the same tan caps and highway patrol flight suits with patches on the shoulders.

The project was headed by Dr. Jim Schamadan, who had been a medic in Vietnam. After leaving the Army he was recruited to work for ASU and later to take the lead on the AMES project. Schamadan remembers: *"The question was: 'Could or should this type of operation be done by a police agency, medical, national guard, or what?' The answer was: 'Yes to all.' Arizona was chosen because of its high altitudes, snow, desert, heat. All the environmental and weather-related aspects could be tested here."*

The patrolmen and pilots were all given extensive medical training so we could handle emergencies—or at least stabilize a patient until we could get them to a hospital. We were awarded a diploma by the American Academy of Orthopedic Surgeons for care of the sick and injured.

We would be asked to undertake a variety of missions ranging from locations in the hot deserts where temperatures soared to 120 degrees, to the snow-covered mountains reaching up to 12,000 feet. Arizona is considered a hostile environment for helicopters. Rotor blades, tail rotors and engines would wear out much faster in the desert areas because of the sandy, rocky terrain. Particle separators were required on turbine engines to filter out dirt and sand. It would be a challenge and I was excited to be named the chief pilot.

Two new FH1100 Hillers, which had been configured especially for our purposes, were dedicated to the AMES program. None of us liked the seating arrangement. The pilot sat in the right front seat and the medic sat directly behind him, while two stretchers filled the left side. All flights, with or without patients, would be in this tandem configuration, meaning there was no visibility from the left while on searches, law enforcement missions or flights of any kind. But it was what it was, and we learned to deal with it.

The Hillers were new to us, but the flight back from the factory had given us enough time in the machine to feel comfortable. It had the same engine as the Bell JetRanger, but a different feel and tended to fly nose down when loaded. It had a stabilization called SAS. There was a button on the cyclic control that, when pushed, would hold the cyclic in that position. It was possible to fly hands-off for a short period of time, but it was more like a trim on an airplane. We also had the latest navigation systems: VOR (Variable Omni Range) and ADF (Automatic Direction Finder), plus multiple police and fire channels. By the time the program started we had enough time and training in the new birds and were comfortable with them. Jim Schamadan remembers, *"AMES pilots were all Army trained and knew their machines. They didn't get into a helicopter, they strapped it on and became a part of it."*

Arizona Helicopters at Scottsdale Airport was our base of operations. We had a ready-room equipped with two cots for the on-duty crew. Our operation was staffed, everyone had been trained, and we were ready to go.

We tried to keep one ship at Scottsdale Airport with a crew manned and ready. The other ship was sometimes on satellite duty in a different location during busy holidays or weekends. In the early days we visited hospitals and law enforcement agencies around the state to familiarize them with our operation, and were warmly received everywhere we went. It was a much-needed and appreciated service; especially in the rural areas.

Our missions varied between medical and law enforcement calls of all kinds. Following are examples of the variety of missions we took on.

July 4: This holiday weekend provided a test to the ability of the FH1100. Pilot Lance Steward and Paramedic Robert Martin were on satellite duty in Payson when at 4 p.m. they received a call of a fatal accident north of the town on Highway 160. They arrived 20 minutes later and landed next to the highway. There were two dead and two badly injured. The terrain was tall trees and the altitude was 7000 feet. The crew administered first aid to the injured and loaded them in the helicopter. The pilot made a downwind takeoff and threaded his way through the trees. Within

20 minutes of leaving the scene patients were in the hands and care of the Payson hospital.

Pilot Lance Steward later said that even at that altitude, loaded, and with an unfavorable wind, the engine power limits were never exceeded. Further, even with fading light, the Hiller had no problems except the uncomfortable nose-down attitude when heavy.

That mission made us feel good about the FH1100. We were all learning with every flight what our machine would do under different circumstances.

July 29: Paramedic Waite Blake and I received a call from the Grand Canyon Hospital. A helicopter had crashed and the pilot was burned over 80 percent of his body. He needed to be flown to the Burn Center at Maricopa County Hospital as soon as possible. We departed Scottsdale at 5:40 p.m. for the one-hour and fifteen-minute flight to the Grand Canyon airport, where we refueled and flew to the hospital a short distance away, landing at 7:40 p.m.

The patient had been covered completely with a sterile sheet and was given morphine to help with the pain. As we carefully began to load him in, he started screaming when he realized he was being placed in a helicopter. He was given another quarter gram of morphine by the doctor in attendance and it seemed to help.

I'll never forget him looking at me and pleading for me to be careful. When I told him we were with the highway patrol it seemed to help. He could hardly be understood because of the tracheotomy. He also had two IV bottles attached. Even the slightest movement caused him pain and the doctor asked me to make it as smooth and fast as possible.

We took off at 8:20 p.m and climbed to 10,000 feet looking for smoother conditions. There had been heavy rain in the area earlier and there were still scattered showers around, causing turbulence at different times. Our patient would scream or moan when we hit a pocket of unstable air.

This man had crashed in a helicopter, and that knowledge made a psychological difference for Waite and me on the flight back. I imagined all kinds of things that could go wrong; things I normally never thought about. Blake and I were totally spooked by the time we arrived in Phoenix.

We landed at County Hospital shortly after 10 p.m., where the hospital staff was waiting at the helipad. They whisked him to the burn unit where he would get the best care possible.

Sadly, the pilot died from his injuries a few days later. For Waite and me it had been another one of those learning experiences. That flight had been the first time I had truly been afraid in the air. It was a wakeup call for all of us, as we thought, *There, but for the Grace of God, go I.*

August 10: There was one instance when we disagreed with a doctor already on the scene, but we had to follow our training. Paramedic Waite Blake and I were at Northern Arizona University on static display when we were alerted to an accident north of Sedona. We departed the hospital at 5:25 p.m and landed at the scene 15 minutes later. A doctor had arrived at the scene and provided Blake a rundown on the female's condition. Her biggest problem seemed to be shock and we could find no broken bones. When Blake asked the doctor to take her vitals he refused, saying that getting the girl to the hospital was more important. Our training and instructions required that we take blood pressure and vitals before departing a scene, as doctors on the other end would be asking for them. Blake told the doctor that's the way it was going to be. We took the vitals, loaded up and left. The doctor wasn't happy, but Blake was correct in his actions. The patient was released from the Flagstaff hospital two hours after we delivered her. The incident was our first and only run-in with a doctor out in the field.

August 20: Hospital transfers were the most frequent of all AMES missions. But this one with pilot Kramer and paramedic Schultz would be different, as our crews had not yet encountered a call for an infant. This patient was only 14-hours old, and suffering from spinal problems. Before takeoff, the crew removed the top litter so that an incubator could be placed on the bottom litter. But when they arrived in Yuma they were caught off-guard, realizing there was no way to power the incubator.

The doctors there were able to figure out a way to provide oxygen to the infant. The outside temperature was 111 degrees, so keeping the baby warm wouldn't be a problem, and within two hours the little baby was put into the loving hands of one of the Sisters at St. Joseph Hospital in Phoenix.

After this incident, both AMES helicopters were modified to include additional power outlets for any kind of life-saving equipment.

August 23: One of the most personally frightening rescues took place at the bottom of a dam. In late August, Paramedic Glen Schultz and I were dispatched to Alamo Dam about 80 miles west of Phoenix. The report indicated that a man was trapped under an elevator at the bottom of the dam. Injuries were unknown. We were told an employee of the elevator company was on the way and we were given a description of his car. We followed the highway north out of Wickenburg hoping to spot him and pick him up, but with the rain and spotty visibility, were unable to do so.

We landed on top of the dam at 4:45 in hard rain and strong winds from an overhead thunderstorm. On shutdown, the rotors nearly hit the tail when a droop stop failed, allowing the rotor blade to flop up and down. The Hiller didn't have a rotor brake to stop it, but somehow the rotors missed the tail and finally stopped. It was a close call.

The victim's partner gave us good news and bad news. He said the victim wasn't trapped under the elevator, but had fallen off a ladder from which he had been doing work. He had a badly broken or displaced shoulder and was in a great deal of pain.

The bad news was that the thunderstorm had knocked out the power. The elevator wouldn't run, and the only way down was a steel ladder which ran the length of the shaft. With no power we would only have was flashlights to guide us. As we peered down the shaft all we could see was the victim's flashlight shining 15 floors below. I was starting to get spooked big time.

Glen and I looked at each other and finally he said, "I'll lead the way and don't you fall on me." He started down and I was right behind him. It was cold down there and the steel ladder felt icy. I held on so tightly that my wrists and fingers were becoming numb. About halfway down we had to stop, wrap our arms around the ladder and let the blood start flowing again in our hands. After about 15 minutes we made it to the bottom.

We found our victim sitting against a wall with a big grin, but obviously in pain. We made him as comfortable as possible then we were out of ideas. The only way to get him out of there with his injuries was in the elevator, and that would take electricity. We stayed in touch with men at the top using our two-way radios. The power finally came back on, but the elevator still wouldn't budge. We pushed every button and circuit breaker we could find, to no avail.

About 45 minutes later the elevator technician from Phoenix arrived and started to work. He found the problem after a few minutes and gave us a sequence of buttons to push. It worked! The elevator light came on and we started up with the technician operating it from above. It was slow and jerky, then it stopped, the light went out, it dropped a few feet and stopped again. I thought I would wet my pants and seriously considered getting off at the next floor. By this time the steel ladder was starting to look pretty good. When the elevator started again, this time it went all the way to the top.

As the steel doors opened we all gave a big cheer and quickly got our patient out of the elevator before something else could happen. We laid him on the floor and I went to get the litter out of the helicopter. To my dismay, it was still windy and stormy.

We carried our patient to the helicopter and loaded him up. With the winds still gusting I tried to start up, but had to abort when the gale began whipping the main rotor up and down. We had no idea how long the wind would continue, so Glen decided we should put the patient in a car and get him headed to the

Wickenburg hospital. Since laying in the back seat was too uncomfortable, we put him in the front passenger seat and off they went.

It was only about 15 minutes later that I was able to make a successful start. We quickly found the car and made the exchange. Rather than put the patient on a stretcher, Glen decided he should ride on the stretcher and let our patient take his seat, since sitting up was much less painful. That selfless gesture by Glen Schultz was typical of the highway patrolmen I worked with.

August 29: Helping law enforcement, particularly the highway patrol, was also a major part of the AMES mission. Pilot Ellery Kramer and paramedic Sgt. Richard Sandheger were standing by at the Sedona airport on a satellite mission when they were dispatched to Jerome on a kidnapping call. The victim was a Yavapai County Deputy Sheriff who was being held at gunpoint by two bad guys. That was all the information available.

Many units were heading for the scene and the highway patrol airplane was already overhead in Jerome, but hadn't spotted the marked cruiser. The AMES crew arrived in the area a few minutes later and was notified that a highway patrol cruiser had spotted the abandoned patrol car on a dirt road. Another cruiser was five miles behind in pursuit of the kidnapper's pickup truck.

The AMES crew spotted the patrol car. The patrolman in pursuit radioed Sgt. Sandheger that he was going to slow down, because several people had already been run off the road by the fleeing blue and white pickup. A few minutes later the chopper crew spotted the truck, flew low over it and identified it as that of the kidnapper. The highway patrol aircraft also made a low pass. The driver, seeing that he was just about finished, pulled over and slid to a stop. He could be seen laying something in the back of the truck, which we later found to be the deputy's pistol.

Pilot Kramer landed in the road about 75 feet from the man who was now standing in the middle of the road. Sgt. Sandheger immediately stepped out with his shotgun to cover the man and, after securing the controls, Kramer assisted in taking the man into custody. A Letter of Commendation was awarded to Kramer and Sandheger by the Department of Public Safety.

September 1: Holiday weekends were always busy for us and this Labor Day would be no exception. At 3:45 p.m. paramedic Glen Schultz and I left Scottsdale for the Apache Lake area. The Maricopa County Sheriff's Office (MCSO) had deputies en-route to a possible accident with injuries, but were still 30 miles away. We arrived in the area half an hour later and began searching for accident victims. The patrolman radioed he had found the car, a white Plymouth loaded with drunks. The car had been hidden in the bushes and was now fleeing the scene. Police were in pursuit.

The terrain around Apache Lake was mountainous, with a winding dirt road and fifteen-hundred-foot drop-offs … and the route was heavy with holiday traffic. The patrolman radioed that several people had been run off the road by this maniac and that he was going to discontinue the chase and let us find him. Several minutes later we spotted the car moving toward us on the narrow road at a dangerous rate of speed. I flew ahead of him about a mile around a blind corner, and stopped to a hover just a few inches above the middle of the road, facing his direction. When he turned the corner he could see the dust and hear our loudspeaker siren. He hit the brakes, but couldn't stop in time. I rose several feet and let him pass underneath us, then landed in front of him so he couldn't go anywhere.

Over the loudspeaker, I ordered everyone to put their hands up. All the occupants complied, and when the patrol car arrived we took the five passengers into custody. They still had two cases of beer in the car.

We had to calm down a number of people who had nearly been run off the road by this fool. Everyone present agreed that had we not caught and stopped this car, someone would very likely have been killed or injured.

When we began the AMES project it was intended to be a six-month test period. However, we were granted a three-month extension so we could test the program during the winter months as well.

By the time the test period ended, we had manned the operation 24-7 the entire time. We had flown nearly 1,200 hours and during the course of 213 missions, had evacuated 225 victims of accidents, animal bites, burns, and other injuries or trauma. In addition to the medical-related missions, we flew another 613 missions involving manhunts, searches and surveillance. There were never any accidents with the helicopters, for which we were thankful.

After the final analysis and results were in, it was obvious this was a successful and much-needed operation. Tug was happy because it meant more income for him. I was happy because I had been part of a test project that would be accepted and copied all over the world. We were the first trained flying paramedics in the state, with the first helicopters dedicated to civilian patients. In the 1960s and 70s there were very few law enforcement aircraft. Soon after the AMES project ended, various state agencies began to form their own air rescue units. It was the beginning of air ambulance services all over the world: and it began right here in Arizona.

Highway patrol helicopter and crew

PART THREE

Chapter 19

A New Direction

Did you ever read about a frog who dreamed of bein' a king
And then became one
Well except for the names and a few other changes
If you talk about me the story's the same one

I Am I Said - Neil Diamond

In the spring of 1971, while Dianna and I were trying to figure out how to avoid going to Nepal, I received a call from an Arizona broadcaster that would totally change the course of my life.

Homer Lane was the general manager of KOOL Radio and Television in Phoenix. He explained that the radio station wanted to start doing daily traffic reports, and they were shopping around for an aircraft and a pilot–reporter. I agreed to meet him for lunch at the Biltmore Hotel the following Monday.

I was excited, because it sounded like they wanted to lease a machine from Arizona Helicopters, and I anticipated that we'd make some money on a deal I had set up. Was I wrong!

I walked into the dining room at 11:55 and was met by the hostess, who said, "Mr. Lane is expecting you. Right this way please." We introduced ourselves and sat down. I liked Homer Lane right away. He looked just as he did on television, with short black hair, thick-rimmed glasses, and wearing a dark blue suit. He had a thin build and a pleasant smile, but was all business.

"Mr. Lane," I said at the first opportunity, "AHI has a full line of Bell Helicopters. Which one were you thinking of, Sir?"

Homer replied, "We are planning to buy a McCulloch J-2 gyroplane."

This was *not* the answer I was expecting! He smiled at my surprise, and explained, "Other markets have airplanes flying traffic reports, but we are going to try something a little different."

"A little different" was an understatement. I had read an article on the gyroplane and thought that McCulloch should have stuck with making chain saws. But I kept quiet.

Homer Lane

"Jerry, we have the machine on order and it will be delivered in six weeks. When it's ready we would like to have you be the pilot-reporter. You would fly an hour during each morning and evening rush hour, and have weekends and holidays off. We also own a Cessna Skymaster and you will be called on to fly news crews around the state covering stories. "

"We need someone experienced with helicopters and airplanes because the gyroplane is a little of both," he continued. "Would you be interested?"

It was a wonder I didn't pass out cold. "Mr. Lane," I said, "I'm going to be honest, Sir. I'll need to think about that and talk to my family. "

"That's understandable," he said, "but I will need an answer in the next couple days."

The salary sounded a little low, but his next statement made my ears perk up. He had watched the "Death in the Desert" special on Channel 12 that I had done with Duane Brady, and he believed I could be trained to be a news reporter. Homer said that in addition to reporting on traffic jams, I would be looking for news stories such as accidents, fires, airplane crashes and searches for missing persons.

I was still stunned as I left the Arizona Biltmore and drove back to work. *Wait until I tell Dianna and Mom,* I thought.

Tug was after me to get a passport and all the shots that going to Nepal would require. What a dilemma. Do I go to Nepal or turn it down and try broadcasting? Do I give up a great career flying nearly every kind of general aviation aircraft to fly a gyroplane? I had a lot to consider.

That night we had dinner with Mom and told her about this opportunity. Dianna didn't want to leave Arizona and couldn't for a while because she was expecting our second child. Mom was negative on Nepal from the very beginning. "Keep Arizona your home and tell Mr. Lane about the Marines before you're hired." Dianna's father said the same thing and encouraged me to give it a try.

The next day I called Myles Ruggenberg and was surprised to learn he knew all about it. "Homer Lane is a good friend of mine and I told him I thought you were the guy for the job."

I should have known Homer didn't call just because he saw me on Channel 12. Once again, I had a little help from my friends.

Two days later I met Homer for lunch again; this time in the airport coffee shop at Sky Harbor in Phoenix. I told him I would like to have the job, but there was something he needed to know. I blurted out the whole miserable story. Homer looked me straight in the eye and said, "That makes no difference at all to us. You have the background for this job and I am very particular about who flies my Skymaster. How soon can you start?"

"Two weeks," I said, and I was ready to embark on a new career.

That evening I told Tug I was going to tender my resignation and would like to leave in two weeks. He was surprised and not very happy, but he was a business man and understood the concerns I had given him. He said he would appreciate my bringing Florine and Jack up to date on my duties and responsibilities and I was free to go.

I felt bad about leaving and hoped I had not made a mistake. Tug had given me a golden opportunity and I would always be deeply grateful.

Ten days later I reported for work at KOOL. Homer took me to accounting where I completed all the paperwork of a new employee. Then he introduced me to Bill Lester, who would be my new boss. *How difficult can it be?* I thought. Then it hit me that I would be reporting live on the radio, and I worried again. *Live on the radio. Me, a broadcaster, with my use of the English language and no formal education. Would I stutter or freeze up? What was I thinking, accepting this job?*

But I had accepted it, and I'd do my best. Homer told me the delivery date for the gyroplane had been moved up, and it would be ready for pickup in about 10 days. He wanted me to go to Lake Havasu and attend the McCulloch flight school, then bring the little J-2 home. Things were looking good.

I followed Homer out to Sky Harbor Airport where he showed me the hangar for the SkyMaster twin Cessna 337. This red, white and blue aircraft, with blue crushed velvet interior, was Homer Lane's pride and joy. I would later fly it all over the Southwest covering news stories.

Homer explained the log books and, since I had time in 337s, he just gave me tips on how to get it in and out of the hangar and how he liked the cockpit and cabin to be left when the flight was over. He was extremely picky, and made me nervous. But he would be a great mentor to me during my time at KOOL.

He said he might have a flight for me the next day and would call me later that night with the details. I was now officially on the payroll as the company pilot. I drove home that night with mixed feelings. I was happy to have a five-day a week job (and my family would be delighted) and I knew I could handle the gyroplane alright. But those traffic reports had me worried.

About eight o'clock Homer called to confirm the Saturday morning flight. I was to meet station owner Tom Chauncey at the hangar at 7 a.m. and fly him to Winslow where he had a ranch a few miles out of town. Mr. Chauncey would be met by the ranch manager and should return to the airport about two hours later for the flight home. Homer said Mr. Chauncey would probably ask me to go along to the ranch with him, and he assured me that the boss was a nice guy and I would be just fine. "You will probably be home by noon, so enjoy the rest of the weekend."

"My first assignment!" I proudly told Dianna.

She said, "I thought you were going to be off weekends."

"That's what they said, but you know how things sometimes come up," I told her.

"Oh sure, I know all about that!" she said.

The next morning I woke up, looked at the clock, and saw that it was ten 'til seven. I couldn't believe I had forgotten to set the alarm. I was going to be *very* late. I jumped out of bed, quickly dressed, combed my hair and flew out the door with my electric razor.

I drove like a mad man and arrived at the airport at 7:30. There wasn't a soul anywhere to be seen. No Mr. Chauncey; no one. I opened up the hangar and rolled out the airplane, hoping he would show up. By eight o'clock I knew I was in trouble; *big* trouble. I went into the terminal and called Homer.

He had already talked to Mr. Chauncey, who had returned home. Homer asked me why I was late and I told him the truth. "Sir," I said, "I forgot to set my alarm. It's the first time I have ever been late for a flight, and it will never happen again."

Homer said, "Well, the boss isn't happy and wants to see you first thing Monday morning."

"Yes Sir," I said. "What time?"

"Seven a.m. sharp." Homer replied.

It was the longest weekend you can imagine. I couldn't do anything but stay home and worry and then worry some more. I knew I had gotten off to a terrible start and didn't know if I would even have a job by Monday. I had screwed up my first assignment, and I painfully remembered one of the things Homer had told me: they were looking for someone reliable. Of all times to forget to set my alarm.

I hardly slept at all Sunday night, and at 5 a.m. I was up and ready to go. By 6:30 I was sitting in the KOOL parking lot, nervously keeping an eye on the time. I was taking no chances on being late again. At 6:45 I walked into Homer's office. He was very kind. "Jerry I don't know what Mr. Chauncey is going to do, so you're just going to have to wing it. Go on over to his office. And good luck.

Homer got out of his chair, came around his desk and shook my hand. "I told you that reliability is one of the most important assets our employees can possess, and the other is loyalty. See you later, I hope."

As I started out the door, I realized I didn't know where Mr. Chauncey's office was.

"Sir, I don't how to get there," I said.

Homer smiled and said, "Follow me, flyboy."

I was glad he took me, because the KOOL Radio and TV complex was huge. We went through an alley into another massive building and then into a large garage. There was only one car there; a blue Cadillac De Ville. Homer pointed to a set of wooden doors and said, "You're on your own. See me when you're finished."

At seven o'clock sharp I walked through the doors into a comfortable looking outer office. I was intimidated and it must have showed. Audrey Herring stepped around her desk and offered her hand. "Hi Jerry. I'll tell Mr. Chauncey you're here. Would you care for coffee or tea, or a soft drink?" she asked.

"Coffee would be great," I squeaked.

She disappeared into another room, saying, "Make yourself comfortable."

A couple of minutes later she returned with a tray holding a cup of coffee, cream, sugar, and a small bowl of fruit. "Mr. Chauncey knows you're here," she beamed. "Now let me know if you need anything." Patting me on the shoulder, she softly said, "Relax, Jerry, he's a very nice man."

Oh boy, I sure hope so, I thought.

It was difficult to relax, with my mind going in a dozen different directions. I would try to think positively, only to have a doom and gloom thought counteract it. *Well if he is a nice man then maybe I'm okay. But his mind is probably already made up.* I was afraid it would be a very short meeting.

Shortly before 8 a.m. several men and a woman, all wearing business suits, walked in and exchanged morning greetings with Audrey. She smiled and pointed to the other room, telling each one to go right in. When the last person entered, she got up and closed a large oak door.

I just sat there. Every now and then Audrey and I would exchange meaningless conversation between her answering calls, taking messages, and doing all those things a good secretary does. I was very impressed by her efficiency and manner. *I bet she's reliable and loyal*, I thought.

A little after 9 o'clock, I had been joined by two men who had appointments with Mr. Chauncey. Audrey told each one that the Monday morning staff meeting was just about over and it might be just a few minutes. Soon afterward, the big door opened and everyone walked out. Their smiles and conversation indicated a happy mood, and I began to hope that I might leave the same way.

By now I had convinced myself that Mr. Chauncey knew about my discharge and was going to fire me. The stress was causing my thoughts to run rampant.

Two more hours passed: the two men who had appointments were gone, and there I sat. I had been waiting four and a half hours. The one cup of coffee I'd had was making itself known. I had been reluctant to look for a restroom for fear that's when "the boss" would call for me. I couldn't risk not being there when he was ready.

I finally couldn't hold off any longer, and stood up to ask Audrey where the restroom was, when Mr. Chauncey walked into the outer office with a poodle in each arm. "Audrey take my little ones out to the alley please," he said.

"Okay, come on in, Jerry," he said, turning to go back into his office.

Not even a smile, I thought. I knew I was going to wet my pants before I got out of there.

The office was intimidating and quite large. A huge desk stood at one end of the room, and the other end held two comfortable-looking black leather couches facing each other, with matching chairs flanking them. A large coffee table stood between the couches, topped by a bronze stagecoach and six running horses. The office decor had an old western theme.

"I need to make a call," he said. "Sit down. There's a restroom right over there if you need it."

I must have been walking cross-legged, because that was music to my ears. I wasted no time and just barely made it. When I returned I sat down across from "White Cloud," as he was affectionately known by employees. I guessed him to be in his early seventies. He was small and thin, but not frail, and had a full head of beautiful, pure white hair.

He was still on the phone talking to his wife about a horse. There were so many knick-knacks and things sitting around that I wanted to examine more closely, but I wasn't there for a tour. I kept my eyes straight ahead like a good Marine waiting to hear from his commander.

Tom Chauncey

Finally, he put down the phone and looked straight at me. "*You* are responsible for making me wait Saturday morning. *You* are responsible for me missing an important meeting. And *you* are the reason I had a bad weekend. What's your excuse?"

"Mr. Chauncey, I forgot to set my alarm, Sir. It's the first time I have *ever* been late for a flight and I promise it will never happen again."

We sat there looking at each other for a full minute. Then he leaned forward, and in a very stern voice asked me if I had learned anything this morning.

I thought about it and realized why I had sat in the outer office all morning. "Yes Sir," I said. "You don't wait for me; I wait for you."

He stood up as the two poodles came bounding back in, and said "Audrey, meet the new company pilot."

"Congratulations!" she said, giving me a nice hug.

White Cloud walked around his desk, held out his hand, and welcomed me to the KOOL family. "Go see Homer," he said.

Leaving his office, I could finally breathe again. I was back in the broadcasting business and was never late for work again. Lesson learned.

Since there was still no bird to fly, Homer gave me a week off, saying it would give me a chance to relax and recover from my meeting with White Cloud. But first he said, "When you start work, between 6:55 and 8:06 a.m., and 4:35 to 5:35 p.m., come hell or high water, your skinny little ass had better be in the seat of the 'copter doing traffic reports."

Then he smiled and said, "Have a good week off, then come back refreshed and ready to go."

I had no idea what a great adventure it would turn out to be.

Chapter 20

KOOL Radio and TV

Dianna and I had a great time that week. We were expecting our second little one in a few months so we did some shopping and planning. Uncle Phill had sent us a hundred dollars for new baby stuff. We had dinner at Guggy's nearly every night that week. My mother was so proud and loved to show off Dianna and little Andy. We spent nearly the whole weekend out in the desert with Dianna's family, racing around on the dirt bikes and doing the little things families do. By Sunday night I was feeling like a family man again and looking forward to a new career. For the first time, I was starting a job where my bosses already knew about my past. There would be no more looking over my shoulder. It was a great feeling.

A couple of weeks later, in early summer, I took the McCulloch shuttle to Lake Havasu City on the western Arizona border. The chainsaw magnate had built a large factory and was cranking out the little gyroplanes. My first close look at the little half-breed was very positive. Part airplane and part rotorcraft, it combined the best of two worlds. It had the simple control and economy of fixed-wing aircraft along with the maneuverability of a helicopter. It was really small, and kind of cute. The fuselage was about the size of today's Smart Car. There was room for two people—two *small* people—and not much more.

McCullough Gyroplane

Now imagine an engine mounted to the rear of the Smart Car, with a two-bladed prop and a three-bladed, freewheeling rotor on the top. The fuel tanks were mounted on each side and served a dual purpose as stubby little wings and mounts for the landing gear. I was convinced they were more for show than lift. The fuselage was fully enclosed with doors on each side. It was very stylish and modern looking for the time. I loved that little "Pollywog," as I would call it. It was a new concept in the aviation world.

The pilot had a lever on his left side with a twist-type throttle. Before takeoff, the lever was pushed down to engage the rotors and the throttle was twisted to bring them up to speed. Then the handle was released to give the rotors lift and full throttle, while the propeller on the back pushed the little machine forward.

It took only about 50 to 70 feet of ground run for the J-2 to get in the air, but it was necessary to level off right after takeoff to build up the airspeed. Then it would fly just like an airplane. The pusher propeller made a lot of noise and could be heard for quite a distance. It was much noisier than anything I had ever flown. Headsets helped, but I was afraid noise was going to be a problem in urban areas.

Landing was the most fun. With just a little wind it was possible to land on the apron of a runway and turn off in less than 50 feet. The cruise speed was around the 65 to 75 miles-per-hour range and could be slowed down to about 25 mph for slow flight. The pusher engine was a 180 horsepower Lycoming. It was underpowered, but perfectly safe when correctly flown.

I spent three days with an instructor, flying a total of 10 training hours. I also spent a good deal of time with the engineers, learning what the little Pollywog could and could not do. I was impressed by McCulloch Aircraft. The training was first class and so were the employees. By the time I was ready to head for home I felt comfortable with my new little friend and was excited about getting back to work.

I took off early in the morning for the nearly two-hour flight back to Phoenix. I flew high, then low, down canyons and up and over little hills. I just played with my new toy until I saw the Valley, and then settled down for my landing at Sky Harbor. About 10 miles west of the airport I called the tower. The reaction of Lou, the tower controller on duty, was priceless.

Me: "Phoenix tower, this is gyro 9-6-0 Alpha Mike, 10 miles west, landing Sky Harbor."

Lou: "Aircraft calling, repeat type and number, please."

Me: "Sir, this is gyroplane 9-6-0 A-M, 10 west, landing Sky Harbor."

Lou: "Did you say gyroplane? And if so, are you a single seat, home-built gyroplane?"

Me: "No Sir, I am a McCulloch factory-built J-2 gyroplane."

It was obvious that Lou and the other controllers were not up on this latest toy and, following a long pause, Lou came back with, "Okay 960 A-M keep it coming this way and report one mile final for runway 26 left."

Just before I reported one mile, Lou came over the radio again: "960 A-M, we have you in sight, cleared to land runway 26 left. What will be your final approach speed? There is traffic about eight miles behind you."

I replied, "About 35 miles-per-hour on short final for Alpha Mike, but I will kick it up to 60 and land short. I should be clear, Sir."

There was no response from the tower so I continued on. About 200 yards from the runway I slowed down to 25 mph. Once over the fence, I was down to a fast walk, and by the time I got to the runway apron I touched down and rolled about 10 feet, made a left turn and cleared the runway.

Lou came back on and said, "960 Alpha Mike, you are cleared to parking. I saw it, but none of us in the tower can believe what we saw. That was impressive!"

I was home, and had the first indication as to how my little Pollywog would be received. We kept it in a large city hangar right next to Saguaro Aviation, where Les Taylor had taught me to fly. Les loved having it so close, because I usually attracted a crowd going in and out of the airport.

The next order of business was a number of meetings at KOOL radio. The plan was simple enough. All I had to do was be in the air each morning in time for my first report at 7:06. The morning disc jockey was an old radio pioneer named Len Engebretson, and in the afternoon I worked with DJ Johnny Johnson, reporting from 4:35 to 5:35. If there was a traffic jam or something big going on, I was to stay up and continue reporting it as a news event.

Since we were a CBS radio affiliate, we carried the national news at fixed times and couldn't interrupt programming for a local event. My reports were to be no more than one minute unless it was breaking news. There was a lot to learn, and my nervousness about being on the air was returning.

KOOL had both an FM and an AM station, located in two large, sound-proofed glass rooms across from each other. The television newsroom was next to the radio booths in the same building. I was working only for the AM station, which was dedicated to the older crowd, while the FM side was classic rock.

Both Homer and White Cloud listened to the AM station. It was clearly Homer's favorite and he stayed involved with the operation, though my immediate boss was the station manager, Bill Lester. Bill had a physical disability that required the use of crutches. I came to have a great deal of respect for him, as he took a lot of time with me over the years and never raised his voice. His work ethic was remarkable. My misuse of the English language was the biggest problem for Bill. He would tell me to use a noun or pronoun or whatever, and it went right over my head. Now I was paying for being a know-it-all and disregarding the need for a proper education. My blind desire to be a Marine—face down in the dirt under fire—had cost me. Another lesson learned.

For the next couple of weeks most of my flying time was spent ferrying station VIPs and friends of the bosses around the valley. I sneaked in rides for Mom and Dianna. The broadcast quality of my two-way radio was the biggest problem I had to overcome. The engine noise was overwhelming, and even with noise-canceling microphones, I could barely be heard over the racket. Our engineers tried different types of mics, but none seemed to work well. With the inaugural day of the traffic reports closing in, we were all under pressure. Mr. Chauncey called everyone into his office for a brief statement: "Get the problem solved." The pressure was on.

That first day was upon us and the noise problem still wasn't solved. It was better, but not really broadcast quality. The station had planned a celebratory party at the Left Seat Restaurant at Sky Harbor Airport. Many dignitaries and VIPs attended, including Governor Jack Williams, Sheriff Jerry Hill, and Phoenix Police Chief Larry Wetzel. The gyroplane was parked on the ramp right outside the door, and at the appropriate time I got in and taxied about 100 feet to the runway. The tower cleared me for takeoff, and off I went. I wound up the rotor and gave it full throttle while holding the brakes. At full power I released the brakes, rolled about fifty feet and was airborne. They loved it! I could see the crowd clapping and smiling as I took off.

I headed west toward the Black Canyon freeway, looking for traffic jams or anything interesting to report. By now I was a nervous wreck. I was just a few minutes away from my first live report, and I really felt the pressure. Morning rush hour traffic was heavy, which would at least give me something to report. Through my headset, I could hear the station and my two-way radio. I made notes on weather and known heavy travel spots.

The noise through the hand-held mic had me worried. If my voice couldn't be heard over the engine, this could be a disaster. In addition to the concern about them hearing me, I also worried about whether or not I'd be able to hear the cue from the station. If I couldn't, I'd have no idea when to begin speaking.

Len Engebretson gave me a two-minute warning. I heard that. So far, so good. He then threw it to Homer Lane who was handling the live remote from the airport. Homer introduced the new "Skywatch Program," then said, "Let's go live to our pilot-reporter, Jerry Foster in Skywatch."

I opened my microphone and started talking, but heard engineers on the radio telling me to try different things. I was totally lost and spooked. All I could do was push the mic button; if that didn't work I was out of ideas. Homer went on the air, explaining we were having a technical problem. Then I heard the engineer tell Len that he forgot to push the switch that would put me on the air. By this time Len was rattled and had started playing another record. The engineers told Homer what the problem was and that we would try again at the end of the record. I was just relieved that the glitch wasn't my fault.

During the long wait I had an idea. I pushed the throttle full forward and started a fast climb. I leveled off just as I heard Len say, "Well, let's see if we can talk to Jerry Foster in Skywatch ... Jerry are you there?" I pushed the mic button and heard myself say, "Yes sir, Len, here I am!"

The sound was barely audible so I reached up and pulled the throttle back about half way and *Bingo*! I heard my voice loud and clear as I started talking. It wasn't bad, considering I was slowly gliding toward the ground. I talked about the weather, then the traffic, and by that time I was getting pretty low over the freeway, so I closed with the words I had written, "From the KOOL Skywatch Gyroplane, I'm Jerry Foster!"

Another thirty seconds and I would have been *driving* down the freeway. We had pulled it off and I was now officially a pilot–reporter. Until technology caught up with us, I would have to report from a higher altitude so I could glide with the engine at flight idle while broadcasting. A couple of times I misjudged the altitude and had to abruptly drop the mic to save myself from crashing into the ground.

There were also times when I just couldn't hear my radio cue over the noise and I completely missed the report. That usually would get Len rattled in the mornings, but during the afternoon reports, Johnny Johnson was a master at ad-libbing. He was fun to work with and we had a great time on the air.

Len Engebretson was a very nice guy, but he was old-fashioned and set in his ways. He had done his show for years with good ratings, and sometimes forgot that I was up there whirling around the valley, or he'd occasionally forget to turn on the two-way radio. One morning I had been up for nearly half an hour before a frustrated Homer Lane stopped at a pay phone on his way to work to call the station. He had the switchboard operator send someone to the other building to find out why I wasn't in the air. I was *in* the air; I just hadn't been *on* the air.

For the next several months I did morning and evening traffic reports, and nothing more. My weekends were free and life was starting to get back to the way it was at Madison Aviation.

We arranged for the gyroplane to be maintained by Arizona Helicopters. I think my old boss Tug saw an opportunity to sell a few of these little half-breeds. According to the sales people at McCulloch Aircraft, 83 machines had been sold and many more were on order. Tug sent a mechanic to Lake Havasu for a two-week maintenance school, but decided to wait a while before buying a demonstrator and becoming a dealer. The little machines were more expensive than an airplane, but cheaper than a helicopter. KOOL felt it was something new that would attract attention and boost ratings, which would then bring in the revenue. All of that was for the station to worry about, not me. I was the pilot and had plans of my own.

Our second daughter was born that October, and we named her Barry Michelle, in part after Barry Goldwater, who had become a good friend. Dianna now had a full-time job at home with the two girls.

The two Barrys

Chapter 21

Becoming a newsman

I was doing my morning reports one day when I heard Jim Murdock, our radio news anchor, talking about a young couple who had been missing for two days. They had last been seen near the Hassayampa River, 40 miles west of Phoenix. It was summertime and the temps were soaring upward of 100 degrees, so there was cause for concern. The Maricopa County Sheriff's Office was rounding up their volunteer posse to start a search. After my last morning report, I landed and called Homer Lane.

Homer listened to the radio on the way to work, so he knew what I was talking about. He listened to what I had to say, and said he would call me right back. Fifteen minutes later he called and said he had talked to the sheriff, and that a deputy would be at Saguaro Aviation in a few minutes to fly out with me. "Be careful and send back radio reports. I'll let Bill Lester know."

A few minutes later a sheriff's car drove up with a uniformed deputy. I don't remember his name, but I will never forget his size. As we walked toward the helicopter I asked, "How much do you weigh?"

"Oh, about 220, 230. I dunno," he said.

The lawman wasn't fat, just big. I told him with full fuel we were probably right at the gross weight and should be okay. We climbed in, or I should say, we squeezed in. His door wouldn't close with the chrome .44 cannon on his gun belt, so we got back out and talked it over. I suggested he leave the gun belt in his car and just bring his portable radio. He agreed, and a few minutes later we climbed in again. I had to turn sideways to close my door; that's how tight it was. We felt like a couple of sardines, but we were in. I fired up and headed for the runway as I explained how we couldn't talk without headsets and showed him how to use the push-button mic. He was concerned about hearing his own police radio, so I suggested he only cover one ear with the headset and hold his radio to the other ear. It wasn't rocket science; you just do what you gotta do. I was anxious to get out there and find those two kids. This had all the makings of another story like the "Death in the Desert" one I so vividly recalled. I hoped this would have a better ending.

First I had to get us off the ground. I went through my checklist, which took several minutes, and by then we were both soaked in sweat. It was still morning, but already close to 100 degrees outside; and much hotter in the enclosed cockpit of the J-2. I considered calling off the flight, but I really wanted to try and find the couple. The runway was more than a mile long and I figured I would make my final go/no go decision half way down.

"Tower this is gyro 960 AM ready for takeoff and requesting a straight out departure."

The Phoenix tower came back, "You're cleared for takeoff, straight out departure is approved."

Well, here we go, I thought. I wound up the rotor, applied full power and we started forward—both of us sweating like we were in a sauna bath. I always leaned forward in my seat as though that would help us move faster. The little machine picked up speed and about a hundred feet later we were in the air, although only about three feet off the ground. I leveled off and picked up speed, then started a climb; not a fast climb, but at least we were going in the right direction.

With no air conditioning we were cramped and soaked to the skin. There was just one small vent in each door and one in the nose that did nothing more than let in the hot air. I'm sure the deputy was second-guessing his decision to fly with me.

We had only been up a few minutes when Jim Murdock came on the company radio saying, "Jerry, come on back. The sheriff's office just found them and they're in good shape. They were stuck in a wash."

I was glad it ended happily, and I learned a lot from that flight. First, I was going to have to set a maximum weight limit for passengers. Second, this little gyroplane could be used as a search and rescue tool, and who knew what else.

The company radio was also used by the TV crews out covering news stories. Sometimes we had a conflict when a photographer or reporter needed to contact the base. On one occasion I was just getting ready to do a report when one of our photogs came on the radio, excitedly saying, "Some dumb-ass just rear-ended me."

That went out over KOOL AM clear as a bell. The guilty party had turned his radio volume down to hear a tune over another radio station and had forgotten about it, so he didn't hear me getting time cues.

The next morning I was in front of Homer and White Cloud along with our morning jock and radio news director. The result of that meeting was that from then on anyone using the company radio had better pay attention or suffer the wrath of management. Many times I would direct news cars from the air to various events, ranging from fires to shootings.

I asked station photographer Gil Rickert to show me how to use one of the film cameras—a wind-up Bolex that held 100 feet of film. Gil said I could use the extra camera, and he'd let me know if someone else needed it. He said he knew that Duane Brady over at Channel 12 had slipped me a Bolex when I was flying for the highway patrol on the AMES project. I thought we had gotten away with that! But Gil knew what I was up to and was solidly behind me.

He gave me some extra rolls of film and said, "We won't tell Close," referring to Bill Close, the TV news director.

Holding the J-2's control stick between my knees, I practiced using the camera as I circled an intersection. After a while I was able to keep the Pollywog steady in a turn long enough to capture whatever I was shooting.

Learning to film stories

It wasn't long before my efforts paid off. I was flying near the McDowell Road overpass at Black Canyon freeway during the evening rush hour when I heard the report of an overturned gasoline tanker about a mile away. When I got there it was a mess. Traffic was at a standstill and vehicles were being re-routed where possible. The news cruisers couldn't even get close, but I could. I was 300 feet above it all and shot my first roll of film.

I called the news desk on the radio to let them know I had film of the overturned truck and arranged for a photographer to pick it up at the airport. Chuck Hawley met me at Sky Harbor a little after 5 p.m., and a few minutes later the film was being processed. The processing took about 25 minutes and then the film was edited into a thirty-second clip and rushed across the alley to the TV control room.

From a photographer's standpoint it wasn't pretty, in fact it was pretty bad by today's standards. I had to shoot through the plastic window of the door frame, and there were shadows, sun streaks, and my own reflection on the film. To say it was ugly is probably being too kind. But to me it was a masterpiece. My first news film hit the air.

The tanker was the lead story on the six o'clock news that night, and no other station had it. All they could do was talk about the aftermath, while we had film of the "Flames, Smoke and Mayhem." I had really hit the jackpot. From that time on my little Pollywog and I started gaining some respect from the news side of broadcasting.

Unfortunately, there is always a price to pay when you try something different. Homer Lane was the general manager, but in the newsroom I reported directly to Bill Close, the anchor and news director. We often had a contentious relationship, and he preferred that I just do my radio job and nothing more. Now he was unhappy with me because he hadn't been consulted and hadn't given permission for me to use one of "his" cameras.

I worked for radio, not television, he said, and he demanded to know who had given me the camera and film. I politely told him I wouldn't say who, but in the future I would check with him. He wouldn't let it go, again demanding to know who had given me the camera. I remained silent and just looked at him, until he pointed his finger at me and said, "Am I to assume that you stole that equipment from the camera locker?"

"Mr. Close," I said, "you can assume anything you like!"

I got up and stalked out of his office.

In the years ahead Bill Close was a lot of help to me, but in those early days our working relationship didn't look very encouraging. I was allowed to keep the Bolex and I set up a camera bag that could be taken on each flight.

Eventually the Bolex would be replaced by a Canon Scoopic, which made life a little easier. It was battery operated and I could hold it with one hand and fly with the other. It was so much easier to operate, and it had a zoom lens. I was on a roll.

Chapter 22

Rough times

I had been at Channel 10 about a year when our seven-month-old daughter Barry became violently ill. We rushed her to the hospital where she was admitted right away. Her condition continued to worsen daily, and Dianna spent every minute she could at our daughter's side. Barry's little brown eyes were nearly swollen shut, and tubes and needles seemed to protrude from every part of her. Whenever anyone in a white uniform came near her she began screaming, afraid of being stuck again with another needle. It was heartbreaking for all of us.

The hospital staff did everything they could to make things easier for us. Dianna was given a bed in Barry's room and I was permitted to use the heliport in front of the hospital. Someone in the family was with her 24 hours a day. Doctors tried everything they knew, but were at a loss as to what to do, as our little girl's condition steadily worsened.

On the eighth day, doctors said they had done all they could and they would like to send Barry to UCLA Medical Center in Los Angeles. We were devastated. Unbeknownst to me, my close friend Dr. John Bull had kept Homer Lane informed of Barry's condition for the last several days. Mr. Chauncey's secretary, Audrey Herring, called to tell us that arrangements were being made to move our little baby to California. She told Dianna that White Cloud would pay all our expenses and that we should stay with Barry until she was ready to come home. When Dianna told me that, we sat on a couch in the hospital chapel, just hugging and crying.

Before the transfer took place there was an intervention that I will always believe was a miracle. Mother and her good friend

Dr. Ruth, a family physician, paid us a visit. Dr. Ruth consulted with our doctors and looked at all the data collected. She had seen a case like ours several years before and thought it could be a form of salmonella. She suggested direct blood transfusions and the doctors agreed to try it. My blood type matched Barry's and so we proceeded with the transfusion. In a matter of 12 hours, Barry's condition improved from critical to stable. A few days later we took our baby home, and a month later she was fully recovered.

We will always be thankful to our friends, doctors and staff for all they did, and of course to White Cloud for what he was willing to do for an employee. I wasn't the first nor the last he helped out of a grave situation: the list is long. KOOL was a great place to work.

An unpleasant adventure occurred the day Uncle Phill showed up at Mom's for a short visit. I invited him to ride with me on a morning run, so he met me at the airport. As we walked up to the gyroplane, he noted, "Kind of small isn't it?"

I could tell he was looking for a way out. After climbing in, we had trouble getting his door closed, but finally we were ready to go. On takeoff, my dear uncle didn't say a word. He didn't look left or right, just straight ahead. We departed the airport to the north and I continued climbing. I had a report due in two minutes and I needed altitude.

Len Engebretsen, the morning guy, cued me before I was fully ready. I abruptly pulled back the power and nosed the machine over, grabbed the radio mic and started my report. But before I could say, "Good morning," my uncle, still looking straight ahead, took off his baseball cap and upchucked into it.

I tried looking the other way, but when the smell hit me I gagged, then got the dry heaves so bad that I could not finish my report. I put the mic down and made a turn back toward the airport. Between dry heaves I managed to squeak out to the tower that I was returning with a sick passenger. I advised the station of my situation.

Landing with the heaves is not a pleasant experience. The

smell is inescapable. My eyes immediately started to water and my whole body felt white hot. The vents in the gyroplane were so small we got very little fresh air.

On the ground we headed for the hangar and water hose. I never did upchuck myself, but only because my stomach was empty. Uncle Phill had earlier enjoyed a big breakfast at Guggy's with Mom.

From that time on I never left the ground without a supply of barf bags and I always told passengers where they were and how to use them. I also warned my passengers that if *they* got sick, it was very likely their pilot would too.

After he recovered, my poor uncle told me that when I got a "real" helicopter he would try it again. Another lesson learned.

I was always excited to go to work, and saw a good future as a pilot–reporter. I dreamed of someday having a real helicopter and becoming more involved in the search and rescue missions I had trained for years earlier. The little gyroplane was doing a great job for the radio station, and I often filmed a spot news story that would make the evening news.

On the downside, we received many noise complaints. The gyro's two-bladed wooden propeller made an irritating screaming sound, especially on hot days when I ran high power settings. During the hot months I often had to fly solo in the afternoons.

The winter months made flying easier, but provided a new rash of stories and issues. The early 1970s brought some of the worst floods ever to the valley. Bridges were washed out, resulting in major traffic jams as vehicles searched for alternate routes across the river. The Phoenix area was literally cut in half by the raging Salt River. The valley and state were a mess. More than thirty people died from the storms during those years, and almost a thousand homes were damaged or destroyed.

Many people—especially those new to Arizona—don't think it can flood in the dry desert of the Valley of the Sun. But Phoenix and the surrounding areas are scarred with thousands of dry washes, until the rains come. Those washes suddenly fill with rushing water, catching motorists unaware. Streets dip down into these washes, which normally are not a problem; but when flooding is imminent, barricades are set up to close the roads. Often, drivers don't realize just how much the pavement dips, and they drive around the barricades intent on continuing their journey through what they believe to be a few inches of water. But those "few inches" can turn out to be several feet of fast-moving rapids which can lift a vehicle and float it downstream.

The gyroplane's role in reporting the news became more crucial. I was reporting and filming flash floods as they carried cars, cactus and other debris down the rivers. It was critical to have up-to-date traffic reports, and the rising waters required several rescues from police and firefighters on the ground.

When those big storms came through the state Homer would let me rent a real helicopter and it paid off. We were able to beat the pants off our competition for several years. The only "News Only" helicopter in town was us. Our viewers came to trust that the KOOL-News helicopter would be there when the big story broke.

About three months into flying the gyro, the problems began. Cracks were appearing in the tail boom, and the FAA was issuing safety bulletins announcing mandatory changes. Sometimes the mechanics worked through the night to have the gyro ready for the next day. On other occasions I was grounded for days at a time and did traffic reports from my news car; but it sure wasn't very effective.

It was a nightmare for Arizona Helicopters maintenance people. They were having trouble getting parts from McCulloch, or any other help for that matter. Other users around the country were having the same problems.

Homer Lane and I met with Tug about the future of my little flying machine. Tug was honest with Homer and told him they were doing their best, but the aircraft was a new concept. In addition, rumors had it that McCulloch was looking for a way out. There was no way to predict the future, so Homer told Tug we would give the little Pollywog more time.

And then it crashed. Or at least, it "landed real hard."

I had earlier met Deputy Skip Carnes from the Maricopa County Sheriff's Office (MCSO), who was in charge of the search and rescue operations. He was interested in how I could help, and promised to call me when they had a search. I told him if I was available, I would respond as fast as I could. "Even on weekends?" he asked.

"Even on weekends," I replied.

True to his word, Skip called me for a manhunt out beyond Wickenburg, a small town west of Phoenix. A murder suspect was being hunted near a cotton gin that happened to have a small dirt landing strip nearby. About all I could do was provide an aerial lookout in the desert areas, since the gyro just didn't have the power needed to cover the rugged mountainous terrain. Again I thought, *If only I had a real helicopter!*

After we had flown over the area for an hour or so, Skip asked if we could land on a little strip near the search command center. "Piece of cake," I said.

We landed and I shot some ground film while Skip coordinated the search. The suspect was soon nabbed while hiding inside a large pipe next to the cotton gin. I got film of him being handcuffed and hauled away. There was no way we could have spotted him from the air, but we were there and I got the story. All that was left to do was make the short flight back to the airport, get the film to the station, do my evening reports and go home a happy guy. At least that was my plan.

Skip and I loaded up and prepared for takeoff. The little runway wasn't much more than two vehicle tracks in a flat part of desert right next to the cotton gin. It ran approximately 600 feet to a stand of mesquite trees, and then took a sharp left turn. I had a lot more room than I needed even with no wind to help. I wound up the rotor, applied full power and away we went. About 100 feet later I lifted off and leveled to build up my airspeed.

As the airspeed hit about 60 mph, the engine started missing and coughing. Those trees were coming up fast, but I was well past the point of no return. If I pulled the power and stayed on the ground we would hit hard and crash. I had no choice but to try and clear the trees and take my chances landing on the other side. They were about fifteen feet high, and it was obvious we weren't going to get over them. We bullied our way through the top branches of a couple of trees, then broke out into an open field that was used to store cotton trailers. It was flat as a pancake, and I made a "no problem" landing. When we came to a standstill, Skip and I both sat there utterly speechless for a few moments. When we were sure we had survived, we started laughing and joking. Several deputies ran up, having watched the whole drama. One of them brought up the old saying, "Any landing you walk away from is a good one," and we all had a good laugh.

While it was funny, it was also troubling, since it was another issue to add onto the long list of problems with the J2. *We* may have been able to laugh it off, but Homer wasn't going to be smiling about this one. The sheriff's dispatcher called Arizona Helicopters, who would be sending a service truck and flatbed trailer. It was three hours before they arrived, and the mechanics loaded my gyro onto the trailer. They hauled it back to Scottsdale Airport while a deputy drove me back to Sky Harbor to get my car. We would know in the morning how serious the problem was. I called Homer from Saguaro Aviation to brief him. As I predicted, he told me to do tomorrow's traffic reports from a news car and then come to his office.

By the time I arrived home, it was 7:30 p.m. Dianna had made my favorite spaghetti and meatballs for dinner, and I started telling her about the search. Then it hit me—I still had the film I had shot of the captured fugitive! I dropped my fork, then bolted into the living room, grabbed the phone and called the news room. It was now 8:30. Bill Close was home so I talked to Dave Nichols, the 10 p.m. anchorman. I explained to Dave what I had shot and why I had forgotten it. "Don't worry about that," he said. "Just get your butt down here ASAP; that's going to be my lead story. How long will it take you?"

"About 45 minutes," I said. "I live in Mesa and I can leave right now. I'll have everything ready to go."

"Just hurry!" he said.

I yelled goodbye to the girls and I was gone. I arrived at the newsroom at 9:15 and found Louie Villa waiting in the film processing room. When he was done the film editor, Coleman Rusnak would edit. He usually complained about what I shot from the air because it was shaky and I never got enough. Coleman was always grumpy, but everyone liked him in spite of it.

The pressure was now on the film guys, and I figured my job was finished, until Dave Nichols walked up and handed me an Associated Press bulletin outlining the story I had filmed. "Hot off the wire," he said. "I want you on the set. This will be our lead story."

"What? I've never done a story live on the set!" I pleaded.

"You have plenty of time to write it, so get on it," he said.

I found an empty desk with a typewriter and started writing. I had taken typing in school and I was pretty good. It was one of the few courses I had liked and the only one I passed with a "B." Newsroom typewriters were large print and the copy paper was in triplicate with a line down the middle so the words would fit in the teleprompter. One copy went to the news producer, another to the teleprompter operator and the last one went to the director in the control room.

Four large TV monitors hung on the newsroom wall and were tuned to the network stations in our area. The volume was down, but speakers in the radio news booth were always on. The company frequency and several police and fire scanners blared constantly. If there was a serious incident of some kind, the report would be heard and someone would let the assignment editor know.

Competition between the stations was fierce. When I did rush hour traffic reports, an intern sat in the radio room and monitored the frequencies. If there was a particularly bad traffic jam or an accident, the intern called it up to me. Anyone walking in off the street would think our operation was an out-of-control madhouse, but somehow it all worked.

Now I was struggling with writing the copy to accompany

my film footage. Dave wanted no more than a minute of copy. That may not sound like much time, but would feel like an eternity to me. The plan was for me to sit beside Dave in the weatherman's spot. As Dave read the introduction, the cameras would change to a two-shot of us. When I started reading my script the camera would switch to just me, then run my film as I spoke, coming back to me for the close. It all sounded simple enough and I really wasn't that concerned. It was one of those times when your back is against the wall and you know it's something you have to do. It looks so easy when you're home in the recliner watching the news, but when that huge studio camera is aimed at you, and the little red light comes on, you had better be focused.

It was 9:58 p.m. and one of the camera crew called out "Two minutes!" Everybody was on the set; weatherman Joe Dougherty, sports guy Bill Denney, and Dave Nichols between the two of them. I was standing off to the side ready to slip into Joe's seat during the station break.

The cameraman continued calling the times: "One minute! ... 30 seconds!"

My brain went into mush mode. I heard the tagline for the station break: "Blessed is the Nation whose God is the Lord. K-O-O-L TV, Channel 10, Phoenix."

"We're in the 30 second open. Standby, Dave."

The floorman pointed at Dave with one hand and at camera with the other. I saw the single shot of Dave on the monitor and the behind-the-scene commotion began. Bill Denney and Joe Dougherty both left the set. I slipped into a seat and waited for the intro. Cameras were being jostled around and one was pointed right at me. All I remember is being aware of the two-shot and Dave saying: "Our pilot-reporter, Jerry Foster participated in that search and is here with the details. Jerry?"

"Thanks Dave," I said, and then noticed another commotion going on. Someone was frantically waving their arms. Mic! mic! I heard someone say, and realized I hadn't put my microphone on. It was hanging on the back of my chair where Joe had left it. I was so "fried" with excitement or panic that I had forgotten it. I reached behind me, put it around my neck, and began reading the teleprompter. When the film was finished so was I. I closed with, "That's it Dave, back to you."

"Thanks Jerry, good story!" he replied.

I knew I had done a miserable job on the air, but I had done it and now I knew I could do it a lot better. Since this was something that might come up again, I was going to pay more attention to the anchors and reporters from now on. I would develop my own style, but right now I didn't know what it would be.

Exhausted and hungry, I pulled into my driveway about eleven o'clock. I tip-toed into the house, dark except for a nightlight in the hall. The girls were sound asleep alongside Dianna in our bed. I hadn't eaten anything but a ham sandwich and a couple of Cokes provided by the sheriff's office earlier that afternoon. I turned on the kitchen light and there sat my plate of spaghetti, just the way I'd left it. I got the message: I was in the dog house again; big time.

Dead tired, I crashed on the couch.

Chapter 23

End of the Pollywog

At 5:45 the next morning, the phone startled me out of my sleep. It was our mechanic: "Hey Jerry, we got your Pollywog fixed and it's ready to go. We found that one of the magnetos had failed, which caused the loss of power and the rough-running engine. Come and get it!" he said.

I got up and saw that the girls were still asleep; at least Dianna was pretending to be. I showered, dressed, and headed out. I would drive to Scottsdale Airport, pick up the gyroplane and do my morning reports. Later I'd land at Sky Harbor and try to get a news car to drive me back to Scottsdale to pick up my truck.

I was in the air just before seven a.m. and checked in on the radio. Jim Murdock in radio news answered and was surprised that I was flying this morning. I told him it wasn't a major problem and asked him to call Len over in AM and let him know I was up. A few minutes later Jim called back. "Len was told you wouldn't be up and he has his show programmed. He says he's not going to change it."

"Ten-Four, Jim, Thanks. Can you send a news car to pick me up at the hangar?"

"Ten-Four on that Jerry, News Base clear."

"Skywatch clear."

When I got to the station, the first guy I ran into was Bill Close. In his terse manner, he said, "My office, please."

I followed him into his office. "Close the door, please." Now his voice became louder as he asked me why my film wasn't on the "Big News."

"Well, sir, after my close call in the aircraft, I totally forgot I had shot the film. I didn't remember until I got home. Then I called Dave and we got it on the late news." (In the early 1970s there were only two evening newscasts a day.)

"I don't care about the late news," he shouted. "The 'Big News' is the showpiece for this station. I don't want you to ever appear on any live news program again without my permission, and without wearing a jacket and tie. And by the way, forgetting is no excuse!"

I am not proud of the way I handled myself at times with Bill Close. The truth of the matter is, I have always had a quick temper and said and done things I regret. I am quick to apologize after a blowup, but by then the damage has been done and an impression has been left. I have learned that in a disagreement, the one who gets mad and loses control loses the argument. I regret that I came to be known as a "hot head" in some circles. I'm sure I was, and I'm not proud of that.

About to get another chewing-out from Bill Close

Usually though, I was able to hold my temper in front of my boss or superior. I was raised to be respectful and Marine boot camp reinforced my early training. But for some reason, Bill Close was able to set me off like dynamite. When he did, I would stand up and walk out, usually with a parting expletive. After a harsh word or two by both of us, I was out of there. I have never before, nor since, met anyone with such a huge ego, and I was learning the hard way to deal with it. I realize now that both of us were wrong. The bottom line and reality was: he was the commander, and I was the soldier.

Just before my afternoon traffic report I was summoned to Homer Lane's office. I was surprised to see his door closed, but his smiling secretary told me to go right in. I was also surprised to see the morning-drive man, Len Engebretson, sitting in front of Homer's desk. Neither one of them was smiling. "Sit down," Homer instructed me firmly. This meeting was to be much shorter than my previous encounter.

"You are both doing a good job and our ratings are number one in the morning. But if either one of you intentionally keeps the other from doing the job he was hired to do I will replace you." Neither of us said a word. "Skywatch is now a part of our programming and we will use it as much as possible. And we will use it wisely." With that he excused Len, asked him to close the door and focused on me.

He wanted to know the story behind having to send mechanics and a trailer out to haul the gyroplane back to the airport. I explained the incident from beginning to end and he was satisfied. Homer never talked to me about the expenses, but he let me know Mr. Chauncey was very concerned about the mounting problems and the machine's reliability. He did say it was costing as much as a helicopter would have, and that was a problem. Homer was very pleased with my radio reports and aerial shots, which by now were becoming better and more useable on the air.

Our conversation was interrupted by a phone call, during which Homer listened for a moment and said, "He's sitting here right now."

Two minutes after he hung up, White Cloud strode through the door, sat down, and immediately began speaking. "My concern is that someone is going to get hurt if we continue flying that thing," he started. "You have had some close calls and we've been lucky. If we have one more failure, I'm going to get rid of it and we will continue Skywatch with a small plane or a news car. *You* have worked out much better than your aircraft." And with that he was gone.

Homer recognized my worried look and assured me that if the gyroplane was axed, I would still have a job. He was always great about reassuring me of my job security at KOOL, and understood how sensitive I was underneath my tough exterior.

He wrapped up the meeting by going over my mistakes, the first of which was not getting my story on the six o'clock news. "You can always call someone to meet you and pick up the film. The story is everything, but never compromise safety to get it on the air," he said. "Second: when you're on a TV broadcast please

190

wear a jacket and tie. That is newsroom policy," he said. His message was loud and clear that the department heads ran their own show and made their own rules subject to Tom Chauncey's approval. From then on, when asked to report a story live, I wore the proper attire.

The gyroplane was due for an annual inspection that would take several days to complete, so Dianna and I planned a little vacation to visit Uncle Mac and Aunt Wanda at Lake Powell. On my last day of work before the inspection, I spotted a house fire and shot aerials, then arranged for Chuck Hawley, the photographer, to meet me and pick up the film.

I had worked out a system with the photographers for getting the film to them. I would fly in low over some power lines at 19th Avenue next to the freeway, over a plowed plot of land that was now furrowed and planted with some sort of produce. I'd swoop down over the field and drop the can of film near the photographer. If we could connect and get the film to the processor by 5:30 we could have the story on the air at the bottom of the six o'clock news. Bill Close had begun to warm up to the idea of having my shaky film on the air, since it beat the competition. My stuff was always "Exclusive," as the TV people love to say. I was the only game in town.

This day I went over the telephone lines at about 50 mph, and came down low over the field. As I got to where Chuck was standing I tried to add full power, but the long throttle rod bent over ninety degrees and froze.

I was only about twelve feet in the air, and barely moving fast enough to stay there. With no power, I had only one choice, and that was to land straight ahead. I dropped the can of film and, since I was moving forward, it went straight back into the wooden propeller, splintering it. Pieces of the prop flew into the rotor blades, causing a serious out-of-balance situation. I stood the gyro on its tail, killed off the remaining airspeed, leveled the machine, and—with the help of a good headwind—was able to land level between the rows without sliding over the furrows and flipping over. It was, without a doubt, one of my prouder moments. I sat in shock, realizing I had survived what could have been an ugly crash. The only damage—a broken propeller blade and a missing chunk from a rotor blade—was not that serious, but it would be expensive.

Chuck radioed the station, who notified the police department, who then informed the fire department of the downed aircraft. A few minutes later there were more fire and police units than I had ever seen in one place. Pretty soon Bill Close and Homer Lane were also on the scene. I must have explained the story a dozen times to investigators and the media. I had asked Homer what I should tell the media. "Just tell them the truth," he said.

When everyone had cleared the scene, a lone policeman was assigned to guard the forlorn little gyrocopter until mechanics could haul it off. I confess that as we drove away, the sight of my little friend stranded in that field brought tears to my eyes. I knew that was the end of an incredible adventure. While I had always wished

Abandoned in the field

and hoped that someday I would fly a real TV news helicopter, on this day I mourned my little Pollywog.

Homer told me to go ahead and take the week off; when I returned he would have an answer to what the future held for our Skywatch program. Dianna and I bundled up the kids and drove north to Lake Powell for a little relaxation, and a lot of worry. We had fun with Uncle Mac's family and used their houseboat for a couple of days. I thought about the incredible night I had spent on the lake when I had flown to Wyoming. I would spend many nights on beautiful Lake Powell in the coming years, and it would become my personal hideaway from the world.

Back at KOOL, I spent the next two weeks driving the streets in a news car, listening to my police and fire scanner and reporting what I heard on the radio. I hated that. At least from the gyroplane, I had a bird's eye view of the predicament and could report whether it was blocking traffic or was just a minor situation. I heard of house fires, overturned vehicles, and police chases, but was powerless without my whirlybird. By the time I arrived on the scene in the news cruiser, it was all over.

Meanwhile, the gyroplane was sitting in hangar C with a big red maintenance tag that read: "Do Not Fly." Homer said when Mr. Chauncey decided on a new program he would let me know. "Any idea how long it'll be, or what we are going to get?" I would ask hopefully.

"Jerry, you will know when it's decided. Just keep up those traffic reports."

The whole station was buzzing with curiosity. Would White Cloud really *buy* a helicopter? A news station with its own helicopter was unheard of in 1972, but I felt confident he would want to be on the cutting edge. The gyroplane had come along at just the right time and planted a seed that would spread like a wildflower in the broadcasting business. We had been able to get a lot of shaky aerial videos on the air that scooped the competition; and beating our competitors was always the bottom line.

I always wanted to learn more and be better at my job, so between morning and evening traffic reports, I spent a lot of time with station photographers learning as much as I could about film and cameras. I also went out on stories with reporters and watched how it was done. I raced to spot news stories in a station car and shot film of it.

I politely and honestly told everyone I didn't have a clue what was going to happen, while I tried to keep a positive attitude. I didn't want anything negative getting back to Homer or White Cloud. Until they made their decision, I planned to stay under the radar and keep my mouth shut, which was very difficult.

For two weeks I was home a lot and crossing some things off

my "Honey-do" list. My little girls were so much fun, and it was such a thrill to watch them grow. My heart just melted when they interacted with me in such a loving way. I was their Daddy and they let me know it.

I was the Daddy, but Dianna took care of their needs. I had been so busy with my new career that I was only around for the fun parts. By the weekend I was so tired that all I wanted to do was eat and sleep. It was beginning to wear thin on Dianna, and I knew deep down she was dreading the thought of another helicopter taking up my time. "It can only get worse," she said.

Pete also talked to me about the future. He stayed in the middle of us and encouraged Dianna to "hang in there." Pete and Dottie were among my best supporters. My mother and Uncle Phill were also solidly behind me, and they were all proud of how far I had come.

Mom and I talked practically every day, and naturally she worried a lot when I was flying the gyroplane.

It wasn't just the station and my family that had had enough of the gyrocopter, though. Even McCulloch was selling out. The little J-2 was ahead of its time. The accident rate for the eighty or so machines they had sold was alarmingly high, and their maintenance records weren't much better. Everyone thought I had dodged a bullet. Who knows, maybe they were right. But it sure was fun while it lasted.

On a Monday morning, right after traffic reports, our radio dispatcher told me I was wanted in Homer's office at 9 a.m. This could only mean one thing, and I was excited. "Okey dokey," I replied, and headed toward the station.

Just as I came up on a busy intersection I heard a crash, as one car slammed into another one making a left turn. Traffic came to a standstill, so I jumped out of my car with my Scoopic camera and captured the nasty accident on film. Now I was running a few minutes late for the meeting, and of course right at 9:02 Bill Close's voice came over my radio. "This is KFG617 News Base calling Unit 2, Jerry Foster, over."

"Yo Bill!" I replied in my cocky way.

"You were due in Homer's office two minutes ago. What's your 10-20 and ETA?"

"Bill, the signs are going by so fast I can't give you a location, but I should be skidding in there in about 15 minutes."

He was not amused. "This is KFG-617 to Unit 2, Jerry Foster. This is not a joking matter. There is no excuse for being late. This is KFG-617 News Base clear with Unit 2."

I explained to Homer why I was late but he already knew about it from listening to the radio traffic. "We are expected next door," he said, leading me out of the room.

We walked into Tom Chauncey's office at 9:45. I honestly didn't know what to expect. My anticipation had been building for weeks. My blood was flowing so hard that I could feel the veins in my neck popping out. Talk about pressure. This day could be the best day of my life, or one of the worst. I just didn't know what to expect. White Cloud had me totally intimidated.

As we entered, he was at his desk and on the phone. He spotted us, smiled and waved us in. *This is a good sign,* I thought. He finished his call, then turned to me and said with a smile, "I notice you are late again, and Bill Close says it's because you covered an accident after your traffic reports. Nice job." Before I could say a word he gave me the news I'd been hoping for.

"Homer and I are going to put you in a Hughes helicopter to do traffic reports and cover TV news. We have a machine on order that will be ready next week."

From that point on my mind was racing, and I had to pay close attention to avoid missing part of the conversation. I was bursting with excitement and couldn't wait to get out of that office and spread the word. I was getting a helicopter! I felt like a little kid at Christmas, finally getting the bike he had yearned for.

"… and Homer will give you all the details. I'm investing a lot of money and I want to see you make this work."

"Yes, sir," I replied meekly.

As we stood up to leave, I built up my courage and said, "Mr. Chauncey, if you will also buy a CP-16 camera just for the helicopter, I can make your investment a lot better."

Both Homer and White Cloud looked at each other and I thought I might have pushed my luck. Homer just shrugged his shoulders, and the boss said, "Anything else?"

"No, sir," I answered. And with that we were out the door headed back to Homer's office.

This was a big day for me. A Hughes 300C was on order and so was the camera I requested. I would be leaving for Culver City, California next week to pick up my new toy. I called Mom and Dianna, and we arranged to meet at Guggy's for dinner at six o'clock, along with Dianna's family. Homer told me not to say anything on the radio about the change because it would be announced at the "appropriate" time. Everyone in the newsroom knew about it from the look on my face when I walked back in. Of course Bill Close had to tell me *he'd* known about it a week ago.

I walked back to the TV newsroom and promptly got into a wrestling match with sportscaster Bill Denney. We fell over a desk, knocked over a trash can, and Denney had me pinned on the floor, when Bill Close walked in. "That will be quite enough!" he roared.

We quickly regained our composure and stood in front of the boss while he carried on about our playful jousting in, of all places, *his* newsroom. It was all we could do to keep from bursting out laughing. When Mr. Close asked, "Who started this?" we both pointed to each other, then totally lost it. With giggles and teary eyes, we were both now practically incoherent.

Close spun around and walked toward his office. Just before going in he turned and said to me, "Oh, by the way, that accident you shot turned out to be a double fatality. It's our lead story on the big news at six and you'll be reporting it."

"Whoa," I said, "I have dinner plans at six!" He gave me that famous Bill Close TV smile, which meant "No, you don't," as he said, "Be sure and wear a coat and tie."

I was a little late for dinner that night and had learned a very important lesson in my new broadcasting career. Do not make personal plans that cannot be broken. Like a policeman is sworn to uphold the law 24 hours a day, on or off duty, a dedicated "news chaser" better be there and ready to go when the call comes in.

Chapter 24

Hughes 300

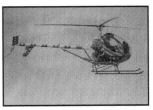

The "Bug"

I was one happy pilot the day I walked into the Hughes plant in Culver City. I was met at LAX by our Hughes sales rep, Roger Schuster. I spent two days with an instructor learning everything I could about the little bird. I had flown more than 300 hours in the Hughes 269 at Ft. Wolters, so I felt right at home.

It's difficult to describe what a big event this was in my life. Having vertical capabilities and the ability to land nearly anywhere was huge for covering news. During these years, the Federal Aviation Administration was busy dealing with a rash of airline crashes and was not paying much attention to us news guys.

I wouldn't do anything stupid. As long as I continued to use good judgment and didn't endanger anyone or anything, I was good to go. When a complaint came into the station it was sent straight to Homer. If it was something we needed to talk about, we did.

As soon as I got back to Phoenix with the new machine, which I had already named "the Bug," I contacted a friend who owned a radio shop. Bob Miller's specialty was radios and scanners, and his passion was gyroplanes and helicopters, so we made a great team. Bob fixed me up with a radio that would allow me to talk to the station on channel A, and switch over to channel B and talk to the sheriff's office dispatcher. I would also have two scanners that picked up police and fire frequencies statewide. In my new career as a pilot–reporter, I wanted to be armed to the teeth, and I took the initiative to make it happen. This new bird was the perfect starter for what I had in mind.

Even though it seemed I had everything, there was one more project I really wanted to be a part of. The Arizona Department of Public Safety created a new unit within the highway patrol called Air Rescue; an offshoot of the AMES program I had participated in a couple of years earlier. DPS now had three turbine-powered Bells, each capable of carrying two patients on stretchers, plus a pilot and a medic.

One unit would be based in Phoenix, another at the airport in Flagstaff, and the third would be used for back-up. I would have joined that unit in a flash, but I always remembered what the Scottsdale chief had told me about felons, so I didn't bother to apply. Even so, I would share an incredible relationship with DPS Air Rescue throughout my entire career.

Following KOOL's announcement and press releases about the new chopper, I was reporting traffic the next week. The new Hughes 300 was a three-passenger hot-rod painted red, white and blue, with stars and stripes; it drew a lot of attention. I strapped it on and away I went! I had a max forward speed of 75 mph, but I could fly forward, backward, sideways, and straight up and down.

A landing pad was built on the roof of the KOOL building, making it faster and more convenient for me to hop in and go. The Hughes was much quieter than the Pollywog and the broadcast quality on my two-way radio was very good. I could dial in the agency I wanted to listen to on my scanners. This was 1972 when electronics were relatively new. The Motorola two-channel radio weighed more than forty pounds. On a 110-degree day with full fuel, I still had to fly alone, just like in the gyro. That was another reason I learned to shoot my own film. If I was alone up there, I wanted to be prepared. It is absolutely gut-wrenching to get over a major news event and not have a camera; or worse, have a camera but no film.

I made all those mistakes and more. If the camera had more than three dials, I was usually confused. I didn't know a thing about photography, so it was a slow process for me. I learned the hard way and suffered the wrath of the people at the station who had to deal with my film. It sometimes got real ugly in the editing room when I sent the wrong can of film to a waiting Coleman Rusnak, who would rant, "Does that Dumbo fly like he shoots film?"

I would always hear about it later, and when I was at the station I would go to the editing room, slap him on the back and ask him if he had been talking about me. That would get him going. Other photographers editing their film would chime in with remarks and it sometimes got out of control. Bill Close would always magically appear and remind us all that we had jobs to do.

The new Skywatch caught on right away. With my sound camera strapped into the middle seat I still had the capacity to take one passenger. Our promotions department helped out by keeping a schedule. VIPs had priority for the extra seat, so I was fortunate to meet and fly with most of the Arizona movers and shakers. I had friends of my own who needed to get up every now and again, so at times there were two passengers showing up for

Skywatch

the single seat. On those occasions I cut the flight in half and both passengers were happy.

I was still an FAA pilot examiner and still giving flight tests for both helicopter and single and multi-engine aircraft, so I was doing a lot of additional flying outside my news job. I was also involved in FAA programs such as the Safety Pin Award, and was attending seminars all over the state. I became great friends with many of the inspectors who transferred in and out of the local office. Sadly, I also stepped on some toes along the way, but overall, this was a good time in my career. I tried very hard to make everyone like me, and it would be years before I figured out I hadn't succeeded. My style of flying would worry a lot of people. I was definitely a "cowboy" and made no excuses for it. The fact was, Homer Lane and the station encouraged that persona, as long as I stayed safe and within the law.

Chapter 25

Dr. John Bull

There's a saying that people come into your life for a reason, a season or a lifetime. Dr. John Bull was all three. He definitely came into my life for a reason, he was there for a season, and would have been in it for my lifetime—had he lived long enough.

I met Dr. Bull soon after starting at Channel 10. He rented a hangar next to Saguaro Aviation where the gyrocopter was kept, and one day he wandered over to take a look at the strange little Pollywog. We enjoyed talking aviation, and began getting together for coffee after my morning traffic reports. We'd meet on the little porch overlooking the flight line and swap flying stories. I told him about my family, and I learned that he was married with four children, and was a practicing plastic surgeon in Phoenix. Over the next few months we became good friends.

After our friendship was established, John became my personal physician and remained so for most of my TV career. He was careful to prescribe medicine that wouldn't affect my flying, and he watched over me very closely. On a couple of occasions when I was sick or worn out, he ordered me grounded. I always listened to him. By keeping me healthy, he played a big part in my success. John was six years older than I, and like the big brother I'd never had.

He was also one of the most generous people I've ever known. I mentioned to him over lunch one day that Dianna and I needed to get away and were planning a long drive up the California coast, all the way to Oregon. He said "Why don't you go in style. Take my Jag."

I couldn't believe what I was hearing, and tried to refuse. His Jag was a sleek charcoal XKE hardtop with a V-12 engine; a dream car. He kept insisting we take it, and I'll admit it was hard to resist. It would have been a wonderful trip anyway, but driving that Jag up the coast just made it that much better. It was the first time I had driven such an expensive and sporty automobile. My mom thought I would get a handful of tickets for speeding, but we never even got stopped. That was one of the best vacations Dianna and I ever had, though it got off to a shaky start.

We were just 60 miles outside of Phoenix, heading west on Interstate 10, when the V-12 engine suddenly quit. I pulled over onto the shoulder and coasted to a stop. This was not good. I looked at Dianna and said something like, "I wish we had taken the Volkswagen."

It was still about 50 miles to Blythe, California. The closest telephone was five miles down the road at a truck stop. In desperation, I turned the key back on, hit the starter, and *VAROOOOM!* That big Jaguar engine roared to life. It scared us both, and then we started laughing and clapping our hands. "Hooray," I said, and dropped that beast into low gear and took off.

But wait! Something was still wrong. In second gear all I could get was 30 miles per hour. When I pushed the throttle down all the engine would do was gasp and then drop back down to 30. So down the interstate we drove on the shoulder of the road at 30 miles an hour, feeling very depressed. What a sight that must have been to motorists flying by.

A few minutes later, which seemed like an eternity, we made it to a truck stop. I found a mechanic who looked at the car and suggested I call the Jaguar dealer in Phoenix. "Too fancy," he said.

I dreaded calling John, but I was out of options. I caught him at home, explained the problem and the symptoms, and right away he knew what it was. He took the phone number and a few minutes later called me back.

John had talked to his mechanic and they agreed it was a faulty fuel pump which had been a problem in the past. He said I should go ahead and drive the car to the airport in Blythe. He and the mechanic would fly down in his Baron and get us going again. Driving the car wouldn't hurt a thing, he assured me.

After creeping along for over two hours, at 30 miles an hour, in the emergency lane, with flashers on—but looking sharp!—we arrived in Blythe. John and the mechanic were waiting when we arrived.

It's a very humbling feeling when you play with someone's toy and it breaks. I felt responsible and guilty and just hated that I broke it, but that all fell on deaf ears. John was truly happy that he could save our trip and felt guilty because the car malfunctioned.

An hour later we were back on the road. Our trip took us to San Diego then all the way up the coast to Portland where we visited friends. For the rest of our vacation we didn't have another problem and I was able to return the car just the way I had found it.

Our two families became close. My family often had dinner at their home, and we all did fun things together, including a fishing trip in northern California. The only issue that made me uncomfortable was that John would always pick up the tab for whatever we did. The cost of the fishing trip was staggering to me, but John would have it no other way.

During my entire career at KOOL I never made more than twelve thousand dollars a year. Dianna and I had been through some tough times financially. Both her family and mine had helped us out several times, and up to this point I had still not been able to pay them back. I sometimes had to borrow money from Mom between pay days, just for the bare essentials.

I think John understood our situation, and didn't want to put us in a bind. He was a great influence on me, and I enjoyed his friendship and needed his counsel. He would be especially helpful years later, during one of the darkest times of my life.

There were times we'd be relaxing and chatting over coffee, when I'd be called to go out on a breaking news story. If John was free, he would go along. At 5' 7" and 150 pounds, he was a lightweight, so I never worried about how much extra weight I'd have on board. He was with me during my first major news story that went national.

One hot July day, I had just finished my morning traffic report, landed, and met John for coffee. I no sooner arrived when a call from the station informed me of a search being launched near Gila Bend, 60 miles southwest of Phoenix.

A group of 10 immigrants had entered the country illegally from Mexico, gotten lost and ran out of water. It was an all-too familiar story for Arizona lawmen and the border patrol. The Gila Bend Gunnery Range sits on hundreds of square miles of desert and shares an unsecured border with Mexico.

The range had to be closed so that the sheriff's office could get in to conduct a search. In an emergency like this the sheriff's office has jurisdiction, which was a sore point with the Air Force.

Eight survivors had been found, but two more were still missing. It was the middle of July and time was running out. The previous night's low temp was just under 100 degrees and by noon it would soar to 112.

I invited John along and we took off. Flying time to the range took about 40 minutes. Enroute I contacted the sheriff's office, which told me several ground units had found the survivors late yesterday and they were in bad shape. When I got a little closer I made contact with the deputy at the scene to let him know I was on the way, but stopping for fuel at the Gila Bend airport.

I only had a little over two hours of fuel when the Bug was topped off, so I tried to never pass up an airport if we were headed into rugged country. That is exactly what the Gila Bend Gunnery Range is; 2.7 million acres of beautiful and pristine Sonoran desert.

The range serves all of America's armed forces, and is primarily operated by the U.S. Air Force. Fighters and bombers test nearly every kind of ordinance in their arsenal, and the testing goes on nearly every day and night of the year. So when someone or something shuts down the range for any reason, the Air Force gets real grumpy. On this occasion, trespassing immigrants and deputies out on their range had forced them to shut down air traffic. That made them hard to work with. Now toss in a news helicopter on the way to the search, and their day was ruined.

That was the scene Dr. Bull and I were unknowingly blundering into. The rules governing this type of situation were yet to be made. It was the first time the gunnery range had a news helicopter invading their territory.

My next step was to contact the Air Force tower located at an auxiliary field with an 8500 foot runway used for emergencies.

Me: "Gila Bend tower this is helicopter 960 Alpha Mike, five miles north, inbound for the city airport for fuel, then we will be inbound to the search area. Over."

Tower: "Helicopter 960 Alpha Mike you are to remain clear of our airspace. We have an emergency in progress until further notice. There is an Air Force helicopter in the search area. The range is closed. Over."

Me: "Tower, we were dispatched by the sheriff's office to help with the search and I have a doctor on board. Over."

Tower: "Are you a sheriff's helicopter or a news helicopter?"

Me: "Tower, we are both, but right now inbound as a search

tool. Over."

Tower: "Helicopter 960 Alpha Mike remain clear of our airspace. Out!"

Thanks to mountaintop radio repeaters we were in contact with the newsroom. I told KPNX news director Jim Murdock the problem and he said he would work on it from his end. I then called the sheriff's dispatcher and told them what was happening. Now I was out of ideas so we just stayed at the airport under a shady tree and waited. The temp now was 108 degrees and it was only a little after 10 a.m.

It was a very uncomfortable wait. The airport is unmanned and you have to call a number just to get someone out to pump fuel.

After countless radio calls and total frustration I got a call on the sheriff's frequency authorizing me to enter the restricted range and assist with the search. When I asked if that was okay with the Air Force the reply was simple enough. "The sheriff called the commanding officer at the gunnery range and advised you would be assisting his office with the search and we would worry about the jurisdiction at a later time."

This was my first disagreement with a large bureaucratic organization and, to say the least, I was a bit nervous as John and I lifted off from city airport and headed south for the short five-mile flight. We were finally on the gunnery range a little after noon. It was still getting hotter, even with the doors off. I called the tower to advise them of my intentions, and this time I got a response.

Tower: "Helicopter 960 Alpha Mike land at the center of runway. You will be escorted from there. Over."

Five minutes later we landed on the runway and were advised to follow the pickup to parking. The pickup had a large sign on the back that said, "Follow me." After a short hover flight behind the truck, we landed on a square helipad. After I shut down, an Air Force staff car pulled up and and a colonel with a clipboard in his hand stepped out.

He didn't look happy as he walked up and told us he was going to allow us entry into the range and I should expect to hear from the Federal Aviation Administration, as he planned to file a violation.

John and I were asked to sign a "hold harmless" document that basically said we would hold the Air Force harmless for anything that happened in their airspace. After we signed the form, the Colonel said, "Very well," did an about face and was gone.

Back in the Bug, fired up and ready to go, I called the tower for takeoff clearance to the south:

Tower: "Helicopter 960 Alpha Mike south departure will be at your own risk."

We took off and headed south into clear skies and 110 degree temps. I was grateful that we left the doors off during the summer, since we had no air conditioning. In the 1970s we were not yet spoiled with that luxury. The only way you don't sweat in the desert is if you're dead. I hear Easterners say, "Yes, but it's a dry heat," and that is true, but so is my oven. It's not comfortable!

The Sonoran desert is beautiful any time of year. Every kind of desert plant and creature can be found here. The range is relatively untouched except for roads leading to and from various areas. This is where the fighter pilots and helicopter jocks come to play and train with all different kinds of weapons and lots of secret stuff.

We immediately noticed small parachutes scattered on the ground, which had floated down during the night missions with flares hanging underneath to light up a target. We crossed over a couple of ranges with mock targets representing trucks and tanks. We saw mockup bombers and fighters that had been nearly blown to bits and would soon be replaced. It was anything but a dull flight, and we were seeing it from about 50 feet above ground. There are mountains that rise several thousand feet scattered around the area, which had to be detoured around by hikers. Getting lost was easy.

Twenty minutes later we landed next to a patrol car in the search area and were briefed. Tracks indicated the group had been walking in a large circle and moving only at night. It was hard to

206

tell, because of the heavy usage by others. This group had made it about 10 miles north of the border.

Back in the air, I set up a pattern flying north and south to avoid looking into the sun reflecting against the Plexiglas windows. There were small mesquite trees and bushes we needed to look under, where a person might find a precious little bit of shade out of this relentless heat.

Dying of hyperthermia is said to be a painful and agonizing death. As first responders, we realized the desperation of the poor souls we were hoping to find. We had water on board, which we were desperate to share with them.

I was just getting ready to tell John we would have to go refuel when he said over the intercom, "Jerry, come around. I see something."

I circled to the right, and over John's shoulder, saw the young man step out from under a spindly little mesquite tree. I circled long enough to call over the sheriff's search frequency that we had found a survivor, then landed next to him.

John was quickly out with a canteen of water. It was a pathetic sight. The poor guy was wearing jeans and a once-white t-shirt that was nearly torn off. He had cuts and scratches all over his body. When I got to them, I pointed my Scoopic camera and recorded the scene.

The man's long hair was soaked with water from the canteen and he was struggling with John for more. John was making him drink only small amounts to begin with. I had to help John restrain him until help arrived a few minutes later.

The man was so delirious we were not able to get any information from him about the last remaining victim. When the Air Force helicopter arrived with a medic, he helped John administer an IV and prepared him for transport.

After he left we fired up and headed back to Gila Bend to refuel, planning to return and try to find the last missing man. Just before we cleared the gunnery range we heard over the sheriff's frequency that searchers had just found the last body under a bush.

As we cleared the gunnery range boundary, I gave the Air Force tower a call, not really expecting an answer. "Gila Bend tower this is Helicopter 960 Alpha Mike, we are clear of your airspace to the north and will be changing the frequency."

They responded, "Helicopter 960 Alpha Mike, understand clearing our airspace. Have a good flight and thank you!"

I never mentioned the run-in with the Air Force and I never heard a word about it from the FAA.

When I called the news department to tell them we were on the way home with film, Bill Close advised me over the radio that I would be on his news show that evening. He added, "Be sure to wear a coat and tie."

Despite the miserable conditions, misunderstandings and tragedy, we made a difference on a successful search that saved a life. There is no better feeling for first responders.

Most exciting for us was seeing my film of the survivor getting his first taste of water from John on the CBS Evening News with Walter Cronkite. I had hit the big time.

A new character was being molded by the press and I started to feel the pressure of trying to live up to the "Fastest Newsman in Town" ads in the newspapers. That image was being built up by the KOOL promotions department. They took a photo of me in a field of wildflowers with the helicopter in the background. The caption read, "Take Time to Smell the Flowers." My new persona was "Helicopter Cowboy" and my bosses loved it.

The stellar news ratings pointed to a public viewing audience that approved of my style of reporting and flying. Focus groups interviewed by the TV station plainly showed our Skywatch program was a big part of the news operation

This new celebrity status was somewhat difficult to deal with. I was becoming well-known while doing something I truly loved, but had to take the bad with the good. I would much rather have been just one of the boys over at Air Rescue than signing autographs at some staged event. I certainly struggled, as I felt it was a complete invasion of my privacy and my soul. I had secrets and worried constantly about someone doing an investigative report on KOOL's pilot–reporter. What if someone from one of our competing stations did some digging into my past?

Homer and I talked about it several times and he always assured me that he and Mr. Chauncey would stand behind me all the way, as long as I didn't do something dumb. With that assurance I continued building this character I was now living.

Chapter 26

Traffic Reports

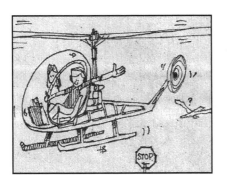

It took me a good year to really get into the traffic reports. It can be very dull, particularly for my friends in the small airplanes. When I was in the gyroplane I had to spend a lot of time flying the machine. It was a totally different aircraft, one which I felt was always on the edge of doing something I wasn't going to like. The little Pollywog had my full attention. I also flew it higher than I would have a helicopter because it was so noisy. I discovered it was hard to talk—especially on the radio where you know thousands of people are listening—while trying to stay in control. Sometimes the DJ would call for a traffic report and I would miss it because I was busy with other things, like paying attention to flying, or concentrating on those frequencies that had something going on. We tried using a sound to get my attention— the a bell sound. It helped get me on the air on time, but in the newsroom I now had the nickname, "the ding-a-ling."

My tension level was reduced when we got the Hughes 300, since much of the training I had done for the U.S. Army at Ft. Wolters was in a Hughes. In no time I was back in the saddle flying a "real" helicopter, and was able to put more of *me* into the radio traffic reports. I developed two different styles, both centered around the DJs. In the mornings with Len Engebretson, I was more reserved and didn't crack many jokes. His show was a bit slow for me, but we still got through it. The afternoons were more fun and usually a lot busier. Johnny Johnson was the evening DJ, and he always made it interesting. We had a good relationship. If the news was serious that's how we played it, otherwise we kidded around with each other and made it fun for the listeners. I never missed a cue with him because he always checked to be sure I was in a position to give a report, which made a huge difference.

Johnny and I had so much fun that we were called in to Bill Lester's office a couple of times for an update on Broadcasting 101 as it applied to our station. Nothing serious; just reprimands for

Flying and filming over ASU

our discussions about flying over swimming pools and trying not to look down at the scantily clad maidens. This was back in the 70s when broadcast codes and morality were much different than today.

Another DJ, Joe MacNamara, did an afternoon show and filled in for Johnny and Len on various occasions. When it was Joe in the morning and Johnny in the afternoons, I could count on it being a good day.

KOOL-AM was very conservative and our audience was primarily the older generation. At that time it was one of the strongest radio stations in our market. KOOL-FM targeted the younger listeners and was one of my favorites. I tried for years to do reports on the FM side, but it never happened.

Every workday started the same. At this time we were living in a Scottsdale housing development. A 20-mile, 40-minute drive took me through the city to the hangar. It took another 15 minutes to pull the aircraft out of the hangar and give it a quick look-over. I soon understood that the quicker the response time, the better the story.

I knew on the day I picked up the Bug that we were going to see a lot of each other and I needed to figure out ways to cut my response time down. I made that one of my priorities.

My first traffic report followed the CBS news at 7:06 a.m. so I was usually in the air by 6:45. An intern in the newsroom listened to police monitors and let me know what was going on in the valley. If there was something happening, I was on it. If not, I just wandered around in the air. I'd give my traffic report, a brief weather forecast, and hand it over to Jim Murdock for the local news.

My first radio call was usually to the tower at Sky Harbor Airport, five miles from downtown Phoenix. The airport control area was a tricky place. I had to monitor the tower for other traffic and stay well clear of arrivals and departures. Whenever I flew within a five-mile radius of the airport I was required to check in with the tower to enter their control zone. I did this every morning for years, and got to know tower controllers by name. The conversation was something like this:

"Good morning Phoenix tower, this is Helicopter 960 Alpha Mike, five miles east to enter the control zone low level and north of the airport:

"Good morning, Jerry, request approved. Let me know if you need to cross the runway centerline."

That meant I was cleared into the control zone and I was restricted from crossing to the south side of the airport without permission. The single-runway airport was always busy, but not as rushed as it is today. A little chat between pilots and controllers was common. My day always seemed to go best after a friendly "good morning" from the tower.

From the airport I headed downtown and then out into the suburbs. At that time, there was only the Black Canyon Freeway which runs north and south as Interstate 17 to Flagstaff. In the morning the freeway and all major streets were clogged with stop-and-go traffic as commuters poured into the downtown and State Capital areas.

I gave a traffic report every 15 minutes, making the last one at 8:06, after which I landed at the station to see what was going on and what the assignment desk had for me. Sometimes reporters would ask for aerials of an area they were covering or the assignment desk would have a story for me out of town.

Depending on the circumstances, I might take the helicopter or it might be Homer's Skymaster. The great thing about my job was never knowing what the day or night held for me. The only "knowns" were my morning and evening traffic reports. Homer had made that very clear when I started; although breaking news had first priority over everything.

Afternoon was my favorite time. Johnny and I would kid around and talk about what was happening in the valley. It's called "happy talk," but people enjoyed it on their slow drive home. One particular day I spotted a cat up on a telephone pole and a group of kids and adults all looking up at it. They started waving at me and pointing to the cat, expecting me to do something about it. I couldn't just fly off and disappoint them, so I made a very low pass over the telephone pole. When I was about 10 feet away the cat looked at me and shot down the pole. I had discovered something else a helicopter could do. As I flew away I could see the girls blowing kisses at me and the boys waving like crazy. We talked about that on the radio and people just loved it.

Helicopters were still something new and different. People had a fascination with them and I flew low enough to wave and interact with people on the ground. I also had favorite places I liked to fly over. We have lots of homes with swimming pools all over the valley. You cannot imagine how many people swim in the nude during the warm months. I once shot some aerials of a nude couple waving at me, then getting out of the pool and waving again. I was raised very conservatively so I was shocked, but I got used to it. That film never made it on TV, but I'm sure the editors in the back room enjoyed it.

Whenever I could, I flew over the home of a very special lady, Mary Jordan. Her daughter, Devoney, worked at KOOL as a secretary to one of the vice-presidents. Mary and her husband Joe owned two Mexican food restaurants, one of which was downtown near the station. I ate there a couple times a week and became friends with the Jordan family. Whenever Mary heard my rotor blades she would come out and wave, while her little dog would run around the backyard. For years I enjoyed dinner at their weekly family get-together, referred to as "Taco Tuesday." Dianna and Devoney became close friends and we all enjoyed each other's company. Devoney also dated my friend Buzz for a while, and we have all have remained friends over the years. For the rest of my career, "Mother Mary" as I called her, was always there to wave when I flew over. As I write this book, Joe is gone, but I recently attended Mother Mary Jordan's 100th birthday party.

I could fly from one side of the Phoenix metropolitan area to the other in about 15 minutes, so when I heard a police or fire call of interest I could get there quickly and catch the action. If I saw breaking news I would call the DJ and get right on the air. That is, if Len had the volume on his two-way radio turned up. If not, I did a slow burn, shot the film and reported the story when Len got around to it. He truly was the nicest guy; just set in ways. And I guess I was easy to forget.

Many times I circled a scene, flying with my knees and feet. I controlled the throttle and pitch with my left hand and held the camera with the right. My right eye looked through the camera viewer, the left eye looked ahead, and my hearing and instinct reported back on how my little bird was feeling and flying.

I did this every day and was able to make a takeoff and landing without touching the cyclic (the control for movement forward, sideways and backwards). I was the brain for my mechanical hummingbird and felt like we were in tune with each other. Some people talk to their machines, and some don't, thinking it silly. I do: always have, and always will. Ever since I was a young man driving my first car, motorcycle, airplane and helicopter, I have always chattered to them like a parrot, believing my machine has its own spirit with which I could communicate. The gyrocopter had been"Pollywog" and the 300 was "Bug." On a hot day with a heavy load, there would be a strain in my voice as I lifted off the helipad, coaxing, "Okay, Bug, up we go, now over the power lines ... oooh ... keep it climbing ..." until we cleared the obstacles. If I had a passenger, I would keep it to myself or flip on the intercom and give them a show. I always treated both birds with the utmost respect.

Doing traffic reports from a helicopter is much different than from an airplane. Airplane traffic reporters had to maintain at least one thousand feet above populated areas, per FAA regulations, but a helicopter could operate at any altitude that would permit a safe landing in case of an emergency.

The FAA rules were so ambiguous that they had a tough time enforcing them. There were so many variables that it came down to using common sense and consideration. I always got a fair shake from the local FAA office. It was a different era and generation. The FAA motto used to be, "We're here to help." And they were very helpful. Like everyone else, inspectors were still learning about helicopter operations and how they would evolve. We were all learning together.

I liked to fly with my door removed unless the weather was bad. Depending on the neighborhood, I generally flew at between 300 and 500 feet over the valley. If I was working a story I would go lower. A car chase, for example, was easier for me to fly and film from 500 feet, but if searching for a lost child or a drowning victim I needed to be much lower. In the rural areas I skimmed just above the cacti, so I really got to see what was going on. Good judgment and common sense were necessary, and sometimes I may have pushed it just a little.

One evening during traffic reports, I listened to a conversation between deputies trying to stop a motorcycle for traffic violations. The machine was a high-powered dirt bike that apparently was not licensed for the road. The chase went from the city streets to the desert and was creating a lot of excitement. It was only a few minutes away so I headed in that direction.

From the conversation, it was obvious the biker was just playing with the deputies. When a deputy got close, the biker would simply climb up on a bank of the dry river bed, sit there and watch them, then speed off for a short distance and repeat the process.

I had no trouble spotting the sheriff's four-wheel drive trucks, but I didn't see the motorcycle right away, and the deputies had lost track of it. After a couple of minutes I saw the biker about a half mile up the sandy wash, trying to hide under some mesquite trees. When he saw me and realized I was the enemy he took off again. By now there were six patrol vehicles on the scene.

The biker headed down the wash toward all the patrol units. It looked like the keystone cops in action. They were no match for the bike. The biker would get close to one of them, wave, and then leave the deputies in the dust. Circling overhead, I shot some film then gave a traffic report which included the on-going chase. When my report was over I dropped down on the desert floor right behind the motorcycle.

I followed close behind, matching his maneuvers for several minutes until he made a big mistake. When he hit a stretch of moguls and ruts he had to slow down. But he was too late and he partially lost control of the bike. Down he went with the bike going one way and him the other. By then I was right on top of him. When the bike stopped rolling I set a skid on the front tire. He was unhurt and when he stood up he flipped me off. By then a a swarm of deputies was all over him.

Every day it seemed we found another unique use for the helicopter. There was just no way a motorcycle in the desert could outrun or out-maneuver that little Hughes 300.

Surprisingly, there was seldom a complaint called into the station about me. My orders from Homer were to return all calls of complaint and explain my actions. There were times when the complaints went to Homer and some went to the FAA. When the FAA received it, one of the local inspectors would invite me to their office for a chat. I explained to the inspector what I was doing and why. No violations were ever issued until years later when I became their problem child.

Some days were non-stop flying except for fuel and personal pit stops. Our news department relied heavily on the helicopter to capture breaking news. I cruised around, smiling and waving at people, reporting on whatever was happening. On busy days I zipped from one end of the valley to the other, checking out various reports coming from the police scanner: accidents, house fires and police situations of all kinds. Some days I might have several different photographers with me for stories needing aerial shots; some days it seemed there was a big story in every part of town; and other days there was nothing going on.

Fires were a different kind of call. If I was busy in the east valley and heard about a house fire on the west side, I only had to glance across the skies to see if there was smoke. I didn't get excited about a little wisp of white smoke, but if it was grey or black, the race was on between me and whatever fire department was en route. I usually won during the early years, but as their response times improved, I only had minutes to get to the scene before the fire department was there to put it out.

So many times my little Bug would be maxed out at 75 mph, racing toward the column of black smoke only to see it—*psssst*—begin to turn white and gradually disappear. Whenever I filmed house fires I always felt bad for the homeowners. I'd put myself in their position and think about how I'd feel if I had just lost everything. In many cases, the victims didn't have a lot to lose in the first place.

Even though my goal was to get film of the fire—the story—in my heart I was rooting for the firemen to win this race. Several firefighters told me that when responding to a fire, their goal was to beat me to the blaze. When they got back to their stations they cheered when my aerial shots showed they had saved the house. We had a rivalry; but a fun and worthy one.

Everything I carried had a place in the cockpit. Items I might need quickly, such as a camera, film, scripts, snacks or water, were kept where the center seat used to be. We eventually built a small cabinet that fit between the cockpit and the center seat space. Now I could only take one photographer—and that was just the way I liked it: no more flying the station VIPs around. The Bug was transformed into a dedicated TV news helicopter. We were a new force to be dealt with in the broadcasting industry. Locally, we were way ahead of all our competitors.

Now that we had a heliport at the station, I spent the day in the newsroom or covered ground stories between drive times. Most of my down time was spent wandering around the station learning what made up a mega-broadcast company. I had joined a professional team of people who truly loved the challenge of building a dominant television news channel. It was amazing to see all the activities in the control room, programming, news, sales and the many other departments. I found it mind-boggling. Technically, it was way over my head and I spent a lot of time learning just enough to get by. I refer to these as the "Golden Years" because I am flooded with so many good memories of trying and doing things that were not being done elsewhere. I loved where I was, who I was with, and where we were all trying to go. Every single day was an adventure.

A New Era

In 1973 I resolved a huge problem: shortening the time and distance between me and my Bug. It was taking me at least an hour to get in the air and I worried about missing big stories at night or on weekends. The solution was to have the helicopter live where I lived. I just needed to find a home I could afford, with enough space for the Bug.

Dianna's dad found it for us: a cute little three-bedroom in a rural area with a huge, fenced, three-acre lot. It had a second-story addition that served as an office. Before we bought it, Dianna, Pete and I canvassed the area and made lots of friends, so the neighbors would understand there would soon be regular helicopter traffic in the area.

This proved to be an excellent arrangement. If I was called out by the sheriff or the newsroom at night or on weekends, I could be there in a flash. Neighbors loved it and we never had a complaint.

It made a big difference at home. By parking the machine in my back yard, I was able to get home sooner and I didn't have to lift off until 6:45 each morning. I could sleep until 0600, then thank-you-dear, kiss-the-kids, and I was gone. I would lift out of my back yard and head straight for my mom's house in Mesa. She came out every morning to wave and seldom missed a day.

It seemed as though the big stories usually happened right before my last traffic report of the evening, after which I'd end up on the set for the six o'clock news. By the time I got home it was seven or eight p.m.; just in time to kiss the kids goodnight, which might be the only time I got to see them, since I usually left before they were up in the morning. Many nights I didn't get home until Dianna and the kids were already in bed. I remember Dianna often saying, "Well at least your kids get to see you on TV."

I knew I was being a miserable father and husband, but I just couldn't resist that new guy I had become. In the middle of the night at home, a call would come in from the station or a law

218

enforcement agency, and I would literally be in the air and on the way within 10 minutes.

This job had become a lifestyle.

A Happy Recovery

HELICOPTER RESCUE OF 2-YEAR-OLD BOY

I wasn't scoring a lot of points at home, but my relationship with the sheriff's office was becoming even tighter after several successful searches. My first real big moment came on a search for a little lost boy in a rural desert area near Apache Junction. Skip Carnes, the MCSO search and rescue coordinator, called me before sun-up one morning and explained that searchers had combed the desert all night for a two-year-old toddler they thought had wandered from his house into a desert area.

It was only an hour until daylight, and he wondered if I could possibly help out. I told him I would be in the air in 10 minutes. He gave me his location and I was ready to go. I jumped out of bed and went through a well-rehearsed routine that had me out the door and in the helicopter in less than five minutes. Another five minutes and I was in the air.

It was about a 20-minute flight to the search area, and I could see all the red emergency lights flashing from miles away. A deputy lit a flare indicating where I was to land. With my landing light illuminating the still-dark sky, I settled behind the flare and shut down.

Skip explained that the boy's parents noticed him missing about ten o'clock the previous evening. Deputies responded immediately, searching on foot. They called for the DPS helicopter, which continued the search until about 3 a.m. The outlook was grim, and they were having to consider the possibility that the toddler had been kidnapped. It would be highly unlikely that wild animals played a part. Of the many scenarios I went through for search and rescues, when kids were involved I always asked myself, *What would I do if this was my kid?*

I could feel the urgency and desperation as I watched Skip, the other rescuers, and especially the parents. I had an urgency of my own and wanted to get in the air. I kept remembering the tragic search for the grandmother and kids a few years earlier, and I wanted this one to have a better outcome. Then I'd think—DPS had used a searchlight and didn't spot him, so what could I see that they missed? If the little guy was up and moving, Air Rescue would have found him.

At 5:15 a.m. with Deputy Skip Carnes on board, I lifted off from the boy's front yard. We both felt he was going to be close to home. I moved about a quarter-mile away from the house and began a low, slow circle. It was now light enough to see under the brush and small desert trees. I stayed about 20 feet high so the rotors gently moved the branches around. I hadn't even made it half way around my circle, and there he was.

Skip and I both saw him at the same time; standing near a bush, looking up at us. I quickly set the helicopter down and the boy didn't make a move. Skip jumped out and ran toward him, as the little boy held his arms out to be taken. When Skip picked him up, the toddler wrapped his arms around the big deputy and laid his head on Skip's shoulder. I'll never forget how my heart just melted.

We flew the little guy back home to a happy reunion, and I shot some great film of Deputy Carnes handing the boy to his mother. The sun was now bright enough to clearly see the toddler's face, which held the remnants of his adventure: some scratches and bruises, quite a few grimy tear stains, and a great big smile. That's one of my treasured memories.

We figured out that he must have become tired of wandering around and crawled under a bush for the night, which was why my Air Rescue friends hadn't spotted him.

That was my first mission directly from home. I had been called for help and arrived at the scene less than 30 minutes later. The payoff for the station was that I got the story and made us a lot of friends.

The payoff for me was also huge. I realized the mutual

benefit that could come about between a news helicopter and agencies responsible for public safety. The sheriff's office was happy and so was KOOL. But there were also those who would later criticize me for becoming part of the story, but for now this was a small victory.

That emergency call-out was the beginning of a different mission for me, and from that time on I never strayed far from my little Bug. My goal was to be in the air within 20 minutes after being called.

Deputy Skip Carnes with found toddler

Chapter 27

The Senator's Antics

 My friendship with Senator Goldwater continued to grow, as we shared a love of flying and genuinely liked each other as individuals. Over the years we traveled to many different places, within Arizona and beyond. In 1974 I began flying him around for his campaign for the Senate, and did so again during the 1980 campaign. Sometimes we'd take a fixed-wing plane and other times a helicopter. Sometimes I'd fly, other times he would, and I was the back-up pilot. I was paid well for these flights and enjoyed seeing the various parts of the state with Barry.

When I realized I would be spending a lot of time with him during these campaign trips, I decided to come clean with him about my past. By this time I had come to like and respect him enough that I didn't want anything in my background to come up and tarnish his campaign. I thought I'd tell him what I had done, and he could replace me as his pilot.

It was hard for me to tell this highly respected general, senator, and nationally known public figure that I had a felony in my background. In true Goldwater fashion, he took it in stride and said it wouldn't change a thing.

The managers of both TV stations I worked for—Homer Lane and Tom Chauncey at 10, and later, Pep Cooney and Karl Eller at 12—all approved flights with Barry to anywhere in Arizona. They could all see the news value, and I believe they liked and respected him enough to allow whatever he wanted.

What I refer to as the Goldwater days, or "the Golden Years," were an incredible time. I became close to the family, and was invited to their parties, on their yacht, and to Hollywood events that included Barry. There were several of these, as he was often invited to be a guest on talk shows, such as The Dinah Shore Show, or to participate in the Hollywood "roasts" that were popular then. I would fly him over and back, and I often attended the events as well.

A Cheap Date

One of these trips stands out in my mind, partly because it was my first experience with getting the "royal treatment" that was accorded to people like Senator Goldwater, and also because of a little-known quirk of his that would come to aggravate me. On this particular trip, I had flown him to Los Angeles where he would be one of the guest speakers for a roast of Johnny Carson. We were met by a black stretch limousine driven by Katie, a beautiful, long-legged blonde, wearing a "hot pants" outfit that looked like it had been painted on. Hot pants were a fad of the early 1970s, when short-shorts were considered dressy and were worn for all occasions, even fancy events. Katie's outfit was topped off with a chauffeur's cap. She was hot-looking and cute as a button. The limo was stocked with a small bar, fresh fruit and snacks, and conveniences like radio and TV. According to Katie she stayed busy every day driving the rich and famous.

When the roast was over Katie was there to drive us back to the airport. During the drive back Barry told me to give her fifty bucks. Now, one thing about Barry that drove me nuts was that he never carried cash. Somehow he got away with it, but usually at the expense of those with him. This was one of those occasions. I said, "How about twenty?"

He said, "Fifty."

I grumbled, and even said I only had twenty on me, but he knew better. In the end I grudgingly forked over the fifty bucks. On the flight back to Phoenix we didn't talk much, but as we were close to landing, I said, "Next time bring some cash or a credit card along, willya?"

I told him that I wasn't bringing any money on the next trip, and he said he wasn't either. He never did. I think it was a point of pride with him that he could get what he needed with no credit card, check or cash.

At first I just accepted the losses when I had to pick up the tab. Soon though, his secretary, Judy Eisenhower, pulled me aside and said, "You don't have to eat those expenses, just send me receipts for anything you pay for, and I'll see that you're reimbursed." From then on I relaxed and paid up.

While Barry was a great friend, he could also get me into trouble quicker than anyone else ever did. Two instances come to mind when the FAA was all over me because I followed his instructions.

Secret Service Scare

In 1964 Barry Goldwater had been the Republican nominee for President of the United States. His opponent was sitting President, Lyndon B. Johnson. It was a bitter battle and my friend was soundly defeated. The last round of that feud was on January 29, 1972 in Tempe, Arizona at ASU's Grady Gammage auditorium. I was not really aware of the depth of their animosity until this day.

The event was a memorial service for the late Senator Carl Hayden, who had served Arizona in the Senate for 57 years: the longest-serving senator in history. The tributes would be given first by former President Johnson, followed by Barry. The memorial was to begin at 11 a.m. The schedule called for Johnson to land at Sky Harbor Airport at 10 a.m. and be flown by a National Guard helicopter at 10:30 to the ASU stadium. The helicopter would land and Johnson would be taken to the auditorium by motorcade.

I was scheduled to land with Goldwater at the stadium at 10:45 and he would be driven to the event in a police car. It was all laid out and looked to be a good plan. In a Secret Service briefing the previous day, I was told to be sure I didn't land before the motorcade had cleared the stadium. The agent in charge told the assembled gathering that "timing was everything."

On the morning of the service I landed in the driveway of the Goldwater home at 10:15 to pick up the senator and the Arizona head of the Republican Party, Chairman Harry Rosensweig. By 10:30 Barry and Harry were strapped in and ready.

I heard the Phoenix tower clear the former president's helicopter for takeoff to the east, which was my signal to lift off and head for the stadium. We lifted off and also headed east. It only took the Guard chopper about five minutes to arrive at the stadium and start an approach.

Three minutes after he was on the ground we were circling and waiting for the motorcade depart the stadium: my cue to land. As we passed over the auditorium, Barry suddenly said over the intercom, "Jerry, I want you to land down there on the lawn next to the auditorium."

"What?" I said, "You have got to be kidding! The Secret Service is going to be pissed and the FAA will take my license, that is if they don't shoot us down."

"Land right there," Goldwater said, firmly pointing to a wide open lawn that bordered the auditorium. It was a beautiful area, roped off to keep the public away from the main entrance. But what he had asked me to do was crazy, and I told him that as I started my approach.

Barry picks up the story from there in his own biography with Jack Casserly:

Barry: *"There!" I said, pointing to a patch of clear grass to the side of the auditorium.*

"Aw, shit!" Jerry hollered, and put the bird down.

Jerry was right. The stuff hit the fan. It seemed every cop in town was bearing down on us—Tempe and university police, the highway patrol and Secret Service.

President Johnson's motorcade turned off Mill Avenue toward the auditorium. I stepped out of the helicopter and walked to greet the

President in front of the building. The police flew by me to grab Jerry. I greeted Johnson, laughing so hard I couldn't stand straight. The President felt I'd upstaged him. When we'd arrived by helicopter, the crowd had turned our way instead of toward his motorcade.

I could hear Jerry shouting in the distance, "Go talk to Goldwater. He's the guy who did this. I'm only the pilot. See the senator, guys. Arrest him — not me!

Jerry finally managed to convince the police I was the instigator. He avoided a Federal Aviation Administration citation. I never heard any more about it — except from Jerry, who still taunts me from time to time: "So you finally beat Johnson! Yeah, you had to beat him!"

The next morning the *Arizona Republic* published a photograph on the front page of us walking away from the helicopter. I was tucking my shirt tail in, Barry was straightening his tie, and Harry Rosensweig was adjusting his suit coat. The only one smiling was the senator.

Goldwater told us that was the best day of his life since losing the election. I was happy to be a part of it and never heard another word about it; at least not officially. But the FAA never got over it.

Trespassing

The second event took place several years later. We had flown to Tucson for an event, and from there to Ajo, about 125 miles directly west. At least it would be directly west if it weren't for the restricted area of the Gila Bend Gunnery Range.

The range has been here since 1942 and is used extensively. Nobody knew it better than Goldwater. He trained here as a fighter pilot throughout his long Air Force career. He had been checked out in nearly every jet fighter during his career.

I was preparing to detour around the range, but since we were running late, Barry said "Just go through the restricted area."

When I objected, he asked me to radio the FAA Flight Service Center and see if the range was open or closed and said, "tell them we want to go directly there; we're running late, dammit!"

I radioed for permission, but got the expected denial. The gunnery range was closed to all air traffic. Barry reached over and turned the radio off, saying, "We'll tell them I was flying."

I could not believe what he had just done. When I looked over at him and started to object, he looked at me with that mischievous grin and pointed straight ahead. We didn't just cut a corner of a restricted area, we flew right through the center of it, directly to Ajo, Arizona. That was Barry. And I still got in trouble for it.

Two days later I got a call from an inspector at the local FAA office telling me about a storm that was brewing within FAA.

Ironically, a few years later the Air Force renamed that area "The Barry Goldwater Gunnery Range."

Family Trip to Mexico

One of the most memorable trips with Barry didn't get me in trouble with the FAA, but it almost cost our lives. I was flying Barry and his family to Las Cruses, Mexico to celebrate the holidays and his January 1 birthday. A large group was going, so he had rented two planes for the trip. I flew a Cessna 402 with Barry in the co-pilot's seat. Mrs Goldwater, four other family members, and Ollie Carey—widow of the well-known actor,

Harry Carey—were in the back. The rest of the party was on the other plane. Before takeoff I looked for the maps I had purchased, then realized they were in the other plane, which had already left. Barry said, "Don't worry, I know Mexico like the back of my hand."

We had to land in Mexicali to go through customs, which was a long ordeal. Barry was impatient at the delays, but as far as the customs agents were concerned, he was just another gringo tourist. We were finally cleared to take off again. A couple of hours later dark clouds began moving in, obscuring our visibility. We couldn't see the ground and knew there were mountains in the area, so we dropped down below the clouds to get our bearings. Then we lost contact with the other plane, as well as the directional signal from La Paz.

Checking fuel gauge, with nearly zero visibility

Barry said he didn't recognize anything. The maps would have come in real handy about now. In addition to the dense cloud cover, we were now flying through heavy rain. And then we were almost out of gas; in fact, it was dangerously low. The passengers in the back who had earlier been chatting and singing, were now quiet. Even Barry had a concerned look on his face. We were flying at just one hundred feet above the ground when we spotted a small coastal village with a landing strip and touched down there.

We piled out of the airplane, hoping to buy some fuel. Barry assured me that he spoke Spanish and would take care of it. But the few words he knew weren't the ones we needed. No one in this little fishing village spoke English, and all the gesturing in the world wasn't helping. Then eighty-year-old Ollie Carey stepped up and, in fluent Spanish, asked for a telephone and fuel.

The storm had knocked out the lines for the one telephone in the area. They did have fuel, and it cost us one hundred dollars for a 55-gallon drum, but we were in no position to haggle. We were given a handwritten receipt, stating "Nota de Venta, Vendido a Barry Goldwater, Fecha 27-12-72." We fueled up, providing entertainment for those hanging around watching the "rich gringos" who didn't know where they were or how to get where they were going. None of the locals could agree on which direction La Paz was, and were pointing all over the place. We gave up, deciding to take our chances, and took off again.

We were again flying through rain, black skies and lightning flashes, but at least we had fuel. Everyone was quiet as we concentrated on staying the course. Finally, we heard the beautiful sound of the VOR beep from La Paz; the clouds broke, and we could see the lights of the town. We landed and found that the other plane in our party had arrived sometime earlier. The tower had closed and shut down the VOR, but our other pilot insisted they re-open for us. Without his help, we might not have found La Paz at all.

We scouted out a place to eat and then went looking for hotel rooms, since it was very late and we were too tired by now to go on to Las Cruces. Unfortunately, there were no rooms to be found, and we headed back to the airport planning to sleep in the planes.

For whatever reason, the Mexican airport authorities would not allow that. They didn't know who Barry Goldwater was, and didn't care. They were gracious enough to offer cots to Peggy Goldwater and Ollie Carey in the airport jail, but the rest of us were supposed to sleep on the hard benches or chairs.

As soon as the authorities were out of the way, Barry said "Come on, I'm going to get some sleep in that damn plane!" We hightailed it out of there and locked ourselves in the Cessna.

The next morning, after a decent night's sleep, our group gathered outside near the planes. Barry's khakis and an old red sweatshirt were rumpled from sleeping in the plane, and he was unshaven. We were arguing with the authorities over some trivial incident, when fate intervened. Another plane landed at the little airport, carrying the Secretary of Mexico; an office equivalent to our vice-president. He also happened to be a good friend of Goldwater's.

He recognized the senator's famous smile and made his way to greet Barry, giving him a big bear hug. The attitude of the airport authorities changed drastically, and we were soon given whatever assistance we needed to be on our way. We finally reached our destination of Las Cruces. After everyone was off the plane I flew back to Arizona to pick up Dianna, because Barry insisted she and I also be his guests at the celebration. It was one of the best vacations we'd ever had.

Unbeknownst to us during this trip, then-President Nixon had been frantically trying to reach Goldwater. Even after being told he had left on vacation, Nixon insisted he be found. Now!

All the Secret Service agents had been able to discover by going first to Barry's house and then to mine, was that he was on his way to Las Cruces, Mexico. More than 24 hours passed before Nixon was able to find him and get a call through. His important message? "Best wishes on your birthday! By the way, how's the weather?"

I happened to be present another time when the senator was talking with Nixon on the phone. Barry was yelling at him "You sonofabitch, you'd better retire or you're going to ruin this country!" Nixon resigned shortly afterward.

Barry never did pull any punches.

Chapter 28

School Visits

One day I was called by Audrey to see Mr. Chauncey. These messages didn't come along very often and I was always a little paranoid. Even when Homer called for me, I'd sometimes wonder, *could this be the time?*

When I reached the reception area, Audrey motioned me into the office of White Cloud with a cheerful smile. Her greeting was usually a barometer of his moods. If she waved me in without even making eye contact, I was probably in trouble. But if she was smiling, I could relax.

Everything must be okay, I thought, as I walked into his mammoth, intimidating-shrine-of-success office. He offered his hand and gave me a welcoming smile, then got right to the point as I sat down. "Jerry, I have an assignment for you. I would like you to take the helicopter over to the Little Sisters of the Poor school for show-and-tell with the kids. But first, I want you to drive over to the school, pick up one of the sisters and bring her back to the station so she can fly back with you."

He handed me a piece of paper with all the info neatly typed. "Make it happen, Jerry. Sister Superior is a long-time friend of the station."

White Cloud then reached for the two little poodles sitting quietly in their beds. They didn't make a sound until he spoke to them. I was always impressed by their control: even the dogs knew who was boss.

It was easy to see why everyone at the station held this man in high regard. Mr. Chauncey had power, and I'd heard he could be intimidating and frightening, but so far, I had only seen a very gentle man. I was happy to complete this easy mission for him.

The next morning I landed on the station roof helipad after my last report at 8:15. There was plenty of time to straighten up the helicopter and clean out the inside of my unmarked news car before picking up the sister at her school 10 miles away.

A huge welcome awaited me as I pulled up in front of the school. The staff and several classes were outside to see their teacher off. I met all the "Little Sisters of the Poor," strapped in my passenger, and drove around the circular drive to head back to the station—all to loud cheers. All this hooplah and we weren't even in the helicopter yet. The sister was very nice and told me how the kids and staff all thought I was such a good role model. I was very flattered and vowed to do a good job for the kids.

We arrived at the station and parked next to the stairway that led to the heliport. Homer Lane was there to open the car door for our guest, and all three of us climbed the stairs up to the Bug. I strapped myself in while Homer helped the nun into her seat and secured her belt. He waved and shouted, "Enjoy the flight, Sister."

We were off for our five-minute flight to the school. I circled to recon the landing area, then made a fast pass down the field to show my passenger off and let her wave to the cheering throng of kids. I came back around and landed in the designated spot, shut the engine down and helped the sister out.

The kids were brought to sit closer while I told them about flying the helicopter, shooting film and using the radio. I answered questions from the children and several of the nuns and they presented me with a school T-shirt. I lifted off and put on a little air show and headed happily back to the station.

After lunch I was sitting in the newsroom writing up a story about an accident when Audrey called: "Jerry, Mr. Chauncey would like to see you right now."

Of course, I thought, *he wants to thank me for a job well done, maybe even give me a raise!* "I'm on the way," I said, smiling.

But when I walked into the reception area, Audrey wasn't smiling. She continued looking at her typewriter and pointed for me to go in Mr. Chauncey's office. I went in to find the boss sitting at his desk with his hands folded. I knew right away this was the side of White Cloud I'd been told I didn't want to see.

"I cannot believe that you went out to that school and embarrassed me and the Little Sisters of the Poor," he started.

I was completely stunned and didn't know what to say. I just stood there looking at him.

"Where do you park your car?"

"Sir, in the news garage, because I fly in from home."

"Let's take a look." He got up and motioned for me to follow him. My mind was in mush mode, as I just couldn't imagine what I had done wrong.

We walked into the garage where my news car was parked. He walked around to the back and pointed to my bumper. I immediately saw the trouble. On the lower right bumper was a sticker that said simply, "SHIT HAPPENS." I was shocked! How in holy hell did that get there? This was huge.

"Sister Superior would like an answer to this. What do I tell her, Mr. Foster?"

"Sir," I started. I just did not have an answer. I would never put that on a company car or even my own car. "I didn't know it was there. It's got to be an inside job, because this is where my car is at night. I am very sorry, sir."

White Cloud stood there looking at a very humbled man and finally said, "You call Sister Superior and set up a time to go out and apologize to her and the school. Are there any stickers on the helicopter I should know about?"

"No, Sir," I said, "and this will never happen again, Mr. Chauncey, Sir."

"See to it." With that he turned around and walked out. Several people had walked though the garage with funny looks and snickers, and they knew I'd been set up. I would just take it on the chin for now and be a good sport.

I called Sister Superior's office and made an appointment for three o'clock. When I arrived I was shown right in to the sister's office. She stood up, immediately came around her desk and embraced me.

"I didn't mean for Tom to get all over you," she said. "He asked how your visit was and I told him how much we all enjoyed your presentation. I was worried that you didn't know that awful writing was on your car and that you would be embarrassed. Only Sister Ruth and I noticed it so I asked him to let you know."

"Sister, I just wanted to apologize to you and the school. I should have checked my car just like I do my helicopter, and I am sorry. I promise that won't happen again."

From a very bad situation, I made some good friends. A few days later I received a copy of the sister's letter to Mr. Chauncey. He had scribbled on it, "Well done."

I would visit that Catholic school for many years to come, as well as about 3,000 others during my career as pilot–reporter. These visits became one of my favorite activities.

Imagine excited students all looking up, anxiously awaiting a visit from me in the helicopter. When I landed in the school yard I had their undivided attention. My photographer and I would give them a tour of the little Bug, the cameras and all the equipment. We stressed the dangers of being around a running helicopter.

And since we were role models, we used that leverage to preach safety, to say no to drugs, and to stay in school. We answered questions and put on an air show for them, with my little helicopter hovering like a hummingbird or flying laterally like a pendulum. My photographer would watch from the ground, and then for our final trick, I hovered while he climbed up onto the skid and into the cockpit.

If I was alone I did the flight demo with a fast pass and a goodbye wave. It was always a lot of fun, and I had some great experiences with the kids. If something was going on at the school and I had a photographer with me, we would shoot film and do a little feature story for the bottom of the news. They didn't always make it on air, especially if it was a busy news day. I always worried because I knew how disappointed the kids would be. What bothered me more were the times we had to cancel a school at the last minute to cover a news story. I was a hero one minute and a zero the next to all those little kids down there waiting. I hated when that happened.

During all my years at KOOL, Homer Lane was my number one mentor and supporter. He watched my every move in and out

My favorite part of the job. John Bass at right

of the station, and I met with him several times a week. An avid aviation fan, he was also a licensed pilot and very active in the aviation community.

Homer owned two percent of KOOL Broadcasting along with the two major stockholders, Tom Chauncey and cowboy legend, Gene Autry. Homer had a straight-laced appearance, with black hair parted in the middle, and thick-rimmed glasses. His on-air delivery was serious, and he seldom smiled. The dark suit and tie he wore made him look thin, and his shirt was usually too big around his small neck. His role on the air was to provide an editorial at the end of the six and ten o'clock news broadcasts. He made it clear that his editorials stated the position of the KOOL Broadcasting Company and its owner, Tom Chauncey.

During that era, Homer and Chauncey were very powerful men, and were strong supporters of aerial news coverage. Without their guidance and support, I would have never become a broadcaster. I would very likely have ended up in Nepal, still working for Tug and Arizona Helicopters.

While Homer looked stern and serious during his editorials, his off-air personality was quite different. He loved to attend functions with his wife, Doris, and he was always smiling and cordial.

One year Dianna and I attended the Black and White Ball, an annual charity event. It was a black-tie affair and we were Homer's guests. I couldn't remember ever having so much fun. It was our first formal outing.

My old boss, Chief Walter C. Nemitz, who had fired me from the Scottsdale Police Department years ago, also attended this event, and was pure class. When he walked up and offered his hand I really felt honored. He told me I was doing a nice job and to keep it up.

I stood there with my mouth open until Dianna came to the rescue and quickly introduced herself. We were both introduced to Mrs. Nemitz. We had a very pleasant chat and the chief said they were both Channel 10 viewers and enjoyed my aerial coverage. I felt their sincerity and appreciated the way Chief Nemitz handled the situation.

I had felt a slight sense of paranoia when we first met. Here was a Chief of Police who knew all about me; yet I was still here and very much in survival mode.

It had been a very emotional night for Dianna as well. She would later tell me that she felt out of her league. I had trouble understanding why, because she is so beautiful, inside and out, and was always devoted to me and the kids. It really sunk in to both of us that we were traveling first class without a ticket.

Looking back, I recall a newsroom full of good, fun-loving and dedicated people. I never sensed an undercurrent in any of the departments. It was an organization that ran like a Swiss watch. Management was very much respected by the workers and vice-versa. It was a money-making machine and my friend Homer was a major reason for its success.

Chapter 29

The Dirty Dozen – 1972

 When I was still a young boy in Wallace, Idaho, my Uncle Phill showed up one day riding a British Triumph. He sat me in front of him and we took off. We went so fast the scenery was a blur, but the sound of the engine alone was a huge thrill. The feelings I experienced would stay with me for years, much to the dismay of my dear mom. Later she would update her list of what I was to stay away from to include helicopters, airplanes, motorcycles and dirt bikes. She was okay with a boat.

My fascination with bikes probably had a lot to do with my real dad, whose biker name was "Swifty." Though I had almost no memory of him I think there was some kind of fascination that attracted me to bikers.

When I turned 16 I bought my first machine, an old beat up Triumph. I hid it at a friend's house until my mom got used to the idea. From that time on I always had either a street bike or a dirt bike, and most importantly, my step-dad's blessing.

Now that I spent all my time in helicopters, I didn't have much time to ride anymore, but the fascination was still there. One Sunday afternoon I was flying back from covering a story in Flagstaff when I spotted a group of bikers heading south on Interstate 17. From 300 feet above I could hear the unmistakable rumble of the Harley Davidson engines. These motorcycles were referred to as "choppers" and the riders as "outlaws" There must have been fifty chopped-down Harleys riding in a perfect two-across formation. They rode in a tight pack in the high-speed lane, but stayed at the speed limit. Behind the pack was a white two-ton truck with "Dirty Dozen" painted in large black letters. About 100 yards behind them were two highway patrol cars, just hanging back and watching the show.

And what a show it was! They looked like the Hells Angels. Every bike was on a custom frame, some with kicked out front ends and high-rise handlebars. They were all different sizes and colors, and most were created in someone's back yard or garage.

There was a friendly little game of "Cat and Mouse" going on between the bikers and the highway patrol on outings like this. Each side knew the other was there, and as long as no one did anything dumb it would remain a quiet Sunday afternoon.

After a few minutes I peeled off and headed for the station. I found the event interesting and wondered, *Who are those guys? Do they work? Are they as mean as they look?* I decided to look into it. If I was curious, our viewers might be. That was the start.

Biker gangs had their beginnings in the post World War II era, and had continued to grow, gaining a reputation for illegal activities along the way. The gangs were glamorized by movies such as the 1955 *Rebel Without a Cause* and *Easy Rider* in 1969.

It didn't take long for me to track down the leader of the group and explain over the phone what I wanted to do. Billy Burr identified himself as the president of the Dirty Dozen. He let me do all the talking. When I finished he said, "I understand and will get back to you." He hung up before I could say anything more.

A month went by before I got the call. The voice on the other end identified himself as Mr. Clean, the vice-president of the Dirty Dozen. "Billy says for you to be at Cave Creek Road and the Carefree Highway Saturday at 7 p.m. for a club meeting," he said. When I repeated it back and asked for an address my answer was another hang-up.

So I had a date and time, but still didn't know the location. The area he gave was nearly 30 miles from downtown and there was no way I would fly out there. It was very remote and it would be dark by seven o'clock. This whole thing was starting to spook me. I had three days to think it over. I sure couldn't ask one of my deputy friends to go along.

The more I thought about it, the more I knew I wanted to do it. This could really be a good series, and I was determined to go. The next day I had a plan. I asked my good friend Peter Cronk to go along on a story with me, but I didn't tell him what it was about. I only said it was one of those stories he would like ... and he bought it.

That Saturday evening we left my place at 5:15. On the way I explained to Pete what we were really doing. It was too late for him to back out since I was driving and he was along for the ride. But he had a ready answer. "While you're doing your investigative stuff I'll wait outside in the car with the doors locked and windows closed to make sure no one bothers it," he said.

We laughed about how safe he would be sitting in a locked car out in the middle of nowhere. For the next 45 minutes we joked about all the different scenarios we might encounter, like being surrounded by bikers. "Pete," I said, "how long do you think you could hold them off in a locked car with the windows up?"

We had a ball during the long drive to what seemed like nowhere, and arrived early at the designated intersection. It was dark, lonely, and spooky. There were few lights in sight, and only a stop sign for each direction. In the first 10 minutes only one car passed by. We sat there for a half an hour getting more spooked by the minute.

Pete looked at his watch and said, "It's 20 minutes past the meeting time. Let's go home." I was about ready to get out of there myself when a pickup truck pulled right up beside us with its lights off. Pete and I both nearly had heart attacks. The passenger side window came down and a voice ordered us to follow them. I tried to ask how far, but they were already moving. *These guys don't do a lot of talking,* I thought!

Five minutes later they turned onto a narrow dirt road marked only by a mailbox. Sitting about 100 yards off the road was a house with a circular drive. The first thing we saw was a large campfire with at least 20 bikers sitting and standing around the flames. It looked like a nice house, and I could see horse stalls and a barn on the property. Parked in front of the house was a mass of choppers lined up around the driveway.

By this time Pete and I were not so cocky about this meeting. As we pulled behind the truck, a biker walked up and told us to follow him. Pete and I both jumped out of my car without a word and followed our guide to the huge fire.

Our guide told us to wait there, and told the others to go inside for their meeting. We suddenly found ourselves all alone by the fire, way out here in the boonies, surrounded by chopped down Harleys and men wearing biker patches and toting guns. It was a scene right out of a biker movie; surreal to both of us and very uncomfortable.

A few minutes later a tall man wearing a stocking cap and biker garb walked out of the house and straight toward us. "Uh oh, here we go," Pete whispered.

The man stood there for at least 10 seconds, then extended his hand and smiled. As I took his hand and got a closer look I realized I knew this guy! As we shook hands, he said, "My biker name is 'Mr. Clean,' but you know me as a whole different guy."

What a shocker this was. Oh yeah, I knew him alright, but didn't dare say his name. For a moment I thought maybe I had stumbled into a sting operation. "Do these guys know who you really are?" I asked, looking quickly at Pete, who didn't have a clue what was going on.

Mr. Clean & Raggs

"Yes, Jerry, they all know that you and I worked together at the Scottsdale Police Department. That was then and this is now. When the meeting is almost over you will come inside to meet the club and answer some questions. I'll send someone out to get you.

Your friend will have to wait here. See you later." With that he went back into the house.

"What the hell was that all about?" Pete asked.

I told him, "When I worked at the Scottsdale department, Phil and I were on the same shift working patrol. He was the neatest and most organized man I have ever known. He always cleaned the interior of his patrol car before each shift and wore a fresh uniform every day with spit-shined gun belt and boots. His hair then was short and neatly trimmed."

Now Phil's hair was long, but he was, by all appearances, still the same guy, wearing a white t-shirt, jeans, polished boots and a cut-off Levi jacket with the club name on the back.

"What happened and why the change?" Pete asked.

I was at a loss for words. A few minutes later another biker emerged from the house, walked up to me and held out his hand. As we shook hands it was another surprise. Again, it was someone I knew quite well. His biker name was "Pappy," but I knew him as Deputy Bill Carroll. He had been with the Maricopa County Sheriff's Office and I had ridden with him on patrol a number of times when I was working for Scottsdale.

Bill had retired and was now a biker. I also learned this was Pappy's house. He told me the club was ready for me, and told a nervous Pete he would have to stay by the fire until after the meeting. On the way in I asked Pappy if there was anyone else here that I knew. "You never know," he replied, as we walked in the door.

There wasn't a sound as we entered, and all eyes were on me. Bill Burr, the president, was standing in front of the group. He motioned for me to stand with him and told me what the club had decided. "Some of the 'brothers' don't like the idea of you snooping around, but we have voted to let you come around for awhile before you bring in any cameras or do any kind of stories. Some guys don't want their faces shown and you need to know who's who and then we'll decide if we trust you."

"Anybody have any questions?" Billy asked the group. There wasn't a sound and no hands were raised.

"Okay, that's it, the meeting is over." I walked outside with Pappy and spent the next hour talking to anyone who would talk to me. It wasn't a very friendly crowd and not what I expected.

In many ways these guys were very similar to the mining camp families and kids I had grown up around. Back then it was mostly automobiles that took center stage and brought people together. Here it was the motorcycle and was considered "Sacred."

I learned a lot that night about bikers likes and dislikes, including the "Three Golden Rules:"

1. *Never mess with a brother's bike unless you ask permission*

2. *Never mess with a brother's "old lady"*

3. *Never mess with a needle* (referring to drugs that had to be injected.)

Anyone who violated any one of those rules paid a stiff price.

"How stiff," I asked?

"You don't need to know," was the response to most of my questions.

During the next few months I went to parties when I could, as well as special events like a Christmas party, a New Year's party, and an Easter party at a city park where kids were treated to an egg hunt. Dianna and I spent the day there with our two daughters and we all had a good time. It didn't take long for them to get to know me and soon I was given permission to go along on a Memorial Day run.

I asked my friend and photographer, Bill Leverton, if he would go along and shoot film of the ride. He was up for that because he also saw the story value, and he liked the challenge. My pal Pete Cronk also volunteered to go along and help.

It was an awesome sight as we pulled into the meeting place at 9 a.m. There were about 70 motorcycles with riders, passengers, the club truck, and several other cars following behind. Bill's first response was, "Oh, my God! What have I gotten into?"

Pete said, "Maybe we should just roll up the windows and lock the doors until we see if they're friendly," referring to our first meeting in the desert. We had a good laugh and a good story going. When we stepped out of my truck, it was into another culture.

Everyone, including Pete, Bill and me, was dressed similarly; jeans, shirts, boots, and some with caps; but the "brothers" wore their club colors. The "old ladies," as they called their women, wore mostly jeans, and looked like any typical woman. There were exceptions, as in any group. Guns and knives hanging in holsters and sheaths made their men look intimidating. Their club colors had different patches and symbols, some of which were offensive, as was the very salty language they used. It wasn't at all hard to see why they clashed with authorities, and why they were called "outlaws," a term they relished as much as the press and the public did.

On a long ride like this, the group stopped about every 70-80 miles to gas up. Many of these machines had small gas tanks and only held 2-3 gallons. If someone ran out of gas it was available on the club truck, so the group would usually stop, because then it was time for another beer, which was also on ice in the truck.

On the road the pack was led by the president and vice-president. The riders were in no set order, except that non-members rode in the back of the pack, in front of the club truck, and cars brought up the rear. The pack was stretched out at times on the highway, but going through a city or town it was a tight formation and straight line of bikes. People along the route would stop and stare at the spectacle of all those rumbling Harleys and their colorful riders.

The outlaws' internal police are called warlords. Their job is to enforce the peace and, if necessary, take a brother off his bike if he's drunk, high or poses a threat to himself or others.

There is also a road captain who is responsible for keeping the pack orderly and safe. On this run it was "Fat Al" who took cameraman Bill Leverton on a ride he will never forget. Leverton needed film from all angles as the bikers rode down the highway. They rode alongside for close ups, in front, in the rear, and right through the middle of the moving pack. It was sensational film.

Reservations had been made to rent space from a bar owner right on the Colorado River. There were rooms for those who wanted them and a large party room next to the bar. That was the home of the Dirty Dozen for the next two days.

Occasionally a highway patrolman or Parker police officer would drive through the lot and wave, or stop and talk. I had the impression the bikers liked the attention. It was all part of a game and was usually friendly on these kinds of outings.

The more I found out about this group, the more interested I became. I kept a file on everything I could find regarding so-called outlaw bikers. Were these guys a club or a gang? Were they a danger or threat to the public? The answers depended on who I asked. I considered writing a book, and thought *Chopper to Chopper* would be a good title.

I actually felt comfortable with my biker friends. They took me back to my roots and reminded me of the rough-and-tumble, foul-mouthed miners and loggers I grew up around. Miners loved their cars and bikers loved their motorcycles. If a stranger was foolish enough to start trouble at a party or bar, they threw him out. By the same token, if one of their own stepped out of line they straightened it out internally.

Balancing these two cultures—journalism and law enforcement with the Dirty Dozen—was never a problem for me. I didn't try to hide any of my off-duty activities or relationships. If I was called to assist law enforcement agencies or someone in distress, I did my best. If one of my biker friends needed help I tried to be right there.

One of the more bizarre instances of living my "two sides of the street" occurred one New Year's Eve. Dianna and I attended a formal, dressy party at the Goldwater's home. After an unbelievable, glitzy evening, we changed into jeans, jackets and boots, and took off with our biker friends for a road trip, where Dianna was dunked in a lake to be "initiated" into the group. These two events were so extremely opposite, we still laugh about the irony.

I never acted as an informant for anyone. But I did act as a newsman and heard a lot of great stories and adventures from both sides of the street. However, my new friends tended to make the law enforcement side a little nervous.

Lieutenant David Paul (MCSO) remembers, *"We didn't like where we saw Jerry going, and it made us worry about him a little bit. Some people around the office turned against him when he started to hang out with that group. But I'll have to say, he never let us down and he never betrayed our trust or confidence. I know without Jerry we would have been hung up a lot of times. He showed up. He was available 24/7."*

I didn't live the life of policeman, but I believe I was judged by some as a sworn officer. I was not. I was simply a citizen doing my job and a volunteer citizen in time of need.

On a run with the Dirty Dozen. I'm the guy in the white hat.

Chapter 30

Buzz

My time with the Dirty Dozen brought me one of the best friends of my life. He's the Sundance to my Butch Cassidy, Robin to Batman, Tonto to the Lone Ranger; my silent, steady partner in so many adventures.

Allen "Buzz" Stalcup was born in Great Bend, Kansas in 1946, and came from a family of aviators. His grandfather, father and uncle were all pilots who died together in a plane crash when Buzz was just six years old. His mom remarried, moved to Hutchison and gave birth to little sister Suzie.

Buzz loved motorcycles from early on, and spent quite a bit of time building his own with money earned from yard work and odd jobs. His family moved to Arizona when he was 14. Buzz was a good student through high school and community college. He enlisted in the Army, as was expected of a healthy, able-bodied young man in the 1960s. Students who were late to class were reported to the draft board back in those days, and Buzz always had a problem getting up before the crack of noon.

After serving tours in Germany and Vietnam, he was honorably discharged and headed back to Phoenix; his mind still freshly full of wartime horrors and his mom not-so-gently suggesting any career other than flying. He continued pursuing his love of motorcycles and worked at various cycle shops around Phoenix, where he met and befriended members of the Dirty

Dozen. After an altercation, one member was voted out of the club and Buzz was voted in.

In the late 1960s, and early '70s, anyone who chose the chopper lifestyle was labeled an outlaw, and there weren't many social clubs for people who enjoyed riding. Members of the Dirty Dozen were hounded by police at every turn for the actions of a few. Less than one percent of the club's members were "heavies" who were involved in illegal activities (pot, guns and gambling). For the most part, Buzz's new friends were a brotherhood of family men. They were plumbers, electricians and professionals. They also gave each other the most unfortunate nicknames. A man who was burned in an accident was named "Torch;" another guy whose girlfriend beat up his bike with a two-pound hammer was called "Two Pound;" a woman who fell off a motorcycle was named "Tumbles," and Buzz was given his forever name by his mom, who accidentally uttered the long-forgotten childhood nickname of "Buzzy" in front of another biker friend. My nickname was "Gar" after the Garfish. Don't ask me why.

Members of the Dozen truly loved to ride motorcycles, and some didn't fit in socially anywhere else. The "gang" label was grudgingly accepted as part of the motorcycle lifestyle.

In 1972 Buzz opened The Wheel Shop at 16th Street and McDowell in Phoenix, and that's where I met him. I was drawn to his quiet, easy-going manner. Buzz is the person I would choose to have by my side in battle, for his calm demeanor and complete loyalty.

We quickly became friends and I'd hang around the shop talking when I could. When a call came in, I would often take Buzz with me. I figured if anyone asked, he could act as a cameraman and later a back-up pilot; but the truth was, I just enjoyed his company, and he made the long hours a little less tedious.

Buzz remembers, *"Jerry would hang out at the shop, playing darts or just talking. He was there one day when a call came in for him and he asked me if I'd like to go along. I was surprised, but said 'Sure.' From then on I went with him every chance I got."*

The calls often sent us to a scene filled with law enforcement officials and media. Buzz has never been comfortable around cops, and he never wanted to project an outlaw persona. He told me on more than one occasion, "You shouldn't take me to these things. I'm an outlaw. I don't wear a white hat."

But he always went along; a picture of quiet stability—and he even started dressing better for the occasions. Buzz was a great escape for me from the pressure of high-flying, and we did quite a bit of partying together. I was never much of a drinker, but I would have a couple beers now and then, and occasionally smoked pot to relax when I knew I wouldn't be flying. Groups of us would go camping and there would be lots of drinking, campfires, bullets thrown into the fire, running like hell, and laughter; so much laughter.

Buzz is still my closest friend to this day. We've been through a lot; together and individually. He had never had any trouble with the law; in fact he had always been an upstanding member of the community, with civic memberships and community involvement. Buzz had been a cub scout, a serious student and a business owner who never received even a parking ticket. But he dabbled in illegal substances throughout his life.

By 1973 we were good friends and had already shared many adventures in the air and on the ground. Buzz had always loved to fly, but never considered it because of his mother's fear for him. After he flew with me on traffic reports, searches, and mountain rescues, he decided to go for it. He used his G.I. Bill to get helicopter flight training. I arranged for him to take a flight test with my old friend Myles Ruggenberg at FAA. Buzz passed and was awarded his Helicopter Pilot Certificate. As anyone who has done it will tell you, it requires a ton of study and practice. I was very proud and so were his mom and step-dad.

One morning just after traffic reports I landed at the airport for fuel. As I was shutting down the engine, the station called to let me know that an airplane had crashed on takeoff from the Williams airport, about 190 miles north of Phoenix. Two people had been on board and their fate was unknown.

248

I told the station I would be on the way in 10 minutes; just as soon as I refueled. I called Buzz. He really wanted to go and said he would be there shortly. I waited an extra five minutes and when he didn't arrive I started the engine, engaged the rotor, and contacted the tower requesting a northwest departure. As I lifted off I saw his van skid to a stop in the parking lot. I knew he was watching so I continued the takeoff, and as I passed by I flipped him off. *That will teach him.* I flew another mile before requesting a return landing. When I got back on the ground I huffed up like a junkyard dog, put my finger on his chest and told him I would never wait for him again. But I did, because I needed the help and he would do whatever needed to be done.

Less than two hours later we were circling over the crash site. The single-engine Cessna had gone down in a stand of trees about a mile off the end of the Williams runway. We spotted two people around the crash and presumed them to be Coconino County Sheriff's detectives. As we circled and I shot aerials, the two men stopped what they were doing and one of them waved at me to get out of there. Then they began stringing "keep out" evidence tape around the scene. "Not a good sign," I told Buzz.

As I approached to land, the men both waved me off again. This happens every now and then and I went ahead and landed about 300 feet away, between the small trees and well away from the crash. I shut the machine down and grabbed my backpack, which contained the recorder and the color adapter; a total weight of 40 pounds. Attached to the recorder was a six-foot-long kinky cable that attached to the camera head. Buzz carried the backpack and I carried the five-pound camera. That meant Buzz had to stay within five feet of me or we ran out of cord.

We started toward the two men, who were walking toward us. They didn't look happy, and Buzz said, "I don't think they want us here. Maybe we ought to make another plan."

"No way," I said, "we have a right to be here as long as we don't interfere. Just stay close and I'll do the talking."

I could see the perspiration on his forehead and knew he wasn't comfortable with what was about to happen. The older of the two deputies was a detective sergeant who was clearly in charge of the scene. As he and his partner stepped back for a little strategy session, Buzz whispered in my ear … "I'm holding."

That's all he said, but it was enough to freeze me in my tracks. The two lawmen turned back to us and the sergeant said, "Either get back in your helicopter and leave, or you are going to jail."

Before I could answer, Buzz insisted, "Whoa, whoa, let's get out of here, Jerry; it's not worth it!"

I ignored him and told the sergeant that if he didn't allow us access to the crash he would have to take us to jail. I put the camera on the ground, faced the two lawmen and held out both arms, saying, "Go ahead and put the cuffs on because I am not leaving without the story I was sent here to get."

I looked back at Buzz, who reluctantly slipped out of the backpack, placed it on the ground, and held out both arms for handcuffs. Then we all stood there and looked at each other. "Your move," I said calmly.

Turning to Buzz, I told him he could fly the ship back to the station, but to video my arrest before he left. He was soaked with sweat by now and quickly put on the pack, picked up the camera head and started recording.

The wily old sergeant looked at his partner who just kind of shrugged his shoulders. Then both men focused on me. "Here's what we're going to do. I will walk you and your cameraman around the accident scene and let you get the shots you need. The only on-camera comment I will make is that there are two fatalities as yet unidentified and we are waiting for the FAA to arrive. We would appreciate you not showing the bodies. The only info I can give you is that it's an ongoing investigation. Does that work for you?"

"Yes sir, that works and we'll make it quick," I said.

As the investigators led the way I started shooting video of the scene, careful not to show the victims. After a few minutes I had everything we needed and we all headed back to the helicopter. I gave both investigators a little tour of the helicopter.

We had all loosened up from our confrontation and were now conversing like old friends. We talked about how we both had a job to do and by working together, we all got what we needed.

This wasn't the first time I'd had a run-in with skeptical lawmen and it certainly wouldn't be the last. The helicopter was new not only to the broadcast business, but to law enforcement as well. In the past, when an accident or major story broke, the press was unable to get to the scene of an incident in remote areas and relied on the law enforcement agencies involved to report the facts and take photos. But with the helicopter, we could not only get there fast and locate the scene, but could evacuate the injured if necessary, before lawmen got there. In some cases, as with the National Park Service at the Grand Canyon, the agencies didn't like that we could access what had been their private domain. Things were changing and rules were being written which sometimes had to be broken.

As we packed up and started to leave, I asked the sergeant if he would like to have a look at the crash site from the air. He said he'd rather stay on the ground, but if his partner could take his camera, it would sure help with the investigation. After giving the investigator a tour, I dropped him off, picked up Buzz and we headed for home. In the years ahead I never had another problem with the Coconino County Sheriff's Office, and we worked together on many search and rescue missions.

We stopped in Prescott for fuel and a sandwich, and talked over the incident. Buzz had been so nervous because he had forgotten about a joint hidden in his shirt pocket. I explained that if we had been arrested, the story wouldn't have been the plane crash, but the two newsmen arrested for interfering with an investigation and carrying illegal substances in a helicopter. I had his promise that would never happen again, and it didn't.

On another outing, Buzz would give *me* some valuable advice. One Saturday afternoon we took a short ride on our bikes to Canyon Lake, about 40 miles east of Phoenix. The helicopter was down for an engine change so I was able to get away. We spent the day with my father-in-law, Pete, and my daughters, swimming and water skiing from my boat. We had lunch and left around four o'clock to head back home.

In Apache Junction we rode past a small bar with 10 or 12 chopped Harleys sitting out front. Buzz waved for us to go back and shouted for us to stop in for a cold one. As we rolled up to the front, several bikers came out to check out the new arrivals. Buzz said he didn't recognize anyone, but we walked inside and sat at the bar. Several men and their ladies were playing pool and the juke box was blaring. It was a typical biker bar; dimly lit inside, creating a blinding white flash of sunlight when the door was opened. It took a few minutes for our eyes to adjust before we could even begin to tell who—or what—was in the bar.

We made our way to a couple of barstools, and the bartender asked what we would like. "Bud Light" said Buzz, throwing a twenty-dollar bill on the counter. I ordered a Coke and got a strange look from the bartender, who asked, "You a cop?" as he set the Coke in front of me.

"No, I 'm not," I replied. As he walked down to the end of the bar I told Buzz that I had a bad feeling about these guys. About then a skinny biker walked up to Buzz and introduced himself as "Bones." He recognized Buzz as being the owner of the Wheel Shop. Several other guys stopped by when they realized who was among them. Friendly hellos and banter continued until a few minutes later.

I was seated at one end of the bar and Buzz was talking to someone on his right, when a huge, dirty-looking hombre came up to my left and set his beer down right next to my Coke.

"Hey, ain't you the hot-shot helicopter pilot on TV?" he said. "You spying on us, hot-shot? How 'bout you take your Coke and go drink it outside with the kids; that way a real man can use that bar stool."

It was pretty obvious this was a 300-pound drunk looking for trouble. Before I could say a word Buzz was off his stool like a lightning bolt. One hand had this giant by the hair and the other hand was around his throat. Next thing I knew the biker was flat on his back in a stranglehold that Buzz didn't release until the guy was helpless.

When Buzz released his neck the giant put both hands out, wheezing and coughing, pleading with Buzz that he'd had enough and was only joking. When he was able to get off the floor he apologized to me and disappeared into the bathroom.

We finished our drinks, said our goodbyes and headed for the front door, followed by most of the bikers. Unlike our entrance, our exit felt like we were parting with old friends.

In Buzz's world, this was the way it was done. No need for the police. Justice had been served. Now it was Buzz's turn to share advice with me. "Next time, order a boilermaker and a Coke chaser. That way I can drink the jigger of whiskey when no one is looking and you can drink the Coke."

That's what I did, and we never had a problem again. Thanks Pal!

On a ride with my friend Buzz

Chapter 31

Meeting President Nixon - May 3, 1974

6:55 a.m. - My morning started like any other weekday. I took off from my back yard, contacted the station and checked in for my morning reports. There wasn't much going on, and everyone was busy getting ready for the president's speech that night at the Phoenix Coliseum. For the next hour I reported on the streets and freeway that were busy in all the usual places. It was a typical Friday morning, with just enough activity to give me something to say. After my last report at 8:06 I landed at Sky Harbor to refuel before heading downtown to the station heli-pad.

8:50 a.m. - I arrived at the station and found a note to call Senator Barry Goldwater's office in Washington right away. I knew he would be coming in for the president's speech later that day. His administrative aide, Judy Eisenhower, answered the phone and said the senator wanted me to pick him up in the helicopter on his return from Washington. Barry came on the line and said "I'll be coming into the Air National Guard on Air Force One, and would like you to fly me to the house. Can you make the necessary arrangements or should Judy?"

"I'll take care of it here," I assured him, "and if I need any help I'll contact Tom [Dunlavey, his aide in Phoenix] and have him make some calls."

We discussed the landing arrangements I had already made with the Department of Public Safety, and the transportation to and from their heliport at the coliseum. "Be sure to reserve the JetRanger, since there will be four of us going to the coliseum," he reminded me. "The president asked me to ride in the motorcade with him, but I'd rather fly in the helicopter."

I asked, "Will there be a problem landing the chopper at your house during a presidential visit? And what should I plan to do after I drop you off at home?"

"You just stay with me, and after Nixon leaves I'd like you to fly me back to Sky Harbor so I can get back to D.C. on the red eye. Wouldn't you like to meet President Nixon?"

"Oh, I sure would!" I answered.

"Okay, Jerry, I'll see you at the National Guard at 4 o'clock. By the way, does the JetRanger have dual controls?"

I replied that it did. I knew he was itching to fly it.

9:10 a.m. - During the next hour I made telephone calls to the DPS, the sheriff's office, Phoenix Police Department and the United States Secret Service. Each agency called back to confirm my request to land at the Arizona Air National Guard site, which was located at the south end of Sky Harbor. Agent Wilson from the Secret Service contacted me, and to my surprise, said it appeared the arrangements we had requested could be worked out. He said he would send an agent to the station to interview me, and that he would need background information on me and my family. "Why is this necessary?" I asked.

"You will be around the president and we have procedures that must be followed."

I next spoke to Allan Schmidt of the DPS, who informed me I would not be able to land at their heliport, because the DPS chopper would be involved and would need to land there. We worked out a suitable landing area just east of the DPS heliport.

10:15 a.m. - A Secret Service agent walked in the newsroom and asked for me. He identified himself and said there were a few questions he must ask, including my previous employment and who I socialized with. It didn't strike me as a "security clearance" kind of interview, and of course my mind went back into mush mode. I just knew I was going to be asked about my military service. But it never came up at all. I passed the interview and was handed a lapel pin to wear during the evening's events. The agent left and I calmed down, feeling like I'd squeaked through another tricky situation. I called DPS again and arranged to have a car standing by to take Senator Goldwater and me to the coliseum and return us to the helicopter after the president's speech.

12:15 p.m. - I left the station and flew to Sky Harbor Airport to wipe down the KOOL helicopter and make it presentable and ready to go. Then I drove to the Scottsdale airport, inspected the JetRanger, left fueling instructions, and drove home for a short visit with the kids.

2 p.m. - Just before I reached my house, the news base radioed me to contact Senator Goldwater's office right away. Figuring something was wrong with the plans, I landed at home and hurriedly called the senator's office. I was told my clearance with the Secret Service was approved and I should plan to be at the National Guard base by 3 p.m. I should land in space number six and stay in the helicopter until I was escorted by the Secret Service to a waiting area. I would be instructed what to do from there.

I showered, shaved, put on a suit and drove back to Sky Harbor airport. Upon arrival, I pulled the KOOL chopper out of the hangar, made a final inspection and took off for the Air Guard.

3 p.m. - As I approached the landing area, I could see the entire facility was buzzing with activity. A "Follow Me" truck escorted me to landing-space six and before I could shut the machine down, a Secret Service agent was standing beside the helicopter, looking it over. As I got out, he asked if I carried any weapons on board and asked to see my pilot's license and identification. He then pulled out a tape measure to ensure proper separation between the helicopter and the parking spot for Air Force One. There were 50 yards between the two spaces—just enough room. The agent politely told me I could wait in a shaded area next to the hangar that was reserved for the president's welcoming party. For the next hour I stood talking with an elite group that included Governor Jack Williams and other state dignitaries, and all the loyal Republicans who wanted to be seen. It was an impressive gathering. I was in tall cotton, so to speak.

3:45 p.m. - Secret Service agents began lining up the welcoming party to greet the president. They were firm, but polite, and there was very little confusion as they told each dignitary where to stand. They always knew who belonged where, and if they didn't know who you were, they certainly weren't bashful about asking. We were all lined up as Air Force One was on final approach on the south runway. The welcoming party was in position on the ramp, while newsmen and spectators were behind ropes about 100 feet behind us, with an adequate number of Secret Service agents to keep them controlled.

I was standing right behind the Governor and Mrs. Williams—not because I belonged there, but because I had that little pin on my collar that allowed me into the inner circle. I wanted Senator Goldwater to see me when he stepped off the plane. At this point in my career, this was the most exciting thing I had experienced, and I was flattered beyond words to be part of such an elite group. *If they only knew,* I thought.

3:55 p.m. - As Air Force One taxied to a stop, I noted how beautiful and spotless the aircraft was, all polished aluminum with blue trim. The familiar "United States of America" seal was on the fuselage, and "The Spirit of '76" was in blue on the nose. Those huge jet engines were screaming at a deafening roar. Agents began plugging telephones into the belly of the plane before it even came to a stop. Once it was still, the ramp was moved into position and two agents climbed to the top of the stairway and opened the door. A few seconds later President and Mrs. Nixon stepped out onto the ramp to a huge roar of the welcoming crowd. What a thrill!

As the president's party descended the ramp, there was more applause and a surge of national press trying to move in closer. Not a chance ... as agents had no trouble holding their line. It seemed surreal that I was able to move anywhere I wanted. I noticed a few looks from agents, but was never asked to move away from the president's car. My mind was functioning at three times its normal speed as I watched everything. The President and Mrs. Nixon looked great, and their daughter, Julie, was as beautiful in person as I knew she would be.

The president's secretary, Rosemary Woods, with her red hair and carrying the president's briefcase, could not be missed. As she approached the black limousine, she said "Hello" and remarked on what a beautiful day it was. I'm sure I replied to her, but I don't recall the words. I was completely star-struck. After going through the welcoming line, the president posed for pictures with Arizona's "Maid of Cotton," then headed for the car, holding Mrs. Nixon's hand. When he was within a few feet of me, he said "Hello." I felt someone grab my arm and heard, "Are you looking for me or sightseeing?"

Senator Goldwater was in an unusually good humor. Barry said, "Mr. President, this is my ride home. Jerry ... President Nixon."

"Hi Jerry," the president said, "Wish I could go along."

He flashed a big smile and was in the limo.

As we walked to the chopper I asked Senator Goldwater how the flight was. He said it was a little crowded, but it was always pleasant on Air Force One. The Secret Service agent who had checked the helicopter earlier walked behind us and helped the senator into the machine. He asked me not to fly over the motorcade and said to have a nice flight.

4:15 p.m. - We received clearance from the tower for take-off to the north. As we flew back across the airport we watched the motorcade proceed north on 24th Street. Each intersection ahead was blocked off by a Phoenix police officer to clear the way for the motorcade. From our vantage point it was strange to see 24th Street empty from the airport all the way to Lincoln Drive.

There were three helicopters in the air; DPS, Phoenix Police and our KOOL helicopter. DPS had been assigned to fly just ahead of the motorcade, Phoenix Police was flying to the west of DPS, and we could apparently do whatever we wanted—as long as we didn't fly directly over the motorcade—with full permission from the authorities. Senator Goldwater was interested in watching it, so we stayed close until they reached Lincoln Drive, and then we landed at the senator's home. I shot some very exclusive film of all the action. What a hoot that was!

It took the senator a few minutes to climb out of the helicopter, since his hip seemed to be getting worse every time we flew. He had planned to have surgery done in the summer, but was now busy with the growing discord in Washington and the impending campaign. It looked like surgery would have to wait.

After a brief farewell wave, I lifted off. I had noticed before that whenever I took off from Barry, he would always watch until I was established in flight before turning away. He truly loved watching the helicopter ascend, and was fascinated by the process. And since he also struggled with controlling the machine on his own, he liked watching me come and go.

4:25 p.m. - I landed at Saguaro Aviation to pick up my passenger for the evening news; a good-looking blonde who was the wife of a plastic surgeon. We took off to the north toward a reported accident with injuries at 16th Street and Glendale Avenue. The flight was extremely busy with fender-benders and a large house fire just west of the city. At 5:15 I dropped off my passenger at Sky Harbor and flew to the Scottsdale airport to trade the KOOL Hughes for the JetRanger. I landed, transferred cameras and radios to the JetRanger and departed once again for Senator Goldwater's house.

6 p.m. - There were several cars in the driveway as I approached. His home was surrounded by 40 acres of natural desert landscape, and the front of Goldwater's hilltop home had adequate—but somewhat tight—room for landing a helicopter. I always approached from the north because of the large ham radio antennas lining the west side of his home. There was a large blacktop area in front of and below the main house, and a rock wall separated the garden from the driveway, with stone steps leading up to the front door. The driveway and road could handle 20 cars, but there were only 10 parked now; some belonging to Secret Service, and others owned by the Ham Shack Operators. My landing always brought the senator out of the house, regardless of what he may have been doing. He scrutinized the landing, decided whether it was good, and then turned back to the house.

I shut the machine down and was greeted by the head Secret Service agent, who asked if I would be landing again tonight, and the specific times we would be going in and out. He also asked to see my identification and questioned me at length about the number of times I had been to the senator's home, and how long I had flown for him. The questions he asked seemed casual in tone, but I felt that my answers were being cataloged for future use. After the brief interrogation I went inside the house.

The senator was in his den watching the news along with his administrative assistant, Judy Eisenhower and his aide, Jim Horton. We exchanged hellos and I made my way to the kitchen for a piece of chicken and a glass of root beer.

6:30 p.m. - It was time to go, and the senator made a gesture that got everyone to their feet and moving toward the door. We climbed into the JetRanger and began the start-up procedure. Barry did most of the work with little coaching from me. His hip was bothering him again and he asked me to lift off, but as soon as we were in the air he took the controls until we were ready to land at the coliseum.

On the ground, Lt. Pennington was waiting for us in the DPS car. The short drive was lined with people on their way in to the event, and the VIP entrance was flooded with city and state police cars. The gate was protected by at least 30 police officers, but our car was recognized, and the large iron gates were rolled back so we could drive down the ramp to the rear entrance. I recognized many of the DPS officers from searches and scenes I had been called out on. We were escorted directly to the area where the entertainer dressing rooms were. I had been here before to interview Wayne Newton, so was familiar with the area.

As we entered the crowded room I looked around at the impressive array of guests, which included Congressman and Mrs. John Rhodes, Governor and Mrs. Williams, Representative Sam Steiger, Representative John Conlon; Supreme Court Justice Jack Hays, Attorney General Gary Nelson and Senator and Mrs. Paul Fannin, among others.

A buffet of sandwiches and cheese and cracker plates was set up, along with a small bar in the corner. Most of the guests were seated at card tables and chatting. But when Senator Goldwater entered the room, all eyes turned toward him.

I was amazed to discover that I had a lot in common with many of the guests. Over the past three years I had interviewed each one of them; some of them several times. Still, I felt somewhat guarded, as I was the only person in the room connected with the media, and not a political figure.

6:45 p.m. - The organizers of the rally began lining up the dignitaries for their single-file introduction to the fourteen thousand fans inside the coliseum. Senator Goldwater asked if I had a watch he could borrow to keep track of the various speeches. I said, "Sure," but hoped my Accutron wouldn't wind up going to Washington D.C. with the forgetful Senator.

As the VIPs were introduced, Judy, Jim and I remained backstage talking with the president's press secretary, Ron Ziegler, about the trip to Spokane the following day. Then we were escorted to a group of chairs just to the left of the stage, reserved for White House staff. We had a completely unobstructed view of the podium and would be less than twenty feet from the president when he spoke. Senator Goldwater would serve as master of ceremonies.

The president's motorcade arrived at 7:25 p.m. and the White House staff joined us shortly afterward as the president prepared for his entrance. I sat between Judy Eisenhower and Rosemary Woods. To her right was General Haig, then Dean Burch. During my four years as Goldwater's co-pilot, I had been privileged to sit at the head table with him many times, but on this occasion I felt an overwhelming sense of honor to be sitting with the president's staff.

A voice over the loudspeaker announced, "Ladies and gentlemen, the president of the United States." Balloons were released, noisemakers went off and the crowd went wild to welcome President and Mrs. Nixon. I was close enough to see the American flag pin on his lapel and to watch his eyes and see who he was looking at. As the cheers died down he began to speak. Right away protestors began yelling insults and trying to be heard. The president was somewhat distracted by the interruptions, but recovered well each time.

Governor Williams, who was sitting behind the podium, was visibly upset by the demonstrators. As governor, he probably felt responsible for the disrespect within his state. But the speech went well and the demonstrators were a small minority of the crowd. Most impressive were the Secret Service agents all around and throughout the crowd. I watched their eyes dart around, looking for possible threats, and noticed the way they moved constantly to cover the area. The agents seemed to be living their assignments, rather than just doing a job, with a dedication that was almost intimidating.

I was so impressed by all the activity around me that I had no idea what the president said, even though I heard every word. I was simply overwhelmed with watching the activity in this packed auditorium. It resembled a national convention, complete with signs, buttons, hats and all the excitement of a three-ring circus.

As he finished his speech, the coliseum again came to life with a tremendous roar. Secret Service agents prepared for the president's walk to our seating area, ready for anyone who would dare come close. President and Mrs. Nixon were shaking hands with the guests standing in the front row, and were slowly making their way down the line toward us. As he reached the end of the aisle he was standing next to my left shoulder. He turned and put his hand on my arm and said to the agent next to me, "Okay, let's get to the car."

An army of agents swept him out the door, along with the senator and me. Barry and I were hustled into the DPS car, which pulled out in front as the motorcade was still loading up, and drove out the back gate. The motorcade was a mere few seconds behind us and the security was astonishing. Hundreds of uniformed city and state police held back crowds of long-haired demonstrators with signs. Senator Goldwater told Lt. Pennington to step on it because he needed time to take a leak before the motorcade arrived at his home. The rest of the drive to the helicopter included red lights and sirens.

Back in the helicopter, we fired up and were gone. As we crossed over 19th Avenue, the motorcade was just pulling out of the coliseum parking lot. The flight back to Goldwater's house was just five minutes, but I had time to ask him what he thought of the reception and the demonstrators. His answer surprised me. "If the president didn't have a little interference, he wouldn't feel comfortable. I think it went very well."

8:45 p.m. - As the senator went inside, a Secret Service agent asked me to disable the helicopter so that it couldn't easily be started. I pulled all the circuit breakers and disconnected the battery from the electrical system, then went into the house. Judy, Jim, Barry (after a quick pee) and I sat in the den waiting for the president to arrive.

It was the quiet before the storm. I felt the tension and hoped it would all go well. Even for Barry Goldwater, having a sitting president stop by your home is not something you take lightly. Peggy's being in Washington didn't help Barry's tension level, but so far things had gone well.

A few minutes later there was a flurry of activity as the motorcade snaked up the hill then into the driveway. President and Mrs. Nixon walked up the huge stone steps and greeted Senator Goldwater, who introduced his staff. When he got to me I was introduced again as Barry's helicopter instructor: "He taught me how to fly."

The president asked me if I was responsible for that good-looking JetRanger in the driveway. He said he had invited Barry to ride to the coliseum in the presidential limousine, and now understood why he declined. A handshake with the Nixons, and the party was on.

What an incredible guest list: the president and first lady, his top advisors, General Alexander Haig and Dean Burch, press secretary Ron Ziegler, Rosemary Woods, and several others who I guessed to be White House staffers.

Those top Arizona Republicans who had attended the event at the coliseum were there, as well as Bob Goldwater, some wives, and other guests I didn't recognize. There were fewer than 50 guests present, but at least three times that number in security people outside.

What made all this so interesting was that the president was up to his neck in the Watergate scandal and was here to try to get some support from Barry, who was not happy with the way Nixon was running the country. But at this event they laughed and joked like they were old friends. Politics and the way it's played is way over my head, but it sure is fun to watch.

This was a cocktail party to welcome the president to Arizona, so there was no formal protocol or list of events. Each person simply wandered around looking the place over, sampling a variety of hors d'oeuvres and engaging in conversation.

I was surprised to see the way the president carried himself at this private affair. He milled around speaking to everyone, carrying a drink in his hand. He seemed totally relaxed, joking and reminiscing about previous trips to Arizona. It was very strange for me to be talking to John Rhodes and have the president of

With President Nixon

the United States walk up and join the conversation.

The party lasted about an hour and was very pleasant. Senator Goldwater and Dean Burch were standing together as President and Mrs. Nixon walked over and informed them they were ready to go back to the hotel. As the Nixons said their goodbyes they were escorted to the door. I watched as they walked to their limousine, still shaking hands. Just before getting in, he turned and waved and gave a big smile.

A few minutes later the motorcade was gone and the last of the guests were leaving. It had been so much more than I expected. What a cast of characters this had been.

At 11 p.m. we piled into the JetRanger for the short flight to Sky Harbor. I was able to land next to the jet that would take them back to Washington. From there I flew to Scottsdale Airport to drop off the Ranger and pick up the Bug.

The good news was that there were no traffic reports the following day. The bad news was that my wristwatch was on its way to Washington ... again. And sadly, President Nixon was forced to resign just three months after his Phoenix visit.

President Ford

Senator Goldwater was also the means for me being able to meet President Gerald Ford. A few months after Nixon had resigned, President Ford traveled to Mexico for a state visit. He wanted to meet with the senator while he was in Arizona, so I flew Barry to Tucson, where Ford would be spending the night. There was a receiving line of dignitaries to meet Ford, and after all the greetings had been done, Ford and Goldwater had a brief visit under the wing of Air Force One. Barry asked me to stay with him to film the meeting, even though other reporters were kept at a distance. The Secret Service guys were not happy about my presence, but Barry insisted.

I was excited to meet Ford, and was fascinated as I watched how both of these men so graciously interacted with the public who had gathered for the visit.

Chapter 32

Hard Landing #2

December 15, 1974: Just 10 days until Christmas and it was shaping up to be one of the busier days of the year. Between Thanksgiving and Christmas part of my job involved delivering Santa all over the valley to various shopping malls, schools, or other places where eager kids—and their parents—loved watching us fly in. I had already taken two Santas to their locations that afternoon, then picked up my civilian rider for the evening traffic reports. He was visiting the station and a guest of Homer Lane's. "Show him the city, Jerry. He owns a radio station in Texas and wants to see how you do it," Homer said.

Doing a "Santa run" with kid's show host Ladmo

I explained to my passenger that with the headset he'd be able to hear everything that was going on, and there were several different frequencies, which would sometimes all be chattering at the same time.

As I started the engine and engaged the rotor, I noticed that my rider was sweating and looking nervous. I tried to ease his mind before lifting off, saying, "I've been doing this a long time and have never had a problem."

I told him the same thing I told every nervous passenger, "Watch my face: if I look scared, then it's okay to be nervous."

We smiled at each other and headed north from the downtown helipad. My passenger settled right down once we got going and I was able to give him a good tour of the Valley of the Sun. I even shot aerials of a major accident out near Carefree. As we headed back downtown, the station radioed me to shoot aerials of the holiday madhouse that was Chris-Town Mall at 19th Avenue and Bethany Home Road. Approaching the busy shopping center from the north, we could see the packed parking lot and the surrounding streets heavy with traffic in all directions.

In my usual pilot-photographer stance, I was holding the camera in my right hand, the collective pitch and throttle in my left hand, had the cyclic between my knees, and my feet on the rudders. I crossed over the shopping center then started a slow level turn at 500 feet above the ground. I had just started filming when the engine began revving wildly. The engine and the rotor had stopped communicating. I immediately put the bird into auto rotation, and was gliding it down manually, without the luxury of engine power. By the time I managed to completely close the throttle and shut off the engine, the rpm gauge had surpassed the normal 2700, and gone into the red zone. I threw the camera into my passenger's lap and down we went, heading for a far corner of the parking lot where I had noticed some empty spots. Fifteen seconds later we were on the ground and safe. My guest didn't say a word for a couple of minutes. When he could finally speak again, he said, "Jerry, you said I should worry if you looked scared. Well, you did, and I wet my pants."

As I looked over the Bug, the problem was pretty obvious. The bearing in the idler pulley assembly—the pulley that houses eight fan belts which connect the engine with the rotor system—was gone. No fan belts, no fly.

A few weeks earlier the same part, the idler pulley, had failed on a police patrol helicopter in Hawaii, killing both officers.

Hughes Helicopters, the FAA, and the NTSB were in high gear trying to get the problem figured out. It was another reminder to me that helicopter science had a long way to go. Every moving part on these mechanical birds depended upon the others to make it all work. Knowing this, I found it spooky to look up at the turning mast and watch those man-made parts spinning so fast. I identified with the words of Elton John in the song, Rocket Man, especially in this situation ... *"And all this science, I don't understand. It's just my job five days a week."*

Someone reported my abrupt landing as a crash and in minutes—even before a crowd could gather—a gang of police and firemen were blazing a trail with red lights and sirens. I radioed the station that I had made a forced landing, there were no injuries and no damage to report, and asked them to advise Homer and Arizona Helicopters. Homer was there within the hour, courtesy of the Phoenix Police Department. Instead of reporting a story, we now *were* the story. It was a mess, and other local radio stations had a lot of fun with it. Our competition gleefully made a big deal out of the "what ifs" and all the other rhetoric that comes with this type of event.

I was just thankful we had dodged a bullet; one that could have killed me, my passenger and innocent people on the ground. I was certain that my flying and teaching experience had a lot to do with our survival. I had many thousands of hours in that type of Hughes and over 2500 hours in my latest little Bug. I was so tuned in to that machine that I was able to recognize the sounds and feelings that signaled a problem before it showed up in the instruments. I was thankful my U.S. Army training had taught the importance of touchdown auto rotations, and I had performed literally hundreds of them with students over the years.

That old pilot's saying, "Any landing you walk away from is a good one," came back to me again. As I watched the helicopter being loaded onto the back of a truck and headed for the maintenance hangar, I thought, *That's one you owe me, Bug.*

Chapter 33

Bill Leverton

Leverton stepping out of chopper onto news truck

Although I had been doing a pretty good job of filming news stories myself, trying to do it while flying the helicopter wasn't the best option. When the station began to realize the value of using the helicopter specifically to go shoot news, they began sending a photographer along with me.

The first to fly regularly with me was Bill Leverton, who had been hired from a station in Albuquerque in 1973.

On one of our first trips out, we were doing a story on crop dusters. The company we were filming had an old Bell H3, like the helicopters on M*A*S*H. It was a throbbing, shaking little machine rigged up with these long arms from which the pesticide would be sprayed. Bill was still new at 10, and we weren't really comfortable with each other yet. I'm not sure what he thought about this idea of filming from a helicopter, but he went along with it.

As he tells the story, *"The guy flying the crop duster told us he was going to come up and make a right turn. It was early morning, and I was shooting from the right seat, shooting into the sun, with a close shot, then a wide shot. Just as the crop duster came up and turned, Jerry turned and went over him. It was one of the most beautiful shots ever. I remember thinking, 'This is really neat!' That was one of the most formative experiences of my career."*

Bill had his fixed-wing private pilot license, and got a commercial license soon after coming with KOOL. Later I taught him to fly the helicopter, and he soon had that license as well. During that training period he told his wife, Bonnie, "I scared Jerry, and he says he's not afraid of anything!"

After Bill had his helicopter rating I talked to Homer Lane about having him be my backup pilot. Homer regularly let Bill rent airplanes to do stories, but felt he didn't have enough hours in the helicopter yet.

Bill and I covered some amazing stories together and were also involved in a few rescues. One of the most dramatic involved rescuing a kid from the Gila River. This was an area that was normally either dry or had very low water, and was now swollen from the recent heavy rains. A fourteen-year-old boy had tried to walk across the river, but was knocked down by the rushing water. People don't realize that at eight pounds per gallon, even a few inches of fast-moving water is enough to force a person down.

The kid had managed to grab onto a large bush and pull himself partway out of the water, and was now trapped there. Sheriff's deputies had arrived and were on the riverbank, but couldn't get to the boy. A private Hughes 500 showed up, but wouldn't go out because the pilot felt the power lines were too low. Bill and I arrived to film the rescue, and when we realized nothing was being done, I flew out over the bush.

Bill says, *"I was standing on the skid filming him, and saw a look of sheer terror on his face. Jerry hovered over the bush, while I put the camera inside, reached down and tried to pull the boy up onto the skid. He was terrified and didn't want to let go of the bush. To make matters worse, he had on a heavy wool coat that—soaking wet—seemed to weigh a ton. When I finally convinced him to let go of the bush, I grabbed his shoulders, pulled him up, and he straddled the skid all the way to the shore, where deputies helped him off. The boy lay down and curled up in a fetal position and wouldn't move. He had to have been freezing. One of the deputies criticized us for doing a dangerous rescue, and maybe it was, since we had to fly really low underneath the power lines to get to the shore. But the fact is, if Jerry and I hadn't shown up, the kid would have died."*

I always knew the danger was there, but I also knew whether I could do something safely or not. This was where my period of training Army helicopter pilots at Ft. Wolters really paid off.

Of course not everyone was happy to see us, and I often got in trouble with some authorities who didn't quite see things my way. On one occasion, Bill and I were sent out to an Indian reservation to film a fire at a landfill that was spewing smoke all over the valley. This should have been a simple assignment, until one of the landfill bosses motioned for us to land, which we did. Ten tribal policemen quickly approached and wouldn't let us leave. Homer Lane had to come out and negotiate with them before they'd allow us to take off.

Another time an F-15 jet fighter from Luke Air Force Base had gone down near Sells, Arizona, and Bill and I were sent to cover it. We were flying over the crash site with Bill filming. There were military police and sheriff's deputies on the scene, and one of them waved us down. Naively thinking we were being invited to cover the story, we landed. Instead, an MP approached and insisted that Bill hand over the film.

A discussion followed, during which we reminded the officer that a DOD ruling had come out stating that if a crash is *off* a military reservation, that news film cannot be confiscated. He didn't car, and insisted on the film. The discussion became more heated and I was getting angry. Now the cop had his hand on his gun.

Bill finally said, "Okay, I'll give it to you, but don't you damage it; I want it back!"

I said, "Bill, we don't have to give it to him … don't do it!"

But Bill handed over a canister of film, and I was furious. When we got back in the helicopter, I was still chewing Bill out when he said, "I gave him the unexposed part of the film. I still have what I shot."

271

The camera he was using had a 400 foot magazine with a canister of unexposed film in the front, which wound through the camera with the exposed film going into another canister in the back. Bill simply removed the front canister and handed it over. The MP didn't know the difference and was happy.

One of the best and most amazing things about that era, was that nobody really quite knew what to do with Bill or me, so we were free to make our own stories and develop our own style. We both grew into our jobs with very few rules or regulations.

Bill began a very popular segment called "On the Arizona Road," patterned after Charles Kurault's "On the Road." He searched for unique people, places or events in Arizona, then filmed them, developed a story, and narrated it.

The segments—and Bill—became very popular. His calm, folksy way of speaking created an immediate rapport with his audience. His show provided the "good news." If he wanted to do something he just did it, with very little explanation. As long as it brought in the viewers, the station was happy.

One inter-network survey indicated that Bill and I had more visibility and more likability than any of the other news personalities on any Phoenix station. We kinda liked that!

Bill Leverton On the Arizona Road

Working with Bill was great and every day was something different. If a story was out of town, Bill would go; if it was local, I'd jump in the helicopter and go on my own. We were a good team. When I was doing a story and needed a good photographer

—he was there. When he was doing a story and needed a particular aerial angle—I knew what to do.

We could usually translate what the other needed and make it happen. Although Bill taught me more about photography and I was using better cameras, I still realized what an asset he was to me.

By the time we both ended our careers, I had been the longest-running helicopter pilot and Bill had the longest-running franchise with his "On the Arizona Road" series. They were good times.

Chapter 34

Losing Dad: August 27, 1975

Dianna and I were just finishing up a week of pure pleasure and fun at Lake Powell. This late in the summer the crowd had thinned out, the water was smooth as glass, and the weather had been perfect. Toward the end of the week Buzz and his wife Carol drove up to spend the weekend with us. We'd been invited to have dinner with Uncle Mac and Aunt Wanda on our last night there. I was looking forward to a visit and Uncle Mac's chili—the best I have ever eaten.

Bryan Pace Foster - my hero

I also wanted to get an update on my dad. The previous week I'd learned that he was in the hospital in Fresno, California for tests. I knew Aunt Wanda would have the latest info about her older brother. As soon as we walked in the door I could tell something wasn't right. After the hugs and hellos Aunt Wanda asked me to come into the kitchen for a minute.

"Jerry, I'm sorry to tell you that your dad is not doing well. I just got back from Fresno and the doctors say he has cancer … and it's terminal. Your mother flew up to see him yesterday and left a number for you to call her."

"Dad … terminal?" was all I could say. When I got Mom on the phone she confirmed that he was very sick and was in the veterans hospital. She told me more, but I was already planning my trip from Page to Fresno. Before she hung up I told her I would see her tomorrow and assured her I wouldn't drive like a maniac.

We all sat down for a big bowl of Uncle Mac's chili and a little family time, but talked mostly about my dad and "the good old days."

I thought I would leave my boat in Page and drive directly from there to Fresno. Dianna had to go home,because our two little girls were staying with her family.

Then Buzz came up with a plan that saved the day. He would drive my Bronco, pull my boat, and take Dianna home, and I would drive his Trans Am the 660 miles to Fresno.

With a few stops for meals, gas, a nap, and a shower at a truck stop, I made it to Fresno's VA hospital just after 11 a.m. I had driven a little over the speed limit, but I had used the drive time to adjust to the reality of what was happening. For the past 15 years I had dealt with death in all forms, but this was different. This was the man I had grown up wanting to be like. I promised myself I would be positive and not act like a blithering idiot.

He was in a double room. I walked past the old man in the first bed, past the sliding curtain separating the two, and stood before my dad's bed. The room was typical government: stark, crowded, and depressing.

Mom was sitting next to Dad's bed and they were talking. It had been so long since I had seen the two together that it was a heart-wrenching moment. As Mom and I embraced I got a good look at Dad, and my whole body turned white hot for just an instant.

He had lost a lot of weight and looked like one of the holocaust victims we see on TV. But he still had that smile I knew so well, and it brought a grin to my face as well. Yep … same guy! We talked about the old days in the mining and logging camps and the many places we had lived.

Just before the lunch trays were brought in, Mom said she needed to wash up and she would meet me in the lobby. I thought that odd until Dad said there was something he wanted me to promise him. He lowered his voice, so I moved closer, dreading the serious talk I knew was coming.

It went something like this: "Jerry, I want you to promise me that you will get a good night's sleep, come visit me in the morning, then go home. There is nothing you can do for me except honor my final request."

For a few moments we just looked at each other. As I started to stammer and shake my head, a nurse walked in with his lunch tray.

We looked at each other and he said, "Please, son." I had never heard him ask me to do something with the word "Please" attached. It was a very tender moment—one I will never forget.

I managed a smile and said, "You got it Dad." I gave him a kiss on the forehead and told him I would see him after lunch.

I met up with Mom in the lobby, and we split an egg salad sandwich in the cafeteria and talked about the future. Mom said she had promised Dad she would only stay a few days and then pick up the life she had made in Arizona. We laughed at how Dad was still in charge and giving orders. He may have weighed only 100 pounds, but he was still Dad.

What he didn't know yet was that his mother, my Granny Jo, was leaving Duncan, Arizona with her daughter, Wanda. Granny Jo made it clear: she had birthed that boy and nothing could stop her from being with him. I had to smile. He was no match for 85-year-old Granny Jo. I felt a lot better knowing she would be with him.

We spent the rest of the day just being together. Around 9 p.m. we said goodnight to Dad, had dinner, and Mom and I hit the hay. It had been a long, emotionally exhausting day, and I slept like a log. After breakfast I checked out of the hotel and we headed for the hospital.

We got through it without a single tear, and we said the things we needed to say. I told Mom I would call when I got home and then I headed south toward Arizona. It was the right thing to do, and I felt better about leaving him, knowing he would be surrounded by a loving family.

On September 10 my dad died peacefully. Our family chipped in to bring him home, and he was buried in a family plot. He had a military burial with full honors, on a mesa overlooking his boyhood home of Duncan, Arizona.

Maricopa County Sheriff Dick Godbehere sent two of the Search and Rescue Deputies I had worked with as a sign of respect —a gesture I will always appreciate.

A few years later my precious Granny Jo was laid to rest beside my dad—her son. We miss them.

Chapter 35

The Divorce

By 1977 I had become a media celebrity, and I was working more hours than any one man should. The biggest problem was not that I *had* to work so much, it was that I *wanted* to. The helicopter had become my life. I loved flying, I loved news reporting, I loved the searches and the rescues, and I loved being around my flying buddies like Barry Goldwater. But the long hours and my new inflated ego took a toll on my marriage.

Dianna had known as early as the Pollywog days that a new helicopter wouldn't bode well with family life. From the day KOOL turned me loose with the Hughes, I was like a hummingbird, never hovering in one place too long. I would come home after a long day of flying, and then leave again in the middle of the night, chasing that next big news story, leaving Dianna alone to raise two girls on her own.

She had always been so patient with me, putting up with my long and odd working hours; but everybody has a breaking point, and she was reaching hers. Time after time, she would plan a family outing only to have me cancel. I was often a no-show at family holiday dinners because a news story broke—and I couldn't miss it. I was becoming a stranger in my own home and operating at a speed which was thrilling for me, but completely foreign to my beautiful young wife. She didn't want a celebrity; she wanted a husband.

In the midst of one of our ever-increasing marital screaming matches, she pleaded with me to spend more quality time at home. I kept coming up with reasons why it wasn't possible. Then Dianna laid down this edict: "Jerry, it's either *me* or the *helicopter*."

What could I say? I wasn't letting go of the Bug. "I choose the helicopter," I replied.

She filed for divorce.

In happier days: Me, Dianna, Barry and Andi

I moved out of the house and in with Mom, but only temporarily. My overwhelming need to be close to the helicopter soon had me looking for something near the airport. I didn't need much; just a place to sleep and a bathroom. I scouted around and found a little furnished room just 10 minutes from the helipad, which would allow me to be airborne within thirty minutes after getting a call. If I did happen to finish work early, I could always go to Mom's for a hearty dinner. She was always there for me.

Single life was lonely and very difficult for me in the beginning. Dianna and I had been very close, and during those few occasions we did spend time together, we truly enjoyed each other's company. Even during the divorce, we vowed we would always remain friends and work to make a normal life for our little girls. Still, it was a very difficult time for all of us. I often questioned whether I had made the right decision.

While I was going through the divorce, and even afterward, I was an emotional wreck. I had not wanted to lose my beautiful family, but I was even more afraid of losing the stability and adventure of a job that I loved.

Homer Lane knew everything, and I had job security with him. I couldn't go through starting over, wondering when someone would find out. And I'll admit, I loved being who I was, and doing what I did. Every time I rescued or helped someone, I felt I had taken another step toward vindicating myself.

I was trying to explain all of this to my friend John Bull during one of our morning coffee breaks. He and his wife Ann had both been very supportive as I went through the divorce, and now he had noticed the dark shadows under my eyes. He could see that I wasn't myself, and asked me what was going on. I had to confess that I was depressed, not eating well, and having trouble sleeping.

John insisted—as my physician—that I take a few days off. Of course I never wanted to take time off, and tried to reassure him I would be fine. But the more we talked about it, the more I knew he was right. I was not in the best shape, and I needed to get my head straightened out. It was decided that I would put the helicopter in the shop for its annual inspection, and then take a little vacation.

I went to Lake Powell with my friend, Tom Gerczynski, who was also going through his own painful divorce. We moped around for the first couple of days, anchored in a dead-end canyon; sleeping, drinking, smoking and feeling sorry for ourselves. But after a week on the lake we had talked our problems over, done a lot of thinking and realized we were two lucky guys. Tom's photography business was doing well and so was my broadcasting career. When we headed for home it was with a whole different attitude and acceptance of reality.

New Living Quarters

Back at the station it was business as usual. In so many ways one day was just like the next. I started off with the morning rush hour and ended with the evening rush hour. A traffic reporter will tell you that after awhile you don't need to be looking at a situation—you just know it's jammed up.

On a light day I chased everything, and if I couldn't find anything, I would go sit up on one of our mountaintops like a little hummingbird and just wait. That was fine on cool winter days with the doors on, but there was no air conditioning in the chopper, so I had to leave the doors at the station during the summer.

I talked Homer into putting a storage shed on the rooftop helipad so the doors and other needs could be stored. Since the Bug and I weren't living at home anymore, I had to rearrange some things.

One of those needs was living quarters close to the station. I was a single man now, and on a mission. The little room I was renting was feeling cramped. It wasn't a dive, but it wasn't much more. I found a nice apartment building just six blocks from the station, close to the old Phoenix landmark, the Westward Ho Hotel. There was a vacant apartment that faced downtown, on the 10th floor of the 11-story building. From the balcony I could see my little Bug sitting on the station heliport. This was perfect! The bad news was that in six months the building would be renovated and the units would then be sold as condos.

"Sign me up," I said.

I would worry about the rest of it when the time came. I called Mom, whose first question was whether or not it was furnished. I told her it was partly furnished, which was close to the truth, though it only contained a mattress and a kitchen table with matching chairs. "Ok, Jerry, let me know when you get possession."

I moved in the next day, since I didn't have a lot of personal possessions to move. I tease Dianna to this day that all I got out of the divorce was my pickup, Harley, and toolbox. I would need to buy everything else to furnish my new place.

Saturday afternoon Mom rang the bell downstairs and I buzzed her in to come up. Pretty fancy, I thought. After all the oohs and ahs, she whipped out her little tape measure, and got busy measuring and jotting down notes. I pleaded with her to keep the costs down, and tried to convince her that I really didn't need a cutting board or any of those other accessories. She just nodded and said, "And before I go I need a key."

"A key for what?" I asked, sounding as casual as I could.

She just held out her hand, and of course I gave her the extra key. You don't argue with your mother. A big hug and a kiss, and she was gone. I walked out onto the balcony and watched her get into her new Oldsmobile Tornado. She hadn't said a word about it, but Uncle Phill had told me over the phone he bought it for her.

A few days later I got home late after chasing some story. I opened the door expecting to walk into my dark apartment. But it was brightly lit, and there sat Mom, surrounded by my new furniture—at least new to this place. She had hired two of the restaurant busboys to rent a truck and bring my old bedroom set in, along with other furniture. My apartment was now very modestly, but thoroughly, furnished; right down to the dishes, silverware and yes, even a cutting board.

I was thrilled, even after she handed me the bill. I was reminded again that night of her love for me and that we had come a long way together. I may have been in my thirties and a hot-shot helicopter pilot, but I still needed my mom.

As I admired all my "new" possessions, Mom told me to just pay her when I could, a little at a time. I did just that. We also talked about those early dark days and whether they were gone for good. "You have to put it out of your mind," she would say.

And I would think, *Mom, you just don't understand.* It was true, because inside, I still feared being exposed.

I settled in and got down to business. The helicopter was well-equipped and from my new perch I could see it sitting on the pad. The years ahead would serve me well from this building. When the renovations began, the builder offered me a good deal, and I was able to buy my apartment. I was learning that a helicopter ride turned people into friends, and in this case it paid off. I appreciated the builder's generous offer, and was thrilled that I would be staying there.

When the time came to begin the remodel, I was moved to a one-bedroom apartment across the hall. It was exactly the same as mine except that everything was reversed. This balcony faced to the north, so I could no longer keep an eye on the Bug. I could see the Channel 12 TV station, but since they didn't have a helicopter they were no worry to me. My biggest concern was that a downtown drunk would get a wild hair to climb up on the roof and try to steal "my" helicopter. That worry took care of itself when, a couple of years later, the Phoenix Police Department built their headquarters right next door to Channel 10.

Six weeks later I moved back across the hall to my new condo. I felt so much more comfortable when I was able to see the helicopter. I kept binoculars on my balcony and checked it often. Living right downtown was interesting: beautiful at night, but always busy and noisy with the harsh sounds of motorcycles, trucks, trains, and the countless sirens as police and fire fighters kept the city safe.

When I got in late I would sometimes sit on the balcony with my binoculars, watching the people of the night come and go. It was quite a show at times. My view to the south included the tall downtown buildings, Sky Harbor Airport, and all of South Mountain with its twinkling TV towers.

Most importantly, I felt comfortable with my response time, since I could be in the air within twenty minutes.

Somewhere along the way I had instituted my own "twenty-minute rule." I vowed I would never be more than twenty minutes from my helicopter, unless I was sick, on vacation, or the chopper was in for maintenance.

The rule kept me within about a 10-to-15 mile radius of the station, which limited my activities quite a bit. But at that time, the helicopter was my life, and nothing else—other than visiting with Mom and the girls—interested me anyway. I adhered to my self-imposed rule, and rarely broke it, unless there were circumstances beyond my control

There were times when I was sent out on a story that kept me away for a couple of days, and there were times when I had a Goldwater trip and had to be gone. But I don't ever recall missing a big story. I was lucky. My friend Pete Cronk could fly for me with a photographer if needed.

Around two o'clock one morning I was called out on a three-alarm fire at a hospital. I waited in front of the elevator for a couple of minutes before noticing it was stuck on the third floor. *Uh-oh*, I thought. I ran down all 10 flights of stairs with my camera bag on my shoulder. When I reached the lobby I saw that it was full of boxes and a rental truck was parked right outside. Someone had the elevator blocked while moving in. Right then I was on a mission and didn't have time to voice my displeasure.

I still made it to the helipad within my allotted twenty minutes, and was in the air headed north. Just as I rolled in over the Sunnyslope hospital to have a look, I heard over the fire channel: "All units cancel at hospital and return to quarters." It was a false alarm within the hospital system. It happened a lot that way: false alarms used up expensive flying time, but if I waited until the code-four was given, the action was over. I always used my best judgment, and I never heard a complaint from Homer.

I returned home, and as I pulled back into the Embassy Court the rental truck was still blocking the circular driveway.

That's a no-no and by golly, I was going to do something about it. I parked, walked into the building and climbed the stairs to the third floor. As I walked down the hallway I could see one of the condo doors open. I stopped and knocked, and was ready to huff and puff when the largest man I had ever seen stepped into view. He was awesome big: tough big, not fat. And not smiling.

My mind quickly went into survival mode. "Hello, sir, I was just wondering if you needed help. I live up on 10 and saw the rental truck."

He walked over to me, ducking as he cleared the door. I couldn't move. "I'm Danny," he said.

I looked up—way up—and saw the smile of a very gentle man. "I sure hope I didn't hold you up with the elevator," he said. "I been working hard as I can, sir, and I'm just about done."

Danny was a guy I liked right off the bat. As we talked, it got even better. I learned that he was going to be the new night security guard while attending college by day. I introduced myself and he said, "Oh, I knew who you was right off, and anything I can do for you, Mr. Foster, you just let me know."

I had kept my mouth shut—admittedly out of fear rather than tact—and made a new friend. From that time on he would always call me Mr. Foster. He was a big help in the coming times, just keeping gawkers off my floor. I was going to have to give him a ride when the weather got a little cooler. No … make that a *lot* cooler. A person who weighs 250-plus pounds is a mouthful for the Bug.

Lesson learned. I happily walked up the seven remaining stories and enjoyed it. I realized I should walk up more often, and sometimes did just that. It was a great way to stay in shape. Now I needed to get a couple hours of sleep before my morning traffic reports at 7:06.

My personal life was starting to feel normal again. I was recovering from the emotional trauma of the divorce, but my new-found peace wouldn't last long. There just seemed to be too many changes in my life.

By this time Dianna's parents had also divorced, and her father was now living at Saguaro Lake as the new manager, overseeing the restaurant, boat docks and marina. He remarried almost immediately, which was a shock to all of us.

Dianna spent a lot of time at the lake helping her dad out, and always had the girls with her. I saw a lot of them that first year. I'd fly to the lake to see the kids, and Dianna would come out onto the balcony to smile and wave as I landed.

Andy and Barry would come running out, sometimes carrying their little overnight bags to stay in town with me for the night. We all had a good relationship, though I usually had to swallow hard when I saw Dianna. She was so many good things; I knew what I had lost, and I knew she was deeply hurt.

Sadly, most of us know just how emotionally painful a divorce is, with all its ups and downs. So it sent me reeling when I found out Dianna was dating an Air Force guy who worked part-time for Pete at the lake. I was beginning to spend more time at Saguaro Lake now that the sheriff's office had a first aid station with a helipad there. Once or twice a week I'd fly out and have coffee with Pete and the deputies assigned to Lake Patrol.

Dianna and the girls were usually there, and everything seemed to be going well for them. But I still had trouble adjusting to the idea of her having a boyfriend. John was a nice guy and I liked him, but I found myself keeping a distance from both of them, while trying to stay as close to my daughters as I could.

Barry and Andryea were about six and eight years old, but still my little babies, and I could tell they were proud of their dad. It crossed my mind that they could drift away from me to John, and I hated that thought. It was sad and about to get worse.

Six months after she'd begun dating John, Dianna called to tell me they had married and were moving to Sacramento in two weeks. I was stunned and shaken, and needed time to process this news.

It really made me think about my decision to choose the helicopter over my family, even though I knew it was now too late to change anything. I realized it had been selfish on my part, but once I discovered flying, I'd had a plan and a dream; and that's all I could focus on. But now, flying was more difficult and less fun with watery eyes and a heavy heart.

As I usually did when I was going through a rough patch, I called my friend John Bull. We had lunch and mulled over this new turn of events. He wisely pointed out the realities and told me I needed to accept where I was and keep moving forward.

He said I should be relieved that Dianna's husband seemed to be a good man and would be a good father. John assured me that my kids would always know me as Dad. "It just may be a blessing in disguise for both of you."

I knew he was right. But when I looked into Andy's and Barry's little faces, filled with love for me, it was hard to accept.

After Charmaine and I had divorced, she remarried and her new husband wanted to adopt Kari Jill. My life was such a mess at that point, I figured he would be a better dad to her than I ever could, so I relented. I'd had very little contact with her over the years, and now I was afraid of losing my other two daughters to another man.

On an already cold, gray, November day, Dianna brought the girls out to Falcon Field for a goodbye. It was also cold and gray in my heart, as I stood with them by the helicopter. We talked about how we would keep in touch and we promised to love each other forever.

Dianna and I are both proud that our girls never heard an unkind word from either one of us about the other, during or after our divorce. She always has been a class act, and we remain great friends to this day.

We all cried, hugged, kissed, and cried some more. Then they were gone.

With Barry (left) and Andi (right)

Chapter 36

Catalina

The Hughes 300 had proven beyond a doubt helicopters were here to stay. KOOL was receiving inquiries from broadcasting companies all over the country, wanting to learn more about our operation. Locally, rumors were floating around that Channel 12 was looking into buying a turbine-powered helicopter.

One day in early April, Homer called me into his office. He was assigning me to the Special Projects department to do an hour-long feature story on Catalina Island. Mr. Chauncey had leased a Hughes 500 from the factory at Culver City for the project, and they wanted me to evaluate it for our own news operation.

I saw this as the assignment of a lifetime, and—more importantly for me—a chance to move into the jet age of helicopters.

"Homer, does this mean we're going to buy a turbine?" I asked.

Homer replied with his usual non-committal answer, "We shall see when the time comes."

That was all I needed. *I* heard him say "yes" even though the word never came out of his mouth. Just knowing the subject of a turbine had come up with White Cloud was great news to me. It was going to happen somewhere in the country, and I wanted to be the first. Homer and Chauncey must have heard the rumors that Channel 12 was considering one.

Before I left his office I asked, "Homer, what's the big deal about Catalina Island?"

His quick reply, "Check with Special Projects."

The Special Projects department—headed by Bill Miller—was located just above the newsroom, looking down on the rest of us. Manny Garcia was the chief photographer and a master with film; a true pioneer when video cameras came along. Bonnie James, who would later become Bonnie Leverton, was a brand new producer and writer ... and the one who did the real work.

I always enjoyed working on projects with this department. They traveled to various Arizona locations and developed spectacular feature stories about its people and beautiful places. I had already been featured with the Bug in a half-hour special titled "Arizona as seen by Eagles."

Bonnie gave me the briefing, explaining that we would film a one-hour-plus documentary of the history, beauty and wildlife of Catalina Island. This spring was forecast to be the prettiest in more than a decade. While it sounded like a great assignment, I was still curious about why we were doing a special feature on a location outside of Arizona. I quickly learned.

I had heard rumors during the years that Mrs. Chauncey was related to the "chewing gum family," but I'd had no idea she was the daughter of the late William Wrigley. The Wrigleys had owned a majority interest in the Catalina Island Company, and lived in a huge house perched high above the town of Avalon.

Dorothy "Deedie" Wrigley Chauncey was an impressive lady. I was around her several times, and on one occasion when Dianna was with me, she insisted we call her Deedie.

Two days after checking in with Special Projects, I was in Culver City, California at the Hughes Helicopter plant, meeting with sales rep Roger Schuster. I had been in touch with him often over the years, and he usually kept me informed about what was going on in the industry. I was nervous when he told me Channel 12 had indeed inquired about a new Hughes; but when he went on to say they had turned down a demo ride when offered, I relaxed a little.

As we approached the dark blue Hughes 500, I admired the look of it. Roger and I climbed in for a practice run to Catalina. The white interior was just as classy as the deep blue outside.

Flying over the ocean I was totally in awe of the view beneath us: the water, ships and sailboats were all new to me, a desert rat.

We landed at the small private airport on the island. At the time, fuel was not available to the general public, but because I knew somebody with influence, we had a fuel truck at our disposal. After a brief stop on the island I took off,

Testing the Hughes 500

climbed up to about 1500 feet and headed back to Culver City to drop off Roger.

I was very impressed with the new helicopter. Everything about it felt so different, and my mind was spinning with the potential of this powerful little bird. My job for the next few days would be to fly this beautiful jet-powered helicopter all over the island of Catalina. I could not wait to meet our crew at the airport the next day.

Hughes put me up in a very nice hotel in Culver City and I had dinner with Roger Schuster in the dining room. Roger was about my age and liked to "put on the dog," so to speak. He was tall, blond, good-looking and had a way with words. Every female at this huge hotel knew him by name. We were friends throughout my years of flying a Hughes, and he could always be counted on for a great dinner.

I had a good night's sleep and was up at the crack of dawn. At 6 a.m. I would meet Deedie Chauncey and the crew at the Catalina airport, and I wasn't going to be late.

It was a bit misty as I lifted off from the airport at Culver City, but the early morning sunrise gave me a spectacular view of Marina Del Rey and provided a ten-mile visibility in the haze.

Identifying myself as "Helicopter 10 TV," I contacted Los Angeles tower, gave my location, and requested radar following out to Catalina.

The feeling of speed at 500 feet above the ocean is overwhelming. I flashed over fishing boats and vessels of all kinds, and nearly everyone had a friendly wave. I even spotted a pod of dolphins following a small boat.

I dropped down to 50 feet and watched the airspeed indicator hit 175 mph … until I saw a very large pelican coming up fast. I realized how careless I had been and came back to reality. Bird strikes with a helicopter or airplane are very unpleasant. That could have been disaster. I immediately slowed down and kept my eyes glued straight ahead.

It was like being in your own new car for the very first time. Everything was brand new and worked. It smelled different and sounded like what it was: One Bad Ass Machine!

There was a period when I could no longer see the California coastline behind me and could not yet see Catalina ahead. It reminded me of flying out to the oil platforms off the Gulf Coast. One big difference, I thought … no alligators!

The distance to Catalina was less than 30 miles, and I was surprised at how quickly I got there. The private air strip sat atop a high meadow, and I landed at six on the dot.

I could see a van parked near the windsock, and as I climbed out of the helicopter I was met by the crew and Mrs. Chauncey, who would be directing our little movie.

Deedie Chauncey had arranged for the crew to stay at a hotel in the little city of Avalon. I was concerned about the Hughes spending a lonely night at an abandoned airstrip, so I planned to sleep inside to make sure no harm came to it. We were there to film the wildlife, which I assumed would include big and mean critters. After my adventure in the Louisiana swamps years earlier, I wasn't real eager to take on anything wild.

No need to worry though; my new Bluebird—as I had already named it—and I were going to be put up in what Bonnie referred to as the "Homestead." I was thrilled, to say the least. The beautiful Wrigley mansion sits on the highest point of the island, overlooking everything. My room was very comfortable and elegantly furnished. I could walk out onto my patio and see Bluebird just 50 feet away, sitting on a pristinely manicured lawn.

That first morning we flew all around the island getting a feel for where we should *not* fly because of wildlife concerns. We all put on headsets, and Bonnie and Manny sat in the rear seats while Mrs. Chauncey was up front with me, giving us a tour of Catalina and sharing personal stories of growing up here. The Wrigley family loved the island, and had once owned an 88 percent interest in it. Three years earlier, in 1975, all of the Wrigley shares were deeded to the Catalina Island Conservancy to ensure that it would always be maintained as one of the most beautiful places in the world.

The crew for this trip; Bonnie James, Manny Garcia and Gerry Grunig, were all hard-working, dedicated people, and a joy to work with.

Bonnie had been working at Channel 10 since before I started there, having joined KOOL straight from her junior year at Arizona State University. She started as Johnny Johnson's program secretary at KOOL radio, moved on to Promotions for a short spell, then moved into Special Projects as a girl friday. Once in that department, she continued up the ladder to research director, associate producer–writer, and finally to her then current position of self-made producer–writer. Bonnie was whip-smart and one of the nicest people at KOOL. In the early days she was often the one who would be dispatched to pick up the film I dropped from the gyroplane. We were always in a hurry; if Bonnie had the film by 5:30, the story could make the six o'clock news.

Years later I asked Bonnie to share some of her memories of those times. Her response made me smile: "*I didn't know Jerry Foster well. He was kind of scary … and rumors of his moodiness and "mean" personality were rampant. One of my early encounters with him took place when he was still flying the gyroplane and doing traffic reports. I was sent out to retrieve some film he'd shot. It had been raining earlier, but had stopped by the time I got to the pick-up location. When*

Jerry tossed the film container out to me, it landed directly in a huge puddle. To retrieve it, I had to wade into the muddy water in my nice dress and heels, which were soon a mud-splattered dress and soggy heels. Jerry, of course, thought it was hilarious."

Another time the canister came open and the film went trailing out behind the chopper. No story that day.

Bonnie was a cute little thing, and I liked to tease her and chase her around the newsroom, but she wasn't interested in playing my games. She was tall with long brown hair, and in great shape. When she came through the newsroom in such a big hurry, some of us would try to slow her down. Bill Denney and I could really push her buttons and sometimes we hit the jackpot.

One day I harassed her so much that she just lit into me. As she started up the stairs to her office, I tossed out one more smart aleck comment for her, and she turned and flipped me off, shouting the words to go along with it. There was complete silence while everything came to a standstill. No one could believe she'd finally stood up to me. I'll admit, I couldn't get away with that kind of behavior today, and back then, it was all in fun.

Bonnie and me on Catalina

When Bill Leverton arrived at KOOL, he and Bonnie hit it off right away. They were a pair for all the years I was there and eventually married. Even then I couldn't let well enough alone. They were married in Bill's back yard, and as Joe Betancourt was singing the beautiful *Wedding Song*, I flew over and circled the house. It's a wonder they didn't shoot me down!

Manny Garcia had been with the station a long time and was our chief photographer. His talent with film projects had already become legendary; another reason White Cloud had sent him on this project. Manny was always a pleasure to be around and to work with, but he had two hurdles to contend with on this Catalina trip; the first being the recent transition from film to the new video tape. Video was still new technology and Manny would have to work a little harder to make it look like film, but we knew he could do it. His second challenge, a little tougher to deal with, was his impending divorce.

Our technician, Gerry Grunig, was a tall, quiet kid from engineering who was sent along to keep things running, since he had a good knowledge of the new video equipment. Every night they would play back all the video that had been shot that day. It sounds so simple by today's standards, but in the 1970s all those recorders and monitors were much larger, with dozens of wires to contend with.

Unfortunately, Gerry suffered from extreme airsickness, and could not fly with us. I felt bad for him, but we couldn't take the risk of him hurling on that equipment, much less in the new helicopter that we did not yet own.

There was one close call, however, when Bonnie was in the back seat with the recorder, and Manny was up front with the camera head. Bonnie had to watch the recorder while Manny was shooting, to make sure it was running. Constantly looking down was starting to affect her, but she didn't say anything. When we landed on a huge cliff overlooking the ocean, Bonnie got out and hightailed it away from the helicopter out of our sight. Manny and I knew she had finally barfed. It made my day, but we didn't let on. We knew she'd be embarrassed.

Bonnie remembers, *"My first real opportunity to work with Jerry came during the Catalina trip. When we arrived, we found that Mrs. Chauncey had arranged for a hotel in Avalon to open up part of its premises and give us an entire floor, since it was off season. Manny, Gerry and I each had our own room, and there was another empty room where we set up all our viewing equipment.*

"Each day we'd meet Mrs. Chauncey in front of the hotel at 6 a.m. After a long day of filming, we'd get back to the hotel about 8 p.m. and go

to the viewing room to watch video until around midnight. Then we'd do it all again the next day. This made for long days and nights.

"Jerry wasn't involved in the actual production, and—poor baby— didn't stay at the hotel with us. He had to make do at the Wrigley homestead.

"We didn't film aerial shots every day, but when we did, we got some spectacular footage. Catalina is a gift from nature, and all the flowers, trees and greenery made for wonderful video.

"Early on Jerry decided he couldn't let Grunig go up with us, as he had a bad stomach for flying, and Jerry didn't want anyone throwing up in his chopper. He said he'd throw up if anyone else did, and wouldn't be able to control the helicopter, making for an unsafe flight. I didn't tell him that I get massive motion sickness and that flying was actually torture for me. For the most part, I did fairly well. But after one flight, when Jerry set down so Manny could film a particular area, I ran over to a cliff edge and let it all out. Jerry didn't say a word, and I was surprised that he had been so nice about it.

"After we returned to Phoenix, I worked on the footage, wrote a script ... then told Jerry to follow my guidelines, but to ad-lib what I had written so it would sound more like him. I was surprised to learn that he wasn't as sure of his ad-libbing skills as I would have thought him to be ... and he just read my script verbatim.

"The whole Catalina experience was an eye-opener. I discovered that Jerry wasn't the bogey-man he'd been made out to be. He was quiet and could sometimes be a little moody, but he didn't take it out on us. He joked around with us and flew us anywhere we wanted to go."

After thirty-plus years, much of the Catalina trip is just a blur to me. What I remember most was the thrill of flying that Hughes 500. I wasn't needed to fly all the time, and could come and go as I pleased.

Mrs. Chauncey made a car available to me so I could go out and see things, but I preferred staying at my room just looking at the helicopter and daydreaming of having one like it. I took a couple of flights each day for evaluation purposes, since that was the main reason I was sent to Catalina. I spent a good deal of time writing a report for Mr. Chauncey, comparing the 300 to the 500. I made it factual, but try as I might, I couldn't find a bad thing to report.

When I did fly with the crew, Manny knew exactly what he wanted and was very pleased with the way his video was turning out. We all had dinners together in Avalon, and on the final night Mrs. Chauncey hosted a beautiful dinner for us at her home. It had been an experience that this crew would cherish for the rest of our lives.

The next day we said goodbye to our new friend, Deedie, and went our separate ways. We all felt it had been a job well done.

My last flight of the trip was back to the mainland and civilization. I had just spent four days in paradise, and flying over the coastline, I felt myself re-entering the reality of life and all that was ahead. But I had no doubt I would soon be flying one of these beautiful, fast machines again. Hopefully, this one!

I reluctantly landed at Hughes, turned in the Bluebird and headed home.

Deedie Wrigley Chauncey and me at Catalina

Chapter 37

End of an Era

I returned from Catalina wondering if Mr. Chauncey and Homer had reneged on their promise of the Hughes 500. Roger Schuster, the sales rep at Hughes Helicopters, had told me before that it was all but a done deal, but nothing was happening. About a week after I got back I called him again; he said no one from KOOL was returning his calls. To make matters worse, rumors were running rampant that Channel 12 was going to buy a helicopter to compete with us. Everyone knew it was coming.

Homer finally let me know that a turbine machine was just too costly right now, but they would review it again for next year's budget. I went home that night feeling pretty low. You didn't argue with Chauncey or Homer if you liked your job. I went back to traffic reports and chasing news stories in my little Bug.

A couple of weeks later I got a call from Al Buch, the news director at Channel 12. I was surprised, and felt like a traitor for even taking the call. He got right to the point; they had heard I was unhappy about KOOL's decision to not buy a turbine machine. He said Karl Eller, the owner of KTAR, had given his approval to purchase whatever they needed to compete with 10, and that the purchase of a Hughes 500 was already in the works. My heart had been sinking as he told me they would be competing with 10, but it nearly stopped when he said Mr. Eller wanted me to fly it!

I knew they had me even before we hung up. We arranged to meet for lunch two days later at the Left Seat restaurant at Sky Harbor Airport.

Al, who had only recently been hired by KTAR, had been studying the market research and focus groups relating to news broadcasting. He recalls, *"The message we were getting was basically "No helicopter, no news business" so we knew that Channel 12 had to get a helicopter quick. We started poking around and found out that Jerry would love to have a jet helicopter, and that KOOL was not going to buy one.*

"I called Jerry to get a feel for whether or not he might come over to 12. He sounded very interested, so Pep Cooney and I talked to Karl Eller and decided to go ahead and try to get him. We would have bought the helicopter whether Jerry had come over or not, but getting him was a bonus. However, we wanted to take it even a step further: we wanted to use the term "reporter" in conjunction with his flying and filming.

I felt I needed to be honest with Homer, so I told him about the call and the upcoming lunch. His entire demeanor totally changed. I had never experienced his "icy" side until that moment. He told me they would not get into a bidding war with Eller and if I moved "across the street" I'd lose the respect I'd gained over my years with Channel 10. It was not the reaction I had expected, so I tried to soften the impact of my news by telling him, "They would have to promise me the moon for me to leave KOOL."

Homer didn't say a word. The meeting was over and I knew I had been sternly warned.

I was highly conflicted. On the one hand, I felt a sense of loyalty and gratitude to KOOL, and especially to Homer Lane. But my feelings were hurt because I knew that most reporters were making almost triple my twelve thousand dollar annual salary, while I was working triple the hours of everyone I knew. I was locked into the morning and evening traffic reports, which were getting mighty old after seven years. On top of that, I was chasing TV news all day and night, and making myself available 24/7.

My biggest concern was my past. Homer and Mr. Chauncey knew all my dirty little secrets. If I walked over to the competition, would I be reading about myself in the morning paper? My friend John Bull strongly urged me to move on. "It's the opportunity of a lifetime, and if they do make it public, they are the ones who will look bad, not you. But if you go to 12," he cautioned, "tell them all about your past before you make a deal."

My family felt the same way and encouraged me to go for it. I knew they were right, but I kept one concern to myself: I did not *ever* want to relive another public humiliation. I felt disgraced in the Marine Corps and again with the Scottsdale Police Department. If it happened again it would be a much longer way to fall, with a much larger audience and a lot more friends and critics. It would be ugly, especially for my family.

It was a long two days until the lunch with Al Buch. After the morning traffic report I landed at the station and went straight to the newsroom for a cup of coffee. I piddled around there most of the morning, trying to stay out of sight of Bill Close. The last thing I needed was a run-in with him. No such luck. He walked up to my little cubicle, pulled up a chair and sat down. *Uh oh*, I thought, *here comes trouble!*

He leaned over and very quietly said, "I know about your lunch today and I just wanted to tell you to take the time you need to make your decision. You have more security and freedom here than you would ever have at 12."

He patted me on the arm, got up and went back to his office. I had assumed he knew, and now he wanted me to *know* he knew. But he did surprise me with his gentle advice and it gave me a good feeling. It was one of the best "Close Encounters" I'd ever had with him.

Shortly before noon I took off from downtown and flew to Sky Harbor. There were two helipads right in front of the Left Seat Café. On one of the pads was a Hughes 500. It was the very same machine I had flown to Catalina Island—Bluebird! As I landed next to it I saw Roger Schuster, the Hughes rep. He gave me a big wave and smile, as did the two men who were standing with him: Channel 12's General Manager, C.E. (Pep) Cooney and News Director, Al Buch.

After I shut down the engine the two men approached. The surprise on my face must have been obvious. After the introductions, I said, "You guys set me up by having Roger bring this beautiful machine over here. A classy move."

We all had a big laugh, which got us off to a good start for what turned out to be a great afternoon.

Roger put me in the pilot's seat and off we flew to a little restaurant called the Mining Camp at the base of the Superstition Mountains. It was decked out like an old mining camp chow hall with benches, tin plates and mugs, sawdust, mining paraphernalia and family-style servings of food.

While we ate they began selling me on the idea of coming over to Channel 12. It wasn't a hard sell. Pep asked if I would be interested in a meeting with Karl Eller when we got back and I told him I would like that. We discussed the mechanics of where the machine would be kept at night. They had plans in the works for a rooftop helipad at the Channel 12 station and assured me I would be able to operate for them as I had been at KOOL.

I could get used to this and was getting more excited every minute. I was afraid it was a dream, and that I would wake up any moment. After lunch I flew them down through the canyons on the Salt River, and over Saguaro and Canyon Lakes. These were my old stomping grounds, and it made me very aware of the higher speed of the 500, which was twice what my little Bug could do. It also had a much roomier interior, including a back seat and other high-tech features. Al Buch said there was a device that would enable me to go live while over a news story. It was the first one ever built with a tracking system that would lock in the signal.

Al Buch later explained, "I had met a guy who owned an engineering firm in San Diego, which made microwave radios to be used as tracking devices for the government. I asked him if they could convert the device to transmit video. After several meetings, and a lot of playing around with slide rulers, he determined that it could be done. As a result, KTAR Channel 12 was the first in the country to use live reports from a helicopter."

I was elated at this news! Film drops in empty fields would be a thing of the past, and so would the Bug!

We landed at Sky Harbor, where I said goodbye to Roger and gave the Hughes 500 a fond pat, hoping it would soon be mine. Pep and Al drove me to Channel 12 and led me up a private staircase that went straight to Karl Eller's office. It was another huge, impressive office, but completely different than White Cloud's.

Mr. Eller was sitting behind a large desk that butted up to a conference table; more business than show. I had done a little research on my own and knew this was a very powerful man.

Karl Eller was an Arizona boy who had grown up in Tucson and attended the University of Arizona. This was the same "Eller" of Eller Outdoor Advertising, whose name was seen on advertising billboards nationwide. Photos of many of those billboards adorned his office. In 1968 he merged his outdoor advertising business with KTAR Radio and TV to create Combined Communications.

During the ride to Channel 12, Pep had told me that Karl Eller didn't waste words or time. He was an entrepreneur who wanted more than anything to beat his old nemesis, Tom Chauncey, in the TV ratings.

The four of us made ourselves comfortable around the conference table. Mr. Eller sat across from me and came right to the business at hand. "Jerry we are very impressed with what you have done at Channel 10. I don't know what you are making at KOOL, but here's my proposal:

"Number one: I will double your salary and give you a contract for however long you want.

"Number two: I will give you a turbine helicopter of your choosing and let you operate the same way you have done at KOOL.

"Number 3: You will have the first 'live' capability plus a video camera that can be easily taken out of the helicopter for ground shots just like you have at KOOL. Al Buch will see to it you have whatever you need to do the job. That's my deal, what say you?"

My mouth was so dry I didn't know if I could get the words out. I started by asking, "Mr. Eller, you own AM and FM radio stations. Would I be required to do daily traffic reports?"

Mr. Eller looked at Pep, Al and then me. "No traffic reports," he said.

"There is one more thing," I squeaked. I told the story of my past and left nothing out. When I finished, there were a few seconds of silence that felt like an eternity. Eller looked straight at me and said, "That was in the past. Your performance since then has been outstanding. If it should ever come up I will defend you with everything in my power as long as you're doing the job I hired you to do. Anything else?"

"No, sir," I replied. "I guess that makes me your new helicopter pilot. I'll need to give Homer two week's notice." He stood up, shook my hand and welcomed me to Channel 12. The meeting was over and I had a new job. Al Buch drove me back to the airport, gave me his phone numbers and asked me to call as soon as I talked to Homer.

I got in my little Bug and flew back to the station to see Homer. Now came the tough part ... the part I had been dreading. I had become close to Homer and it was thanks to him that I had been able to make a go of it at KOOL. I had worked there nearly eight years; the longest I had ever held any job.

I landed on the roof and headed straight for Homer's office. It was shortly after three o'clock and I had traffic reports to do in less than an hour. But I couldn't put this off until tomorrow.

Homer was on the phone when I got there, and he motioned for me to sit down. When he finished his phone call he put the receiver down and looked at me. He clasped his hands together and waited for me to start.

I had my opening statement all thought out. "Homer, they promised me the moon and a deal I couldn't turn down. I can give you two week's notice, Sir."

Homer said, "That won't be necessary. Leave the helicopter on the roof and turn in your company car and equipment to Bill

Close, as well as your key to the building. You're fired as of right now."

"I'm sorry, sir," I tried to say. But he interrupted me, saying, "That's all, Jerry. I'm very disappointed in you."

That's all there was to it. I left the building and went to my apartment to unpack my car. Soon afterward Bill Close was trying to get me on the two-way radio. I didn't answer. Later that evening he called, demanding to know why I hadn't turned in my gear. I politely told him that I would do that in the morning and I hung up. Later that night, when the ten o'clock news was over and the place was deserted, I drove to Channel 10 and left my news car and equipment locked up in the garage. I put the keys on top of Close's desk and walked the five blocks home.

I had already called Al Buch and told him. He wasn't a bit surprised that Homer had fired me. "That's the way it's done in this business. Take a few days off and I will be in touch," he said.

Al remembers, *"Soon after we had an agreement with him, I met with the rep from Hughes over dinner, and handed over a check for a quarter of a million dollars from Karl Eller for a new jet helicopter. It was definitely the most expensive business dinner deal I've ever been involved in."*

What a day it had been. I went home and slept like a baby, knowing my new course had been charted and an exciting journey would soon begin.

But there was a good deal of sadness and remorse that went along with it. The next morning I woke up at five o'clock as usual, and couldn't get back to sleep. I opened the curtains and looked over at the little Bug sitting on the KOOL helipad. I tuned in the Len Engebretsen show on KOOL Radio. There was no mention of traffic reports or me. I went through all the mood swings. That job at KOOL would have no shortage of applicants and I was going to have competition. I began getting calls from the media; newspapers in particular.

My line was that Channel 10 said "No" to a turbine helicopter and Channel 12 said "Yes" and made me a good deal. I let it go at that. My move surprised a lot of people and sent a signal that TV news had a new tool.

KOOL wasted no time getting their helicopter in the air for traffic reports and chasing news stories. That afternoon I watched the little Bug lift off the Channel 10 heliport to the north. They flew right over my apartment and gave me a big wave that I returned. It hurt that someone else was flying the Bug and doing a job I had done for so long. KOOL hired a pilot and used a reporter to give the traffic reports. At least it took two people to replace me, I told myself with satisfaction. But the truth was, I took a big gamble and was more than ready to fight for my turf.

After a week off, I reported to work at Channel 12.

PART FOUR

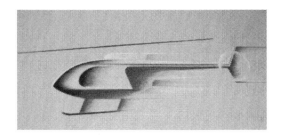

Chapter 38

Transition to the Jet Age

 Feeling a little nervous on my first day at Channel 12, I hoped to sneak in unnoticed and go directly to Al Buch's office. That didn't happen. He was holding a meeting in his office, and as I entered I was facing Al's back and the entire newsroom staff. So much for a quiet entrance.

Somebody in back hollered, "The competition is here!" The room erupted in clapping, whistling and some comical exchanges. But it was all in fun and I felt relieved. I had entered the room feeling like a defector, and a bit self-conscious. But once Al made the introduction, I immediately became part of the team.

I already knew most of the reporters and photographers from working the street news. Several of them told me they hadn't believed I would actually make the change; that I was just looking for a healthier contract. Little did they know that most of them were making more than I was at KOOL and that I never even had a contract there.

When I had a few moments alone I looked around the 12 newsroom and wondered if I had made a huge mistake. I was surrounded by a cacophony of noise in a smoke-filled room. Nearly everyone smoked, including me. *That*, by the way, is the worst thing I ever did to my body and I so regret it. But ash trays were as common as pens and paper on every surface.

It was always very loud. That's just the way newsrooms were then. The phone lines were answered by whoever was in the room at the time, and the ringing never seemed to stop.

Al Buch assigned me a small office right next to his and made sure I had a typewriter and all those little things necessary to start work. The huge newsroom consisted of an assignment desk and about 20 desks pushed together for reporters and producers in the center. Several private offices lined the main room walls on both sides. Four large TV monitors hung over the assignment desk so we could keep an eye on the competition and the network. Police and fire scanners blared out their needs for all to hear. The sounds, smells and activity were identical to those at Channel 10. If I closed my eyes I couldn't tell the difference. *Now* I felt right at home!

The dispatcher, Bill Sherman, had a little room in the back where more scanners squawked. Bill answered the phone, kept the assignment desk up on what was going on, and dispatched our ground units to breaking stories. However, he spoke so fast over the radio we could hardly understand a word he was saying. He was also the newsroom spark plug who entertained and offended anyone who would listen. He was good at his job, but the feeling was "a little of Bill went a long way," resulting in Al Buch occasionally stepping out of his office and yelling, "Bill shut up and close your door!"

Adding to the noise was the constant thumping of the typewriters ... big, heavy, bulletin manual typewriters you really had to pound because the keys had to punch through several carbons. There were never enough typewriters for everyone. When a reporter left the room, that typewriter was immediately grabbed by someone else.

The closer we got to a newscast the more noise: producers, reporters and anchors all shouting at each other to be heard. It was incredible, but I would come to love it.

That first day I went to lunch with Al Buch and station manager Pep Cooney. We talked about delivery dates for the helicopter, cameras and a hundred other things. It was a good time for me to evaluate my bosses. They were both great guys and let me know I had their support. Most importantly, I had their promise I would be flying a news helicopter and not a corporate limousine.

We also settled the financial end of our deal. My starting salary was more than five times what I was making at KOOL. I would also receive a clothing allowance, a company car and expenses. Things were suddenly looking not just good, but *real* good. I signed a three-year contract.

My first day was a huge success and set the stage for what would be an incredible adventure. I went home that night feeling relieved, knowing this change was the right way to go, although I still worried that my past would surface and blow the whole thing. I was a celebrity now and wasn't prepared to be in the position I was in. It was truly one step at a time.

I had some thoughts on what I wanted to do with my new bird. I didn't have traffic reports to deal with now, unlike the past eight years, when I had been obligated to give morning and evening reports.

My tenth-story condo was just across the street from the station. From my balcony, I could see where the Channel 10 helicopter rested to the south, but I couldn't see the Channel 12 pad on the north side. I would have to do something about that.

I hadn't been gone from KOOL more than a month when they announced they had purchased a Bell JetRanger and were looking for a pilot–reporter. I had known it was coming and so had everyone else. Our delivery date for the new Hughes was less than a week away. Sales rep Roger Schuster said he would be happy to deliver it and I told him I would be unhappy if he did. I wanted to be the first to fly and bring it home. I cannot describe how excited and eager I was to get that bird and get to work.

On September 27, 1978, I picked up our new Hughes 500D at the plant in Culver City, California. The jet was a beautiful red, white and blue with blue interior. It was egg-shaped with a "T" tail, a five-blade rotor system, and was powered by an Allison 250C-20B turbine engine which put out 420 horsepower. It could seat three passengers snugly in the front, and two in the cramped back seats. It wasn't a Cadillac; this was a sleek little Corvette with all the bells and whistles. It was state of the art for its time.

Even the radios were luxuries for me. We now had two VHF radios with VOR, ADF and transponder, two police and fire scanners, and a programmable two-way radio capable of storing multiple frequencies. We added a fuel tank in the back that gave us an additional three hours flight time. But the most expensive toy on the ship was the microwave setup that would allow us to go live. While others had been experimenting with live broadcasts, Tayburn Electronics in Carlsbad, California built us the first system that worked.

Talk about luck! I was in the right place at exactly the right time and found myself the center of a TV helicopter war. It was my news director at Channel 12 who had come up with the solution that put us in the lead.

The idea for automatically tracking a flying camera platform for news gathering had its genesis in the mid-1970s with two journalists in California. Al Buch and John Lander were co-workers in the McClatchy Broadcasting Company. Al was news director in Fresno and John was the state capitol correspondent based in Sacramento. One day they were brainstorming the future of TV news and the tools that would be neat to have. Lander had met the folks at Tayburn and thought they might be able to help with miniature microwave transmitters that could be mounted in an aircraft.

When Al Buch later moved to Phoenix to take the news director slot at KTAR, he got things moving in the direction of live broadcasting from a helicopter. Hiring me was just the first step. As Al remembers it:

"The first thing General Manager, C.E. (Pep) Cooney and I did was conduct a series of focus groups to see what the Phoenix market thought of television news programs. Bottom line: Only KOOL-TV (Channel 10) was considered to be in the news business because they had a helicopter. Our viewers told us if KTAR (Channel 12) wanted to stay competitive in the news business, they must have a helicopter. (I've

never seen such a clear guidance from any market research, for any company since that project.)

"Pep and I took that information to KTAR's owner, Karl Eller. He immediately gave the okay to buy a jet helicopter and handed me a check for the down payment—$250,000. Hughes Aircraft got the order for a new Hughes 500-D and we were on our way. Pep and I had heard that we might be able to hire Jerry Foster from KOOL if we were to offer him a jet chopper and good money. We did both and Jerry quickly moved across town. Sky 12 was born."

Channel 10 wasn't far behind us with their helicopter operation known as "Skywatch." They hired an ex-Vietnam pilot who had been shot down several times during the war. Bill Dimond was a nice guy and I respected him. I was intimidated when I first heard about his war record, but the first time he showed up on a big story all that changed. I never knew him well and I didn't want to, simply because he was the competition. But he never beat me to a spot news story unless my machine was down for maintenance.

Many times the mechanics at Arizona Helicopters would work all night to complete whatever needed to be done and get me back in the air ASAP. We had all worked together for years, going back to the time when I was part of their team. I never once had to question a maintenance decision or worry about the work they did. They were as proud as I was when I continued to arrive on the scene first, as being first was everything.

My biggest advantage over Channel 10 was response time. While flying with the AMES project for the Arizona Highway Patrol, I had learned getting there quickly could mean the difference between life and death. The same applied to news stories. When I was at KOOL I gave myself a 20-minute window to be airborne. I had been doing it that way for the past eight years and I would continue to do it now.

My only real rivals in that area were the Air Rescue crews at the Department of Public Safety. When I was flying the little Bug I missed a lot of big stories in the rural areas because by the time I got there it was all over. If it was a bad accident or a plane crash for instance, then I could shoot film or video of the aftermath. But now I would be able to get there for the action—and to get there first was everything to me and the station. It wasn't a job, it was a lifestyle; and I loved it.

During the daylight working hours I would scramble off the roof with a photographer. If no one was available I would go by myself. The Hughes 500 made it much easier for me to shoot my own video. After about 100 hours of flying my new machine, I felt bonded to it. I didn't have to think about flying, it just came naturally. I was as comfortable flying as most people are driving a car. Drivers don't think about pushing the gas pedal or making a turn, they just do it. I felt the same in this chopper. Unlike the Bug, the turbine engine had a governor which maintained the rpm. That was a tremendous help, allowing me more freedom to shoot film or tape.

My tenth-floor condo remained a problem for me. I needed to be able to see KOOL's helipad and keep an eye on them, but I could not see my own machine. Being able to see "my" helicopter was as important to me as a mother being able to keep an eye on her kids playing in the park. I solved the problem by buying the top floor apartment on the southeast corner (one of four penthouses) so I could see Sky 12 sitting on the roof as well as Channel 10's white JetRanger. Since I was always either at home or at the TV station, my 20-minute window was a piece of cake. On weekends and at night my competition's pilot had to be called out from his home in Scottsdale. By the time he was in the air I was long gone and maybe on the scene.

My first year at KTAR was the best year of my life up to that point. I never took a day off. When Sky 12 was in for maintenance we would rent a machine from Arizona Helicopters just to have a bird on the roof in case a big story broke. That's how competitive the Phoenix TV market was at the time. It may sound hokey, but being ready to go was the key to our success.

It didn't take long for me to realize my days of operating solo were over and I needed help. Up to this point I had been pretty much on my own. Over the next 10 years I would team up with four photographers and one producer. When my news director, Al Buch, recognized that I needed help, he let me choose my partners. It was a much needed blessing, as my schedule now included community events and school visits.

Having a photographer along, when one was available, was a big help. What I really needed though, was a full-time shooter; someone who could jump out on a rocky cliff to get ground shots or guard the tail rotor on starts and shutdowns when we landed in a school yard or public place. There were so many advantages to a full-time photographer that I didn't have to convince Al Buch.

My first partner was Howard Shepherd, who was more than willing to take on the assignment. He was good with a camera and with meeting the public. The only drawback was his size: he weighed well over 200 pounds and stood six-foot-four. A big guy with a big heart, Howie was everyone's friend, and we got along just fine. It was this gentle giant who taught me the ins and outs of Channel 12. He had a knack for never getting angry or upset, even if he was relegated to the cramped back seat when we had a special passenger.

One afternoon we were just lifting off the downtown pad with a ride-along guest. The plan was to let our guest sit up front until we came up in the weather segment for the 5 p.m. news— about 15 minutes away. I intended to set down in a field and let Howie get up front to handle the camera shots. But before I could land, we heard over the Phoenix Police emergency frequency that homicide detectives were chasing a murder suspect near Sky Harbor Airport.

Since Howie had a camera in the back seat, I told him to power up and be ready, as we were only five minutes away. I called the control tower for permission to enter their control zone, and then intercepted the chase near 24th street and Interstate 10.

Howie was shooting from the left rear seat. He had to put the camera in his lap in the cramped space where he sat all scrunched up. I flew with the nose crabbed to the right so he could see the van. The chase left the interstate and snaked through a housing development, going over lawns, around trees, and the wrong way down one-way streets. The driver was desperate, eluding police for a good 15 minutes before finally ending up back on the interstate access road. When he tried to make a U-turn he was bottled up by patrol cars and ran into an overpass abutment. The car was surrounded by unhappy police officers with guns drawn. When one of our ground units arrived we broke off and headed for the station.

Howie had not missed a single shot. To this day, I'm amazed at how he was able to do that under those conditions. We won an Emmy for covering that chase and police departments all over the country would use it in their training departments. It was the first high speed chase any of us had ever seen from the air. Many more would follow.

With Howie, there was never a dull moment. He could relax me when things turned tense. He just kept shooting and always got the shot I needed. Over the years the catch-phrase, the "Howie Factor"

Cameraman Howard Shepherd (right)

became attached to him, because of his proclivity for things to go wrong. Once he was first on the scene of an aircraft that had slid off the runway at Sky Harbor. He arrived while passengers were still being taken off the plane. It would have been great film, but he forgot to load his camera! Another time he was chasing the police who were chasing a bank robber, and Howie ran out of gas. There was a spectacular crash and shootout that left the robber dead, but Howie missed it all.

The Howie Factor only struck once while we were teamed up. After lifting off the downtown helipad I was just crossing over Central Avenue with the doors off on a warm day. Howie was changing batteries in his camera and the heavy battery fell out the door, landing squarely on top of a Volkswagen!

Howie spent nearly a year with me before deciding he needed to slow down and spend more time with his family. I knew he had been getting pressure to start being a full-time dad again. I understood, and we parted the best of friends.

Chapter 39

New Cameraman, New Technology

John Bass

Now that Howie had moved on, I started looking for a new shooter. Al Buch suggested John Bass, and I whole-heartedly agreed. John was happy to come on board, and recalls, *"I didn't even have to think about it. I could shoot film, I knew journalism, and aviation had been in my blood for as long as I could remember. This would be serious fun. I soon traded my coat and tie for boots and jeans. Since Jerry had developed a routine over his years in the Phoenix market, I learned the way things would work. I'd help care for the 'copter and be available 24/7 to do the job. It also meant overtime for me, and that was important.*

"This was all before the microwave system had been fully operational. The engineers were still doing tests and working the bugs out. In the meantime, when the "bell" rang to go chase spot news or do a story, we were out of the newsroom and up a flight of stairs to the roof. We could be airborne and ready to shoot within five minutes."

During my first year with Channel 12, the competition worked hard to get their live capability up and running. John and I listened nearly every day as Channel 10 pilot, Bill Dimond, and the engineers were on their company frequency talking back and forth, tweaking and adjusting, trying to figure it all out. Every time they tried a live shot and failed, John and I would look at each other and smile. But they were getting close and we knew it.

The engineers from Tayburn, Ev Shultz and Ed Black, had arrived in Phoenix days after I brought the new machine home. These two had designed the system and were on hand to help our chief engineer, Leon Anglin. For nearly a year it was a race to see whether Channel 10 or Channel 12 would be first to go live. It was a nightmare for us until the engineers finally got the automatic tracking antenna to lock onto the helicopter's transmitter. We got it figured out the day after KOOL tried to go live with their system. But their system required that a satellite truck be nearby to pick up their signal and transmit it back to the station, and their bird had to remain at a hover while this was happening.

Fitting the antenna to the chopper

John Bass: *"Just before the microwave unit was fully operational, Jerry's old station, KOOL, and his old nemesis, pulled a stunt designed to upstage our live capability. They sent their JetRanger up with a portable microwave unit used for ground relays, to shoot a signal to their downtown station's receiver. When the very short "live" was over they came back to the anchor and news director, Bill Close, who—with a defined smirk on his face—said, 'You saw it here first, and it won't be the last time.'*

"Okay, they were first to show someone in a helicopter shooting a live signal back to the station. But the picture only lasted a few seconds and was jittery the whole time. They did it as a cheap shot and it worked. That infuriated the Tayburn Electronics guys and by the next morning we were ready to go."

My auto tracker was different. I could fly at any speed and automatically be tracked. We had the winning ticket for the time being, but it wouldn't take other stations long to catch up.

John Bass: *"We tweaked and tested all morning, just waiting for the noon news. At the right time our anchorman, Bill Stull, said, "Let's go live to Jerry Foster who is in Sky 12 over downtown Phoenix. Jerry?"*

Our very first shot was tight on the JetRanger sitting on its pad at KOOL. John then pulled back for a wide shot of the downtown buildings.

I said, "Folks, that's a live shot of downtown and what a beautiful day it is ... "

About that time the signal started to weaken and I kicked it back to Bill Stull. Our first live broadcast was a huge success and sent a message to our competition to "bring it on." From that time on, we kept working to perfect the tracking system, and within a few months we were doing live shots for nearly every newscast, leaving our competition in the dust.

All that technical stuff about microwaves and cost of operation went right over my head. Al Buch and Pep Cooney had all that covered. I only cared about flying. It wasn't all sunshine-and-roses by any means, but our engineers did a great job and every time we had a glitch they were on it. Within a year our system was up and running and the ratings gap began to close. The helicopter and microwave cost about $500,000, plus around $120 dollars per flight hour: not cheap by any standard.

Early on I hadn't realized what a big deal this new microwave system was to broadcasting. It allowed me to do live reports of accidents, plane crashes, floods, drowning victims, searches and whatever else I could find.

While the struggle to be "first live" was going on between KOOL and KTAR, the actual first had already taken place at KTLA in California many years earlier.

Ed Sharpe, Director and Lead Archivist for the SMECC[1], relays, *"Sometime in the 1950s, CBS engineers placed a camera in a Bell*

---

[1] Southwest Museum Of Engineering, Communications and Computation

helicopter with a 100-foot-long cable running down to the camera chain equipment in a remote truck. Under the right conditions, this afforded a high perspective for the television viewers. It provided a great view, but was not really mobile.

KTLA-TV's chief engineer, John Silva, created the idea of a "Telecopter"—a flying TV studio—with a microwave link back to Mt. Wilson. He then convinced the station to spend $40,000 on equipment that might not even work. KTLA hired Richard Hart and his staff at National Helicopter Service & Engineering Company to supply the Bell 47-G2 and the aviation engineering expertise that would provide a stable platform for the equipment. Silva's challenge was to trim down the equipment to a manageable weight. The Bell G-2 was put on a trailer and stashed behind Richard Hart's house. Surrounded by trees, away from the prying eyes of the competition, they began assembling all the parts in strict secrecy.

On July 3, 1958, Silva and pilot Bob Gilbreath, vice-president of National Helicopter Service, took the first flight to test the equipment. The engineers on the ground radioed that they were not getting any video. While Gilbreath hovered, Silva stepped out onto the skid, unlatched the box holding the microwave transmitter, and discovered that one of the vacuum tubes was not functioning.

That evening Silva improved the insulation and cushioning of the box to protect the tubes from excessive heat and vibration. On July 4th they went up again. When Silva aimed the hand-held camera toward Hollywood homes, this time the excited engineers on the ground reported seeing the images."

Years later John Silva told Air & Space magazine, "I never thought about being a pioneer, all I ever wanted to do was get us there and get the picture—before the competition got it."

From that moment on, TV news was never the same.

Veteran KTLA reporter Stan Chambers recalls in his 2008 book, KTLA'S News at Ten, "The Telecopter became the envy of every news department in the country and it was many years before anyone was able to match it."

Even then, being first was everything.

Me, Bill Denney and Kent Dana chuckling over KOOL's "loyalty oath"

Around August 1979, my good friends Kent Dana and Bill Denny shocked the local news public when they left Channel 10 and joined me at 12. Kent had been a news anchor along with Bill Close at 10, and Bill Denney had been the sportscaster. They would be filling the same roles now at Channel 12. Their defection brightened my life, since we had always liked each other and enjoyed kidding around. And now I wasn't the only one who had "crossed the street" from 10 to 12, which eased my guilt a bit.

Kent remembers, *"Jerry was one of the most unique persons to ever work in the business. Very competitive, engaged, eager to learn, and just cocky enough to know he was the best helicopter pilot around. He was also fun-loving and brought a magnetic personality to the job that everyone enjoyed. He was the first to tell you that he was trained to be a pilot, not a journalist, yet nobody worked harder to get the story right and get it first."*

After that move, KOOL-TV asked their employees to sign a loyalty oath, promising not to leave and go to a competing station. That didn't go over well with their employees, and it was soon dropped, but now we had their attention.

Leatham, Gerczynski and Mell

In 1978 I started shooting photos for the Arizona Republic and the Mesa Tribune if they couldn't get pictures of a major news story any other way. I preferred to take their photographer up to shoot, but sometimes that just wasn't possible. My only stipulation was that if they used the photo it would be credited to "Skywatch" when I was at Channel 10 and then to "Sky 12" after I defected.

During my broadcasting career hundreds of my photos were used for every kind of news story, and many were front page.

My very close circle of friends included two professional photographers: Nyle Leatham and Tom Gerczynski. Between the two of them, I learned enough about shooting 35mm to get by (kind of like I did with a lot of things.) I know there is a saying "A little knowledge is a dangerous thing," but in my case it was necessary. I did a lot of flying with both of them and netted some incredible photos from all over the state, especially while on trips to the reservations with my favorite senator.

Nyle Leatham was the chief photographer for the Arizona Republic. I met him in the mid 1960s at a plane crash, took him up for a photo of the scene, and we became close friends over the years. This friend was a Mormon; a "Good Mormon" and family man. Whenever Nyle was around we cleaned up our language and showed this gentle man the respect he was due. He was a good sport and sometimes showed up with home-baked cookies.

Susan Sorg, (she was Susan Berry back then) who would later become my Sky-12 producer, remembers, *"Nyle was quite a bit older, with adult kids and eventually grandchildren, so he was a sort of the 'Dad' of Sky-12, and gave us encouragement when times were rocky. He was also the master of soundbites. No matter what the story was, if he was with us, we could always count on him for a succinct, almost poetic soundbite that said it all in 15 seconds. Nyle Leatham had a wicked, dry sense of humor and a chuckle I can remember 30 years later! Losing Nyle to liver cancer a few years ago was very hard on us all; we lost a member of our family. Each of us has our own, private 'Nyle' story. Thank God for our wonderful memories of him!"*

On the other hand, Tom Gerczynski reminded me of myself. He and I met at my friend Buzz's birthday party. He lived in a section of downtown Phoenix that was going through a change. The old neighborhoods that made up the Encanto Park District were being upgraded with restored or remodeled homes. Tom's home was a large two-story house that included two apartments.

It was in need of just about everything. Over the years I watched my friend refurbish that old place with the patience and skill of a master builder. Walls, floors, plumbing, electrical, and even cabinets—he did it all. One of the first things he installed was a super bad stereo system with two of the biggest bass speakers I have ever seen. The woofers, tweeters, and robust power supplies gave me one of the best "music moments" of my life.

As we sat on boxes at his place late one night, Tom introduced me to Pink Floyd and *The Dark Side of the Moon*. From that night on I was a devoted fan.

Tom was running his freelance photographer business from home, and he did a lot of work for our promotion department as well as for other stations. Tom and I both lived close to downtown and I enjoyed spending time watching him work. If I got a call ... off we went.

It took him about three years to complete that place and he turned it into a beautiful combination studio and home that today is one of the sharpest in the Encanto District.

Between Nyle, Tom, and the Channel 12 shooters, we photographed every out-of-town event I participated in. Today I have photos of nearly everything I have written about in my broadcasting career.

In the late 1970s, Tom introduced me to a man who referred to himself as a "starving artist." Ed Mell is an Arizona native who grew up loving to draw both mechanical and landscaping scenes. He spent two years at a junior college then majored in advertising and design at the Los Angeles Art Center of Design, graduating in 1967. He then spent two years in New York as an art director for a large advertising agency.

Yearning for the Southwest, the smell of cow pies, and blazing heat, he returned to Arizona and spent two years teaching art to children on the Hopi Reservation. It was here that he began developing a style that would earn him worldwide attention.

We took Ed with us on a photo flight in Sky-12 to the Hopi-Navajo reservations, where he got a look at the beauty of Arizona and Indian country from a different perspective. Ed weighed no more than 150 pounds; small enough to endure the back seat of a Hughes. He wore glasses and came off as a bit timid and unsure around the helicopter. He is such a likable guy with his dry sense of humor, that he became a favorite of the crew right away.

Ed recalls his impression of seeing the landscape from the air. *"With the helicopter, you not only saw the front of a rock form, but could explore the sides, the back, and finally perch on it like a bird. It was an aerial voyage that shaped—and continues to shape—a new visual perception of the plateau from top to bottom."*

Chapter 40

RTNDA Conference

In September of 1979, when Sky 12 had been in operation for a year, I got a call from Al Buch who was attending a RTNDA (Radio-Television News Directors Association) convention in Las Vegas. Al would be giving a briefing about our operation to several hundred news directors the following day, and he wanted me to fly to Vegas the next morning and display the helicopter. Since Bell Helicopters had a machine on display, Hughes did not want to be outdone and had offered to pay our expenses to fly in. We still had the only microwave system that could be tracked automatically. The system that Bell was showing off required a satellite truck to be underneath the helicopter and they both had to remain in one place or the satellite would lose their signal.

Hughes Helicopters and Tayburn Electronics had a display area, but no chopper hooked up to their system. Al needed me there by 2 p.m. for the seminar and told me I could land next to the Bell JetRanger in the parking lot at Caesars Palace.

The next morning John Bass and I were up early and headed out to Scottsdale Airport to have the helicopter, which we had now dubbed "the Dog," shined up for the Vegas adventure. I made arrangements to have a rental helicopter and pilot standby at the station. We would head for Vegas about 11:00. That would give me time to refuel at McCarron International airport then head over to Caesars Palace.

It was all going according to plan until I got a call over the two-way radio from the station advising me of a school bus accident just west of Prescott. I immediately turned north. It would be about 30 minutes out of our way, but there was no other option: the news came first. Anytime a school bus was involved, it was an automatic go until we heard if it was serious or minor. It took us 20 long minutes to get there. I always dreaded these kinds of calls, and I hoped this wasn't serious, but I had a plan if it was. I would first circle and John would shoot aerials, then if I could, I'd land and we'd get ground shots.

My luck—and that of all the kids—held, and I was relieved to find only a minor accident. The bus had been struck from the rear by a pickup truck whose driver was the only reported injury. The dozen or so kids were in a group, jumping up and down and waving as we circled overhead. I circled twice, then gave everyone a big wave before heading south, climbing as fast as I could. I needed to get back in touch with the station, beam the newly shot video to them, and get ready to do my regular weather report on the noon news. The assignment desk radioed that I would be live at the top of the newscast with anchorman Bill Stull and we would talk about the accident. Even though it was minor, Channel 12 had run a live crawl over regular programming when the call had come in. Now they would need to inform worried parents that everything was under control and no kids were injured.

I climbed to an altitude of 8,000 feet then leveled off and prepared to send my video of the accident back to the station. This required that John first rewind the recorder—located in the middle front seat—then push the forward button. When the video started to play on our TV monitor, mounted on the floor in front of the recorder, he would pause the recorder and turn on the microwave transmitter. I would then call ENG (Electronic News Gathering) on the two-way and let them know we were transmitting a signal.

I'd give them my compass bearing from the station, and advise them I was ready to transmit our video for them to record.

Channel 12 had two locations for the two-way radio. One was the assignment desk and the other was ENG, the engineering department. By remote control, the engineer would turn on the receiver—a large antenna on a nearby mountain—to tune us in. I had three antennas on the helicopter skid, and within 35 miles of the station, I could push a button to lower a small Omni antenna that allowed me to circle a scene and stay connected. If I was in a hurry I could use a forward or rear-shooting antenna that was good for 100 miles or better, but I had to fly in a straight line. Going west now, and behind schedule, we chose the rear shooting horn:

"Sky 12, calling ENG, over."

"This is ENG, go ahead Sky 12."

"ENG, I'm about 75 miles west by northwest, 8,000 feet and powered up."

At this point the engineer would fine tune the signal and when he was satisfied, he would advise me to roll the tape that was on freeze frame. We would then roll the video we had just shot, which was now being recorded for use on the noon news. When I was on the air and started talking about the accident, the control room director would roll the video. The TV viewer would see the accident and hear my voice. After about 30 seconds of the video the director would switch back to me and Bill Stull. It sounds complicated and I guess it was. All the helicopter pilot can do is turn the switch to ON to roll the tape. If it doesn't work, you try it again, and if it still doesn't work, you get back to the station as fast as you can and report the story from the studio. Or they dump it.

In this case, things worked just fine. At the top of the news I reported the story, armed with the basic facts that our assignment desk got from the sheriff's office. Ten minutes later Stull came to me again to do the weather. Everything went smoothly and we did it all at about 150 mph. Since Nevada is an hour behind us in time, we still made it to Vegas by 1 p.m.

We landed at McCarran, refueled, then headed to Caesars Palace. Las Vegas sparkles at night, but even in the bright light of day, the neon, marquees, traffic jams and people make Las Vegas a one-of-a-kind city.

As we circled the hotel I spotted the roped-off parking lot and saw there was lots of room. A Bell JetRanger and a Hughes 500 were already there, but that Hughes did not have the live capability we had. Competition between the two companies was as intense as within the TV industry. Al Buch stood in the middle of the parking lot, waving his arms and pointing to a white X that indicated my landing spot. Sky 12 was the only machine with a microwave system installed. I was about to find out how big a deal this new high-dollar contraption was to the helicopter and TV industry.

After I shut down and had a short visit with the helicopter reps, Al, John and I grabbed a quick lunch at a hot dog stand. As we stood there wolfing down our lunches, Al explained the plan. He'd be with a panel of experts who would discuss the new things happening in the broadcast industry. After a question-and-answer period, Al would invite anyone who was interested to go outside and see Sky 12. Sounded simple enough. All I would have to do was let anyone who showed up look at the helicopter, answer a few questions and then we could either fly home or stay the night. That was a no-brainer for me. I couldn't be out of there quickly enough to suit me. While others might have enjoyed a free night in Vegas, I wanted to get back home and back to my real work!

When we finished our hot dogs Al and I headed for the meeting, leaving John with the ship. I was surprised to learn the conference was being held in the showroom of Caesars. When we walked in I was stunned by the number of people in attendance. The showroom was nearly full and people were still coming in. Al told me to take a seat and that he would see me outside by Sky 12 afterward. As I looked around the showroom, I started feeling out of place. I was the only man in the crowd not wearing a jacket, or a white shirt and tie. The ladies were all dressed in business attire as well, and everyone carried a briefcase or notepad. There I sat: blue jeans, boots, gray sweater, and I really needed a haircut.

Onstage, the four experts sat at a long table facing the crowd, with a microphone in front of each one. A moderator gave the order of presentation: First was Jane Cohen, Vice President of the National Association of Broadcasters, Don Gale of KSL-TV, Reese Schonfeld, president of Ted Turner's new Cable News Network, and Al Buch of KPNX TV. Each expert discussed new changes and challenges to the broadcast industry.

The time came for Al Buch and his presentation on helicopter technology. He explained how the new microwave transmitter came into being by Tayburn Electronics, and what it did for Channel 12 in Phoenix. He then showed a 20-minute tape of Sky 12 doing a myriad of local breaking news bits, weather segments and stories of people being rescued from the tops of their cars during floods. It ended with a homicide suspect in a panel truck being chased by police through the streets of Phoenix, crashing into a bridge abutment and being taken into custody.

Al then told the audience about my flight from Phoenix that morning: how I was able to tape the school bus accident near Prescott, beam it back to the station, cover it live a few minutes later on the noon news, broadcast the weather 10 minutes later, all while on my way to Vegas. It was just a routine day in the life of the Sky 12 pilot, but to these TV bosses, it was their first time seeing the full capability of a TV news helicopter. The presentation was very effective. When the applause died down, Al introduced me and I got a standing ovation. He then invited those interested to see Sky 12 for themselves.

In the parking lot we were overwhelmed by the number of TV people who showed up. It was nearly three hours later before I was able to fire up Sky 12 and head for home. It had been an incredible experience for me, John and for Al. Newspaper and magazine articles would later say that we had stolen the show at the convention of broadcasters. And nobody cared that I was in jeans.

John had been able to shoot some video at the convention, which we beamed back during the two-hour flight back to Phoenix, while I did a live report on the six o'clock news. I refueled at Sky Harbor, checked to be sure the KOOL helicopter was on its perch, and returned to the station helipad. It had been a very good day.

Chapter 41

The Rains Came - January 1980

John and I sometimes worked around the clock. Our office was the cockpit of the Hughes 500, and we were always set up and ready to go. John kept the cameras and related gear in good working order. At the end of the day we topped off the fuel tanks and settled the bird on the rooftop helipad.

We tried to keep the ship as light as possible, so a small storage shed next to the helipad stowed extra equipment like oil, cleaning gear, scuba gear, medical bag, and survival equipment. When the helicopter was in service it was ready to travel and so were we.

John Bass was a big reason we were doing so well. He had the knowledge and experience that our operation needed to operate in this high-tech war. I understood just enough about cameras, microwaves, and people to get by. With John, I could be the helicopter pilot and he could be the technician.

In the early 1980s, heavy rains and flooding really put our operation to the test. We pulled people off the tops of their stalled cars, flew patients who were cut off from ground transportation to hospitals, and did whatever else was necessary. It was a time of desperation and uncertainty as the heavy rains—more rain than any of us had ever seen in Arizona—poured down on the Valley of the "Sun"—a title that didn't quite fit just then.

The rain in the mountains to the east and north of Phoenix was intense, filling up the watersheds and lakes to their capacity. When the water level got too high and threatened the integrity of the dams, the flood gates were opened, allowing the normally dry river beds to help carry the load. All of that water eventually filled the Salt River and flowed through the Phoenix metropolitan area.

In no time the water releases into the Salt River turned the usually dry riverbed into a raging torrent. In some places the width of the river spanned a quarter of a mile. Then the bridges connecting Tempe and Mesa to Phoenix began to wash away, dividing this huge urban area in half and causing traffic nightmares as drivers sought other routes.

For the next 10 days it rained nearly every day. By 6 a.m. we were over the river giving live reports to our early morning news watchers, showing the massive traffic backups as well as the flooding in many homes and businesses. All the law enforcement agencies were swamped with calls. The situation worsened as bridges over the Salt River were damaged and had to be closed. Finally, all that remained open to traffic were the bridges at Central Avenue and Interstate 10. The railroad bridge between Tempe and Phoenix was put into use to ease the load of pedestrians trying to get across the river.

The Salt River was just one of the problems. Most of Arizona was saturated, affecting every little town and community. There were detours and closed creek and river crossings all over the map.

In the northern part of the state the Arizona National Guard put their helicopters to work hauling food and medical supplies into the Navajo and Hopi Indian reservations, which had now turned into mud. Hay was dropped from the air to feed the livestock. It was a heartbreaking time for a lot of people, pets and livestock. In many areas, helicopters provided the only way in or out.

By 1980 Arizona had seen more than its share of so-called one-hundred-year floods. We had already experienced a couple of them during in the 1970s. Hurricanes on the West Coast turned into powerful monster storms by the time they reached Arizona. Between October 1977 and February 1980, seven regional floods occurred, and Phoenix was declared a disaster area three different times. There would be a total of 18 people dead before it stopped raining this time. More than 600 homes were destroyed or damaged and 6,000 residents had to be evacuated.

Susan: *"Jerry and John were working around the clock. They never complained—at least not that I heard. They were tired, stressed, and worn out, but still doing the job. I knew sometimes the flying itself was dangerous, and rescues only multiplied risks. It was obvious to me they were both running on empty a lot of the time. This was also a time when the whole newsroom was overworked, but we all put our hearts into it and did the job."*

John Bass: *"Our morning started at sunrise, shooting the overnight damage. We were live from the helicopter for all the news shows; 6 a.m., noon, and 6 p.m., weather permitting. For the 10 p.m. show Jerry would write a script, record it and I would edit a package together.*

"We flew over homes, fields, and dairy farms that were under water, and we sometimes stopped and did stories while farmers and residents tried hard to save their livestock and personal property before the rising water could take it. It was all very sad wherever we went."

Tempe police called me about two o'clock one morning. I was in the air in five minutes and at the scene within thirty. A father had picked up his son from the babysitter after having been out drinking. He went around the barrier, got caught in the rushing water, and the car started spinning around.

I landed next to the river where the fire truck was, then I jerked off the front doors of the helicopter and said I needed someone to help me. A fireman stepped up and I explained what he needed to do. I showed him how to stand on the skid and what to hold onto when I put the helicopter skid on the car. He was to grab the little boy first, shove him in the front seat of the helicopter, and then get the father if he could.

As we got close we could see the father sitting on top of the car holding onto his son. The car was starting to move and I knew we had to get them on this try, otherwise that car would be gone.

I put one skid on top of the car. This was much more difficult at night, since I had only my landing light and water was rushing by, spraying us and making visibility a problem. I had to really concentrate or I could lose sight of the car. Worse, vertigo could set in, in which case I'd have to abort the attempt and try again ... or crash.

The fireman grabbed the little boy and got him inside, then he grabbed the father. As soon as he had him, I lifted up, got back to shore and landed. By the time we looked back, the car was *gone!* There is no doubt that if I hadn't been there, it would have meant the death of that little boy and his dumb-ass father, who had irresponsibly driven around barricades into a raging river.

John and I had spent that whole day on the go, being dispatched by the newsroom or handling one emergency or another.

John Bass: *"One evening just before the five o'clock news, we got a call over the sheriff's emergency frequency requesting us to fly north of Phoenix to New River, a small community along Interstate 17. As we approached we saw sheriff and DPS units, but couldn't see any problem other than a closed bridge over Interstate 17 that had traffic backed up for miles. Jerry landed, jumped out and joined the deputies, who seemed worked up about something to the south of us. In a couple of minutes Jerry jumped back in, belted up and said, 'There's a mobile home about a half mile downstream that has been turned over and neighbors think people might be trapped inside.'*

"We popped off the ground, turned south and there it was—a huge 12-by-60-foot mobile home that had been turned on its side by the raging torrent. It had been carried about a hundred yards down the normally dry river bed, with the front door and windows exposed on top.

"Jerry said something like, 'I'm going to set you off right by the front door. If you can, open it and check inside for people or pets. I don't

have to tell you to be careful. If you should fall in the water look for a skid to grab onto. I'll be there!'

"'Are you crazy?' I yelled. Jerry just smiled and said, 'Here we go!'

"As I climbed out onto the skid, I looked down at the river rushing underneath us. Between that, the sound and vibration of the helicopter, and the fixed position of the trailer, my perception short-circuited. I felt an attack of vertigo and I started to lose it. I closed my eyes and took a moment to focus. When I looked up at Jerry, he gave me a reassuring look.

"I made up my mind that I was going to do this. But I was going to make every move count and take advantage of every handhold I could find. Jerry put the right skid of the helicopter down close to the front door of the trailer and I made my move, stepping off the skid onto the trailer. Then I went to a prone position, hanging on and scooting over to the door. I sensed the helicopter moving away as the downblast of wind and water from the rotors started to calm down.

"What had looked like a stable structure was actually bucking under me with strong rhythmic pounding from the river. I wanted to get this over with quickly. I tried the door and it was unlocked so I managed to get it open and laid flat. I leaned into the trailer and looked around. I could hear the dirty water lapping throughout, and could feel the trailer moving. It was much colder inside than it was outside. All I saw was floating furniture and debris—no people. I closed my eyes again to stave off the vertigo, and then took one last look. No people here, I declared to myself, then backed out and gave Jerry the signal to pick me up.

"I had a graceful technique for getting back aboard in a school yard, but not today. When the skid got close enough I reached up and grabbed it with my arms and legs. As Jerry pulled away from the trailer I managed to climb up and into my seat. When I got my headset on I told Jerry there was no one inside that I could see. He radioed the deputies with a 'Code 4,' meaning, 'Everything okay.' Yep. Just another day at the office."

Deputies later told us the mobile home only lasted another 15 minutes before it broke into pieces and disappeared. We also learned that Wally Athey, our chief photographer, had been on the bank and captured our adventure from start to finish with his camera.

Susan Sorg: *"That was the top story on NBC Nightly News. For nearly two weeks we had the lead story locally and many times nationally."*

John Bass on mobile home going downriver.

Chapter 42

Rescues and Chases

Shortly after that incident, we were getting ready to do a live insert (interrupt live programming for a "news bulletin") on the current flooding situation. I was looking off to the left for other air traffic when John hit me on the shoulder. Before even looking at him I saw the problem. A yellow warning light on the enunciator panel was lit up.

It was the engine chip-detector warning system. We both knew what it meant. This had happened a couple of times before, and both times it was a defective indicator. But you never know, and the risk is too great to not have it checked ASAP.

If the metal detector was working properly it meant the engine was making metal, indicating that something in the engine was coming apart.

John called the station and cancelled our live as we headed to ASI to have the problem looked at. Air Services International, which used to be Arizona Helicopters, was still run by my old friend Tug Wachs. He had built a large facility at the Scottsdale Airport industrial area and transformed Arizona Helicopters into a worldwide operation. There is no better feeling for a helicopter crew than knowing the people who work on your machine are competent and dedicated. We were about to put them to the test.

I landed on the ramp in front of the hangar and was met by Richard Dick, the maintenance manager. (We called him Dick Dick.) As he walked up to the idling helicopter I pointed at the flashing warning light. He nodded and headed back inside for a dolly to roll the machine into the hangar.

Scott Smith, Tug's right hand man, was very knowledgeable about helicopter operations and keeping the contracts coming in. He spent a lot of time traveling abroad, buying and selling helicopter parts and related equipment. When Sky 12 was being worked on I usually covered the station with one of ASI's machines.

John and I joined Scott in his office and talked about all the serious flooding going on and what we had seen, when Dick Dick walked in with the magnetic chip detector in his hand. He held it out for me to look at and I let out a groan. The magnet was full of little metal shavings, indicating that indeed, something was coming apart inside the engine. Technology is great, because back in the old days you didn't know there was a problem until the engine quit. Then it was too late.

"How soon can you get us back up?" I asked, knowing full well I wasn't going to like the answer.

"Three days, *if* I can use one of our spare engines," he said, looking straight at Scott, who shrugged his shoulders.

"I'll have to talk to Tug," Scott replied.

While Scott was talking to his boss I called *my* boss and told him the sad story. Al Buch didn't hesitate: "Do whatever you have to do and get that bird back in the air."

With all the flood stories going on, this was a bad time to be without a helicopter. I pleaded my case to Tug, and he assigned two mechanics to do an overnight engine change.

I asked John to stay and shoot video of the engine change for a story the following day. We needed to do a payback to Tug and what better way than to do a story on his aircraft maintenance people. John was exhausted, but did what I asked.

John: *"I wasn't thrilled about putting in another 24-hour day, but I stayed long enough that night to shoot them pulling out the old engine. I had enough to do a story so I spent a few hours sleeping in the lounge.*

"The next morning Jerry made the test flight shortly after 5 a.m. It went well and by 6:00 we were reporting live on the rain storm moving in once again from the west. Our mechanics were in the back seats. It's a good sign when your mechanics will ride along after a major fix."

ASI was our best friend when we had a problem. We stopped there nearly every day to let the mechanics look over our bird, refuel, wash, or just hang out and wait for something to chase. When the machine was due for a 100-hour inspection we took a couple days off. During the annual inspection, which took at least a week to 10 days, we would take our vacations if nothing big was going on.

Mountain Rescue

Late one afternoon we were sent out by the sheriff's office to find a glider which was reported missing somewhere in the Estrella mountains, 35 miles south of downtown Phoenix. Rising more than 4500 feet above the desert floor, this rugged range of mountains is very rocky and steep. A doctor in town for a conference had rented a glider from Estrella Airpark, a glider school located on the south end of the mountain range. He was overdue and presumed down.

John and I had just finished the 5 p.m. weather so we headed out to the Estrellas. It was a short flight and as we approached the south end of the mountain we spotted the glider right away. It was upside-down near the top, and we could see the pilot laying on a rock next to it. John started shooting video and caught the man waving his arms and pointing at his legs. They were both broken.

Wrecked glider and injured pilot

While I relayed to the sheriff's office what we had found, John fired up the microwave and advised the newsroom. The producer of the 5 p.m. newscast wanted a live report in two minutes and wanted to end the show with shots of the glider and victim.

With John holding the shot, I gave our viewers a quick update and promised more info at six. That done, we moved in closer to look over the terrain and find a place to land. There was no way to set the 'copter down. It was nearly 3,000 feet to the desert floor; much of that straight down. I reached down and took our portable radio out of its charger and handed it to John. We both knew what had to be done. We had done this before.

John Bass: *"It was an easy off to a large boulder about 75 feet below the glider. When I got to the man it was obvious he was in a lot of pain. He was shivering and cold so I took off my jacket and gloves and gave them to him, hoping to stave off shock that might set in. He told me he had caught a weak thermal going up, but got too close to the mountain and a downdraft drove him into the rocky cliffs. It's a miracle he survived. Jerry radioed that he had contacted the sheriff's office and they were sending a mountain rescue team, but it would take a couple of hours to get them to the base of the mountain. I asked him to be sure they* *brought heavy coats for us, along with food and water. It was starting to get dark and cold, and it was going to be a long night."*

There was nothing I could do until the rescue team got to the airpark. At the top of the six o'clock news I did an update on the rescue in progress. Then I landed at the glider airpark at the bottom of the mountain and shut down. I briefed deputies on the scene, then took off all the doors and removed unnecessary gear to get the ship as light as possible. By now it was nearly dark, there was no moon, and the winds were starting to kick up. The mountain range had turned black as coal and the crash site was on the west side of the mountain—the dark side: no city glare, no nothing.

The six climbers were from the Central Arizona Mountain Rescue Association. I had worked with them over the years and they were helicopter savvy. I explained the situation and told them I had a place to set a skid down just below the downed glider and they would have to climb up about 75 feet. When everyone was finally ready we loaded all the ropes and rappelling gear in the stokes litter, which was crossways in the back seat area. One man sat in the right front seat and the other man stood on the skid holding the litter with one hand and hanging on to a handle especially made for climbers and divers. He also had a safety line, just in case.

I took them up two at a time. The last trip was the hardest because it was now dark and the winds were gusting up the mountain at around 15-20 mph. The sheriff's dispatcher told me an Air Force rescue helicopter was circling just east of our position and was waiting for a signal from me to move in and winch the injured doctor out. That was great news to me. But they had a problem.

John Bass: *"I heard the Air Force pilot tell the dispatcher that, because of low fuel and increasing winds, they only had 10 minutes to stay on the scene. If the rescuers could get the stretcher to a suitable area they would make one try, and if they couldn't get him they would be back at daylight. I told the team leader we needed to get the stretcher down to that big rock we had all come in on. It was the only level spot we knew of.*

"Everyone jumped up, grabbed the litter and down we went as fast as we could. It was miserable and treacherous. The terrain was rocky and steep, with cactus and bushes in the most inconvenient places. We all had a hold on the stretcher and when one of us stumbled the others kept the stretcher stable. We were almost there when we heard the big Bell approaching. Just as we got to the large rock outcropping, the Huey was about 50 feet above us. Now the downblast was hitting us full force. One of the team grabbed the cable as it came down and they began tying off a four-point connection to the litter. Seconds later the stretcher was being reeled up to the hovering Huey. I saw the winch operator reach out, grab the litter and pull it in.

"I looked at the upturned faces of the team as they watched the stretcher disappear into the bird above. This was a happy group of mountain climbers. You just cannot imagine the stress these guys go through under such dangerous conditions."

I had tried to hold my landing light on the rock with the climbers so the Air Force chopper could see it, but the squirrely winds buffeted me around like a ping pong ball. I talked to the pilot on our VHF radio. Once he had the area in sight I backed off and watched the show. I was glad they showed up because there was no way I could have gotten the doctor off that black mountain with the present conditions.

I tried one approach, but as soon as I descended behind the mountain and lost the city lights I could feel the vertigo starting, so I turned away from the mountain. Vertigo is one of the scariest things for a pilot to experience. I knew I was finished until sunrise. I hated leaving John and that team up there, but it was too dangerous.

John Bass: "As we started down the mountain I was number four in line. I was a rookie in climbing, and glad to be with the pros. The only mishap occurred as I was easing my way down a rock chute and then had to drop six feet to the ground below. My left foot landed okay, but my right foot hit a rock. I pitched over and felt something in my ankle pop, then I rolled into a cactus. Helping hands got me up and we took an assessment. My ankle did hurt and the cactus in my butt stung like *crazy, but I felt okay to go on. I did not want to be the reason for another rescue.*

"For the next several hours we made our way slowly down. It was just starting to get light when we finally reached the base of the mountain. Sheriff's deputies treated us to some cold coffee, and then I heard the familiar buzz of Sky 12. My ride had arrived."

When I landed and saw John walking toward me I could not believe it was him. He was always clean and neat, but not this morning. He looked like he had been to hell and back. His clothes were tattered, his boots were skinned up and he looked tired, but he still had a smile on his face. I got him back to the station and he was interviewed by our morning anchor, Bill Stull. After that we had a good breakfast at the hotel across the street. Then he went straight home to face the music.

Sometimes it's many years before the outcome of a story is known. We were covering the police chase of a white pickup truck that was speeding and driving erratically on a highway. Finally the truck went through a fence and crashed in the desert. The police officer pulled up behind, jumped out with gun raised, and yelled for the driver to get out. We were all shocked when the driver turned out to be a 12-year-old boy. When I reported the story on the air, I made the comment, "let's hope there is help somewhere out there for this young man."

Truck after it crashed through fence

We rarely hear what happens to the people in the stories we report, and that was the case here, until 33 years later. In July 2013, I received a Facebook post from the boy—now a 45-year-old man

—telling me that after a long struggle, his life had finally turned around. He wrote, *"After things had gone well for awhile my dad and I were working on a project together when he looked over at me and said 'I guess good old Jerry Foster was right: there was help out there for you.' I would add hope as well."*

I was extremely touched that he contacted me after so many years to let me know he had found that help. I'm a sucker for happy endings.

Chapter 43

Vicki: Early 1980

The morning started just like any other: up about seven, shower, shave, a can of V-8 juice and out the door. Nothing going on that I knew of, so I didn't mind waiting for the elevator. Since I was on the top floor it usually took a couple of minutes for it to get to me. If I was under the gun and in a hurry it could be a very long wait. It didn't do a bit of good to dance around, stand on one foot or scream. I had tried it all. The elevator would get there when it got there.

When the doors finally opened I was happy to see it empty. We stopped on the sixth floor to pick up a resident I did not know, then stopped on the third floor … and that's when my life changed.

As the doors opened, two women stepped in. I recognized one as a tenant, but the other was a stunning stranger. She had blonde shoulder-length hair, combed straight, with bangs above beautiful eyes. I tried not to stare, but I was smitten. I could almost hear Roberta Flack singing "The First Time Ever I Saw Your Face."

When the door closed and the elevator descended, I now hoped it would stop on the next floor and give me time to come up with a plan. But we went straight to the ground floor and I had nothing. As the two women stepped off the elevator, the young blonde turned her lovely head and wished us a nice day.

After I finished the noon news I headed back to my apartment and straight to the manager's office. I found out the third floor tenant was Trula McCarty and the blonde was her daughter, Vicki, who had just relocated from California and was staying with her mother until she found a place of her own. Using my investigative reporter technique, I also learned that she was single. And in my book, she was a "10!"

The building manager was also a cool dude. He said he let her know I would like an introduction, and then suggested that if he arranged a meeting, I could take him up in the helicopter.

I looked him straight in the eye and told him I would give him a ride he would never forget. I was happy to do it, because our manager was also well connected with all the tenants and went out of his way to keep people off the top floor unless they were expected. I very seldom had a visitor and really appreciated the privacy that management and the tenants gave me.

I don't want to give the impression that I was a playboy, because that just wasn't the case. I dated from time to time, but really wasn't looking for a serious relationship. At least I didn't think I was, but when I saw Vicki all that changed.

I had been divorced from Dianna for nearly three years, and my social life was not nearly as active as some people thought. I have always been somewhat shy on a one-to-one basis and it takes me a little time to get to know a person. I would never commit to a date until I knew where the lady lived. If it was out of my 20-minute zone, it was a no go. And just as importantly, I didn't have a lot of off-duty time, so I enjoyed being home alone and having quiet time whenever I could.

I occasionally double-dated with my friend Kent Dana who was also single. He was great at fixing me up with his date's friends. We had good times water skiing at Saguaro Lake and hanging out at my penthouse. Kent found his "10" on one of our double dates at my place. He was dating Janet, a real sweet little blonde who was as pure as the driven snow, until Kent came along. After they married I had to start looking out for myself.

Kent & Janet

I was still hurting for Dianna and the kids. I knew I had to let it go, and because she was now remarried and living in Sacramento, the cold, hard reality was … it was over. I had the girls in the summer for two or three weeks and loved every minute of it, but I still missed their mother.

That evening the building manager knocked on my door. He handed me a piece of paper and I handed him a twenty-dollar bill. Now I had all the info I needed to introduce myself. I took my time, thought about it, looked at my schedule and, Bingo! There it was; the TV Emmy Awards was Saturday evening. I needed a date and I knew just who I wanted to take.

I realized that Saturday was only two days away and she might already have a date, so there was no time to think about it. I had to call now. I reminded myself not to sound desperate. I was actually a bit insecure and almost talked myself out of calling, but then I thought about my friends Kent and Janet Dana, and how I'd like to have my own special girl. Yep, Vicki could stand toe-to-toe with anyone I knew. I sucked it up and made the call.

I dialed her number. Silence. Dang! I was so nervous I was misdialing. I went through the process again, and was just about to hang up when a pleasant voice answered, "Trula's residence, this is Vicki speaking." Her friendliness relaxed me right away.

I introduced myself as a helicopter pilot who lived in the building and had seen her this morning. She laughed that off and came straight at me. "Jerry, I've been here for a week and have watched the news every day. My mother loves you!"

That went a lot better than I thought it would, and we talked for a good while. I finally asked her about being my date for a Saturday evening dress-up function and dinner afterward. She accepted and I was on a roll!

The event was held at a large theatre in Scottsdale. I did well that year, taking an Emmy in the "Spot News" category, which is a big one for me and the station, as well as awards from the Arizona Press Club. Channel 12 won several awards, beating out our rivals at Channel 10. That was huge.

After the awards portion was over I couldn't wait to get out of there. Back in my car, I asked Vicki where she would like to have dinner. She left it up to me, so I told her that I would really rather just pick up a hamburger somewhere and get away from the crowd. She liked that so we stopped at a Dairy Queen and picked up burgers, French fries and milkshakes. We ate in the car, laughed, talked, and began getting to know each other.

After dinner we drove back to my apartment building and sat out by the pool until about 2 a.m. I learned that Vicki was in the process of getting a divorce and had come to Phoenix to start a new life. She had grown up in Missouri with three sisters, and a brother who had been killed in Vietnam. Her mother, Trula, had moved to Phoenix when her marriage had ended, as Vicki had, to start a new life.

The evening ended with a kiss outside her mother's condo, and I went to my place knowing that I had found someone I was excited about. Everything seemed to click and I knew that—like my friends Kent and Janet—it was love at first sight.

The next morning the station called me about an overturned tanker truck on I-17 near Cordes Junction, some 60 miles north of Phoenix. I called Vicki and she readily agreed to meet me downstairs. We were off on our first flight.

I saw her nearly every day for two weeks until she found an apartment in north Phoenix ... out of my 20-minute range. That slowed things down and for about a month we only dated on weekends or when she visited her mother. I soon found a landing spot in an open area near her apartment where I could pick her up, so we were able to see more of each other without violating my 20-minute rule. But we could both see where this was heading.

We decided it would save us both a lot of time and despair if we just teamed up and enjoyed the incredible life I was leading.

We both understood the priorities and she understood that Sky 12 was a lifestyle, not just a job.

One Sunday morning we flew out to my Mom's house for breakfast. She knew about Vicki, but had yet to meet her. Mom had just retired from Guggy's and had married an optometrist, Dr. Ray Jacquet, who I learned to like and respect. He was never like a father, but he was always very kind and never got between Mom and me. They lived about a block from Mesa Lutheran Hospital, which had a large helipad big enough for three choppers. Mom's phone number was on file at the hospital, and for years that was how I visited her on holidays or for family gatherings. I'd land at the hospital and make the five-minute walk to their house.

Mom and Ray liked Vicki immediately, though in private Mom worried about what effect this pretty, blue-eyed blonde would have on me. It didn't take long for her to see the positive change in my life. So far I had everyone's approval except that of my kids, and that would come when they met her.

Vicki moved into my penthouse and immediately set about organizing it. She had a knack for decorating, and I was happy to have her put her own elegant touch on our home. She made it more comfortable, using calming shades of gold and brown. One wall had shelves full of my model helicopters and various renditions of Sky 12, including drawings from school children.

My Emmy awards were displayed along with various other plaques and honors I'd received over the years. It was all the "stuff" I'd had all along, but now it was organized and displayed in a way that was uncluttered and easy to look at.

Vicki also helped to organize my life. She scheduled the various events, school visits, Santa deliveries, and everything else I was called upon to do on a regular basis.

About a year and a half after we'd met, we decided to make it permanent. We didn't want any fuss, so a friend who was an osteopathic surgeon flew us to Las Vegas in his plane. We were married that day and flew home the following day.

Vicki was truly a partner and an important member of what would soon become the Sky 12 Team.

Chapter 44

Chris Greicius: Make-a-Wish Foundation

In 1980 I was emotionally moved by an experience with a little seven-year-old boy. Chris Greicius was the sweetest kid I'd ever met, in spite of his terminal illness. He knew that he was sick with leukemia and would soon be moving to heaven. A U.S. Customs agent found out through a friend of his that Chris was terminally ill and had always dreamed of being a motorcycle policeman. The agent told his story to a group of friends from the Arizona Department of Public Safety, who were determined to make the boy's dream come true.

A highway patrolman in a cruiser picked Chris up at home and drove him to a nearby field where he boarded DPS helicopter Ranger 27. He was flown on a tour around the valley and then to DPS headquarters where he was made an honorary highway patrolman, complete with full uniform, badge, toy gun and hat. He also took a special test for motorcycle duty and was awarded his motorcycle wings and helmet. Chris quickly became a local celebrity and for the rest of his short life he was a happy guy.

When Chris died soon afterward, a service was held during which the church was packed and overflowing with mourners. DPS motorcycles, police cruisers and fire trucks filled the parking lot. After the service in Arizona, Chris was taken to Illinois for burial, escorted by two DPS officers. He was buried in full uniform, along with his DPS hat and helmet, an Air Rescue cap and a Sky 12 cap.

His life was short, but his legacy will go on forever. Those of us who helped make his wish come true knew there were other kids out there just like Chris, who had wishes of their own, but not the time or the opportunity to fulfill them. People with the know-how organized what would become this little boy's legacy. My crew and I put together a video that was shown to civic organizations to help raise funds. This effort would launch the gift which would eventually be shared around the world: The Chris Greicius Make-a-Wish Foundation. It is now the largest non-profit wish-granting organization in the world. In Arizona alone, more than four thousand wishes have been granted to terminally ill children since 1980. I am honored to have been part of such a wonderful experience.

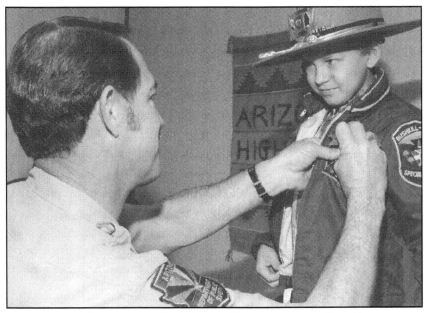

DPS Officer pinning the badge on Chris's custom-made uniform

Chapter 45

Karen Key: Channel 10 Sky Queen

Late in 1980, KOOL made a change in pilots. Bill Dimond was out and a foxy, good-looking lady by the name of Karen Key was hired. We all knew why they had hired the pretty blonde with the vivacious smile. KOOL had us in their crosshairs and I'll admit, they sure had our attention. About all we could do was wait, watch and see.

John Bass: *"It was a good tactical move by Channel 10 to try and steal away Jerry's thunder as the helicopter news leader. Would it work? There were the promos, newspaper ads, billboards, and all their promotion department's hype about the new girl in town: all the usual stuff that a station feeling threatened would do to counter the dynamo that Channel 12 was building."*

I had to admit that Karen had a good reporting style. She started off doing "fluff" stories and would report them live from the helicopter if they could hold a signal long enough. I sensed she didn't have much of a flying technique. Sometimes she'd show up at a story after John and I had arrived and we'd watch her take-offs and landings. She would pop off the ground with the nose high, clear the building, then drop the nose and scamper away. John would look at me and shrug his shoulders. Neither of us thought she had much flying experience.

Shortly after she started at KOOL, the sheriff's office called us one Saturday afternoon to search for a pilot flying a hang glider. He was overdue and had not been seen for several hours. The desert was rocky and full of cactus, sand washes and rolling hills. I was preparing to land on a dirt road when John said, "There it is!" and pointed off to the right.

Sure enough, the glider had run into a large Saguaro cactus. We landed near the scene and John jumped out to check the victim, who had been killed instantly. By now the deputy had driven his four-wheel-drive unit up to us. We talked a few minutes and were ready to leave when we heard the thumping of a Bell JetRanger.

It was Channel 10's new "Sky Flower," Karen Key. Her approach was aiming for a sand wash just below us, and looked good. But as she came to a hover, she snapped the nose around to the right to face us, causing her tail rotor to cut through the top of a five-foot-high mesquite tree. Had she been another foot lower, that could have been her "Waterloo." We all have had bad days and close calls, but it's embarrassing when other people are watching, *especially* your competition. I felt sorry for her and left before she could join us.

From then on we watched her very closely. A few weeks later, with a little more time and experience, she looked like she was getting comfortable. When we met over the scene of a breaking story we'd stay in contact on our aircraft radios, keeping our conversations short and to the point.

I got a lot of kidding about her from everyone; kind of a, "Ha ha, how you doing with the little blonde?"

"What little blonde?" I would reply, "Oh, her!" I always laughed it off and tried to take the high road on that subject, but underneath it all I thought differently. She was sharp, good looking, and had a good TV personality. She was doing what she needed to do to make KOOL very happy and *me* very concerned.

Now that KOOL had their auto tracker working pretty well, we started meeting over the same stories to do "lives." When we were close together my signal didn't seem as strong, so I talked to one of our engineers who told me why. I didn't understand a lot of what he was saying, but I heard enough for the wicked side of my brain to cause me to smile.

In January 1981, John and I flew to Las Vegas to display Sky 12 at the annual Helicopter Convention. It was always my favorite out-of-town event. We were the guests of Hughes Aircraft, and Karen Key was there as the guest of Bell Helicopters. I was getting a little tired of her being at "my" events. From a distance, I watched her interact with different people and groups and could see that she was very popular. I still had not met her face-to-face. John Bass remembers that first meeting.

"She came strolling up to me wearing a bright red, form-fitting flight suit and introduced herself. We chatted a few minutes, but I was very careful not to give away anything. My loyalty to my station's goals outweighed anything she could offer. She wanted to know about Jerry — what he was like — and about our operation. I tried to be friendly and professional, but was glad when Jerry walked up."

I came around a corner and there she was with John Bass. I coolly said, "Hey there, I didn't know you two knew each other," winking at Karen like I had discovered something. We all made some small talk, laughed politely and didn't really say much until John excused himself … and there we were; our first one-on-one meeting.

Karen liked to talk and I liked to listen, so we hit it off in the beginning, until she started telling me that she was looking at something on the outskirts of Phoenix that she was thinking of buying. From her description it sounded expensive. After she told me the part about having a little heli-pad next to her master bedroom patio and pool … I was kind of in a stupor. Did she know that Vicki was looking for a place where I could keep the helicopter at home? Or was she fishing? I played dumb and asked why she would want to do that.

Her answer surprised me. She said, "I would like to be friends with you Jerry, but I want you to know that I was brought in by KOOL to kick your butt and that is what I intend to do."

After that statement I just shrugged my shoulders, turned and walked away.

John Bass: *"Once we were back in Phoenix the war really heated up. One afternoon we had just finished doing a live shot for the evening news north of downtown when we heard Karen on their frequency trying to get a live signal up for a grass fire out west of Phoenix. We had some time to kill since we had another weather shot at the bottom of the news hour, so Jerry headed her way. After determining the little fire was nearly out, we set up an orbit for our weather shot west of the downtown to show the setting sun's red glow against the glass high-rise buildings of Phoenix. We always looked for the artistic stuff when shooting weather segments, and this would be a great shot."*

The moment I had waited for since the helicopter convention had come. I was set up just right for a little fun. When the Channel 10 producer cued Karen two minutes to live, I asked John to power up our camera and give me a shot of the buildings, in case they used it earlier than planned. All the while we were watching Channel 10 on our TV monitor and waiting for Karen to go live. I only had two minutes until my live, so the moon and the stars were aligned and we had plenty of time to pull this off.

John Bass: *"We watched as Karen's producer counted her down to live, and there she was on our little TV. She barely got out a sentence when Jerry powered up our microwave transmitter. We both watched with a smile as her signal started to break up and then ZAP! My weather shot came up on Channel 10. I knew instantly what he had done!*

"Her signal degraded as their receiver's dish became confused by our more powerful transmitter, since we were nearly over the Channel 10 station. Her producer's voice became more and more frantic as their signal faded away and Jerry's smiling face came into view when I swung the camera around to him.

"Channel 10 switched back to their anchor, Bill Close, but not fast enough to block a clear shot of Jerry. We could hear Karen and her producer over their two-way radio. Suffice to say they were not happy"

"Paybacks are hell," someone once said. That little prank started a series of discussions between our general manager and theirs. It ended with a meeting between me and my boss, Al Buch.

Our meeting ended with my promise not to do that again ... purposely ... and then we all had a big laugh.

So I had to tone it down. Another time John and I were in Northeast Arizona looking for a plane crash in the White Mountains. The crash was two days old and the bodies had been removed, but bad weather was keeping investigators out. We were sneaking in to get aerial shots, but had a tough time finding the crash. After about an hour of searching, we finally found it, circled and shot video of the scene. There were spotty low clouds, but we caught a short burst of sunshine on our last orbit and then headed for home.

Fifteen minutes later we spotted Karen's white JetRanger coming toward us. I switched over to the air-to-air frequency and called her.

"Hey, Karen, how's your day," I asked.

She came back all business. "Did you locate that aircraft?"

"Negative," I lied. "It's snowing so hard we got chased out of the area. Good luck. We're headed to something else. See ya!"

I told John that "something else" would make her turn around: I hoped.

She bought it. That night we did a live report using the video to show the crash in bright sunlight. Karen didn't have a story that evening.

Our whole crew turned up the heat and we were never beat to a breaking story by Channel 10. Karen lived in Scottsdale and usually took weekends off. I was always close to my machine. But I tried to keep tabs on that white JetRanger as well. Vicki, listening to a scanner at home, would call me during the day to let me know when Karen took off or landed downtown. Susan was always tuned to a scanner at the station, and John did the same. We had many advantages and used them all.

We continued to meet occasionally out on the circuit when we both attended the same events. At one charity dinner we both served meals and smiled at each other. She was beginning to mellow out a bit and I was once again feeling a little friendlier toward her. Our ratings showed that Channel 10 was no longer

Working together for charity

the powerhouse—we were. What we were doing was working.

Bill Leverton was still at Channel 10, and he remembers Karen as being overly confident in her abilities.

"Karen Key was a beautiful woman; very pleasant and easy to get along with compared to any news helicopter pilot I've known. But she just ticked off Jerry; he didn't like the competition. Why it ever bothered him is a mystery to me. No one was ever going to be competition to him.

"She knew she was good-looking and she knew she was in an elite position. She was a reasonably competent pilot in clear weather and good circumstances. But she didn't have many flying hours or much experience. She once landed at Grand Canyon airport, one of the busiest in Arizona, without talking to the tower. She badly needed experience and a heavy dose of common sense.

"She was well-liked, and when off-duty she socialized with other staff and occasionally with me and Bonnie. There were rumors she drank too much, but I never saw it. She wanted desperately to be as good as—or better than—Jerry Foster. It just wasn't going to be, so she pushed things, got behind the power curve and kept pushing. And every pilot knows that can't be good.

"Station managers, news directors, and people who should have been in charge of guys like Jerry Foster and the pilots who followed him at KOOL—Bill Dimond, Karen Key and Len Clements—just didn't have any idea what they had nor how to manage it. Consequently, the aforementioned pilots were more than a little arrogant and got away with a lot of stuff they never could today. It was the "wild and wooly west" of news helicopter reporting.

"I don't say this unkindly, that's just the way they were. They may have been intimidated by the education and intelligence of the news staff around them, and compensated with short fuses and 'in your face'

belligerence. They were 'Stars' and you didn't tread on them or their shadows."

In my case, I think Bill nailed it when he talked about intimidation, short fuses, education, and "in your face" confrontations. I *was* intimidated by the people in broadcasting. They were smarter and better educated than any group I had ever been exposed to. Everyone had a defined job, guidelines to go by and mentors to watch and learn from: everyone except the helicopter pilots, who, like me, came into broadcasting cold.

It was a new profession, so we had to create our own job description. I knew how to fly and not much else; but there I was, the new kid in the newsroom, making more money and getting more attention than my educated co-workers.

As for the "in-your-face" belligerence, it was a defense mechanism to hide my ignorance or weaknesses ... and maybe even some demons. I worked hard to keep my private and social life to myself, since I felt I had too much to hide and too much to lose.

What I feared most was losing control of the helicopter. It was bought solely for news, but some people at Channel 12 thought it should be used for other purposes. To avoid that, I was determined to do a great job and make that helicopter indispensable to the news department. When the pressure was on, or someone got in my face, I felt threatened and lost my temper. Later I would regret my outburst, and was quick to apologize, but the damage was already done.

By 1981 our operation was doing quite well ... and so was Karen over at Channel 10. That summer the Dog was in the shop getting a required inspection and would be down for a week, so Vicki and I took a few days off and drove to Lake Powell. That's when Karen made a huge blunder.

The Maricopa County Sheriff's Office needed a helicopter to look for a drowning victim in the Salt River. Karen was called and responded about an hour later, just before dark. When she landed, deputies smelled alcohol on her breath and refused to ride with her. They sent her home. A similar encounter a few weeks before that had aroused suspicions and now it was confirmed. It was the beginning of the end for her. Shortly after the second incident she gave notice at Channel 10 and took a pilot–reporter job in Denver. She left quietly, and the reason was never made public, giving her a chance to start fresh somewhere else.

Her replacement was a guy named Bruce Erion from Georgia. His first day on the job, he called me to introduce himself. We had a very pleasant conversation and agreed to sit down and talk as soon as possible. He let me know he was the new guy in town and would appreciate any advice I could give him.

We got together for lunch a few days later at Saguaro Lake. He turned out to be a great guy and we got along very well. Anytime we met on a story we worked together to safely get the shots and information we needed. If either of us had a problem the other helped out. I took him fuel once when he misjudged his flight time, and he brought me a mechanic and a new fuel igniter when mine failed in a remote area. We were friends and it felt good.

LIVE NEWS COVERAGE

Live news coverage is an essential at KOOL News 10. Bruce Erion our Pilot/Reporter brings you live news reports from around the Valley and Arizona. Watch him at 5, 6 & 10PM.

5, 6 & 10PM

Bruce Erion promo

Bruce was a graduate of Harvard and a former company pilot for Bell Helicopter. He was a sharp and good-looking man, probably the first of the "educated pilots" that would one day replace guys like me.

Chapter 46

The Team Grows

Susan Sorg

During that period another woman entered my life. Cute, petite Susan Sorg, who had been an intern at Channel 12 shortly after I was hired, was being considered for the receptionist job in the newsroom.

I first met Susan when she was a dispatcher for the sheriff's office. After starting with Channel 12, she began helping me by writing my weather information. I was hoping to sell Al Buch on letting her work full time with John and me and the Sky-12 operation. But that didn't happen right away.

Susan: *"I interned at KTAR the fall of 1979, graduated from college and started full-time as the newsroom receptionist in January 1980. It was a few years before I was Sky 12's producer, but I could already read Jerry like a book. I knew what kind of day he was going to have by how he looked as he walked in the door or talked on the two-way radio. It may sound like he was high maintenance and sometimes he was, but I always knew two things: If he was needed, he'd go and be the consummate professional, flying as though he was part of the machine; and, he was a very high-strung, emotional guy who tried to carry it all inside. He kept his compassion for victims hidden, but it sometimes brought me close to tears."*

My doing the weather began as a joke between Al Buch and me. I told him I thought the weekend newscasts were being ignored and my crew and I wanted to improve them. He suggested I do the weather from the helicopter at 6 p.m. and do the 10 p.m. weather from the studio.

The weather report from the helicopter usually went smoothly, but when I had to do the weather on the set that was a whole different drama. I was out of my element and it showed. Having lived only in the western part of the country all my life, I didn't have a clue where to find Iowa or Kansas on a blank outline of the USA. I started watching the pros on other stations and found an ally who would help me for years to come ... and no one else would ever know.

Stu Tracey was the meteorologist for Channel 5, at that time

Stu Tracey

an independent station that showed mostly children's shows, old movies, and reruns of old TV series like Red Skelton or the Rifleman. They always had their newscasts half an hour before ours at 6 and 10 p.m. I could watch Stu's weather segments a few minutes before I had to do mine. I would make notes and draw a little weather map on a card, showing cold fronts, rain, snow or whatever. I memorized as much as I could. If Stu was wrong, so was I.

In addition to watching Stu, I watched Willard Scott on the Today Show to get a briefing on national weather for the noon and 5 p.m. shows. One would think with all that professional help over the years I would have turned out to be a pretty good weatherman, but it never happened. I am documented proof that anyone can do the weather on TV.

When the big cameras swung around to me in the studio, and those two little red lights came on, it was "showtime" for the next three minutes. At first I had real maps with magnetic numbers and fronts on them, which I pointed to. Then TV technology improved and I stood in front of a blank green screen. The folks at home see a weather map over that screen, but I had to look at a TV monitor just out of camera range, pretending I was looking at the map everyone else could see. I'd look at that out of the corner of my eye, glancing back and forth to the blank wall and then at the camera. It's tricky and takes some getting used to.

My attempt at reporting the weather

In my mind, I envisioned millions of people from all walks of life out there just waiting for me to make a mistake. Then the telephone switchboard would light up, "Tell that dumbo weatherman he blew it," or "... mispronounced it" or whatever. Sometimes I would get tongue-tied, stutter or even forget what I was talking about. I put on a show that even stressed out my mother, who never missed a chance to see her son on TV.

This was the point in my career when my lack of education really showed. My grammar, pronunciations and sentence structure aggravated and amused a lot of viewers. When Susan came on board with me, she took a lot of weight off my shoulders.

Susan: *"During those early years I learned how to write weather and news stories for Jerry. I tried to adapt to his style and use phrases and words that he was comfortable with. My job was to rip the paper off the US Weather teletype and translate it into "people speak." I also had the duty of putting up the magnetic numbers for temperatures and weather systems on the national and local weather boards. When we eventually went to computer-generated images I had a crash course in using the new system, which took a lot more time."*

When Karl Eller sold KTAR to Gannett Broadcasting it didn't seem to have any effect on my operation. According to Pep and Al, it didn't mean a thing as far as the helicopter was concerned, and Gannett had plans to add 'copters to all their stations. Still, it was an indicator as to where local stations were headed. The days of local ownership were numbered, according to what was happening around the country.

Susan: *"After a year of operating in the "cave," we were about to shake off KTAR and become KPNX. Gannett had purchased the station,* *meaning KTAR radio left the building, making a lot of space available. So it was time for renovation of the newsroom. We had to move into temporary quarters on the ground floor near the news sets. It was a miserable mess for a few months, but when it was finished it was worth the wait. The newsroom took up nearly three quarters of the building. It was very spacious, with cubicles and six edit bays. The live ENG (Electronic News Gathering) was awesome, and soon I learned how to bring in Jerry's live signal.*

"Jerry and John made a great team and I was so proud to be a part of it. There was nothing more satisfying than helping people in need. When they actually saved a life it put them on a wonderful natural high. But when a rescue attempt turned into a recovery, Jerry took those times pretty hard. He stayed to himself in the newsroom and was never one of "the boys." When he blew off steam over the radio or powered down his live signal without a word after his spot was done, eyes in the newsroom would swing to me, asking, 'What the...?' I'd just shrug and roll my eyes; it was just Jerry being Jerry, but we all knew he could save the day if needed."

No doubt, we were on a roll. Every day was a new adventure. Some days we were at a school to judge a contest or to show the kids our mechanical hummingbird. Or we visited service clubs of all kinds, as long as they had a place for us to land. We only turned down a request if we were already scheduled for that time slot. We hauled Santa Clauses, Easter Bunnies, turkeys, pumpkins, Uncle Sam, politicians, celebrities, homecoming kings and queens, and as many of our viewers as we could.

I made it a priority to take fellow employees and their families up in Sky 12 when possible, especially producers and engineers, giving them a look at the many other things that were going on during live reports.

Susan: *"Because of the variety of annual events we covered, we never needed a calendar in Sky 12 to tell us what month it was. January meant Scottsdale Parada Del Sol and rodeo. The Helicopter Association International had their annual convention in February. March meant spring rains, and all sorts of weather issues; spring flowers on nice days,* *or floods on the bad ones. That was also the month of the Jaycees Rodeo of Rodeos. April was the Ahwatukee Easter Parade, and April and May were also when the desert temperatures started rising, and we were doing stories about snakes, scorpions, and the dangers of the desert."*

Every day was different. If we weren't sent out on a spot news story, we generally came up with a feature of some kind. If we had a school visit we would shoot film of the kids waving at the camera, which would usually be shown at the very end of a newscast while credits were being run. We knew all the kids at that school and their parents would be watching and waiting to see the wavers. If the producer was long on time at the end of the show it worked out great, but if time was short, the wavers weren't used. When that happened I could visualize the disappointment in all those little faces watching from home. But back then, as is still the case today, "Breaking news changes everything" in a TV newsroom.

Lake Patrol

During the hot months in Phoenix a popular pastime is getting on the lakes and rivers in boats or inner tubes. In the hot summer months this was the place to be when temperatures soared to over 110 degrees. It was also a dangerous place to be because of drug and alcohol use. We were there most every weekend from Memorial Day through Labor Day, but we were working; the plan being to rescue or recover those who found themselves in trouble in the water. But even the best laid plans sometimes take an unexpected turn.

One Sunday afternoon John and I were working with the sheriff's Lake Patrol looking for a drowning victim in the Salt River. There were hundreds of tubers, many towing ice chests filled with beer, floating down a seven-mile stretch of river designated a recreation area.

On this day we had a drowning victim, but the river was so crowded with tubes, ice chests, and people, that we couldn't see the river bottom from our helicopter. We decided to stick around while John shot video of all the campers and tubers, and toward the end of the day we would pick up the search again. We were heading for the sheriff's aid station when over the emergency channel we heard that a rape had just occurred about a mile upriver and the suspect was riding a black and grey horse.

Within two minutes we had him in sight and five minutes later we had directed deputies to him. We landed about 100 feet away, and John jumped out with his camera while I frictioned the controls and reduced the rpm to flight idle. I had just started walking toward them when all hell broke loose.

John Bass: *"I was rolling tape while the deputies were talking to the suspect, who denied doing anything wrong. They decided to take him back to the scene, and as they started walking, the guy took off running, with deputies right behind in hot pursuit. He was a big guy with long blond hair, wearing shorts and a tank top. I stayed close behind, even with a 20-pound camera and recorder. In less than a minute I heard, felt, and saw the helicopter come right over our heads."*

I had run back to the helicopter and jumped in. While buckling in I twisted the throttle and when it hit 100% I was off the ground and on the way. The deputies and John had just cleared a grove of small trees and were about 30 yards behind the big guy, who was intent on getting away until I got next to him, then forced him into the river where he made a big splash.

John Bass: *"I got there in time to see him floundering in the shallows of the river, trying to get out. I held a tight shot on him as the skids of Sky 12 dropped into frame, holding the suspect where he had fallen until he was taken into custody. He was identified by the victim and later convicted of kidnapping and sexual assault.*

"We found the drowning victim later that day, then beamed both stories back to the station and did a live report for the six o'clock evening news. Never a dull moment."

April 1979

On this April day, which coincided with spring break for many schools, a group of students from the University of Arizona had come up to Phoenix for a boating trip sponsored by the Student Union Activities Board and a couple of sporting businesses. A group of girls would be navigating rubber boats down the normally calm Salt River. But the recent floodwaters filled the lake, causing excess water to spill over the 15-foot diversion dam into the river. When the unpowered boats went over the dam they were caught in a trough at its base and couldn't move forward. Boats and people were all being tossed about.

Two DPS officers had taken the call for help and were headed to the river in Ranger 27, the department's Bell LongRanger. Officer Clarence Forbey recalls, *"We got a call from the Gila County Sheriff's Office requesting help for several college students on the Salt River. The problem location was named as an old diversion dam, several miles upstream from Roosevelt Lake. Pilot Tom Armstrong and I headed in that direction, and as we flew over Saguaro Lake we noticed the Channel 12 helicopter sitting on the pad.*

Tom Armstrong: *The DPS Bell LongRanger was a stretch version of the Bell JetRanger. It was a bigger and heavier aircraft, but with the same horsepower as the smaller JetRanger. On takeoff and landing we had to inject water alcohol to cool the engine turbine and keep us from over-temping the engine. With our gear and crew of two, that didn't give us much of a margin. When we saw Sky 12 on the helipad at the lake we figured we needed to get Jerry Foster along for help. We circled a couple of times to get his attention, and when Jerry came on the radio we described our predicament.*

Forbey: *We radioed Jerry and told him what we were headed for and asked if he would consider helping, as he had always been eager to assist with any type of rescue or law enforcement mission.*

When they contacted me, I agreed to head up to the diversion dam. I had rope with me that I thought would be long enough to reach the victims. When I flew over the trough, I saw two boats trapped there; one with a single female and the other with three or four people. The fuller boat seemed fairly stable, but the one with the lone female was being thrashed about violently. I landed on the shore near Ranger 27 to discuss the plan for their rescue.

Armstrong: *We landed and Clarence went over to Sky 12 to confer with Jerry. When he returned we decided that he would do the* *rescue from Sky 12. It was small and stronger. Ranger 27 just wasn't powerful enough to accomplish the task. I was to get in the air and guide Sky 12 over the scene.*

Forbey: *For us to use the Bell helicopter, we would have had to land and remove the doors and all the equipment before we could begin a rescue. Jerry offered the use of his aircraft, and it was ready, so I decided to give it a try, using his rope. We hoped the girl alone in the boat could grab the line and we could lift her to shore, then return to do the same for those in the second boat.*

As we hovered over the water at the dam, the main rotor of Jerry's aircraft was about two feet from the elevated side of the dam, and the rope was too short to reach the girl below. We backed out from the dam, as the rotor wash was tossing the girl's boat around more violently than the waters were. I climbed out onto the right skid of Jerry's aircraft to have a greater reach of the rope. I was now sitting on the skid, holding on with my crossed legs and one hand.

Armstrong: *I took a position upstream of the dam. Even facing into the wind and alone in the aircraft, I was struggling to keep the engine cool. Jerry, with Clarence sitting on the skid, hovered downwind of the wave, trying to reach the girls. But the wave rose so high they couldn't get into the trough. The boats were being pounded against the dam and the girls were struggling to hang on. Jerry tried again. This time the girl who was alone in a boat slipped out of it.*

My heart sank. I told Jerry we lost her. A few seconds later I saw something pop up downstream, behind Sky 12. This girl was the only one not wearing a life jacket, but she did have one tied to her, and that's what I saw pop up. The girl was still underwater. I directed Jerry downstream over the life jacket.

Forbey: *As I sat on the skid of the helicopter, I had no radio communication either with the DPS helicopter or with Jerry in his aircraft. As the female started floating downstream face down in the flood waters, I attempted to give Jerry hand signals, but could not determine if he was reading them, or if he could do what I wanted done.*

With Tom Armstrong's guidance I could see the problem, and lowered the machine as close to the water as I dared. When my skids touched water I had only about 30 inches clearance between the water and the belly of the aircraft. But I managed to get low enough to allow Forbey to reach the girl.

Forbey: *From my knowledge of helicopter control, I knew this was not only dangerous, but could very easily put an end to both the helicopter and the people attached to it. But as the helicopter dipped further into the water, the girl became within reach and I managed to grab one arm and pull her toward me, trying to get her onto the skid.*

Armstrong: *Clarence lay prone on the skid, with his left arm crooked around the cross tube, signaling Jerry to try to reach the girl. When Jerry dipped his skids into the water Clarence grabbed the girl by her wrist. Jerry then lifted up until the girl was completely out of the water. I was telling Jerry to hurry towards shore.*

When I realized Clarence had her, I lifted up from the water and approached the shore. I saw that I couldn't land at that particular spot, however, and began to back away, gliding about 12 feet above the shore.

Forbey: *I had a tenuous hold on the girl, with one hand holding onto hers, while clinging to the skid with my legs and other arm. When Jerry backed away from the shore, I couldn't hold the weight any longer, and dropped the girl about 10 feet into shallow water.*

DPS Officer Clarence Forbey pulling girl from water and getting her to shore.

Armstrong: *I didn't think Clarence would be able to hold the dead weight of the girl very long. As they reached the shallow water near the shore, he released her. I was amazed that he held on to her for so long, with only one hand.*

There were plenty of spectators—other boaters, tubers and swimmers—who had watched this all play out. Several got to the girl and carried her to shore.

I found another place to land and shut down. Clarence ran to the girl and began CPR while one of the bystanders was attempting mouth-to-mouth resuscitation. The person, while well-intentioned, wasn't well-trained in the procedure, so I took over and we got her breathing again.

Forbey: *This initial breathing—as always—began with coughing up of water and stomach content. This was into Jerry's face and mouth, but he never missed a beat, just spit out the vomit and continued his mouth-to-mouth until the girl was conscious and becoming alert.*

Armstrong: *I landed on shore and rigged the helicopter for the Medevac. Clarence and I loaded the young girl into Ranger 27 and flew her to the hospital for evaluation.*

The girls who had been in the other boat were all wearing life jackets, but still caught in the trough. The kayakers persuaded them to jump from their boat, which they did. Then the kayakers guided the floating girls to shore, where they were all deemed to be in good shape, just exhausted.

Forbey: *I learned after the rescue that while I was on the skid without any way of communicating, Tom Armstrong was telling Jerry via radio what I was seeing, what I was signaling, and how to get me into position to grab the floating body.*

This rescue was a fantastic joint effort on the part of the Sky 12 helicopter and pilot, and the outstanding abilities of both pilots to use small, limited power helicopters to perform a rescue that would seem impossible without the use of a boat and ground crew. Tom and Jerry were given awards by the DPS Director, and I received the first DPS award for valor. The experience of working with two extremely talented pilots, who risked not only their equipment, but their own lives, to save another person, was a solemn and sincere honor, and I'm proud to be associated with them.

It was indeed a joint effort. Without Tom Armstrong guiding me to where I needed to be, and without Clarence Forbey bravely hanging on to the skid and reaching into the water to grab and hold onto the girl, she most likely would not have survived.

Chapter 47

Ups and Downs of Publicity

We had a lot of successes that first year. The live stuff from the helicopter was on most of our newscasts every day. Hardly a weekend passed in the winter months without being called out on a search of some kind. It could be a downed or missing aircraft, a lost child, a manhunt or maybe an overdue couple on a picnic somewhere. The calls were endless but something the whole crew thrived on.

The days were long and sometimes one day led into the next. We always carried a sleeping bag in the baggage compartment for those nights when we just had to land and take a break. Sometimes we stayed in beautiful remote areas. Other times we huddled in the helicopter wrapped up with everything we had until bad weather or low visibility cleared out.

During the sweltering hot summer months if we were on assignment near a lake or river, we knew how to cool off. The Verde River just northeast of the Phoenix valley was one of my favorite spots: there weren't many people and the river was clean and clear. Sometimes we would just lay in the moving water for a few minutes and we were ready to go again.

The Phoenix valley is ringed by mountains in all directions with smaller hills scattered around. At night, with the urban areas lit, it is a beautiful sight, as those little mountains show up as black holes. Camelback Mountain is the best known of the many in the Valley, and it is dotted with expensive homes built on and around it. At one time that's where the rich and powerful lived. Some homes are built into the rocks and one is a replica of an old-style English castle.

I had my favorite places for different things, and I discovered a spot up on the Scottsdale Mountains that was perfect for spending a night on call. The east side of the mountain stands a little over two-thousand feet above the valley. The summit consists of huge sandstone boulders that, over the years, have been carved into cave-like shelters by wind and rain. I would land in an open spot between three huge boulders and shut the machine down. I had my sleeping bag, air mattress, the station's and sheriff's portable radios, and a backpack full of necessary items like binoculars, lights, snacks, and water. I'd walk about 100 feet to a vertical cliff where a small cave had been formed out of the rocks.

From my rock condo I could see the whole Valley of the Sun, from the beautiful Superstition Mountains in the east, to South Mountain and west to the White Tank Mountains. On a clear night I could see the glow of Tucson lights some 120 miles away to the southeast. It was awesome, peaceful and quiet: the perfect place to stop for a rest and take a little snooze.

365

"Nobody knows where you are, how near or how far ... Shine on you crazy diamonds"
　　　　　　Shine On Crazy Diamond - Pink Floyd

Despite my celebrity status and the colorful labels pinned on me—cocky, hot rod, show off, and cowboy, to cite some of the nicer ones—I was comfortable with what I was doing, and I really enjoyed the lifestyle. Now with Vicki keeping our schedule up to date, we usually made it to the right place at the right time.

I started becoming much more comfortable making personal appearances. I got used to signing autographs for kids and anyone else who asked. In the earlier days I had been embarrassed about being thought of as a celebrity, and felt uncomfortable attending awards dinners or public events. I hated being called a hero, although I was happy to see that our work was appreciated.

The attention and praise was exactly what the TV station owners wanted and expected. Sure, I was a cowboy and a show off and I was cocky, because that's what I was being paid the big bucks to be.

The promotion department at Channel 12 made a big deal of our operation just like Channel 10 had done all my years with them. They attributed titles and slogans to me: "The fastest newsman in town," "He's on call to Arizona 24 hours a day," and more.

Every time I went out on a search and found the victim, dead or alive, I got credit on the air and the promotion department made the most of it. They were in business to make money and what they were doing was working. My bosses were happy, but it was all very embarrassing to me, and I knew many of my co-workers didn't like it either.

A lot of people thought the "Jerry Foster heroic stuff" was bullshit. It really wasn't heroic. It was the fact that I was there, and I had the tools to do the job. I would be a jerk and a misfit if I *didn't* do it. It was "damned if you do, and damned if you don't." We did our best and to hell with the journalism critics who said, "You're a newsman, not an ambulance chaser." And they were right: I was a newsman *and* a trained rescue pilot. *Thank you!*

366

I had many critics, and sometimes they nailed me to the wall. For example, New Times, a Phoenix underground paper, did a story about an eagle's nest that was being disturbed by low-flying aircraft on the Salt River. An unidentified "eagle watcher" told the reporter that Sky 12 was seen hovering a few feet above the nest while taking pictures, and the helicopter's downwash blew one of the babies out of the nest. Hogwash! That's what I say!

Even the state's largest newspapers had one reporter assigned as a TV critic, who watched our operation and had a field day with everything from noise complaints and FAA encounters to my grammar and sentence structure. This particular reporter enjoyed labeling me with such titles as "a boorish egomaniac" and "a chauffeur-lapdog for politicians and businessmen," and was overly critical of my misuse of the English language. He seemed to miss the point that I was hired to be a helicopter pilot, not a journalist. I had never claimed to have been trained in journalism, nor to even have a college degree. To his credit, many years later he admitted he had been a young man trying to make a name for himself, and may have been too harsh in his criticism.

I had my share of printed rumors and wild stories, and was often treated more like a celebrity than a news pilot. On the other hand, I got a lot of good press in the form of feature stories and visits to rural areas, where the local reporters were always happy to see us fly in for a community event or a school visit. Whenever possible I took the local media up to shoot film of the story they were covering.

Chapter 48

A New Photographer

Chuck Emmert

John Bass had been with me just over a year when he decided he was ready to slow down and move on. Since he and Phyllis had been married he'd spent more time in the helicopter than at home. We'd had a great run together and built a lifelong bond.

My new partner was a photographer on our staff. He had been with the station for a couple of years after graduating from ASU with a degree in journalism. Chuck Emmert was born and raised on a farm in Ohio. Tall and lanky, he weighed about 160 pounds. Chuck was about to have the adventure of his life and was more than willing and able to take over where John had left off. He was a quick learner and it wasn't long before he was part of my family.

Chuck: *"I was just six months out of ASU and was working the evening shift and weekends at Channel 12. That's how I got to know Jerry. Sometimes he'd grab me and we'd take off. When it came time to switch photographers, he asked me to come on board, and I agreed. I didn't really know what I was getting into. When I took the job with him I was living in Tempe, but moving to Phoenix. That first night I was packing my stuff when we got a call. I rushed downtown but Jerry was gone. That's when I realized that with him, being first really was everything. He waited for no one."*

Vicki, Chuck and I had all learned to scuba dive, which added a whole new dimension to our team. Previously, when we were called to a drowning, we could often fly around and see the victim in shallow water. But we had to wait for the sheriff's divers to arrive. Sometimes, depending on the location, it would be hours before they could get there. If the family was there the waiting was awful for them and awkward for the rest of us.

After we learned to dive, we could be on the scene quickly with three divers. We had dive gear attached to the helicopters, so we were ready whenever a situation required divers. Once we started diving the recovery could take place much faster.

One of the diver's posse rules was that no solo diving was permitted. It was just too dangerous in the dark lakes and canals. But if I could spot the body from the air, we made the recovery, saving volunteer divers from being called out.

The sheriff's dive posse didn't really like what we were doing. Most of them had been recovering victims for many years and we came along and upset the apple cart. It was progress and a new way of doing things, but it took away from what they were proud of doing.

Diving to the bottom of lakes as dark as an unlit closet, was a stressful experience. Feel around ... that's a bush ... make contact ... three tugs on the rope to signal that you were ready to surface. When I made a recovery I'd get the body up and hand it over to someone else, then go back and get the camera to film them bringing it out.

There was one instance when I was covering a drowning in a canal. While flying overhead I spotted the body and landed next to canal. The body started floating downstream, and the deputies were yelling, "We're going to lose it!" None of the

Hanging on to foot of drowning victim

369

deputies were taking off their guns or shoes, so I jumped in and grabbed it. The body was near the surface, so I held on to the foot to get it near the bank so others could pull it out.

To give Chuck and Vicki some experience, we talked Al Buch into letting us take a week off and fly to the Bahamas. Al told us to come back with a five-part series. Chuck took video equipment and rented an underwater camera. We spent six days on *The Dragon Lady*, a 70-foot dive boat, and learned all about deep-water diving. We learned more about diving in the process, and all felt more comfortable with that aspect of our jobs.

An Eerie Sense - February 13, 1982

On a cold Saturday morning Chuck and I were headed north to cover the search for an airplane that had been missing for nearly a week. This was our fourth day of searching, but for some reason I had a feeling that today was the day it would be found.

The missing plane was piloted by Jimmy Gray from Flagstaff. He had flown his Cessna 210 to Phoenix the previous Sunday to pick up his secretary, Dianne Sanders, her husband and their daughter, who were returning home from a trip.

The flight looked good for Jimmy. When he got to the Flagstaff airport it was cold, but the skies were clear. This time of year Flagstaff was covered by a beautiful blanket of snow. The flight would be a cinch for the veteran pilot who had flown the route dozens of times and knew the terrain well.

Jimmy made the trip to Phoenix with no problem and met his friends as planned. Before departing Phoenix, he received a weather briefing from a commuter airline pilot, telling him that Flagstaff was now experiencing low ceilings and moderate snow fall. Jimmy may have had trouble believing that, since he had just departed the same area two hours ago and the weather was perfect. Why he didn't check with the local weather station is unknown. Whatever the reason, it would be a fatal decision. Jimmy and his passengers departed Phoenix and just disappeared.

If the airplane had landed or crashed, time would be critical, as temperatures would plummet to below zero at night. For the next few days the search effort was hampered by a new storm dumping large amounts of snow in the high country, making flying impossible. The search had to be called off twice because of bad weather. To make matters worse, the airplane was white and would blend in with the terrain.

Since the time the plane was reported missing, the Coconino County Sheriff's Office, DPS Air Rescue, the Civil Air Patrol and volunteer search and rescue units, working around the bad weather, had spent 3,000 man-hours covering the flight route between Phoenix and Flagstaff, a relatively short distance of 140 miles.

Almost a week later, on February 13, the skies cleared. Chuck and I landed at the Sedona airport command post. The little airstrip sat high atop a mesa overlooking the town of Sedona. There were at least a dozen Civil Air Patrol planes as well as helicopters from the National Guard and DPS. We were just in time for a morning briefing by Coconino County Sheriff Joe Richards. Areas were assigned for air and ground crews and the massive search was launched.

Chuck and I decided that since there were so many people involved we would just stay out of the way and keep our eyes and ears open. We would build our story with interviews and video. Since today was Saturday, our weekend producer, Rod Haberer, wanted a story at the top of the 6 p.m. broadcast. News was scarce on the weekends, so he told us to stretch out our story as long as we could.

A few minutes after the briefing I was approached by a young man wearing a heavy jacket and a backpack. He was carrying a rifle and was accompanied by a beautiful, white, one-eyed dog he called Sharee.

The man identified himself as Gabe St. John and claimed to be a wilderness guide. He told me he and Sharee had worked the wilderness areas of Arizona for years. Gabe said he knew exactly where the airplane was and had talked to the sheriff and other searchers, but no one believed him. I asked him where he thought it was and he turned and pointed north to a large, high mesa known as Wilson's Mountain, less than three miles from the airport. Not really a mountain, it's a large plateau covered with huge meadows surrounded by forests. The plateau was bounded by deep and beautiful red canyons. We had been all over that area and so had other aircraft.

Gabe St. John and Sharee

Chuck Emmert remembers, *"We had been searching around the Sedona area for the past three days looking for the lost aircraft. There was heavy snow covering the red rocks and that made finding a white aircraft all the more difficult. It was tedious work. Jerry and I had searched, using a grid pattern to thoroughly cover our assigned area. The terrain north of Sedona is high desert, stretching as far as the eye can see, with 12-foot tall pinion trees, their branches spread out wide and nearly touching the ground. Heavy snow had fallen since the airplane disappeared and that sure didn't help.*

"The bright sunlight reflecting on white snow made it difficult for us to focus. We both wore sunglasses, but sometimes it was hard just to keep our eyes open. We were looking for anything that might stand out: a reflection from a piece of cockpit windshield, a piece of metal, or a red stripe along a wing or fuselage. Even if something caught our eye for a second we would have to circle back and have another look.

"We searched flat land and steep canyon walls, creek beds and deep arroyos barely wide enough to let sunlight in. At the same time, I was shooting tape of different areas to be used when we popped up and did live cut-in reports for the station. We also closely monitored the search frequency in case someone found the aircraft and we could rush in and capture the story.

372

"During the search, Jerry seemed driven—as though it was <u>his</u> family missing. He always said that a family cannot even start the grieving process until a loved one's body is found. I felt the same way. That was the down side of our job."

Gabe told me he was a psychic, which surprised me. How many times had I heard about psychics and people talking with the dead? *Mumbo jumbo,* I thought to myself. No wonder Sheriff Richards had turned him down. I also sent him packing and he politely took Sharee and walked away. I felt bad seeing the disappointment on his face, but I thought it best to let him go.

About an hour later Chuck and I were back at Sky 12 preparing to go up and have a look. I had been thinking about that psychic and couldn't get him and his dog off my mind. Maybe Chuck and I would have a look at that plateau. As we were getting in the helicopter a man walked up and identified himself as the father of Gabe St. John, and asked if he could speak to me before I fired up. He seemed so genuine and sincere that I got back out and shook hands with him. I saw Gabe and Sharee standing a short distance away.

Mr. St. John told me that his son had a gift. He said Gabe had been here every day of the search and no one would give him a chance, thinking he only wanted attention. As we stood there and talked, I knew he had me. How many times had I asked for someone to give me a chance? Mr. St. John told me that Gabe and his dog spent a lot of time in the mountains and they would be just fine. They had supplies and everything they needed to stay a while, if they could just get up there. So I agreed to take them.

I looked to where Gabe was standing and waved him over. When he reached me I told him I would take him and his dog up to Wilson Mountain and drop them off wherever he wanted. From what I could tell, Gabe was a clean-cut young man around 20 years old, and I believed he really thought that airplane was up there. It was a dilemma, because he had been turned down by the sheriff and others. If he got lost up there and we had to search for him, I would be toast. But something made me do it.

Chuck: *I was starting to think we would not find this plane until the spring thaw when the snow melted away. That's when Jerry told me he was going up again, but this time I would stay on the ground. He was taking this guy and his dog up to Wilson Mountain and dropping them off. I gave him a second look. We had never taken a dog up. I thought this to be a last ditch effort to try everything."*

Chuck and I briefed Gabe on how to unload himself and Sharee if rocks or deep snow forced me to keep the machine at a low hover. We practiced a couple of times to make sure he understood the procedure. The elevation would be over 7,000 feet on the plateau and Sky 12 was loaded with fuel, so Chuck would stay behind and I would come right back and get him.

I got on the radio and told the command post what I was doing. The only response I got was a terse 10-4, which in police vernacular means neither yes nor no, just that they understood. I knew they wouldn't be happy, but I if I didn't do this and the aircraft was later found on Wilson's Mountain, I would kick myself. My track record for searches over the years was pretty good. There is risk in every search and I knew this was risky.

Once in the air it only took a couple of minutes to reach the vertical red cliffs that jutted straight up for nearly 3,000 feet. After reaching the top we leveled off on a wide plateau that ran for miles with a stand of trees to our right. When I asked Gabe where he wanted to go, he pointed and shouted, "In the middle of that huge meadow, about a quarter-mile from the trees."

The snow was about two feet deep and seemed solid after I set all the weight on the ground. Gabe asked me to tell the command post he would send up a flare when he located the plane. I gave him my best smile and wished him good luck. As I departed into a gentle wind and turned back to Sedona, I noticed Gabe heading the way we had just come. I thought that was strange, but I headed for the cliffs to descend into the airport.

Just as I crossed over the plateau and headed down, I caught a split-second glimpse of something in the trees that shouldn't have been there: the airplane standing on its nose. I couldn't believe what I had just seen. I started to call the command post, but since I had some doubt, I called Chuck on his portable company radio and told him to jump in when I landed; that we needed to check something. My heart was pounding like a bass drum.

Airplane barely visible at left center

Chuck says: "I sat back at the airport cooling my heels until I heard Jerry returning. He called me on the two-way and told me to come right out and get in when he landed; he wouldn't be shutting down the engine. I could tell by his voice that something was up. When I climbed in and put on my headset he said, 'I think I might have seen it.'

"My mind started racing and I knew Jerry wouldn't have said that if he wasn't pretty sure. I made certain my camera and recorder were on and working. As we cleared the cliff Jerry told me we were getting close. Once over the plateau, we came to a stand of trees. Jerry pointed and said, 'There it is!'

"He banked the helicopter into a tight right turn to give me my first glimpse. It took a moment for it to sink in. The airplane was on its side with one wing sticking up in the air like the dorsal fin of a dolphin cutting through the water. My heart was pounding. While we were elated to find the missing aircraft, we were incredibly sad for the people on board, and their families.

"Jerry said he would drop me a short distance from the crash and go back to the command post for more help. As I waded through snow, the helicopter noise faded away. It was so quiet I could feel my ears ring. It was eerie being so close to the downed aircraft, and I said a silent prayer for the victims on board. Jerry and I had been through this before. We'd had to cover many of these terrible accidents, and we always spared our viewers and the victim's families the gruesome images, even though *they would be burned in our memories. It wasn't until later that Jerry told me about the role that Gabe St. John and his dog played in finding the wreck."*

After finding the aircraft, my biggest surprise came when I looked over into the meadow and saw Gabe and his dog heading straight for me. There were no tracks anywhere around him and he still had a quarter-mile to go. Was that why he was headed back the way we came? I could now believe he was somehow tracking that airplane with a power I still do not understand.

I got on the radio and notified command we had located the airplane on Wilson Mountain and there were no survivors that we could see. I landed, picked up a deputy and returned to the scene. When the deputy saw Chuck on the ground he became agitated and told me I should not have left him at the scene until someone from law enforcement had arrived.

With all the tension and stress I had built up over the long search, I blew my stack and told him how stupid he sounded. After I calmed down I pointed out that I did that because I was full of fuel and at 7,000 feet I was only able to carry one person. I did what I needed to do. Nothing more was said, but I'm not sure he ever understood.

I felt so bad for Jimmy Gray and his passengers. He was one of the most experienced bad-weather pilots I ever knew. He had been an Air Force pilot for 24 years and had been flying over and around these mountains for many years. But he'd made a deadly error in judgment, which we see all too often in bad weather.

As we lifted off to head for home I saw Gabe St. John about 100 yards away, working his way toward the crash scene just as Sheriff Joe Richards was landing in a DPS Ranger. I called the pilot of Ranger 28 and asked if he would be sure Gabe and his one-eyed Sharee got a ride home. They assured me they would take care of him.

I will never forget the words from Gabe St. John at the Sedona airport. "Jerry, I know where that airplane is."

Do I believe in psychics and all that mumbo jumbo? Yep, now I'm a believer!

Chapter 49

Sunflower Crash - March 18, 1982

I woke up that morning and knew it was going to be a long and miserable day. I looked out my window towards the Channel 12 helipad, but the low clouds and rain obscured my view of the downtown buildings. A nasty cold front was forecast to move through Arizona today and tomorrow. That meant misery for some, while for others it was the kind of lazy day to stay inside and enjoy the change.

I was glad for a light schedule; the noon weather report, then the short flight to Sun City for a speaking engagement with some retired folks. Our normally mild winters, with sunshine and warm temperatures, are a huge draw for what we fondly refer to as "snowbirds," those who come from all over the country to escape their cold environments.

I enjoyed a peaceful morning and got to the station around 10 a.m. Rain was still coming down, but the clouds had lifted enough that I could fly if needed. Chuck Emmert had already been up to check the Dog, and Susan was getting my weather report together just in case we had to suddenly blast off to a breaking story. Chuck and I each did pre-flights once every morning. That way we knew the helicopter and camera equipment were always ready to go.

Because of the bad weather, the noon news producer wanted me in the air to shoot a live opening with shots of the Valley, after which I would throw it to anchorman Bill Stull. Since I would already be up, I would do the weather report later in the show. I could do my last update at the bottom of the newscast, then land in the parking lot of the Sun City restaurant for my speaking gig.

That was our plan, which of course was always subject to change; and change it did.

I had just started the engine and turned on the radios when we heard traffic coming across the sheriff's frequency about a plane crash.

As Chuck Emmert remembers it:

"We knew something was going on, but didn't know exactly what. The skies were overcast with low clouds and rain in Phoenix, so we knew that north and east in the higher elevations would be worse. We also knew that most of the time, first reports of an overdue aircraft meant it had already landed at some airport to wait out the weather and had just failed to notify the FAA. Being careful not to alert our competition, Jerry called the station on the two-way to advise them we were on the frequency and preparing for take-off. He then called the station on a new cellular phone that had been installed in the chopper the week before. Cell phones were new to us and provided a link that was totally private. Jerry advised the station we would head east until we heard if it was a valid call.

We lifted off from our downtown pad heading east toward Fountain Hills. The weather was exactly as advertised: gusty winds, low clouds and sheets of freezing rain. Then we heard over the sheriff frequency that a twin-engine Cessna with seven people on board had disappeared from FAA radar and was presumed down somewhere in the high desert about 60 miles northeast of Phoenix.

As we headed farther north, Jerry was able to contact the highway patrol helicopter on a frequency that was unlikely to be heard by our competition back in Phoenix. Ranger 27 was somewhere ahead of us and had more details than we did. They told us the Cessna was loaded with seven people: five prisoners and two guards, one of whom was also the pilot. Ranger 27 advised us they were flying over the Beeline Highway and had to land a couple of times because of the low clouds, gusty winds and sheets of freezing rain. Not good! They reported just passing the Saguaro Lake turn-off on the Beeline Highway, where they were picking up a faint signal from a crash locater beacon. After hearing that, Jerry and I looked at each other and knew we would have to give it a try."

The Ranger 27 pilot, Ellery Kramer, was a long-time friend of mine. He and I had flown together at Arizona Helicopters and he had been assigned with me to the AMES project. His partner—and paramedic on this flight—was Mike McArthur. Both men were military vets and knew their business.

This was the kind of mission I loved, as it was challenging for me and the Dog. It was what I had been trained to do and what this machine was built to do. A helicopter is capable of slowing down to a walk if necessary, and there had been several of those occasions.

The clouds were moving across the ground so fast that one minute there was a mile of visibility and the next minute we couldn't see 50 feet. I stayed directly over the highway just enough to see the ground, and several times we had to come to a hover and wait for the clouds to blow by. We could see creosote bushes whipping around like palm trees in a hurricane. It was spooky.

As we continued east the clouds began lifting to a ceiling of around 200 feet—enough for us to see Sycamore Creek bridge about a mile away. By now our VHF radio was picking up the emergency beacon—a warbling sound like an electronic siren— coming from the crashed Cessna. The rain was turning into snow and it was miserably cold.

As I landed behind Ranger 27, Ellery radioed us to keep the helicopter running. His crash locater needle was pointing directly south of us, and as soon as the snow shower passed we would start a search.

According to FAA regulations, all aircraft flown more than 25 miles from their home base must be equipped with an Emergency Locater Beacon. On impact, the beacon is activated on the VHF Emergency frequency (121.5). Without that to guide us, we would have no idea which way to go in this situation. Sky 12 could pick up the beacon, but had no directional indicator. Ranger 27 had a tracking needle which pointed in the general direction of the crashed airplane.

We all felt helpless as we listened to that continuous warbling tone in its plea for help. We knew there were seven people out there and we really didn't believe there would be any survivors. To sit and wait for the weather to clear was torture.

After a few minutes the falling snow cleared enough so we could take off to the south. Ranger 27 went a little east and we went a little west to cover more ground and keep a safe separation from each other. The terrain was rough with large boulders, saguaro cactus and mesquite trees.

Several times I was forced to set down quickly when sheets of sleet passed by, creating zero visibility. Ranger 27 maintained radio contact and reported the same miserable conditions. That eerie, nerve-wracking warbling tone continued to assault our ears, and it was getting stronger.

Chuck: *"We started flying around the little arroyos that make up the terrain. Sometimes we would creep up a wash, careful to keep the rotor blades clear of any obstacles, only to find ourselves up against a sheer wall blocking our path. Jerry would back up enough to turn around if he could, or simply back out if he didn't have enough room to maneuver.*

"My job was to open my door and look back at the tail rotor and be sure it was clear. One wrong move could send a spinning tail rotor into a cactus, and they would be searching for us. Meanwhile, the gusty winds and sleet continued. When we had to land because of zero visibility, Jerry would give me a reassuring smile that all was okay. It was my first time in an aircraft under these conditions, and I was a little nervous, but confident in my pilot."

As we came around a large group of boulders I caught a glimpse of the wreckage. It was an incredible sight. The entire front of the Cessna was smashed in all the way to the door. I landed on a small hill overlooking the airplane and noticed a man standing up against the fuselage looking at us. We knew from his clothes he was one of the prisoners.

I got on the radio and advised Ranger 27 that we had the downed aircraft in sight, but I couldn't give them a specific location because of the low visibility. I shut down the engine and after a couple of minutes they came into view and landed behind the downed aircraft.

Paramedic Mike McArthur jumped out of Ranger 27 and we all cautiously approached the wreck. We knew one guard had been armed with a .44 Magnum. Mike asked the prisoner—who had not moved—if there were more survivors. He nodded yes and gestured inside. As Mike went into the fuselage he yelled at the man inside to drop the gun.

We all froze and then hit the ground. The other survivor had been holding the guard's gun, but dropped it as soon as he was ordered to. Mike took the pistol and handed it to Chuck, who stuffed it into his belt and continued shooting video tape.

The man on the outside was handcuffed and still chained to part of the aircraft. It was a horrible sight. The two guards were killed on impact and partially buried under engines and debris. Besides the man outside and the prisoner who had been holding the gun, a third survivor was still in the fuselage, badly injured,

First view of crash, with prisoner standing outside

unconscious and barely breathing. Another victim was found just behind the wreckage, still chained to his seat, and dead.

Ellery Kramer joined us, carrying the medical bag. He and Mike started doing what they could for the three survivors. First they released them from the handcuffs and chains and tried to make them as comfortable as possible, given the conditions. They were obviously all suffering from internal injuries.

We needed more help, and quickly. Mike wanted two more men to help carry and load stretchers and to bring as many blankets as possible. I went back to Sky 12 to radio the sheriff's office and give them an update on survivors. The dispatcher told me two deputies were on the highway ready to assist. I replied that I was on the way.

Visibility had improved somewhat, but the winds were still gusting and the ride to the highway was full of thrills. As I departed I could see another snow storm heading in. A few more minutes and I would have had to wait until it passed. For now, as I rose up above the huge boulders, I could clearly see the Beeline Highway and all the flashing red and blue lights about a mile away. But that visibility wouldn't last.

The highway patrol had blocked an area of the highway for me to land. Deputy Larry Black with the sheriff's office was on the scene and gave me landing directions. I hadn't been on the ground two minutes before that heavy sleet squall hit us again. Larry hopped into the right seat and everyone else jumped into their cars. It took a good 10 minutes for the storm to pass, during which time I briefed Larry about the scene.

By now there were half a dozen police units on the highway. Larry got out to round up blankets and grab another deputy. Each patrol car carried a blanket, so when Larry came back he had Deputy Larry Wentworth in tow, and both were carrying blankets and first aid kits.

I asked Larry to remove my door so that if visibility got too bad I would be able to see better. Small helicopters didn't have windshield wipers, and snow and ice can accumulate on the Plexiglas, ruining visibility. I would come back and pick up the door later.

Even in cold and miserable conditions the turbine engine can keep the cabin a little warmer than outside with a door off, especially in the cramped rear seat compartment. On the down side, my two passengers, both big guys, sat hunched over knee to chin.

The flight back to the crash scene went pretty well, considering how hard it was to find the first time. But Larry Black didn't like it at all. As he tells it …

"Larry [Wentworth] and I filled up the back seat, and even though I was buckled in tight I still hit my head several times on the ceiling. This was the strongest storm I had ever seen. We were being whipped around like tissue paper. When we landed at the crash I could not believe my eyes. I couldn't imagine anyone living through that. All that remained of the aircraft was part of the rear cabin and tail. The wings were flattened and fuel tanks had ruptured. We could smell the high octane fuel as we got out of the helicopter. It's a miracle there was no fire, otherwise everyone would have died."

We all learned the hard way to be prepared next time. The only ones of us not shaking from the bitter conditions were the crew of Ranger 27, who had come prepared. My photographer never missed a beat. He wore a light jacket and sneakers, as I did, but he never complained. He held a blanket over his camera trying to keep it dry, and he captured the scene from beginning to end. Chuck Emmert was an Ohio farm boy and had come of age as an experienced TV shooter. I was proud of him.

The most critical of the three survivors was placed on a stretcher and carried to the Ranger. It took all of us to carry him because of the nasty conditions. Mike said they needed to get him to the hospital right away if he was to have a chance at all. They loaded up and got him out of there.

As they left, Larry got word over his portable radio that Air Evac was 20 minutes out. The rain had turned to light snow and the visibility had improved, but only a little. I was worried that Air Evac might not land, since their company policy prohibits flying in falling snow.

If the pilot had refused I would not have blamed him a bit. I told him the precipitation was light with strong gusty winds and occasional low ceilings. He replied with, "Roger and thanks. We will be there shortly."

A few minutes later we heard the inbound helicopter. Larry Black guided the pilot in, saying, "Keep coming, we hear you."

Soon the orange "Angel of Mercy" flight was in sight. They circled and watched as I held up both arms to signify the landing spot. Because of the terrain, he would have to land with his tail into a nasty wind. His mind made up, he began a slow approach. I was putting him in the same spot where Ellery had landed in Ranger 27.

Air Evac 2 was a highly maneuverable A-Star, based in Phoenix at a local hospital. It carried a crew of three: Pilot Len DeVries, Flight Nurse Angie Russell and Paramedic Gene Lopez.

As Len started his slow approach, his machine was being violently tossed around by the gusty winds. Despite the erratic buffeting, he stayed with it, never taking his eyes off me until he touched down just three feet from where I stood. It was a perfect landing into a very tight area full of rocks and bushes, not to mention the uneven terrain.

Flight Nurse Angie Russell later said, *"The pilot later told us he didn't want to land. But knowing Jerry's background, he trusted him to bring him into an area smaller than where we normally land. I'd never been to a scene with four dead and three Level 1 trauma patients. It was pretty unusual."*

The patients required expert care at the scene. All three survivors suffered either lacerated spleens or livers and had multiple contusions and abrasions. They would all require surgery. It took nearly half an hour for the medical team to get the patients ready to go and it required all of us to help load them onto stretchers and into the helicopter. When Air Evac had departed and disappeared into the cloudy mist, we were left with a surreal quiet.

It was almost 3 p.m., less than three hours from the time the aircraft was reported missing. It was a team effort that brought us all together to make it happen.

When I woke up that morning I had known it was going to be a miserable day for some. But unlike 10 years ago when Duane Brady and I found that grandmother and those little ones dead in the desert, now there were highly trained medical and law enforcement personnel ready to go with just one phone call.

384

Foster Credited for Sunflower Scene

Reporters often are depicted as hard-driven professionals who clamour for information on deadline and then scramble to report the cold, blood-and-guts details of a human tragedy. It's their job to "get the story", and nothing else really appears to matter at the time.

Jerry Foster is a hard-driven newsman. He is aggressive and gets his story, usually reporting live from his "Sky 12" helicopter for KPNX-TV, Channel 12, Phoenix.

But there is another side of the reporter-pilot. Foster doesn't allow his status as a member of the media to prevent him from providing appreciated—and often vital—assistance to public safety and emergency medical personnel.

Such was the case March 18 when a twin-engine Cessna 401, carrying four prisoners, one male and one female guard and a pilot on a flight to Texas, slammed into rugged mountainous terrain near Sunflower during a powerful wind and rain storm. The guards, the pilot and one prisoner perished; the three other prisoners, handcuffed and shackled, survived but were in desperate need of medical attention.

In a dramatic and potentially perilous search-and-rescue operation, Foster is credited with having located the aircraft, and then having guided and directed Samaritan Air Evac to one of its most skillful and demanding helicopter missions to date.

Reviewing a videotape of the operation on a studio monitor, Foster recalled how he had joined a Department of Public Safety (DPS) helicopter with his own "Sky 12" machine to search for the downed airplane. The Cessna's locator beacon was transmitting a strong signal, but locating the crash site was difficult in the poor weather.

"The weather was absolutely miserable," Foster said, a glance at the monitor confirming his description. "Winds were about 30 miles an hour, and there were freezing sheets of rain. Low-level clouds were hanging right next to the mountains.

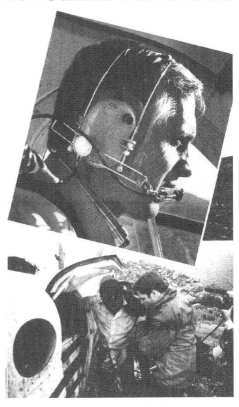

Chapter 50

Taiwan and Korea - June 1982

Quite unexpectedly, I had the trip of a lifetime handed to me. One evening I flew Senator Goldwater to Tucson where he would be giving a speech. For months we had been flying him all over Arizona for his final campaign, hitting the big cities and most of the smaller towns and settlements. For short trips we used the chopper, and for the long hauls we flew a variety of twin-engine airplanes.

After we landed back home from this trip to Tucson, he asked me if Vicki and I would like to accompany him and Mrs. Goldwater to the Orient in a couple of months. I didn't even know where that was, but I very quickly accepted the invitation. Our destination would be Taiwan and South Korea. The next day I told Al Buch about the offer. He gave his approval, but he said he'd have to clear it with General Manager, Pep Cooney. That afternoon we all had a meeting and my trip was approved by Pep. However, he suggested I call the Senator and ask if it would be possible to have Chuck go along as the official photographer and document the trip for a special television report.

I called Barry in Washington and confirmed to his administrative assistant, Judy Eisenhower, that Vicki and I could go on the trip. I then asked if it would it be possible to take my photographer and cover it as a special report. After checking with the senator, Judy called later and gave approval for Chuck to go. He was stunned when I told him the news.

"'We're going to China,' Jerry told me one morning as I finished polishing up the bird for a flight. I wasn't real sure I had heard him correctly, so I said, 'what's happening there?'

"Jerry was already strapped in and beginning the start sequence, and just said, 'I'll tell you on the way.'

"I couldn't believe it; China? Korea? And we were going as the Senator's guests!"

We had plenty of time to get our passports and plan the trip. This wasn't going to be all pleasure, and we had to prepare well for it. We were headed for areas that were torn apart by wars, so we read and learned what we could about the countries we'd be visiting. Chuck had the hardest part to get ready for our trip.

Chuck Emmert: *"I packed extra gear in case something broke so far away from home, and I carried plenty of extra tapes. We packed it all in large metal cases. Our trip to the Bahamas had been good experience for what to take and how to pack it so it didn't get broken. We left from Sky Harbor Airport for the longest flight of our lives. It was the first time I had flown with Jerry that he wasn't the pilot."*

It was hard to sit in one spot for so long. Vicki and I had seats along a window so at least we had a little more privacy than Chuck, who was in the middle section, right in the middle of the largest conglomeration of passengers. It was a Boeing 747 and there was not an empty seat. Every time I looked at Chuck he was sound asleep, usually leaning against his neighbor.

We had learned a little about the Chinese culture before going over the big pond, and discovered that gift-giving was very important to their protocol. The gifts didn't have to be anything expensive, just something that could be handed to another person. Being forewarned, we took along many little things such as business cards, lapel pins, and Sky 12 memorabilia.

We also knew Goldwater was much revered in the Republic of China. He and General Chiang Kai-shek, the country's founder, were good friends and loved by the people of the Republic.

We spent 22 hours en-route with one stop in the Philippines for fuel, before finally landing at Taipei, Taiwan in the Republic of China about midnight. Besides being wide-eyed and feeling like zombies from the long flight, it was exciting and bizarre from the moment we stepped off the airplane.

Everything seemed different. The huge airport terminal was filled with throngs of people scurrying around in all directions, while the PA system squawked endlessly in languages we didn't understand.

The Goldwaters had arrived the previous day, having departed from Washington. We were told that upon arrival at the baggage area we would be met by a government escort. We followed the crowd and surged our way along for about a quarter mile, watching the signs the led toward baggage claim.

A man appeared carrying a sign that read: "JERRY FOSTER PARTY." I had the feeling he saw us long before we saw him. His name was Johnny Chen and he looked like I envisioned an undercover agent for the country to look like. He wore a black business suit, was in his early 40s and was handsome and polite.

Johnny Chen spoke perfect English, as he had been educated in the United States. He would prove to be a pleasure to have as our "government minder." He said our baggage would be waiting for us in our rooms and the car was waiting for us at the curb.

We were in the hands and control of the Taiwan Government and our every visit and move would be watched. Senator Goldwater had told us a lot about protocol and what to expect. He said the Chinese people on Taiwan were the kindest and gentlest people he had ever known. Barry had been here many times before and still showed an excitement about returning.

The Senator said of the Taiwan people, "They have had a taste of freedom and will fight to the death before ever going back under a communist regime." He went on to tell us he would feel safer walking down a street in Taiwan than back home. He also predicted we would have a different view of the Taiwan people's challenges to stay free. Goldwater was right!

Everything we did from this point on was new and intriguing. The 45-minute drive to our hotel was in a heavy rain, but even so, the bicycles seemed to outnumber the cars. It was exciting, but also a bit spooky and strange because nothing was familiar. We couldn't even read the street or store signs. Even at midnight on a wet evening the city streets were busy.

ITINERARY FOR SENATOR GOLDWATER
AND PARTY
Republic of China

Vicki

Saturday, May 29	7:30 PM, Arrive Chiang Kai-Shek International Airport. There will be a brief press conference at CKS Airport. Proceed to accommodations at the Grand Hotel.
	Remain overnight at Grand Hotel.
Sunday, May 30	9:00 AM, Depart for C.C.K. Air Force Base in Taichung via special plane.
	12:00 PM, Arrive Sun Moon Lake.
	12:30 PM, Lunch at Sun Moon Lake.
	2:00 PM, Sightseeing at Sun Moon Lake.
	7:00 PM, Dinner hosted by Mr. Fredrick F. Chien and Mrs. Chien. The dress for the evening is casual resort wear.
	Remain overnight at Evergreen Hotel.
Monday, May 31	8:00 AM, Depart Sun Moon Lake for C.C.K. Air Force Base in Taichung.
	10:00 AM, Arrive C.C.K. Air Force Base. Proceed via special plane to Hwa Lien.
	11:30 AM, Arrive Hwa Lien and excursion to Hwa Lien Highway and Marble Gorge. Lunch afterwards at Tien Hsiang.
	2:00 PM, Visit Marble gift shops at Hwa Lien.
	2:40 PM, Watch dance performance by local performers.
	3:40 PM, Depart Hwa Lien via special plane to Taipei.
	4:40 PM, Arrive Taipei.
	8:00 PM, Formal dinner hosted by Mr. H. E. Fu-Sung Chu, Minister of Foreign Affairs and Mrs. Chu. The dress for the evening is formal long gowns for the ladies and dark business suits for the gentlemen.
	Remain overnight at Grand Hotel.
Tuesday, June 1	7:45 AM, Breakfast meeting with members of the American Chamber of Commerce. This will be a discussion of international trade matters. Terry has provided you with a briefing paper.
	11:30 AM, Call on Dr. Y.S. Tsiang (pronounced Chang), Secretary General, Central Committee of the Kuomingtang.
	12:00 PM, Luncheon hosted by Dr. Tsiang.
	3:00 PM, Call on Premier H. E. Y. S. Sun.

Partial itinerary provided upon our arrival

Our hotel rooms were spacious and comfortable. Our bags had been placed in our rooms, the beds were turned down, and nightclothes and robes were neatly folded on top. A fresh bowl of fruit sat on the table, and soft drinks were in the small refrigerator. Our first night in a real bed after that 22-hour flight was most welcome.

The next morning we had an early breakfast on our balcony. Skies had cleared and the hotel grounds below us were beginning to fill with guests doing Tai Chi, the popular exercise in Asian countries.

The city streets of Taipei began filling with bicycles, motorbikes, cars and people; of every size, shape and description. We sat on the balcony for over two hours, absolutely spellbound with the sights, noises and smells of the city. This was the first rush hour traffic we had ever seen that went on all day.

C h u c k Emmert: *"We stayed at the Grand Hotel, a big, beautiful, five-star facility. It was very ornate, resembling a giant pagoda. The Goldwater party had the 11th floor to ourselves, and we were each given a pin to wear, which*

Grand Hotel

identified us as one of the group. The Senator had security with him whenever he left his room. There was also security around us everywhere we went, though we seldom noticed it.

Later that day we met with the rest of our group for lunch at the hotel. That evening would be the first of a round of formal state dinners hosted by one or another high-ranking government official. The first evening's host was the Minister of Foreign Affairs, H.E. Fu Sung Chu, and Mrs. Chu.

In addition to the senator and his wife, the Goldwater's group included Chuck, Vicki and me, General Bill Quinn and his wife, Michael Goldwater and his wife, Ms. Donna Robbins, Mr. David Lee, and Mr. Julius Kaplan.

The dinner was formal, requiring long gowns for the ladies and black business suits for the men. Formal invitations that included seating arrangements and a dinner menu were delivered to our rooms and placed squarely in the middle of our turned-down beds. An evening snack of fresh fruit and nuts was left in our rooms.

I was starting to like this and so was Chuck. As soon as all the guests were seated, the press was allowed in for a brief photo shoot. When the photo journalists rushed in, they were lined up and then allowed to start taking photos. That's when Chuck would stand up and point his camera at them. That even amused the host and guests. At these dinners there were normally three large tables and twenty guests.

It seemed that everyone in the Republic of China spoke English, at least at these affairs. It is a required class in schools, and even those who served the dinners spoke our language. Dinner was announced with a bell, and every "ding-ding" meant something was about to happen. It could be a speaker, a new course being served, or an introduction to the evening's entertainment.

Our first formal dinner was in the ballroom of the Grand Hotel. The guest list was very impressive and included cabinet members, generals and admirals. We were given very formal invitations, with instructions to RSVP. As if we would turn down it down!

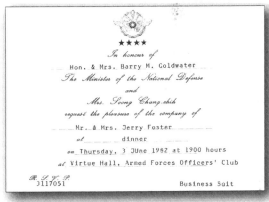

Our formal invitation

The mood was always festive and fun, while polite. At one of the dinners I sat next to the equivalent of our CIA Director, General Chang Shih-ehi, Director of the Intelligence Bureau, who turned out to be a nice guy and a good sport. Before the evening ended I asked him if he knew all about me, Vicki, and Chuck before we came to his country. He gave me a sly smile, looked at me out of the corner of his eye, and said, "We know everything!"

We smiled and laughed, but it brought me back to reality. *They know everything?* I thought.

About 40 guests would be served a dinner like I had never seen or even imagined. The twelve courses included some of the best and worst food I ever tasted. Vicki and Chuck loved it all, but some of the cuisine looked to be still alive and I was having no part of that.

The menu consisted of crispy walnuts, braised shark's fin, "Kung Pao" diced chicken, beef steak in Chinese style, fried mutton, sweet and sour yellow fish, mustard green with scallop, fish and mutton soup, sesame dumpling, and fresh fruits. And to swish it all down, the drinks included Huatiao wine, coffee or tea.

Chuck Emmert: *"One dish in particular stands out. A large silver platter held a lobster tail on one end and the head and claws at the other end, with lobster meat piled up to fill the middle. In place of the eyes at the end of the antennae, little blue LED lights shone. Shark's fin soup was served at every dinner. By the time we left, I hated it, and was just wishing for a cheeseburger. Even the senator said he was looking forward to a taco."*

I thought the formal dinners were going to be stiff and uncomfortable for us, but as it turned out we enjoyed every one.

The afternoon of our final dinner, hosted by Admiral Soong, Commander of the Navy, all the ladies in our group were fitted for evening gowns. Vicki chose a chic, long, black silk Chinese gown, and did she look sharp! The admiral liked it too.

If our dinner was away from the hotel we were driven in a motorcade of unmarked black cars led by a red DeSoto convertible with the top down. Two sharply dressed military policemen sat in the front and two in the back. They all wore chrome helmets and sat at attention holding sub-machine guns. The usually mobbed city streets were blocked off to other traffic until we passed by. We were getting a glimpse into what the power of the world sees and it was incredible, as large crowds of people stood patiently, waiting for our motorcade to pass.

Because the senator was there on business, we chose not to get involved with the political end of this visit and to concentrate on the beauty and lifestyle in the new Republic of China. Everywhere we went and everything we saw was worth a feature story. Vicki summed it up by saying she felt like Alice in Wonderland.

Johnny Chen took us to a different locale every day. One day it was to their manufacturing facilities to show us their booming economy. Another day we traveled to a typical fishing village and saw life in the rural and suburban areas. I had watched all these scenes before on TV programs like National Geographic and various PBS shows, but to be here and observe it in person was just awesome.

Vicki's favorite place was the General Chiang Kai-shek Memorial, comprised of many acres of beautiful gardens and flowers, and a huge pagoda located in the center. It was a long walk in for the public, but our car took a service road and was waved right through, dropping us off at the main entrance.

The beautifully sculptured grounds made a popular wedding backdrop for young couples, while groups of schoolchildren could be seen touring and learning about their environment and heritage. I was charmed by the little kids who gave us precious smiles, but didn't jump up and down or show off for the camera. Teachers had complete control of their classes, and they were a pleasure to be with.

For Chuck and me, the real treat was a one-hour flight in an old C-119 cargo plane that was used by the U.S. Air Force in the Korean conflict. The web seating on both sides of the interior was uncomfortable and the plane was so noisy that trying to talk was useless. We were heading to the Kinmen Islands, within sight of the Chinese mainland. Several times we caught glimpses of our escorts; two F-5 Fighters.

Our destination was Matsu Island, which had been a stronghold during the struggle for Taiwan's freedom when it had been known as Formosa. Since that time little has changed. The island was still a fortress and the struggle to stay free of Communist China continues.

We were met on the ramp by Col. Len Chang-lei, Commander of the Kinmen Defense Force. The first place he took us was to a high point on the island where two huge speakers, 30 feet tall, were pointed toward the Chinese mainland, spewing a war of propaganda toward China, less than three miles away. The colonel told us the prevailing winds were such that the speakers could be plainly heard on the mainland, and seldom were quiet.

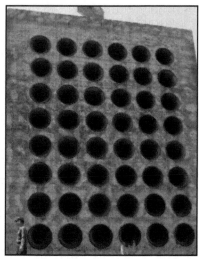

Soldier is dwarfed by giant speakers

Not far away we visited another propaganda operation. Helium balloons were being launched with baskets full of pamphlets, portable radios, and personal items like toothbrushes and soap. According to the colonel, the balloons are having an effect. He said there is not a war against the Chinese people, rather it's a fight against the Communist government for a free China … one China!

Our next stop was at a deserted beach to watch a company of "frogmen" in action. We heard them before we saw the six boats coming in from the China Sea. They were about 24 feet long with a 50-caliber machine gun mounted on the nose and carrying six heavily armed commandos. The boats hit the beach at full speed, ran up on the sand, and even before they stopped, the men started bailing out with all kinds of weapons. It was very impressive and Chuck got it all on film.

The colonel was proud of this unit and allowed us to mingle with his troops and get interviews. The young men, all wearing only shorts, were in perfect physical condition. Every man in the unit wanted his picture taken with Vicki, including the colonel.

Chuck Emmert: *"Our last event of this outing was a reception with the colonel. He brought out sake and challenged Jerry to go shot for shot with him. To his surprise, Jerry accepted and the party was on. Jerry appeared to be drinking, but—as I later learned—during the laughing and joking Vicki was surreptitiously pouring out the sake and replacing it with water. It looked to everyone like Jerry was keeping up with the commander.*

"Later, as we were getting aboard our airplane, the colonel slapped Jerry on the back telling him 'You can really handle that sake.' I thought the same thing: 'For a guy who never drinks, he can sure hold it.' Vicki was real handy to have around."

We had a good time, but the truth is I'd still had enough sake that I almost got airsick on the return flight. I would have never lived that down, so I managed to control it. Chuck had a little sake himself and slept soundly on that noisy C-119 on the way home.

He also had an experience he would never forget when he forgot to wear the pin that identified him as one of our group, and got himself "pinned" against the wall.

Chuck Emmert: *"On one occasion I was rolling off video in the lobby when I saw Barry and Jerry heading for the elevator after a late night snack. I caught up just as the door was closing and jumped in. Two security agents nailed me to the wall until the senator yelled, 'Leave him alone; he flies with me.' I felt very special."*

Johnny Chen did an excellent job for us. It is amazing what a person can see and do in a strange country in just four days. With a car, driver, and our guide, not to mention the government, we had been given an experience we would cherish for the rest of our lives.

Senator Goldwater had been right: We left Taiwan with a whole new opinion of the Chinese people of free China.

The morning of the day we were to depart Taiwan for Korea, Senator Goldwater told me that something had come up in Washington and he was going to have to cancel going to Korea, but that he would appreciate it if I would continue on as his representative. I didn't even have to think about it. I told him I would be very excited to go in his place and he told me it would be *the* experience of a lifetime. I rather doubted that, but the Senator had been right about Taiwan.

General Fred A. Haeffner, Commander U.S. Air Forces, would be our host. I knew him well from when he served at Luke and Davis Monthan Air Force bases in Arizona. I had taken a ride with him in an F-15 and he rode with me in the little Hughes 500D; rides that neither of us would ever forget!

That afternoon we packed up and headed for yet another adventure in another country that had been torn apart by war.

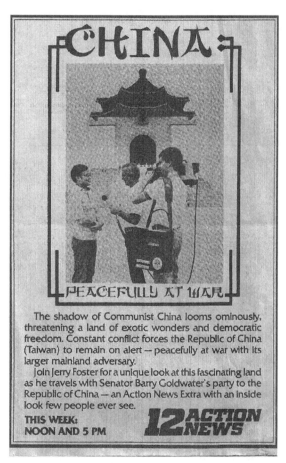

CHINA

PEACEFULLY AT WAR

The shadow of Communist China looms ominously, threatening a land of exotic wonders and democratic freedom. Constant conflict forces the Republic of China (Taiwan) to remain on alert — peacefully at war with its larger mainland adversary.

Join Jerry Foster for a unique look at this fascinating land as he travels with Senator Barry Goldwater's party to the Republic of China — an Action News Extra with an inside look few people ever see.

THIS WEEK:
NOON AND 5 PM

12 ACTION NEWS

Chapter 51

Korea

The relatively short flight took us up the East China Sea and three hours later we were there: Seoul, Korea. It was almost a repeat of what we had seen in Taiwan. The crowded airport seemed a little easier to deal with and most of the signs directing passengers to various locations included some English. We made our way to the baggage area where we were met by a sharp-looking Air Force lieutenant.

Chuck Emmert: *"So far we'd been lucky with our camera equipment. I was careful to pack everything neatly. The tapes we had already used were labeled and packed carefully in a box. I carried them and my camera with me to avoid any problems, like lost luggage. I had a bulky load, but it gave me peace of mind."*

Lt. Jack Reasoner introduced himself as General Haeffner's aide and welcomed us to Korea. Lt. Jack walked us around the long line of passengers waiting to go through customs, to a private area reserved for VIPs entering the country. In a few minutes we were in an unmarked government van on the way to Osan Air Base, our home for the next four days.

Just like Taiwan, South Korea had embraced capitalism full on. Stores and shops were everywhere along the narrow streets of the city and suburbs of Seoul. But unlike Taiwan, South Korea had a much greater military presence. At some intersections armed troops in jeeps could be seen sitting and watching. North and South Korea have been at war with each other since 1950. In 1953 a truce stopped the fighting, but the war continues today, and so does the tension.

Fighting heavy traffic of cars, bicycles, ox-drawn carts, people carrying loads on their heads and backs, and people pulling carts full of items for sale, we made our way through the city. It was the same confusion, but magnified, that we had found in Taiwan, and it lasted all the way to the base.

As we passed through the main gate the difference was immediately felt and seen. This was a U.S. military installation in a war zone. We were asked for passports, and our luggage was inspected because of the metal containers holding camera gear. The tension was obvious. The guards who dealt with us, both American and Korean, were very polite and efficient, and we were quickly passed through.

Lt. Jack gave us a little tour around the base. Noticeable differences were the bunkers for big guns, fighter aircraft and people. There were large maintenance hangars, administrative buildings and a large aircraft ramp for airplanes large and small. It looked like any Air Force base back home. Surrounding all these sights were the sounds of large aircraft and fighters coming and going. This was music to my ears. I could have sat there for hours.

The Republic of Korea also had a strong presence on base. Many civilian jobs were filled by local men and women. ROK troops provided much of the security that sealed off the base from bad guys. All of this was pretty heavy stuff for the three of us and in some ways a bit frightening. The attitude here was that war could break out any minute.

We got to our quarters where Lt. Jack and our driver helped us unload. Before leaving he told us that the general would send a car for us in two hours and would like us to join him for dinner at the officers' club. Two hours seems like plenty of time to get ready for dinner, but I was almost late. When I walked out onto our patio I didn't leave my chair for nearly an hour. I was transfixed by the view. The only thing I unpacked was my binoculars.

Chuck Emmert: *"Was I impressed! We had the rooms reserved for General Officers and VIPs, which were in a large building sitting on a hill overlooking the two runways. It must have been the slow season because we had the whole building to ourselves, and the accommodations were first class; suites with a sitting room, bedroom and kitchen."*

I could have spent the night right there on the porch. The two runways were in plain sight as was most of the base. It was a non-stop air show featuring large four-engine transports and sleek fighters. If I had been there alone I would have been late. It was hard to leave my vantage point.

At two minutes past six an Air Force sedan with one flag on each fender, displaying the star of a Brigadier General, pulled into the drive to pick us up. The driver jumped out and opened the rear passenger seat door. Out stepped our host.

General Fred A. Haeffner was a highly decorated fighter pilot, qualified in nearly every airplane in the Air Force inventory. In Vietnam he shot down a MiG 17, assisted in another shoot-down and was credited with two probable shoot-downs. That made him something very special to his subordinates. He and Senator Goldwater had flown in the same squadron in past years and had remained close friends. He had the cocky swagger of a fighter pilot, but in Air Force circles they didn't come any better than Fred Haeffner.

Walking into a base officers' club with the big boss is quite a thrill. The atmosphere was pleasant, the smell was down home, and everything looked familiar. It reminded me of the club at Luke AFB near Phoenix.

It took a few minutes to get to our table. Some of the officers had served in the Valley back home and were familiar with our helicopter adventures, so that made us comfortable right away. I was amazed at how a commanding general could make himself "one of the gang" and interact; laughing and joking with subordinates of all ranks. The respect he received demonstrated that he was everyone's general.

I will remember my dinner that night for the rest of my days. The thrill began when we first walked in the door and I saw and smelled a plate of meatloaf, mashed potatoes and gravy, and a large glass of milk. It was the first meal in a long time that I didn't have to smell or examine closely before eating. And best of all, I was able to choose it from a menu I could understand. We all had a great evening with our jovial host. The general told us he had several things planned for the Goldwater party, including a day of shopping, a trip to the DMZ, and a helicopter ride to another fighter base. It all sounded good to us.

Back in our quarters I couldn't wait to get my binoculars and watch a real-life late-night movie on the runway.

The next morning, Lt. Jack picked us up for a 7 a.m. breakfast at a base cafeteria. This would be our only day to see the local sights and do a little shopping. Chuck had his camera and a backpack full of tapes. He wasn't going to miss a thing.

We started with a tour of the base and got a feeling for how our troops and their dependents were living. It was very similar to any other military facility except for the security and the number of people on the move, handling all the projects related to the war zone.

We headed off base for lunch at a little spot our guide knew about. I don't remember what I ate; I only know I never ate it again.

Our final stop was a little clothing store our driver knew of. He was a local, working for the Air Force, and he helped us find a lot of bargains that day. We turned off a main street onto a narrow back lane and searched for a place to park. The word "crowded" would be an understatement. We spent about an hour interacting with merchants and customers alike, and enjoyed everything about the day.

Chuck Emmert: *"Stores and shops were everywhere, and everything was inexpensive, especially clothing: shoes for five bucks, and suits for one hundred dollars, which included custom tailoring. We were taken to a small shop with a radio playing so loudly we couldn't get the owner's attention until Jerry reached up and turned it off. The old guy turned around, bowed low, gave us a big smile, opened his arms and said, "'I love America.'*

"As it turned out, that was all the English he knew. It also happened that the old man was our driver's father. Jerry bought a

beautiful western-cut tuxedo from him. It was one-of-a-kind and perfect for Arizona. Jerry wore it often when the occasion called for the best."

That was the only time in my adult life I remember enjoying an afternoon of shopping and actually wishing we had more time. We bought a number of trinkets and had Sky 12 patches made for our viewers, not to mention 5,000 Sky 12 bumper stickers. I paid for everything and spent less than four hundred dollars; tuxedo and a fat tip included.

We had a great day, but these were short diversions from what we had gone there to do: tell the story of American armed forces in Korea and the threat they were up against. The next day we would see firsthand the front lines and the dividing line between North and South.

Korean Cutie!

The following day started a little earlier than expected. I was sound asleep at 4 a.m. when the phone rang. It was on Vicki's side so I let it ring, and finally—after punching me—she answered. I heard her say, "Yes sir, it's Vicki," and then, "Yes sir, I will tell him," then, "thank you, General."

I was all ears and wide-eyed, waiting for her to let me in on this new development. She said, "The general says you should call Chuck and tell him that what happens at daylight on the runway you didn't see and do not photograph."

"What the hell does that mean?" I asked.

Vicki just shrugged her shoulders and closed the bathroom door. As I dialed Chuck I heard a low rumble outside that was building into a roar. Vicki came sailing out of the bathroom, I hung up the phone, and we both headed to the porch just as a second rumble began.

We stood on the porch in a light rain, Vicki in a nightgown and me in boxers, looking at where a huge fighter–bomber sat pointed down the centerline of the runway. Both engines were spewing a light blue flame that was increasing in length as the rpm increased to takeoff power. In a few seconds the ground and windows started to rattle and the huge bird began to roll.

It was like watching a twin-engine rocket blast off. Halfway down the runway the aircraft rotated then established a steep climb. Thirty seconds later it disappeared into rain and clouds; but the bright glow from those massive engines was visible for at least another minute.

What a thrill! I knew immediately what it was: the fastest and highest flying airplane in history. In 1982 the Air Force kept the location and missions of the SR-71 secret.

When the noise stopped, the phone rang. It was Chuck: "Are we at war or what?"

"Did you shoot any video?" I asked

"No, I didn't have time. What's the deal? Was that a Blackbird?"

"I don't know, Chuck. I didn't see a thing."

We had to leave the base around 7 a.m. for a trip with Lt. Jack to the DMZ, about 70 miles to the north from Osan Air Base. The drive would take us into the rural country where we visited a small village and got some great video of Koreans at home and work. My favorite shot was of a mother giving her two-year-old son a bath in a wooden tub outside their small house.

The main highway leading to the DMZ was alive with military vehicles. Stripes on the pavement served a dual purpose: in an emergency the highway could be turned into a runway that would serve military aircraft; both fighters and transports.

Tanks and heavy trucks were stationed at points along the highway, some partially buried with netting over the top to hide them from above. There were also tank traps designed to stop heavy armor.

It seemed odd to see the local farmers out in their fields carrying on with their lives as though nothing was going on. Some farmers had to plow around many tank traps on their land. These are a determined people who, like the Chinese on Taiwan, will do whatever it takes to stay free.

The DMZ is the center of tension; a dividing line between the North and South. Since 1948 this was the hot spot of the cold war when Russia was supplying the North, and the United States was doing the same thing in the South.

The demilitarized zone is a strip of land running across the Korean peninsula, serving as a buffer zone between the North and South. It is 160 miles long, approximately 2.5 miles wide, and is the most heavily militarized border in the world.

At the DMZ

We entered the Joint Security Area (JSA) at the U.S. Army base, Camp Bonifas. As we went through the base gates, military police and armed soldiers watched everything going on. The tension could be felt everywhere. The road to Panmunjom is straight ahead 2400 meters.

At Camp Bonifas we were introduced to a tough Special Forces Ranger, about 6'4" and 230 pounds, wearing a camouflage uniform, highly shined black boots and a Green Beret cap. He was armed and looked dangerous, and was a dead-ringer for John Wayne. Let's just call him Major Wayne because I was so intimidated I forgot his name.

Chuck Emmert: *"The major was one tough dude; the kind of guy you would want on your side in a bar fight. He was perfect for the camera and really knew his stuff. He took us right to the painted line at Panmunjom that divides the country in half, and he gave us a rundown* on *various incidents over the years that have kept tensions high. We saw the famous 'bridge of no return' where prisoners were exchanged during the war. Just beyond the border, about a mile away and up on a hill, we could see that shining 'propaganda city,' with tall towers and modern architecture; but it was all as fake as a movie set. With binoculars, we could see people walking around, but the major told us they were trucked in to make it seem real. It was all propaganda."*

The most interesting part of this childish charade was the confrontational standing on the white line. A North Korean soldier stood with his toes at the line just inches away from the toes of a South Korean soldier; each staring defiantly at each other. When Vicki stood at the line two North Korean soldiers hurriedly walked up within a foot of her. Within seconds two Army Rangers with bulging muscles under white t-shirts had stepped up on each side of Vicki with fists clenched. It was all bluff and bluster.

Our guide gave us a tour of the little building that is used for official meetings between the two sides: that famous building where half the room is on the north side of the line the other on the south side. Even the table straddles the line between the two countries. The guards made it known that if you crossed the line they couldn't be responsible for your safety. There were so many petty things, from the size of each side's flag being the same, right down to the equality of the paper and pens on the table.

Once again, Chuck got it all. We left the DMZ almost in shock at what we had seen. To see all this on TV back home is nothing like being there. Everyone we saw seemed to be walking on eggs and pushing each other to the limit.

There are lyrics in Pink Floyd's album, "The Final Cut" that describes the DMZ:

"The rusty wire that holds the cork that keeps the anger in,
gives way and suddenly its day again.
And as the windshield melts and my tears evaporate,
leaving only charcoal to defend,
finally I understand the feeling of the few,
ashes and diamonds, foe and friend, we were all equal in the end"
                                                    - Pink Floyd

At breakfast the next morning we found out from Lt. Jack that the reason for going to Kunsan Air Base was to visit an F-16 squadron. A flight had been scheduled for Senator Goldwater, and I was going to fill in. I would be going along on a mission with a hot dog group of pilots known as the "Wolf Pack." I was some kind of excited.

We boarded an Air Force helicopter for the one-hour flight to the base. Our bird was an H-3 Sikorsky, a large transport machine that made a lot of noise and shook a little, but I felt right at home. The view from 500 feet was incredible, particularly the beautiful sculptured farmland that dominated the landscape in rich colors of green and yellow. Not an acre of ground was wasted here. Even the mountains and hills were solid with furrows of mixed crops creating spectacular patterns.

A personal welcome!

As we landed on the ramp we were greeted by the Flight Commander of the F-16 squadron and driven straight to the briefing that was about to start in the ready room. I was given a short class on the emergency procedures and met the four pilots who would be flying today's mission. I then listened to the briefing describing what we were about to do.

The next step was to get outfitted in flying gear. I put on a flight suit and was fitted for a helmet, oxygen mask and a G-suit to help withstand the G-forces we would encounter. I had a good time with the pilots, who were typical jet jockeys, and they took bets on how long I would be awake when they started "jinkin' and jiving."

"Give it your best shot," I told them, a statement I would later regret. They had all been stationed around Phoenix and were familiar with my operation, so I felt lucky to be with friends. I wish I had taken notes and written down names, but I didn't, and now that 30 years have passed, my memory only retained the incredible activities of this adventure.

Since I was also the aviation reporter back home, I had flown with the Blue Angels, the Thunderbirds, and had been on missions in front-line fighters, so I knew what to expect. I blacked out at times, but I figured this would be a piece of cake. After all, I was a jet helicopter pilot and I knew all about, jinkin' and jivin'!

Once our pre-flight was completed we saddled up, strapped in, and started through the pre-flight procedures. Our four F-16s were fully armed with guns and rockets, so on the way to the runway we pulled into an armament area to have the rockets checked and armed, then we were cleared to taxi for takeoff. What a thrill already and we hadn't even left the ground. The precision of these guys and their machines was unreal; nothing was left to chance and everything worked.

At our pre-flight briefing the entire mission had been laid out and discussed. Our aircraft would be leading, with numbers two and three flying on each side of us. The plan was to take off in formation then climb to 12,000. At a certain point the flight would make a rapid descent and fly low level along the DMZ to another check point, then climb to 28,000 feet to the Yellow Sea for gunnery practice.

I blacked out on takeoff. When we leveled off I was able to lift my camera up and get a shot of the two F-16s on either side of us. When we headed down I blacked out again and didn't wake up until we leveled out about 500 feet above the ground, with airspeed in excess of 400 knots. We streaked over landscapes and villages for about 10 minutes. I was able to ask the pilot if the villagers ever complained about the noise. He said the jets were the sound of freedom to the Koreans, and they loved it.

I was able to talk, look around and enjoy the thrill. On the radar the pilot pointed out two blips that were paralleling our course about three miles north of us. They were said to be North Korean MiGs that played this little game every time American fighters flew along the DMZ.

When the low level portion was finished, the flight started a climb back to altitude and I blacked out again. I could hear the pilots talking: "Hey newsmen are you still with us?"

"Sure, no problem," I managed to grunt. They knew better.

"Okay, guns are armed and here we go," my pilot said. He rolled upside down and headed for a target being towed by a ship 18,000 feet below. I heard and felt the machine guns firing, but the G-forces were so high I could only hear the action until we leveled off again at altitude. We made two more passes at the target as they fired rockets at the last one. Again I heard chatter on the radio, but missed all the action.

When we started our descent back to Kunsan, I was able to get my senses back and talk without grunting. The pilots were fun and the kidding and bantering was non-stop.

Back in the briefing room, the flight commander asked me in front of the group how I liked the flight, and whether the G-forces bothered me. "Are you kidding? No problem!" I lied. They knew better.

The truth is, I never even saw the Yellow Sea and I spent most of the flight time in la-la land. But what a privilege it was. That was *the* ride of a lifetime.

One thing I've always loved about flying is the ability to see the earth from a different perspective. It was no different flying over Taiwan and Korea. While the flight in the F-16 didn't allow for much sightseeing, my earlier flight in the helicopter and the trip between the two countries gave me a bird's eye view of the landscape below. A long mountain range covers most of the eastern two-thirds of Taiwan, while the western portion is comprised of gently rolling hills and 90 percent of the population.

Korea's landscape is 70 percent mountainous, with its plains being small and widely separated by the mountain ranges. It has been referred to as "rumpled" looking and, from the air, it does give the impression of wads of paper having been crumpled and dropped over the country. But it's all green and beautiful.

After nearly two weeks out of our home country, it was good to be heading back. If I learned anything from that incredible trip it was just how fortunate we are in this country, and how many things we take for granted: Freedom, for one thing, and so much more.

I was a long way out of my comfort zone on that trip. Call it a guilty conscience or whatever, I never forgot the wily smile of the Minister of Intelligence as he said, "We know everything."

Ya think?

Chapter 52

Parades

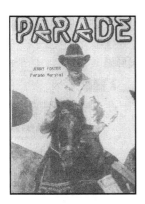

I was invited to ride in many parades, and I enjoyed them as much as anything else I did. Big or small, we never turned one down. Sometimes I was the Grand Marshal and other times I rode in a car or float, or did whatever I was asked to do. I also rode a number of horses loaned to me by someone in the community. My dad had been a real cowboy before he joined the Marines. His mother had a small ranch near Duncan, Arizona, right on the western border of New Mexico. Dad was raised on a horse and passed that ability on to me. I thought I had ridden nearly every kind of horse until I rode one high-stepping stallion.

Easter of 1982, I had been invited to a small community celebration. Susan took the call and got all the information. She could hardly wait to tell me the details and needed to call them back to confirm my attendance. She said I would be riding a beautiful Peruvian Paso, a feisty young stallion that is bred to show off ... and this horse did just that. She said all I'd have to do is smile and wave and the horse will do the rest ... and they promised me a ride I'd never forget.

I swallowed kind of hard because that's what Susan told our viewers when she scheduled them to ride with me in the helicopter. I knew what kinds of unexpected thrills *I* provided on those flights, so was a little concerned about riding this spirited stallion. But after I thought it over I found myself looking forward to it. I did, however, have it in the back of my mind that I could also make a fool of myself if that four-legged hot dog was to pitch off this two-legged hot dog in front of a big crowd. Other horses I rode only trotted when they saw we were headed home. *This could go either way*, I thought.

On Easter morning Chuck, Vicki and I landed at the designated spot in the community of Ahwatukee, where we were met by the parade chairman. He took us by golf cart to a horse trailer where we met Stan Reese, a local cowboy and breeder of Peruvian Pasos. The horse I would be riding nearly took my breath away when I first saw him.

Regal Del Sol was a beautiful Palomino stallion. His blond, muscular body was magnified by a long, nearly white, flowing mane and tail. As we walked up, his eyes locked on mine and I sensed he was sizing me up. I was surprised at his stature. He was shorter than breeds I was used to, but he was well-built, with huge muscular shoulders and neck, tapering down to a trim rear. He was outfitted in traditional Peruvian gear and he was stunning.

Before I could change my mind, Stan swung up into the saddle and gave us a demonstration. That horse went right into parade mode: flared nostrils, head held high, neck arched, ears alert ... he was all business. Stan put him through the paces doing turns and stops that only a man and animal in tune together can do. The Peruvian Paso has a gait which is said to be the smoothest of any breed. Their front leg action is similar to a swimming motion. In other words, this is a breed that "picks 'em up and lays 'em down!"

When Stan slid to a stop and swung down in a cloud of dust, I was ready to call the whole thing off. I had never seen such a spirited horse except in the movies, and I had to force myself to go ahead with this little adventure. I listened as Stan Reese gave me a rundown on his stallion. "Sol," he said, "was trained for the show ring and parades. He is easy to ride and responds best to knee commands and a slight tug on the rein to change direction. A gentle tug on both reins will bring him to an abrupt stop. Be gentle with him and he'll give you a good show. All you will have to do is smile and wave!"

410

Stan handed me a set of Peruvian spurs and said, "You will need these only if he gets distracted by a good-looking mare and you need to show him who's boss."

I almost lost my nerve again, but I held steady enough to reach out for the spurs. Vicki took them from me and knelt down to fasten the straps as I raised each boot. She and Chuck both knew that I was on the verge of walking away from this opportunity.

I jingled my way over to my steed and took the reins from Stan, then took a hunk of the beautiful mane in my left hand. I put my boot in the stirrup and swung up into the saddle—a little too fast—and nearly continued to the ground on the other side. So much for grace, but I was on board and wanted very badly to stay there. Feeling very clumsy, I gathered in the reins, jabbed him lightly with the spurs and nearly went over backward from the fast start into that fancy gait. Once I got away from Stan and Vicki I loosened up, did some starts and stops, right and left turns. I wasn't two minutes into my practice ride when I knew this was going to be fun. Sol responded just like Stan said he would. After about 10 minutes I felt confident enough to ride back over to my group, slam on the brakes, and dismount like a real cowboy in a cloud of swirling dust. I was ready to ride!

I rode the parade without any uncomfortable moments, as that stallion danced and strutted from one side of the street to the other. This parade was the beginning of a totally new lifestyle for me, Vicki, and the crew of Sky 12.

Peruvian Pasos

The following month Vicki and I decided to buy a Peruvian Paso, and a very special one at that. My new friend, Stan Reese, found exactly what I told him I was looking for. Despite our living in a downtown penthouse, we bought him. I nearly passed out when I learned my new steed would cost me twelve thousand dollars, but this was just what I needed, so I swallowed hard and paid up.

Rey de Reyes, which meant "King of Kings" in Spanish, was an elegant, coal-black, five-year-old stallion. He had a long mane and tail and a massive neck and shoulders. Still young, and not fully trained, he was full of spirit. He had all the qualities a Paso is born with, including the natural high-lifting gait. No training devices are used with them—they've either got it or they don't at birth. I arranged for Rey to stay at Stan's ranch and continue his training. He had never been in a parade, but he was well-trained for riding and arena shows. Watching him prance around in an arena, it  was obvious to me that he could put on a show, but he would have to learn some manners and pay attention to his rider. We would learn together.

One of the greatest things about Peruvian horses is their disposition. They are very smart and try hard to please. I spent as much time as I could in Stan's arena, and I had a place to land the chopper, so that made it easy. We finally came to the day of my first parade. By now I had ridden in several parades using Stan's palomino, taking Rey along to get used to all the people and noise. Now, after a few months of training, Stan felt we were ready to "solo" on Rey.

I was slated to be Grand Marshal of the Gilbert Days parade in the town of Gilbert southeast of Phoenix. That day I landed on the high school football field with Chuck and Vicki. The starting point was nearby so we walked over to meet Stan and Rey.

Rey was already decked out in a black and silver parade saddle, with a matching bridle. I thought it best to show him in Arizona western gear since we both were "Zonies." I used a hackamore instead of a bit, to avoid any damage to his mouth.

When he was ready for a parade he was mighty good looking, and he knew it.

Rey was very aggressive around other horses. I had to constantly talk to him and use my spurs to remind him what we were there for. I couldn't sit and talk to other riders without creating a ruckus, but once we started down the parade route, he put on quite a show. Parades were more fun now and Rey was a big hit wherever we went. That black stallion soon became a major part of my life and lifestyle.

Larger parades are usually very slow to accommodate the walking participants. There's lots of stopping and starting for those who move faster. Rey would not just stand in one place in the middle of the street, but I learned that if I rode to one side or the other, and stopped in front of the spectators, he would stand quietly while they touched and petted him. He loved it and would lower his head to be rubbed. Parents would hand their toddler up to me for a picture and that horse would not move.

But when I picked up the reins again he knew it was show time and away we went, cutting back and forth down the street.

At the 1985 Fiesta Bowl Parade we were doing that cut back and forth from side to side, when tragedy nearly struck. We were cutting back to the left when Rey slipped on the pavement and went down on his left side. It happened so fast that he fell on my left leg. For a few seconds Rey lay there with my leg pinned under his side, then he reared his head and started up. All this time there was not a sound. The large crowd was as stunned as I was.

I grabbed my hat off the pavement, picked up a broken spur, stood up, brushed myself off, made sure Rey's legs were okay, and then mounted up.

I took my hat off, waved at the spectators and away we went to a healthy roar of approval. Later I found some scrapes and bruises on both of us. After that we started using rubber pads on his front feet to help with traction and it never happened again. We were still learning. And that rubber pad would save the day at an unexpected time a few years later.

As the years rolled along we became a team and made appearances all around Arizona. Rey went to schools, rodeos, parades, and public events like the state fair. That's where I had a couple of great adventures.

On the final evening of the rodeo at the fairgrounds, I rode Rey into the packed coliseum, carrying a large American flag. He was looking sharp; all decked out in black and silver, with his long, wavy mane and braided tail. He knew he was the star and he pranced and danced and earned himself a huge ovation, which spooked him momentarily.

I was always a little nervous and on guard when he got that way because the truth is, I was really a better helicopter pilot than a cowboy, and in a situation like this, both Rey and I were operating very close to the edge. The last thing I wanted to do was lose control and crash in front of 15,000 people.

The plan was for us to come strutting in and skid to a stop in the center of the arena, stand still while the crowd settled down, then wait for the National Anthem. We had never done this before, but so far all had gone well. As we stood in the center, the lights went out and the lighting guy hit us with a series of spotlights that blinded us both. At the same time, the music started blaring and Rey reared nearly straight up and took several steps on his hind legs. I took a handful of his mane and leaned forward. I know I wasn't smiling, but I acted as if it was part of the show. I thought about bailing out before the flag and I both landed in the dirt.

When his front legs landed I was able to keep him in one spot, but he pranced in place until the music ended and the spotlight disappeared. It had been a close call: video of the event shows that we nearly went over backward. My legs were sore for a week from holding on so tightly.

Parades provided a bit of variety from my normal flying routine. Rey became a trusted friend and an important part of our lives.

Chapter 53

Sky 12 Team - 1982

Bryan Neumeister

Between news and weather reporting, parades, school visits, speaking gigs, and so on, my life was becoming busier and more complicated. Early on I'd had various photographers assigned to me on an "as needed" basis. After some discussion, Al Buch had agreed that I should have a dedicated photographer. First John Bass, and then Chuck Emmert had filled that spot. Now it was time to add someone else to help organize everything I was doing. I talked to Al again, and we decided to bring Susan Sorg on board as a full member of the team. She had been the newsroom receptionist, and for the past year had been working with me part-time, writing my weather and helping out in other areas. Since she was already writing for me, she knew my style of speaking. She would now be the full-time Sky 12 producer, the first television news producer in the country dedicated to a station helicopter operation. She would turn out to be our most valuable asset over the coming years.

Susan: *"It was pretty apparent that Jerry had the freedom to grow his operation, and because he was the biggest draw at the station, didn't it make sense that he should have a producer to manage all his activities? We worked well together, which wasn't the case with everyone.*

"My duties included everything from making sun tea on the roof, to writing Jerry's news stories, weather reports and documentaries. It

was a dream job and I quickly learned what a producer was responsible for ... anything and everything that can go wrong.

I could get hold of Jerry and Chuck any time of the day or night. We all wore pagers, and adhered to a 20-minute response time, sharing the pride of being first to a breaking news story. We were never without those pagers, which were state of the art in 1982. Al Buch reminded us that we were not required to work 24/7, but we did it because we felt as Jerry did ... this was not a job, it was a lifestyle. And I loved it!"

Susan doubled our output right from the start. With the microwave in place and working, we could fly to a story, beam the film back to the station, and by the time we returned to the studio the story was written and my weather scripts were ready to go. My grammar was also greatly improved by reading her scripts. In a day full of deadlines, she took a lot of pressure away from Chuck and me.

Chuck stayed with me about two years. He had done a fantastic job and we had been through a lot in that time, but he was ready to move on.

Chuck Emmert: *"We were so proud to be part of that operation. I'd come back at night to make sure the helicopter was squared away, and I'd just stand there looking at it, thinking, 'Wow, I can't believe this is what I'm doing!' Jerry was a tough mentor, but it was good for me and sharpened my skills. Everything I do now comes from that training.*

"I had two years before I just kind of burned out. I didn't have a lot of personal freedom. I recognized it was a once-in-a-lifetime opportunity, but I couldn't stray too far, couldn't have a date. Jerry had said his photographers only lasted about a year, so I felt good I'd made it another year past the demarcation line."

Our team and alumni now numbered six: Vicki, Susan, Howie, John, Chuck and me. Number seven would be a young man from Burbank, California. I'll never forget the first day I saw him. He drove into the station parking lot in an old dull black Mustang, lowered in the front, with a large air scoop on the hood to make it look like a race car. It certainly sounded like one. I couldn't help noticing the blue smoke pouring out of the exhaust and the California license plate that was two-months expired.

Bryan Neumeister had been recommended to me by both Chuck Emmert and Al Buch. He was an experienced photographer who had been working the overnight shift at KTAR for the past year and a half and wanted to get assigned to Sky 12.

I was still mulling it over and this was the first time I had really focused on him. As he got out of his hot rod, I saw a tall, lanky guy wearing a baseball cap, pilot sunglasses, sloppy sweat shirt and baggy jeans, and carrying a camera bag. With all that and the fact that he really needed a haircut, Bryan appeared to be someone I would like. He didn't try to sell himself; he simply said he could handle it. I believed him and was never sorry.

He and Chuck had been sharing an apartment for the past several months so he already knew the drill and was easy to work with. I let him know right off the bat that he would only be with us for a year because it was a demanding commitment. It was most important that he understand the 20-minute response time was for me, not him. If I got to the station before him I would wait five minutes and then I was gone.

After we had been flying together for a while, Bryan invited Vicki and me to his house for dinner. Since he lived well within our response time, we accepted. When I walked in I was surprised to find a clean and comfortable little pad, nicely furnished, and decorated with a lot of Sky 12 memorabilia. The stunner was his spare room, which had been turned into a musician's playhouse. There were drums, keyboards, guitars, recorders, and a large master panel for producing video and sound. He had a complete studio that would have made Pink Floyd proud. This Southern California kid was a genuine artist and we were quite impressed. From then on, when we landed for me to speak at a luncheon or some event, if there was a piano or guitar present, I would ask Bry to play us a little tune. It went over well: Bryan had come to play!

We had been working together several months when another change would take place. But first, I would experience one of the most emotional weeks of my career.

Chapter 54

A Week in December
December 1, 1982 - 2 a.m.

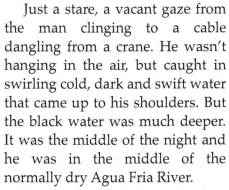

"Mister, can you swim? If I can get to you, can you swim?" I screamed. "Can you hear me?"

Just a stare, a vacant gaze from the man clinging to a cable dangling from a crane. He wasn't hanging in the air, but caught in swirling cold, dark and swift water that came up to his shoulders. But the black water was much deeper. It was the middle of the night and he was in the middle of the normally dry Agua Fria River.

Sixty-one-year-old Donese Tackett gave me that look that said he knew he was going to die. Not if we could help it.

Bryan Neumeister: *"It was our second call that night and I was already tired, cold, soaked, and out of adrenaline. 'I can't believe this!' I thought. We couldn't tell if our victim was dead or alive, but his eyes were open. It was a nightmare scenario, and we were living it."*

This happens so many times in the desert. After a lot of rain, the roads crossing normally dry river beds suddenly become a roaring torrent; yet people still ignore the barricades and get caught trying to drive through the swift-moving water. By the time they realize their mistake, it's too late.

In this case, Mr. Tackett had been with his son, driving down Indian School Road. They had no idea the bridge was washed out in front of them. There were no barricades and no warnings. They were victims of Mother Nature.

It was late at night; cold, crazy winds, and rain showers still in the area. It was tough flying, but I was able to land on a sandbar barely 40 feet from where the victim was hanging on to the cable. He had been washed into a gravel pit and managed to grab a cable from an old crane. There was no way I could see to get to him with the helicopter, so I shut the engine down and tried to establish voice contact with the victim.

The first time I hollered at him I thought I saw his head move, so I knew he was still alive. I kicked off my boots and waded out to my waist in the bitter cold water to get as close as I could to him. As I inched out, my legs started to feel numb. I was afraid that if I swam out to him in the swirling current and he was already unconscious, we would both die. I hollered at Bryan to bring me a rope we carried, planning to tie it to the helicopter and swim out to Tackett, but it was too short.

The outside air temperature was 25 degrees and water temp was 36. Strong, gusty winds whipped the water into a spray that froze instantly on the plexiglass

My brain was in overload. I just didn't know what else to do. I knew if I went out there I would never get back. It was a helpless and hopeless feeling. No one else was around, and I was the only one who could save that man's life at that moment. In that icy water, the clock was ticking and all I could do was shout, "Mister can you hear me?"

We were finally joined by two lake patrol deputies. One of them, Pat Cooper, waded out to me, still yelling at the victim. When I saw Pat, I grabbed onto him and yelled, "Our rope is too short to reach him. I'm afraid to swim out there." He took my arm and gestured back to the sandbar.

Bryan came up with the only option we had, given the circumstances. "Tie me to one end of the rope, tie the other end to the helicopter and get close and I'll jump off and grab him ..."

He was interrupted by Deputy Cooper who agreed with the idea, but objected to Bryan doing it. That was his job. "Let's go," he said, taking off his gun belt and handing it to Bryan.

Bryan Neumeister: *"They had already rescued Mr. Tackett's son. He was on the other side of the river, and was okay. The plan to tie Deputy Pat Cooper to a rope and tie the other end to the right skid of the helicopter, was dangerous for so many reasons, but it seemed the only option."*

As Pat jumped into water the DPS Ranger flew over us with its searchlight illuminating the victim, who was still holding on to the cable.

Please hang on, Mister, I thought. Another two minutes and we would have him.

As soon as Cooper jumped I lost sight of him and realized I had made a big mistake. I should have had him jump from my side so I would have had him in sight the whole time. When I sensed a power surge, I knew I had two people being pulled by the current. Because of the ice building up on the glass, and the rotor blasting the water, I could only see out the passenger side. I was glad we had removed the door.

Clarence Forbey, Paramedic with DPS Ranger: *"We dumped our doors and our equipment. Neither Jerry nor we could get close because of the cable. So we were now supplying light, and Jerry was hovering. The deputy swam over, got the old man off the cable and then Jerry dragged them back to the bank."*

With the light from Ranger 27's powerful searchlight I was able to hold my ship level. Listening to instructions from DPS pilot, Joe Whisinhunt, I started pulling the men toward the sandbar. There was so much radio traffic that I had to concentrate on Joe's instructions, especially when the water spray and ice crystals temporarily blinded me.

Bryan Neumeister: *"I think the rope was about 30 feet long, and then, because he didn't have a floatation device on, Pat Cooper was tumbling in the water, and Jerry started pulling him to shore. The line went taut, and I thought it was going to kill Coop because it just picked him up and dragged him and he was still holding on to Tackett. At the same time, the guys are on the radio, yelling at Jerry to stop pulling. They ran in and dragged Cooper and Tackett out, pulled the rope off, then guided Jerry down so the rope wouldn't go in the tail rotor."*

420

Clarence Forbey: *"We dropped down, picked up the old man and flew him to the west side of the river where the ambulance was waiting. We came back, got the deputy, left our doors and equipment and flew to Maryvale Hospital."*

Bryan Neumeister: *"They took Tackett and started working on his heart—at that time I think his heart had stopped. They were doing CPR and shot him with adrenalin, then flew off. He was in full code at the time, and we didn't know if he'd live or die."*

Donese Tackett was pronounced dead on arrival at the hospital, a combination of hypothermia and heart attack.

When I got to the hospital emergency room where Pat Cooper was, Clarence Forbey jumped all over me. "You almost killed that guy!" he yelled, meaning the deputy.

Clarence Forbey: *"My thoughts were, 'He's going to die now, the deputy, he's going to die of hypothermia and he just got killed for spectacular video!' That was my thought, and it disgusted me. Jerry and I worked side by side for a long time. He's a super, swell individual, but the thought of him taking a chance to kill a cop? I'd have said the same thing to anyone else ... didn't matter what his name was."*

We were all shaken, no doubt about it, and emotions of everyone involved were raw. Thankfully, Deputy Sheriff Pat Cooper was treated for hypothermia and released. Later he would be honored at the White House by President Reagan for his bravery.

After going out on a call like this, with our hearts pumping and adrenalin racing, we'd go our separate ways home. There were times when I'd get home and back to bed, but I'd just lay there staring at the ceiling, because of the realization of what had happened. At the time, we didn't comprehend how much stress we put on ourselves: me, Bryan, Cooper and everyone else who was involved. We were under tremendous stress because we were gambling with somebody's life.

Susan Sorg: *"When I got in that morning the tapes Bryan shot were on my desk. I was struck by what I saw on those tapes, the desperation and also futility of it. Neither Jerry nor Bryan said much when they got in, and I knew to leave them both alone."*

Bryan: *"When we had a mission that worked, we never really said much about it because that was the way it was supposed to go. But when something screwed up, we really took it personally, and it took us days to get back in the swing of things. We'd keep running it through our head, wondering what we could have done differently. It hit us both hard."*

December 7, 1982 - The White House, Washington, D.C.

Five days later, I was about as far removed from that mission as I could be, and that was not intentional. I went to Washington, D.C. to receive the Harmon Trophy, the highest honor in aviation this country can give, usually presented to civilians. Senator Barry Goldwater had nominated me for the award. Now I was about to meet President Ronald Reagan. The senator had planned to escort me, but was recovering from the triple-bypass heart surgery he'd had in November, so he asked a fellow congressman to fill in.

We drove to the White House and walked to the guard shack, where we would receive the badges authorizing us to enter. When the Marine opened the door for me, I wondered, *Does he know about my past? And if he did, would he let me in?* I looked at him for a few seconds before saying, "Thank you."

He looked at me and quietly said, "You're welcome, Sir."

That moment was just incredible.

We walked in the door and were met by a hostess who took us to the waiting room just outside the Oval Office, where the president's secretary was. I met the other current recipients of the Harmon Trophy: John Young and Captain Robert Crippen, Commander and pilot of the first space shuttle; Colonel Joe Engle and Captain Richard Truly, who took up the second space shuttle, and Janice Brown, who flew the first solar-powered aircraft.

We were ushered into the Oval Office, which looked exactly as it did on TV, so I felt as though I'd already been there many times. President Reagan was there and we stood in a little semi-circle around him. The first thing he said was, "Well ...," which he was known for doing at the beginning of most sentences. He was just the *nicest* guy, and then he spoke; first to the shuttle crew, then to Janice, and finally to me.

The president's reference notes stated: *"The 1982 Aviator winner is Jerry Foster, the commercial helicopter pilot for KPNX Broadcasting Company of Phoenix, Arizona. As a volunteer, he has located lost persons, spotted flood victims, and made mountain rescues, all involving a saving of lives."* (Courtesy of the Reagan Presidential Library)

President Reagan commented on all the people I'd rescued in the rural areas and then he looked at me and said, "You did a *marvelous* job!"

He went on to say something complimentary about Senator Goldwater, and I told him Barry was recovering well from his recent heart surgery. The president then said, "Give him my best regards."

And I'm thinking, *Here's the President of the United States telling me to give a United States Senator his best regards!*

I also wondered if he or the astronauts knew about my Marine Corps discharge. It was always on my mind.

Before we left, the president gave me a tie clasp and a bag of jelly beans. After the ceremony we were taken to the opening of an IMAX theater. Before the film began, our host asked us all to stand as he introduced us. I want to tell you, it was overwhelming! As the day ended, we were treated to a pleasant dinner hosted by NASA.

When I returned to my hotel that night, I just lay there staring at the ceiling for a while, just as I had twenty-three years earlier when I thought life would never be good again. It was hard to believe I had been in the White House and been honored by President Reagan. When I turned on the TV, there I was, along with Janice Brown and the astronauts, outside the White House. It must have really happened. It was on TV!

Susan: *"Either NBC or our Washington Bureau fed some tape that night of Jerry and the Harmon winners walking outside the White House. Jerry looked nervous and a little scared. Of course, he was wearing a coat and tie which made him uncomfortable anyway, so I just chalked it up to that.*

423

PRESIDENT REAGAN presented the 1982 Harmon Trophy to six recipients, including the four astronauts that flew the first two Shuttle missions. The astronauts, John Young, Robert Crippen, Joe H. Engle and Richard H. Truly, and two other recipients, Janice Lee Brown of Bakersfield, Calif., and Jerry Foster of Phoenix, Ariz., were selected to receive the trophy, considered one of the most prestigious awards

December 8, 1982, Washington, D.C.

The following morning I was in the hotel room getting ready to check out and fly back to Phoenix, when I got a call from Vicki. Susan had called her a few minutes earlier to tell her that Karen Key, my former competition at Channel 10 in Phoenix, had been killed the night before in a helicopter crash in Colorado. I was absolutely stunned by the news.

She had been working for a station in Denver and was flying in bad weather with her mechanic when the chopper went down. Investigators later learned she'd been drinking.

Those three starkly different events all happened during one week in December 1982. It was a week like no other with one incredibly high point, and two very low ones; but then, that's always been the story of my life. It has been a rollercoaster of a ride as I've made television history and established a list of firsts, while still running from my past.

Karen Key's tragic death would spark an investigation that would embarrass the Washington bureaucrats at FAA and bring TV helicopter pilots under tight scrutiny. The occurrence of her death would kick off a long string of events that would be the beginning of the end for me ... but not just yet.

Chapter 55

An Experiment that Didn't Work

About the time all of this was going on, another plan I had been working on for a while had come to pass.

Although I liked working with Bryan, I had wanted Bill Leverton—whom I had worked with at Channel 10—to come over to 12 as my photographer and backup pilot. We had worked well together at KOOL, coming up with some exciting stories while accomplishing many "firsts" in the news helicopter.

I thought that having another pilot along would be a good idea, and I always felt I could trust Bill and his flying style. He would need experience in turbines, but he could quickly gain that flying with me. I was beginning to realize I would need to slow down before long and thought; what could be better than sharing this adventure with another pilot, especially one I had so much confidence in.

I'd been in cahoots with my news director and general manager to hire him away from 10, and it all came together in early December, 1982. The hard part was telling Bryan, although he knew it before I could talk to him. He was very disappointed, but showed me a lot of respect and said if it didn't work out, he would like to have another shot at it. I really appreciated the way he handled it.

Susan also took the change well, but said it wouldn't work out. She thought Bill would either get his old job back at KOOL or he would get his own feature show on 12, since he was a star in his own right. There was also a lot of coverage from the print media as they continued to report on the "helicopter war" and the "ratings war."

Susan Sorg: *"I had nothing against Bill, who I considered to be an excellent writer, fabulous storyteller and a great guy. But Bryan was and still is just about the best friend I've ever had. One reason we worked well together was because Bryan and I preferred staying in the background, letting Jerry be Jerry and the face of Sky 12. I didn't see Bill playing second fiddle to Jerry. They are both very strong personalities."*

At first Bill and I were able to pick up where we had left off at KOOL. The biggest difference was that the helicopter technology was changing and we had a much more capable machine in so many ways. In no time, Bill picked up on his new duties. We had plenty of news to cover and a calendar full of events like schools, parades, Goldwater flights, and our law enforcement requests for help. Add to that some bad flooding through the holidays and you have busy newsrooms.

Bill came on board in late December. We were just getting ready to do a TV weather broadcast for the noon news when we were alerted by the sheriff's office that a young male was trapped in the middle of the flooded Gila River, about 10 miles south of our present position.

We quickly powered down our signal and told the station where we were headed, assuring them we would be back to do the weather before the show ended in a half hour.

We were on the scene within minutes and spotted our victim in the middle of a flood-swollen Gila River. Thirteen-year-old Justin Stone had been crossing the river at 115th Avenue when his horse slipped, throwing the boy into the rushing water. The horse made it to shore, but the kid didn't, and wasn't going to if we didn't do something.

The only problem was a set of telephone lines that followed the road. They were still up but were starting to lean, and wouldn't hold up much longer. And neither would the boy, who had grabbed onto a bush and was hanging on for his life, just above a five-foot waterfall.

As we got down low it looked like we had enough room between the telephone wires and the top of the rushing water. Bill agreed, but we knew it was tight. We landed on the river bank, dropped Leverton's door with a deputy, and headed back out, this time with Leverton riding on the skid while holding on to the seat frame. We moved under the wires with the skids scudding along the surface of the water.

When we were close enough, Bill reached down and grabbed the terrified boy, who then wrapped his legs around the skid and held on tight. Bill signaled to me that he had him and I backed away from under the wires and delivered our shivering cargo to the deputies. Then we retrieved our door and were back in the air to do our noon weather. It all happened so fast we were not able to shoot video.

Our critics during my day would argue that we were a news crew and were supposed to report the news, not make it. Even though the newspapers reported the story, those critics were quiet on this one, because a young boy's life had been saved by a "news crew."

I tried hard to make Bill feel like part of the team, because I really wanted it to work. But I knew he wasn't happy. When you work closely with a friend for years you get to know each other pretty well. I thought he and management at Channel 12 had worked out an agreement and a contract had been signed.

Bill Leverton: *"By the time I got to 12, Jerry had pretty much settled in to a team that I was never going to be a part of. The whole time*

I was there the only video I shot was with a camera that belonged in the Smithsonian, and was scenic stuff for Jerry's weather segments. Jerry never admitted it at the time, but he was embarrassed by the whole thing, and I was reduced to following him around like a faithful puppy, cleaning the windshield on the helicopter and carrying gear back and forth. Anyone who knew my personality back then knew it wasn't going to last.

"Nobody at Channel 12 had ever bothered to have me sign a contract. When new management came in at 10 I got real humble and asked them if I could have my job back, and they agreed.

"In the last year, Jerry and I have talked about that time and he has apologized for how badly it went wrong. I told him there was nothing to apologize for because it led us both to have wonderful careers. Jerry stayed in the air and I stayed with 'On the Arizona Road.' We're still friends today."

Chapter 56

The Sky 12 Team

The Team - Susan, me and Bryan

In early 1983, Bryan Nuemeister came back as my partner and we hit the ground running. I reminded him again about the one-year-burnout syndrome my photographers seemed to experience, but he took it in stride. As it turned out he stayed with me the next five years.

A team was now in place to give our station what they were paying very dearly for. It was a time in broadcasting which would never be repeated again. The crew of Sky 12 was the first of its kind in television news—and very likely the last. We were living the adventure of our lives. It became a lifestyle for all of us, and we shared the pride.

As the seasons turned into years we developed patterns and habits just like everyone else, but the difference was that every day brought something new. The biggest reason Sky 12 had the market was because we were dead serious about getting there first and then doing it the best. If that meant we were first on the scene and someone needed help, we helped first, and the critics be damned!

Vicki, Susan, Bryan and I were connected by beepers and powerful Motorola two-channel radios that we carried with us everywhere. They weighed a couple of pounds, were four inches wide and10 inches long, but they were lifesavers when Bryan was on the ground and I was in the air. If I dropped him off in a remote spot for a story or rescue, I could always stay in touch. If we couldn't land, at plane crashes or other accidents, for example, I would drop him so he could tell me what was needed and I could call for help.

If our story was about an injured mountain climber in the Superstition Mountains who needed medical help, I would radio either Maricopa County Sheriff's Office or the Highway Patrol, identify myself as "Lincoln 30," tell the dispatcher the problem and request a Ranger (DPS helicopter.) If Air Rescue was unavailable they would call the proper jurisdiction to get officers to the scene.

I would fly them in and very likely fly our victim to a hospital, then return to the scene to fly the officers back to their command post. It sometimes went on for hours or all night. If it was going to be complicated and one helicopter wasn't enough, Air Rescue would get there as soon as they could to help shuttle first responders.

DPS Rescues

Sometimes even the rescuers needed a little help. That was the case during my first year at Channel 12.

In one instance, a Boy Scout on an outing with his troop at the Salt River Canyon, was hit on the head by a falling rock. DPS Air Rescue responded to the call for help, but a mechanical problem caused the engine to overheat. The pilot and his bird spent the night in the parking lot at the bottom of the canyon. Bryan and I were called out to take over. By the time we were coming out of the canyon with the boy, it was so dark that Bryan had to hold a flashlight beam on the rock wall so the blades wouldn't hit it.

Another time a DPS pilot needed help when he was the object of the rescue. The previous day a Hughes 269 helicopter with a pilot and a radio repair tech on board crashed while attempting to take off from the highest peak of the Estrella Mountains, 40 miles southwest of Phoenix. They had just repaired a radio transmitter and were leaving when the crash occurred. Both men were killed.

Photographer Howard Shepherd and I covered the story live from the helicopter. It was pretty grizzly. The little helicopter rolled about 50 feet nearly straight down the west face of the mountain, coming to rest on an outcropping of rock and bursting into flame.

Because of the steep and rough terrain, the Central Arizona Mountain Rescue Association was flown to the scene by a DPS Ranger to recover bodies and bring them up to the small landing pad to be flown out. Before that could be accomplished, however, a thunderstorm rolled in, forcing the recovery to be put off until the next day.

The command center was an old Indian mission located at the base of the mountain range some 4,000 feet below the crash site. By sunrise the next morning the parking lot was nearly full with two helicopters, law enforcement, and families of the victims.

We waited for the sun to get a little higher and eliminate the shadows. I talked over the plan with the DPS crew so we would all be on the same page. My intent was to circle overhead and shoot aerials while they made the recovery. We would both be on the same radio frequency. It was always a good idea to have someone watching your tail when the mission involved risky landing areas, and this one was tricky.

By 7 a.m. the temperature was over 100 degrees, the air breezy on the surface and gusty at 5,000 feet. Humidity was high from last night's rain showers. "Tricky" might be an understatement, but these guys were very experienced and had done this kind of mission many times. They removed the doors and extra gear from Ranger 30 to make it light as possible.

Bob Forsyth was the pilot of the rescue helicopter: *"We developed a plan where we would fly up to the peak and hold power over the small landing pad while a deputy and my medic would get out and load the bodies on board. Then I would fly the bodies down to the command center at the mission and return for the two men and the climbing gear left from last night's attempted recovery.*

"With Jerry circling above, I sat on the little pad, holding full power to keep the ship stable while the medic and the deputy began loading the bodies. One set of remains was placed in the baggage compartment while the other was placed in a Stokes litter and secured crossways in the back. During the night, animals had torn open the body bag, exposing a badly burned head and arm. Because family of the victims was waiting below, the rescuers decided to cover him with a blanket and strap it down.

"Since they were working behind me I kept a running dialog with Jerry. Seeing that they were nearly finished he told me he would head back to the command center and be ready for my arrival. Upon leaving he said, 'Don't do anything heroic; I just powered my camera down.' I assured him I wouldn't."

I wanted to be on the ground to get a shot of Bob landing and to warn the waiting command post that the family should be kept back. It had all gone according to plan up to this point and I was thankful for that. My partner, Howie, who had been with me the previous evening, was home with a sick baby so I was the cameraman on this one.

Bob Forsyth: *"I lifted off the pad heading southwest into the wind, then turned left to head for the mission when there was a loud bang, followed by a severe vibration ... then my anti-torque pedals went lifeless. I tried to attain forward airspeed, but was unable, and started spinning to the left. I reduced power and entered autorotation, but with no airspeed I was just along for the ride. The spinning was so fast that I was held against the seat straps by the force."*

I couldn't have been gone more than 30 seconds when Bob came over the radio and calmly said, "Jerry, I have a problem. I'm out of control. Better come back."

I went from a descent to a full power climb, making a hard left 90-degree turn, and there he was. I was about 2,000 feet below and a quarter-mile away. What a sight! The helicopter was in a spin and headed down fast. We actually talked back and forth. I heard Bob say, "Here we go."

Bob Forsyth: *"I saw the ground approaching fast, and pulled pitch. The helicopter actually stopped a few feet above the ground, and—still spinning—settled onto its skids, then overturned onto its left side. The rotor system beat itself to pieces and finally, when everything stopped, I realized the engine was still running. I shut it down then exited the aircraft through the missing front windshield, moving as fast as I could in case the a/c was on fire."*

I have seen some sights in my day, but that one tops the list. When Bob hit the ground, a huge mushroom ball of dust completely engulfed the machine and didn't clear for at least a minute. I had to circle the crash to wait for visibility to improve. On my second pass I saw a body hanging out of the wreckage and thought it was Bob. I hurriedly landed and before I could friction my controls I saw Bob come running out of the sand cloud straight toward me.

Another helicopter landed that was bringing NTSB investigators in to look at the first accident. They, like me, had seen it all. When I knew Bob was in good hands and uninjured I headed back up the mountain to bring his medic and deputy down.

The cause of the accident was the blanket used to cover one of the bodies, which had come loose and flown into the tail rotor. We were all still learning about operating helicopters in different kinds of situations. All it takes is one little thing unnoticed and bad things can happen. We all learned a big lesson that day.

By the way, I didn't get a single shot of the accident until it was all over. But I got to see a pilot do what he was trained to do in an actual life or death situation. Nice job, Bob!

Upside-down DPS helicopter

The horror of seeing mangled and burned bodies has stayed with me for years. But I gained a lot of respect for the first responders of my generation. The mountain climbers, men and women, were volunteers from the community who formed a posse with the sheriff's office. They would skip work or stay up all night; whatever it took to do the job. In a case like this they had to rummage through the crash and pick up the pieces.

Several years later another DPS helicopter would run into trouble during a search for a missing person near the small town of Camp Verde. A DPS crew was on it and Susan was monitoring the progress while Bryan and I were visiting two schools in northwest Phoenix.

While I was talking to the kids, Bryan was on the radio with Susan. She had urgent traffic for us so he turned up the volume to let the kids could listen.

Susan reported, "The Department of Public Safety just called and said one of their helicopters reported a fuel warning light and he was landing along the river. They are requesting your help. Can you fly some fuel up there?"

Bryan told her to stand by and looked at me for an answer. I turned to the kids and asked them if we should go rescue Ranger 27. About 150 kids were sitting on the grass next to Sky 12 and they all yelled for us to go, even though we had just landed. It was really cute.

After the kids moved back I fired up the engine, came to a three-foot hover, and signaled Bryan to climb up onto the skid and get in. Bryan was like *Spider-Man*. He could run up, grab the skid, and then swing up and into his seat.

We headed to Scottsdale Airport, picked up two five-gallon cans of jet fuel and headed for the location we were given. When we got close I dropped down and flew along the river so we wouldn't miss the helicopter. I thought it odd that Ranger 27 didn't answer my radio calls. We figured he didn't want to waste his battery and cause another problem.

We came around a bend in the river and there was Ranger 27 lying on its side in three feet of water near the bank. I remember Bryan saying, "Holy Cow, Batman, that can't be good!"

The helicopter was next to a tree, with a rotor blade stuck in the branches. I wasn't sure if it had hit the tree or flown into it after the crash. The pilot was shaken up, but seemed okay.

His medic was up on a nearby mountain. They had located the hiker they were searching for, but the medic had to help him down a steep area to the only landing site. Because the helicopter was low on fuel they decided the pilot would go to a nearby airport, get fuel, and then return to pick them up.

As the pilot headed for the airport the fuel warning light came on, indicating there were only a few minutes of running time left. When that light comes on we all know to head for the ground, because it can get real quiet, real quick.

The pilot only had one choice, and that river was it, so he headed for a sandbar. Everything was going according to plan until he changed his mind at the very last second and decided to go for the river bank, about three feet above the water and 15 feet away.

DPS chopper in the river

He didn't make it. The engine flamed out just as he was approaching the bank. His skid caught the side of the bank and over he went. Another few seconds and he would have been safely down.

We felt bad for the pilot, who was a highly respected Army pilot with lots of combat time in Vietnam. But we were glad he was unhurt.

It was a lesson learned for all of us. In the past, when a fuel light came on in Sky 12, I figured I had 15 minutes to get down. But after this shocker my low fuel light never came on again.

Ever.

Chapter 57

Search and Rescue

When Bruce Erion told me he was leaving Channel 10 for a similar job in Atlanta I was truly sorry to hear it. In the short time he had been here we developed a friendly, but competitive, attitude and were able to work together with no problems. I braced myself for whoever was next. I didn't have to wait long, and the selection by the management at Channel 10 was a total surprise.

Len Clements was a young man who had, just a few short years ago, graduated from Scottsdale High School. While a student, he spent summers working at local airports as a line boy refueling airplanes and helicopters.

Len Clements: *"I was a young kid just looking for a sense of direction. I watched Jerry Foster on TV every chance I got and wanted to follow in his footsteps. He was my hero. I refueled his 'copter several times when he landed the KOOL TV Hughes 300.*

"Jerry was always friendly, smiling, and encouraging to kids like me. He was keenly aware of his role model status in a swashbuckling, cowboy kind of way. In the early 1970s Jerry was doing extraordinary things that fired my imagination, along with that of countless other kids of my generation.

"At that time we didn't have cell phones and endless TV channels to choose from. Arizona still had the feel of the Wild West; a vast and still largely unknown land of tremendous beauty and adventure. I developed a deep hunger to know more about this exotic land.

"With his helicopter and a television camera, Jerry brought that beauty and experience right into our living room every night. Watching him was a "Walter Mitty" kind of experience, allowing us to live vicariously through Jerry's experiences. He had the best job in the world as far as I was concerned, and I wanted part of the action.

"I followed my dream, became a pilot and was lucky enough to be in the right place at the right time, to land my dream job. In 1982 Bill Close hired me as the pilot reporter for Channel 10. I was 24 years old and felt on top of the world."

The first thing this upstart youngster did was rent a condo on the north side of the very building I lived in, so that he could see my helicopter sitting on the roof of Channel 12. This kid was serious and I knew the helicopter war was still in full force. But there was a difference: this young man had worked his way up the ladder just as I had.

Len was polite, nice looking, and had a good television presence, even though he had no experience. Our first meeting was in the high-rise where we lived. He was respectful and told me that I was his hero and inspiration when he was a kid, which totally melted my heart on the spot. All I could do was smile, shake hands and welcome him to the business.

Len Clements: *"We needled each other with some good-natured kidding and we always made it fun. Sometimes when we were called out, we happened to meet in the elevator and made small talk, trying to act like we were just going out for a bite to eat. A few minutes later we were both in the air on the way to the same story."*

Len Clements

For the next decade we worked together and never so much as had an argument or disagreement. He was good from the start and only got better. Len was talented and the best natural pilot I have ever known. To this day we are bonded together as close friends who shared the experience of the best flying jobs in the world.

Mountain Rescues

In my early years with Channel 10, police and fire departments would call me for help when a hiker or climber was injured or stranded on one of the Phoenix Mountains; especially Camelback or Squaw Peak [now Piestewa Peak.] I would hover or set a skid on a rock, allowing firemen to load a victim into the right front seat, then I'd fly down to a waiting ambulance. If the area was too tight for the helicopter, rescue personnel would have to carry the victim to an outcropping I could get to.

With the little Hughes, power had been a problem during the summer hot spells, when temperatures might cool down to just under 100 degrees by midnight. Many times I would have to fly firemen up to a scene that was too dangerous to climb, and then wait on the ground for them to get the victim stabilized. This could often take a lot of time. Once we got the victim down and in the ambulance, I would go back up and bring the firemen down, one at a time. Often it was dark by the time the last person was back at the foot of the mountain. If the rescue took place during

DPS helicopter on a mission. I was proud to work with these men

my morning or evening traffic reports, I reported what I was doing. The station was pleased, the victim was glad to be rescued, and I felt good about what I'd done: it worked out well for everyone, although my critics still claimed I was supposed to be a newsman, not a cop.

As crude as the rescues were in the little Bug, it saved a lot of time and hiking for the ground personnel. I made those flights for several years in the Hughes 300, until Phoenix Police formed an Air Patrol, starting off with the same model.

If DPS had a Ranger helicopter available, they would get the call. In those cases, I would stay on the scene and watch their every move. It was a great study for me and I learned a lot from them. Air Rescue was coming of age in the late 1960s and Arizona was the testing ground. There were very few law enforcement helicopters in the country back then, so it was all new to us and every call had its own share of dangers and problems.

Our favorite scenario was to back up the Ranger crew so that we could shoot video of the action and listen to the radio chatter as it was happening. That way we got the news story on video and were still able to help with shuttling rescuers. Every mission was different, and sometimes we lost the patient. That always hit us hard and stayed in our minds until we got the next victim to safety.

We were dependable, and the sheriff's office and other law enforcement agencies knew we were ready when needed. We made a lot of friends, but also stepped on some toes along the way. Not everyone liked me, for a lot of different reasons. Maybe they didn't like my weather reports, or we did a story that offended someone, or I just got it wrong somehow. I know you can't please everyone, but we tried.

I need to point out that not all of the law enforcement folks were happy to see the news helicopter show up. Going back to my Channel 10 days, I was something brand new to all of them, and so was the helicopter. Added to that, I was a newsman and that was a negative. It took time to build up trust, and sometimes I just couldn't make it happen.

When I moved into the Jet Age at Channel 12, with the five-passenger Hughes, I didn't have the capability to put victims on a litter. When it was necessary to fly them out we loaded them in the back seat like we had done in the Bug. I also had the help of a photographer who would quickly become trained and was always willing to do whatever it took to get the job done. We participated in dozens of searches and recoveries, and always carried water, first-aid box, c-rations, blankets, flares and an overnight bag. Since we often dealt with victims in a lot of pain, I also kept a small bottle of Jack Daniels whisky in a secret compartment.

It came in handy when a cowboy fell off his horse and sustained an ugly compound fracture to his leg. A sheriff's deputy requested a DPS helicopter, and since there was not one available, I got the call. The accident had taken place north of the valley near Carefree.

When I landed, the deputy told me the cowpoke was in a lot of pain. We splinted and secured the leg to keep it from moving more than necessary, and got the old man settled into the back seat. I asked if a shot of whiskey would help, and he lit up. He took a long pull, replaced the cap and set the bottle next to him.

The old guy had found a friend. When I landed at the hospital 20 minutes later, the emergency room crew opened the back door to a very happy cowboy and a helicopter that smelled like a bar. We improvised a lot of what we were doing back then, and not all of it was FAA-approved or understood.

We became adept at covering multiple stories at once. In one instance, a hiker had fallen near the top of Camelback Mountain and we had just set down four fireman to prepare the victim for the ride down, when I got a call from base about a plane crash off the Litchfield Park runway 20 miles to the west.

I radioed the fire department that I would be right back. We pointed the nose west and 20 minutes later we were circling the crash. Howie was shooting video as the fire trucks were spewing out chemical fire retardant. We circled twice and minutes later we were back over Camelback when the fireman radioed us that the hiking victim was ready to move. We took off all four doors and carefully stowed them with the fire department.

Firemen carried the victim on a stretcher to an open place near a vertical cliff where I was able to put both skids down. Howie stepped out with his camera and filmed the firemen loading the stretcher crossways in the back seat, while a very brave rescuer stood on the skid holding the stretcher as I flew back to the base of Camelback. A few minutes later I picked up the firemen and their gear, dropped them off, and Howie and I headed for the station. It was only a few minutes before the five o'clock news, and this was in the early days before the live feeds were working. Howie went to the editing room and I found a typewriter to write the stories we had just covered.

We were back in the air for the top of the news and I reported the airplane crash and rescue stories live with video running over my narrative. Ten minutes later I did the weather and followed with an update at the end of the newscast. It had been a busy afternoon, but a very rewarding one.

Channel 10's chopper crew only had video of Sky 12 removing the victim, with the firemen holding onto the stretcher. That really made us smile!

Not all of our assignments went that quickly, however. A few years later, when Bryan was with me, we spent two days in the Superstition Mountains looking for an overdue hiker. Ranger 28 from DPS was in on the search, as well as ground parties on horseback.

Hikers usually stayed on established trails, some of which were along vertical cliffs that dropped straight down for hundreds of feet. It is a very rough and rocky terrain, dotted with Saguaro cactus and desert shrubbery. There are a million places a body could fall and be hidden forever.

The Superstition Mountains comprise 160,000 acres of wilderness about 45 miles east of downtown Phoenix. Its 180 miles of trails, proximity to a large urban area, and normally pleasant year-round weather, combine to entice thousands of people each year to get out for a hike. Unfortunately, many aren't properly prepared. They don't tell anyone where they're going, they don't take enough water, and they don't stay on the trails. An injured person off-trail could be hidden in a crevice or under an overhang, and not be found for days, if at all.

Because the Superstitions are a dedicated wilderness area, no motorized vehicles are allowed to drive in or land. We needed to notify the U.S. Forest Service whenever there was any kind of emergency operation going on. Usually that was taken care of by the responding agency. During my career I made dozens of trips into that area and never heard a word of complaint from them.

Superstition Mountains

On the second day of the search for the overdue hiker, Bryan and I were flying down a vertical rock wall when we spotted two tennis shoes sticking out from a ledge covered by bushes. It was our victim, who had apparently fallen more than 500 feet. Since Ranger 28 had been called away for another mission, we would have to help recover the body.

For more than four hours we shuttled men and equipment from the Central Arizona Mountain Rescue Association to an outcropping just above the victim. Then they had to rappel more than 100 feet down to the ledge. It was a long and tedious operation.

I left Bryan on the mountain with the rescuers so he could assist with landings. Holding up two index fingers, he would show me how close my rotor blades were to the rock wall. Sometimes we had to get within a foot or less to get a skid on the ledge.

The hardest part of these operations was meeting and interacting with the family members who would gather at the command post, desperate for any details about their loved one. For that reason, rescuers made sure the bodies were always secured in a body bag. In this particular case, the victim's parents, wife, and two teenage sons were waiting when I landed. The pain was always shared with family. We knew it could have been any one of us or our family members in the body bag.

During these kinds of missions, rescuers tried to keep it as light as possible when recovering the dead. It was gruesome, and sometimes gory, but it had to be done. For us, the payoff was when we found a lost soul alive and were able to get them out of trouble. There were also times when these missions conflicted with our news commitments. Although we tried to serve both, in at least one case, it made for an awkward situation.

Bryan Neumeister: *"At that time, the sheriff's office did not have a helicopter, so Sky 12 flew about 400 hours a year assisting MCSO on searches, recoveries, or whatever they needed. It was a good arrangement for everyone. We got a news scoop and were part of the story. MCSO got Jerry's skills, the helicopter, and footage they could use as needed. I don't think that would be possible these days, but that's how it was in the 1980s.*

"This particular recovery took place in the White Tank mountains west of Phoenix. It's a hostile, barren environment and a helicopter is really the best possible way to recover anyone with a serious injury in this area.

"A hiker had fallen off a ledge and landed head first; not a pretty picture. He was most likely killed on impact, and our job was to get the body out of the mountains.

"We dropped off Larry Black and a couple other deputies above the fall site. We didn't have a lot of equipment for rappelling yet, so it was going to be one of those situations where we'd try to hand off the body while Jerry balanced a skid on a boulder.

"Larry passed the body to me feet first. What a mess. I literally had him on my lap trying to keep his head outside the helicopter so blood and fluids wouldn't get all over the rear passenger area. With the rotor wash,

blood was going everywhere. I wore a white shirt: at least it had been white that morning.

"It was nearing 5 p.m. and Jerry would need to do the weather live from the helicopter. I would normally shoot weather shots from the rear hand-held camera as Jerry talked to the viewers on the front camera. A switcher allowed Jerry to go between cameras live. Since the camera was mounted on bungee cords, he could also pan to a shot outside. This particular version of Sky 12 was mostly white with a couple of brown stripes.

"We were halfway through this flight down the mountain when it was time for Jerry to do a weather shot. Jerry covered the story briefly and went to my camera. I had the camera balanced on the victim's shoulders, shooting back to the rear tail boom.

"The anchor woman commented on the lovely shot of the red sun reflecting off the tail boom. I thought to myself, 'It's not sunset.'

"The look on the deputy's face as I handed the body over said it all. He looked at the helicopter, looked at me, and was horrified. When we arrived at the hangar and saw the tail assembly of the helicopter, we understood why. Everything was spattered with blood, tissue and brain matter.

"I'm a cameraman, but in Sky 12, you were whatever you needed to be, whenever it was needed, no questions asked."

Many times, on a long ride home after a mission like that, we wouldn't say a word to each other. We all dealt with tragedy in our own way. We had done what we were trained to do and kept it within the parameters of our capabilities and our mechanical hummingbird.

Whenever we could, we filmed every mission as a news story, but there were times when things were happening fast, and capturing the moment wasn't always possible. There was the young woman who tried to drive across a road which had been barricaded because of flood waters. We saw her start from a mile away, and by the time we got there, she was in big trouble. The rushing water turned her car sideways and pointing downriver.

We landed on the highway at the barricades and Bryan quickly removed his door and threw it aside. He stood on the skid ready to go and we were off. I set Bryan down on the car and moved away while he helped the young girl get out of her window and onto the roof. I then went back and picked them both up. In less than five minutes it was all over. That was exactly how DPS would have handled it, except *their* medic would have taken the door off and carefully stowed it. When we recovered our door, it was in the water; broken and bent. But a life was saved, and a lesson learned.

During major flooding in Arizona we went from one situation to another. With the live capability, we seldom ever missed a news spot or a weather segment. Many times we would finish one good news story and beam the video back to the station while on the way to another story.

We usually ate on the run—or in our case, on the fly—and knew every fast food joint with an open area for us to land. As soon as we touched the ground, my shooter was out and sprinting for the door with money in hand.

Our fuel stops were like a NASCAR pit stop. My favorite airport was Scottsdale, and I always landed at Corporate Jets. I would call them on the radio when I was five minutes out and give them notice I was en route and needed a "hot fueling." That meant I needed to get in and out as quickly as possible. As I landed, a fuel truck would pull up and refuel me while the engine was running. I could be out of there in just minutes if we had something going.

Today, news helicopters are just that. They report the news and nothing more. DPS, police helicopters, and Air Rescue have taken over in the search, rescue and recovery areas. And that is as it should be. But when it was all new, and helicopters were coming into their own, we did what had to be done—no questions asked. And lives were saved.

Chapter 58

Diving

When Vicki and I got to spend a little time alone together, we planned our outings with the understanding that "breaking news changes everything," and quite often it did. The first time Vicki went on a drowning recovery with me would be an eye opener for her. We had been dating a short while, and were at my mom's house for Sunday dinner. But the visit was cut short when I got a call from the sheriff's office advising me of a drowning at Bartlett Lake northeast of Phoenix. Back in the air, I contacted the sheriff's office by radio and was told Larry Black would meet me at the aid station at the lake. I switched frequencies and told Larry I would be on the scene

With Vicki on a dive

in about 15 minutes, and that I had my dive gear in the back seat and Vicki in the front.

Larry said a Mexican family had been swimming in a small bay when a six-year-old boy disappeared about 12 feet off the shore. The murky water was nearly 10 feet deep in that area. Larry felt confident about the location the family had given and said he and I would dive when I got there.

By now several deputies were on the scene and guided me into an open spot near the water's edge, approximately 100 feet from where everyone was gathered. Larry and I suited up and prepared for the dive. The family spoke no English so, through an interpreter, Larry asked the father of the boy to point to where he had last seen his son. The man seemed positive, so rather than wait for the volunteer posse to be scrambled out of Phoenix, we walked into the water and floated out until the father was satisfied we were in the right area.

Our desert lakes offer no visibility at all below about five feet. Below that it gets dark quickly, and becomes black as it gets even deeper. Lights cannot be used because they only create a blinding glow in the reflection of water and sand.

As we released our air to descend to the bottom I held onto Larry's weight belt so that we wouldn't get separated. Once on the bottom we started moving around and right away I found the boy's arm, grabbed it tightly, and gave Larry three sharp tugs—our signal that we had found the body. The non-swimmer father had been spot on.

The hardest thing about finding a body was surfacing with the family there. The first sounds you hear after breaking the surface are the pitiful wails and screaming from Mom, Dad and the siblings. We brought the little guy to shore and before we could get him into a body bag, the father pleaded with us to give them a little time with the boy and then they would leave. It was heartbreaking for all of us.

When the family was gone I shot video of the lake shore and the boy wrapped in a body bag being loaded into the back of a sheriff's van.

The sadness stays with you on calls like this. It was comforting to have someone there with you afterward who had seen it all and understood why you needed time to shake it off; especially when it involved an innocent child. Bryan and Susan both understood, having had the same experiences I'd had. And now Vicki understood. This event would spur her on to get her diver's certification. Everyone who participates in a drowning recovery takes home nearly the same feelings.

Another year, my mother made Bryan and me a Thanksgiving dinner to go when we were called out by Susan to a drowning south of Flagstaff in an ice-cold lake. The elevation was around 7,000 feet and this was November. After a full day of diving, we recovered the two fishermen whose boat had capsized in the rough water and gusty winds.

That day at Ashurst Lake was the coldest I had ever been in my life. The temperature of the water was 38 degrees, with surface temps just a few degrees warmer. For the first few minutes we all suffered severe "ice cream" headaches when we submerged into that black water. One of the divers got the "popsicle shakes" and had to be evacuated by a DPS Ranger. When that little adventure was over we were numb for two days.

It was following that recovery mission that Deputy Larry Black persuaded Maricopa County Sheriff, Dick Godbehere, to buy dry suits for the Lake Patrol deputies. From then on, Maricopa County would lead the state in drowning recovery techniques. Every year Lake Patrol divers ran a training school at Saguaro Lake that was always well attended by police and fire agencies around Arizona.

We also developed ways to transport divers to isolated areas on the skids of a helicopter. Search and Rescue organizations in Arizona had come a long way over the past decade and the helicopter had become an integral lifesaving tool all over the world; thanks in large part to those pilots in Vietnam and from the Arizona DPS Air Rescue Unit.

Being associated with the diver's volunteer posse was the hardest and most physically and mentally challenging assignment I ever had. It was a disgusting, sickening, and heartbreaking assignment each and every time. No drowning was routine, and you never got used to it, but there was no choice. It had to be done. A family cannot begin to grieve until that body is recovered. We all know the tragedy of losing a loved one and that's why we do it.

Sgt. Larry Black, MCSO: *"I can remember almost every drowning recovery I was involved in, and every one of them hurt. You became a part of it. You felt the family's grief and became obsessed with finding their loved one.*

Every first responder I ever talked to felt the same way. It was unusual if we didn't come up with the victim in two days. If the location was uncertain, or we didn't find the body within a few days, the divers would be sent home, then we would check the lake or river daily until the body rose to the surface.

The dive operation at the Maricopa County Sheriff's Office was greatly helped in the mid-1980s when the Johnson family of Mesa lost a child to drowning at Lake Powell. From that tragedy came the K.C. Johnson Foundation; a non-profit organization that raised and donated funds to buy the equipment we so badly needed for black and deep water recoveries.

Larry Black: *"When little K.C. Johnson drowned, I remember his family's desperation to recover the child's body. Earl Johnson, an ex-cop, was prepared to drain the lake to get his grandson back if that's what it took. The boy had drowned just out of reach of the family. It was a very tragic story, but it prompted the Johnson family to give us equipment and donations to help find other drowning victims, who, without their help, might never have been found. Thanks to the Johnson Foundation we were able to use special underwater cameras to make recoveries from water too deep for diving. We never gave up until recovery was made. Sheriff Dick Godbehere was also a big reason the Lake Patrol spent so much time on a drowning; he was very supportive, and a member of the Johnson Foundation, as was Jerry. It became a personal thing with all of us in Lake Patrol to find that body and give it back to the family so the grieving process could start."*

Bryan Neumeister: *"One recovery stands out to me. We looked for a young man for two weeks at Bartlett Lake and finally spotted him floating. Jerry told me to get out on the skid and see if I could get hold of him and we would drag him slowly to shallow water, land, and put him in a body bag.*

Jerry put a skid down next to him and I reached out and grabbed a handful of his long bushy hair. Over my headset, I told Jerry I had him, and as we started moving, the unthinkable happened. His scalp came loose and left me holding hair and scalp in my hand. As I moaned in my headset and straightened up, I raised my hand, holding what I had been left with. The expression on Jerry's face said it all and he would later say the same about my own expression. It was an incredibly horrendous moment in our lives. I didn't look at what I had; I just tossed it back in the water.

We had to go at it again and this time I grabbed his swimming trunks and we were able to get him into shallow water. Then I jumped into the water and pulled him to shore as Jerry landed on the bank. Now all we had to do was bag the body.

What happens to a human body after a long time in the water is horrific. The smell, the bloating, the flys and maggots ... it's something you can never forget. When you finally get home and shower, it's hard to wash away the odor that lingers in your nose for days.

We put our victim into a body bag in the rear floor of Sky 12, then flew it to the sheriff's substation. The bereaved family was grateful that their loved one had been recovered. That made it all worthwhile.

Chapter 59

Special Assignments

Producer Susan Sorg turned out to be the MVP of our team. She made sure we knew where to go and what time to be there. We seldom missed a scheduled event unless we were diverted to a breaking story. We never turned down an assignment, never turned down a law enforcement request, and never *ever* turned down a school request.

Each season brought a different challenge. I didn't really have a favorite because by the time it was over we were all ready for a change of pace. Winters were easier because the summer guaranteed daytime temperatures upward of 115 degrees, which is tough on machines, people, and animals.

In April the furnace began so we started doing stories about snakes, scorpions and desert survival. It's the time of year people head for the lakes and rivers, which meant working closely with DPS and county sheriff's departments. And of course there were the many spot news stories that would break daily.

Susan: *"On most spot news stories, Jerry and Bryan would fly to the location and I'd remain at the station, gathering information from my end. When they returned, if there was time before a newscast he'd land long enough for me to write the story while Bryan edited the video, then they would get back in the air for a live report. When time was short, he'd drop off the tape and pick up the scripts I'd written from what I had gathered on the phone and what details he had called back on the radio. Bryan would tell me what he had shot and I knew what to write to.*

"The three of us had developed a rhythm. I had learned how to write so Jerry would feel comfortable with it. I had his "voice," so to speak; knowing how he phrased things, and what words he would use that would sound natural. Working with Bryan brought it all together. He was not only a master with video and sound, he put together some amazing things in the editing booth. Each of our individual strengths made up for the weaknesses of the other two, and the result was magic.

"When we did feature stories I got to go along if there was an open seat. There was nothing I loved more, provided everything worked like it was supposed to. And Jerry expected it to run smoothly, with me briefing him on the story and making sure interviews were lined up. We turned out some great stories, from spot news to half-hour specials. For me, it was a dream job and lifestyle."

Poor Susan—some days her telephone never stopped ringing. Today, when my GPS reports "recalculating," I think of her. Her carefully planned schedules constantly needed to be adjusted.

We seldom took a day off and vacations were normally planned for the hot months, when the helicopter was due for an annual inspection. Even then Susan had us lined up for something fun and cool.

San Diego was a favorite destination. We did a variety of feature stories with the U.S. Navy, Marine Corps and Coast Guard, and we chartered a dive boat and did a series of ocean-related stories. With a little help from friends like Buzz, Tom, and

Fritz, we were able to do a first class job for Channel 12. Despite the effort it took, we always turned it into a good time, and stories we are still proud of today.

One of these trips was particularly good for Susan, as she met her future husband, Ron Sorg, on a Navy aircraft carrier. We had accompanied Senator John McCain on a flight to the USS Carl Vinson, 110 miles off the San Diego coast. It was the first time Senator McCain had been on a Navy carrier since being shot down over Hanoi and spending seven miserable years as a prisoner of war. It was an honor for us to spend this time with him.

We were flown out to the carrier on a twin-engine Sikorsky helicopter, used for shuttling people and cargo back and forth to the beach. Since there was so much to shoot in a short time, Howard Shepard was also with us. The infamous "Howie Factor" hit during an interview when his camera and tripod toppled over, putting a dent in the floor. Some quick repair involving Susan's hairclip and a rubber band saved the day. While Susan and Howie got the interviews, Bryan was out on the flight deck, literally chained to it as he shot video of the jets taking off and landing.

We spent the time on the aircraft carrier as guests of the Admiral of the fleet and the ship's captain. Senator McCain put on an excellent performance, and Bryan and Howie managed to capture it all on video tape. It was an incredible—and exclusive—journey and story.

During that trip I had an emotional moment I will never forget. On our arrival, the first stop was to the "Admiral of the Fleet" quarters for a welcome aboard. I stayed with Senator McCain as his guest while

Bryan, Howie and Susan shot what we needed for a documentary.

As we sat and visited with the admiral and captain my attention was drawn to the admiral's orderly, a young Marine PFC standing off to one side of the room. He was about my size and weight, and wearing dress blues. My eyes began to cloud up and I had to look away several times.

Through that young Marine, I was getting a glimpse of what I had dreamed of being nearly 25 years ago. I wondered how my life would have gone if things had been different.

Chapter 60

More Goldwater Stories

 While most of my flying with Senator Goldwater was for campaigning, speaking engagements, or other work-related trips, sometimes we flew just for fun. I'd schedule a crew and we'd go up north to Lake Powell or other areas, especially around the Navajo reservations. The land was incredibly beautiful, as I had discovered on my solo flight to Casper, Wyoming years before. This area was a favorite of Senator Goldwater. He told a lot of stories about Lake Powell, the Grand Canyon, and Navajo Mountain, where he and his wife Peggy had been part-owners of a lodge and trading post after WWII. Barry was the 75th recorded person to boat down the rapids of the Grand Canyon back in 1939. Since that time the Goldwaters had made numerous trips to Northern Arizona, taking along family and some of his closest friends.

By the late 1970s my cousin Steve Ward had worked up to the position of Public Relations Director for the Del Webb Corporation. Steve got to know the senator very well and shared some stories.

Steve Ward: *"Goldwater's birthday was January 1 and he gathered a group of friends for a yearly get-together. They called themselves "The Grand Canyon Hiking, Singing and Loving Club," and what a powerful group they were: Supreme Court Justice Rehnquist, attorney generals, dignitaries and people of that caliber.*

"He would call me up and say, 'Do you have any tour boats available?' Nobody ever calls for a tour boat, but we would arrange for one and take the group to Rainbow Bridge. Barry would pick up the microphone and talk the entire time, while in the back of the boat they would be playing bridge. When we returned to the marina they went to the lodge, the dining room and lobby and spent the next three days playing bridge and having a great time.

"I first got to know the senator from those excursions, and then when he came to Powell with Jerry, I began to know him in a more personal way.

"One of my favorite Goldwater stories happened at a big reception. I was in a receiving line that included the senator, Jerry, and Page resident, Joan Nevills-Staveley, whose father, Norman Nevills, was the first commercial river runner in 1947. Barry had been one of his first passengers. One of the guests asked Barry how long he had known Joan. The senator's answer: 'Hell, I was there the night she was conceived!'

"During one trip, I was flying with Jerry, Bryan and the senator to Dangling Rope, a marina 40 miles up the lake accessible only by boat or helicopter. We landed at the top of the long ramp that led down to the marina so the senator could have a look and take a few pictures. Apparently, the ranger on

Trip to Dangling Rope at Lake Powell

duty didn't get the word that the senator was on a tour. As we got out of the helicopter and Jerry shut the engine down, I saw the park ranger coming up the ramp.

"It was a long climb and by the time he got to the top he was huffing and puffing and looking irate. He had his citation book out and was headed for Jerry until he spotted Senator Goldwater. His demeanor quickly changed, the scowl on his face was replaced with a big smile, and the citation book went in his back pocket.

"We had a lot of trips on the lake when I would meet Jerry and his crew with a houseboat. Once he even dropped passengers on the houseboat while it was going up the lake. Every trip was an adventure."

There was another trip to Dangling Rope marina to drop off Barry, who was meeting friends on a houseboat. We landed in the same place at the top of the ramp, shut down, and started down the steep, slippery stairs next to the boat ramp. I was in the lead with Barry following me and Bryan behind him.

Bryan Neumeister: *"I was right behind the senator, who was telling us about the time he nearly fell off a steep canyon wall. While telling the story, he suddenly lost his balance and lurched forward. Jerry, with reflexes like a cat, turned around and caught him in midair and put him back on the step. Barry never stopped talking the whole time.*

Jerry and I looked at each other wide-eyed, knowing this would have been a whole different day had Jerry not made the interception. Barry could not have survived that fall.

Staying on a houseboat with Barry was a surreal experience. He would be in the lower bunk, telling amazing stories. I hung on every word, thinking, 'What a privilege.'"

A thrill on those trips was sitting atop of one of the massive buttes overlooking Lake Powell, thousands of feet below us: no sound, no pollution, and no worries until we were ready to leave. Then our only thought was, *O Lord, please let the helicopter start.* The top of one of those tall spires was not a place you'd want to be stranded.

There were so many trips with the senator that it would be difficult to describe them all. A favorite, though, was to the Air Force Academy in Colorado Springs, Colorado. When Judy

Atop of one of the many buttes at Lake Powell

Eisenhower called from Washington to schedule the trip with Susan, she put it on my calendar as a tour of the academy and dinner. I would pick Goldwater up at his house at 4 p.m. in the helicopter, and we would go to Sky Harbor Airport where an Air Force T-39 would be waiting to fly us to the academy. We would return that night in the same aircraft. Sounded pretty straightforward.

When I landed in his driveway and he stepped out of his front door, however, I knew our wires had been crossed somewhere. He was wearing a black tuxedo with a black coat over his arm and he looked sharp. I had a feeling we weren't going for a tour of the academy, but a very formal affair. When he was strapped in and had the headset on he looked over at me and said, "Where the hell is your tuxedo? Never mind, you can stay in the car. I'll fly."

A few minutes later we landed at the Executive Terminal in Phoenix near a beautiful blue and white Air Force jet. It was a small, seven-passenger Lear jet, with a crew of two pilots and a

456

steward. As the steward closed the door, the engines started and we were soon at 35,000 feet, sipping on a cold drink. I was waiting for Barry to tell me what we were headed for. The steward passed us each a pamphlet that was headlined, "United States Air Force Annual Dinner: Featured Speaker, the Honorable Barry Goldwater." Talk about suddenly feeling very out of place! I knew my jeans were not the proper attire.

When we landed in Colorado Springs we were directed to a parking area with a small fleet of business jets like ours. *Must be a big party*, I thought, as the pilot shut down the engines. Before he could roll to a stop an Air Force staff car bearing a white flag with four stars pulled in front of our aircraft.

Barry was out first and it was very impressive to see a four-star general come to attention and sharply salute the senator. They hugged, shook hands, and I learned they were old friends who had served together at one time. I stayed behind Barry until I was introduced to the general.

Barry wasted no time telling this four-star why I had come to the party wearing jeans, boots, and a western jacket. After a good laugh we loaded up and headed for the academy.

The general told his aide to stop at his quarters so he could get me a tie. I offered to just wait somewhere until the dinner was over, but they wouldn't hear of it. They were having a good time at my expense, but I didn't mind.

That night I sat at General Fred Haeffner's table. I had met him at Luke Air Force Base and had been his guest in Korea, so that helped my comfort level slightly, even though I was the only one in a room of 150 people without a tuxedo or dress uniform. I must have met every general in the Air Force that night, along with their wives, and I actually had a great time. Goldwater gave a fiery speech and was rewarded with a standing ovation and a plaque attesting to the love and admiration the Air Force elite had for this senator.

Despite my cowboy appearance and hair hanging over my ears, I was treated with respect by everyone simply because I was a friend of everyone's favorite general: Barry Goldwater.

Chapter 61

Morning Star Ranch

In the summer of 1983, Vicki found the perfect place for us to live. It was a remote 80-acre ranch located north of Cave Creek, about 30 miles north of downtown Phoenix. We couldn't afford the entire 80 acres, but we made a deal to take 10 acres, which included the house, barn, horse stalls, and a guest house.

The ranch was located on a high mesa overlooking Cave Creek, Carefree, and the Tonto hills. It was remote and difficult to reach by automobile. After leaving the town of Cave Creek, it was north about five miles on a dirt road called Spur Cross, then a left turn on Morning Star Road which was not much more than a trail. It crossed through a deep ravine, across the small creek that gave the area its name, and up to the high mesa and the ranch. It had an incredible view ... and very few neighbors.

My closest neighbor, about one-half mile up the creek, was Dick Van Dyke; the same guy who became a household name with his 1950s sitcom, *The Dick Van Dyke Show*. He had recently filmed another series from a studio located in Carefree. He was a good neighbor and I came to like and respect him.

Our ranch was located at the very northern edge of the Phoenix valley. We sat right at the base of high mesas that soared several thousand feet above us and we were surrounded by the beautiful high Sonoran Desert. It was perfect, but before I signed the contract I would need to get permission from my news director to keep the helicopter home at night.

Once again the stars lined up correctly. Pep Cooney and Al Buch gave me the go ahead. As soon as we closed escrow we made the move from our downtown condo to an isolated piece of Shangri-La.

Jim Willi, the news director who would replace Al Buch, later said, *"I'll never forget the first time we landed at Jerry's house. The helicopter pad was tiny—about six feet square. Jerry said that was 'to keep the amateurs out.' After my landing there—I believed it did."*

Landing pad next to the house at Morning Star Ranch

It took Vicki and me a while to make the ranch a home and to adjust from city to country living. But Vicki really came through, and while I chased news and played with the kids at schools, she was taking care of countless details and projects at the ranch. We had a great home for Rey de Reyes and he was quickly joined by a good-looking Peruvian mare named Marascala, which we purchased for Vicki. Over the next years the head count would reach a dozen as our Peruvian family grew.

But it wasn't all sunshine and roses out on the ranch, because there are critters that have lived in the desert far longer than we humans, and they liked to remind us of that occasionally. One day Rey and I were out riding the creek below the ranch, when he suddenly bolted hard to the right, sending me sailing off to the left. While I was still in the air I heard the problem: the unmistakable sound of a mad rattlesnake. I hit the ground on my side and rolled away from where the snake was. Rey had stopped about 50 feet away and looked real nervous.

I got back on my feet and stood still, hoping to see where the snake was. Then I started moving very slowly to join up with my horse, looking all around as I moved. We got back home without seeing the snake again, but I discovered that Rey had been struck on the bottom of the right hoof, on the rubber pad I'd attached to the shoe. After that incident we spent less time in the desert and more in the arena behind the barn.

There were a lot of rattlesnakes in the area and I had plenty of encounters with them around the house and barn. I got too close for comfort a number of times and the snakes came well within striking range. Vicki and occasional visitors also had close calls. In those encounters the snake always warned us it was there. We had to shoot them to protect our horses and dogs. I never liked that, but there was just no other way.

More than once we had "rattlesnake stew," and Vicki made belts and knife sheaths out of the skins, which we wore for years with our jeans and boots.

Scorpions were another desert nuisance. We learned to never put on boots and shoes without shaking them first, and to shake our clothes when we took them out of the closet. Vicki was once stung when she grabbed her towel to dry off after a shower. For the next 12 hours her hand and shoulder were swollen and red. It was 24 hours before she was fully recovered. Stings are rarely more serious than that. No matter what we used or tried, there was no getting rid of them, so we learned to be cautious. On several occasions Bryan and I found the little rascals in the helicopter and started using insect repellent. I finally told him not to tell me anymore because I would rather not know.

My friend Buzz and his wife, Carol, bought a horse property about five miles south of us in a neighborhood of sparsely scattered small ranches. Buzz was a huge help in getting me set up with many of the things a new rancher had to have.

Fritz Holly, whom I had met through the diver's posse, was another good friend and a big help. He was the son of a cotton farmer in the Buckeye area just west of Phoenix. Fritz's passions were scuba diving and flying machines. He had no desire to be a farmer; his heart was set on becoming a helicopter pilot. But he was always willing to help me out with ranching questions.

Fritz was building up his flying time as a fixed-wing crop-duster, then was able to buy a small Robinson helicopter to get his rating and start building time and experience. He flew with me as often as he could, and in time he became a qualified helicopter pilot.

Between Vicki, Buzz and Fritz, we had a fully-functioning ranch within just a few months. Vicki always surprised me. One day I came home to find a wall completely torn out of a bedroom she was remodeling. This little blonde seemed to be able to do it all. She learned about horses and took care of them as well.

Vicki handled the ranch, Susan took care of the Sky 12 news side, and I flew the helicopter and covered the news with my sidekick Bryan. Even though our lives were more complicated now, we started building a team and a lifestyle that was incredible. Bryan and I followed a daily Susy-gram that laid out the schedule for the following day: a schedule that sometimes had to be bumped because of breaking news.

Circle K Riders

After Karl Eller sold KPNX Radio and TV, he moved on and we remained friends. I occasionally saw him and his wife, Stevie, at social functions. At one dinner for a charity event, Vicki and I shared a table with the Ellers. During our conversation we talked about the helicopter and operating it from the ranch. Stevie was excited about our unusual lifestyle and we made a date to have them out for dinner.

Vicki and I both loved entertaining at our ranch, but we kept it to a minimum because it was difficult to plan an event and know that I would be there. When I was on call, which I nearly always was, that meant duty first and personal life later.

The then-Mayor of Scottsdale, Arizona, Herb Drinkwater, and his wife once drove out to the ranch for a Saturday lunch and horseback ride. He was a great guy and we looked forward to spending time with both of them. Vicki had prepared a lovely lunch and decorated a table out by the pool. It was one of those picture-perfect days that just didn't turn out as planned.

Just before the Drinkwaters were to arrive, I got a call from the Pinal County Sheriff's Office to fly an accident victim out of the Superstition Mountains, east of Phoenix. Neither Air Rescue nor Air Evac was available and the patient was critical.

After a quick hug I told Vicki to stall lunch and I would make it snappy. "Just be careful," I heard her say as I sailed out the door. As I was taking off I saw the mayor pulling his horse trailer down through the creek and up the other side. *Good thing he has four-wheel drive*, I thought.

Later that night—and well after bed time—I landed back home. I knew I was in trouble because I had been in this situation before. I should have called. Lesson learned.

When we invited the Ellers out, I told Karl and Stevie that they should have a plan B in case I didn't show up. This time I picked my guests up at the downtown heliport. Twenty minutes later we were at the ranch and I landed in the exercise arena near the barn. By now the horses looked forward to me coming home because I normally gave them a little snack.

After this landing they got a lot of attention and snacks. Stevie Eller loved our black stallion, Rey de Reyes, having seen him in parades. I offered to let her ride him, but as she watched him prance around his stall with ears up and nostrils flared, she declined. Probably a wise decision.

After dinner we sat out on the porch and enjoyed hearing the story of how our guest was able to take over the Circle K Corporation. Karl Eller is an entrepreneur, and a very successful one. Most of the business conversation went right over my head, until he proposed a business deal that got my attention.

It went something like this: "Circle K will pay you four-thousand dollars a month as a sponsor for your horses and any public appearances you make on Rey de Reyes. You provide the truck and trailer painted in the same design as the helicopter, with Circle K logos on both sides. And at those events you will be known as *The Circle K Rider*."

That's how it started. For my remaining years at Channel 12 we rode in parades all over Arizona, some of which were annual affairs. We were invited to events at schools, rodeos, horse shows and more. And while breaking news trumped everything, we seldom had to cancel anything.

If the event was out of town or outside my response time, all I had to do was show up. By the time I landed, Vicki or Buzz would have hauled the horses to the site in the sharp looking Chevy "dually" and matching four-horse trailer with Circle K logos and painted like the helicopter. I'd arrive to find them standing next to the trailer, saddled up and ready to go.

Horse trailer and truck matching the helicopter

We later changed the name to *Circle K Riders*, plural, and included Vicki, Buzz, my daughter Barry, and two good friends who lived nearby and were also Peruvian Paso owners. Jim and Jan Leavette rode with us in many of the events. Jim would dress as a Conquistador and Jan dressed as a lady of times

Some of the Circle K Riders

past. Sometimes I rode alone, and other times any combination of the six of us might be in a parade.

Bryan and Susan would often accompany me, and while I rode in the parade they would find an interesting person, animal or happening. Bryan would film it, Susan would write it, and later I would narrate it for our newscasts.

Vicki was so overwhelmed with the horses, trying to keep them clean, fed and parade ready, that we decided to hire help. We purchased a 10x50 mobile home and had it delivered to the ranch for caretakers to live in. It cost almost as much to have it brought in as it did to buy it. It took five workers almost three days, using a D-6 Caterpillar and a large crane to lift, jack up, and coax the big trailer down into the canyon, across the creek, and back up the other side to ranch. Hairpin turns on both sides of the running creek didn't help the situation.

Once on the property, we set the mobile home in an area that allowed for everyone's privacy. Then we hired a married couple to live on the ranch and take care of it. Horses, tack, and equipment all had to be spotless when we made appearances, and the caretakers took that burden off Vicki. It turned out to be a good move.

We loved the seclusion of the ranch and spent much of our free time riding horses and ATVs, and enjoying our friends. The Morning Star Ranch was my sanctuary for 14 wonderful years, until it all fell apart.

Search for missing family

The weekend had been grueling. It was late August and thousands of Phoenicians had taken to the rivers and lakes to cool off. Temperatures in the deserts were well into the 100 degree range. Recreation areas, like the lower Salt River, were packed with tubers, swimmers, and campers. It had been one of those nightmare weekends for the Maricopa County Lake Patrol and Sky 12.

Bryan, Vicki and I participated in two drowning dives, a plane crash in the mountains north of Tucson, and a successful search for a missing hiker in the Superstition Mountains. We had flown 20 flight hours by Sunday night and were hoping for a day off on Monday. It wasn't to be.

At daybreak Monday morning I was called by the sheriff's office dispatcher requesting our assistance on a search for a missing family. She told me Deputy Black would meet us at the TV station. I said I would be airborne shortly.

I rolled out of bed and called Susan who would have Bryan meet me at the station. I took off from the ranch at sunrise and headed for the downtown pad. Along the way I checked in with the sheriff's office and gave them a 15 minute ETA. I then called Bryan on the portable radio. He was five minutes away.

When I landed downtown and shut down, Larry gave us a quick briefing. We would be looking for 20-year-old Charles Wachta, his 19-year-old wife, Janet, and their 14-month-old son. They were driving a white, modified off-road car.

A neighbor of the family had heard Mr. Wachta say they were going on an overnight camping trip in an area called Seven Springs. According to Wachta's family, he liked to explore old roads and trails, but was level-headed. They had taken supplies for overnight, but this was day three, and they had chosen a very rugged and remote area to explore.

The area was about 20 miles northeast of my ranch in Cave Creek. High desert rises into higher mesas, slashed by steep and rugged canyons, some as deep as several thousand feet. There are hundreds of roads and trails that mostly lead nowhere.

It would take 30 minutes to get to Seven Springs from downtown Phoenix. Since we would fly right over Scottsdale Airport I needed to land and top off with fuel. It could be a long search and I learned to always top off the tanks when going to remote areas. Bry and I carried water and had enough candy bars and snacks to last several days. Fuel would be the problem.

We landed at Corporate Jets and were met by a fuel truck. I bought three box lunches, just in case. We left Scottsdale heading north. Once past Cave Creek and Carefree the high desert gives way to the mountains and valleys, and leads into the Mazatal Wilderness Area.

For the first two hours we flew the obvious main dirt roads that lead in and out of the Seven Springs area. The third hour we were joined by Ranger 30 from DPS. We talked by radio and decided to land at a command post that was being set up by deputies. The search area was huge and included the Verde River, two large lakes and hundreds of square miles of wilderness. It isn't a popular destination, but used a lot by serious off-roaders and explorers.

The sheriff's air posse was called and would send two aircraft. In addition to Ranger 30, DPS would also launch their high-wing Cessna 210. The airplanes would stay 1000 feet above the terrain and helicopters would stay below that. Jeep posses were also being called and would arrive by noon.

Law enforcement pulls out all the stops when the search involves the young, especially the very young and innocent. According to family members, the Wachtas would have run out of baby formula by now and time was of the essence.

We coordinated search areas with the air rescue crew and headed out. It was getting close to time for the noon news and we were getting low on fuel. We checked out of the area and headed back to the airport. On the way, Bryan beamed back video on the microwave and Susan gave me info on the search for a live report at the top of the news.

At 11:30 we landed on the Corporate Jets ramp and were met by the same truck and driver as in the morning. I requested a "hot fueling," which meant I would not shut the engine down, since we were in a hurry. It was like a pit stop in racing terms. Once we were fueled and had fresh sodas on board we headed north again.

By the time we got into the search area it was time for the noon news. Anchor Vince Leonard read the headlines then came straight to me. Over my voice, the director rolled the video of Ranger 30 and the four-wheel drive units pouring into the area, followed by a short interview we had done with Deputy Larry Black at the command post. It was big news and we had ourselves the kind of story that our director loves—an "Exclusive"—a big word in broadcasting circles.

A few minutes later Bryan held a live shot of the rugged mountains and I did my weather segment again using info that Susan radioed to me. That microwave system did the job without a glitch and we were nearly 100 miles from our receiver.

We checked in again with Ranger 30 and headed for our area. All the obvious roads and trails had been checked so if they were around here they were in a canyon. By now we had been joined by pilot–reporter Len Clements in the Channel 10 bird. There were now three helicopters and three fixed-wing airplanes on the search.

After another refueling we checked another area that was more a trail than a road. We were in a large deep canyon with numerous feeder canyons and walls a thousand feet tall. I hated to give up, but we were getting low on fuel again and it was late afternoon. We had been in the air nearly eight hours and this was no place to be at night without at least a full moon.

I pulled in climb power and started going up over a side canyon when I spotted the car in a smaller feeder canyon we had just passed. What luck! As we circled, we could see all three of our victims. The father was waving a towel and the mom was holding the baby and waving. On the hood they had written "HELP." I found a small opening and landed.

I'm not sure who was the happiest, Bryan, me, or them. The car was stuck in the creek, high-centered on a large boulder. Mr. Wachta said they had become disoriented and followed a trail up a narrow canyon that abruptly ended. The trees and brush had them nearly hidden from the air. We could not believe how far up the canyon he had made it. While Bryan shot video, Larry and I helped the family get personal things packed up and loaded in the helicopter. The car would have to stay.

We got back into the air and radioed Ranger 30 that we had the victims and it was Code-4, meaning all victims were safe.

Once again these lives were saved because law enforcement now had the right buttons to push when this family needed help, unlike a few years previously when Duane Brady and I found that grandma and three little kids dead—not 20 miles from where this family was stranded.

It turned out to be a great day for all of us involved, but I sure looked forward to taking a day off. Maybe tomorrow!

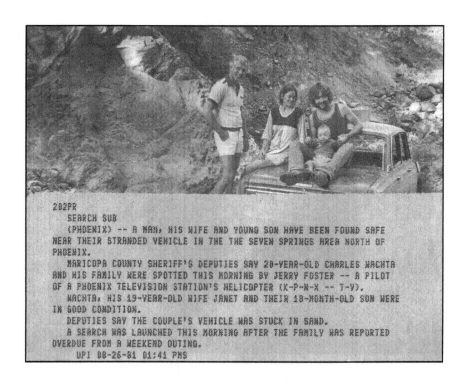

```
282PR
    SEARCH SUB
    (PHOENIX) -- A MAN, HIS WIFE AND YOUNG SON HAVE BEEN FOUND SAFE
NEAR THEIR STRANDED VEHICLE IN THE THE SEVEN SPRINGS AREA NORTH OF
PHOENIX.
    MARICOPA COUNTY SHERIFF'S DEPUTIES SAY 28-YEAR-OLD CHARLES WACHTA
AND HIS FAMILY WERE SPOTTED THIS MORNING BY JERRY FOSTER -- A PILOT
OF A PHOENIX TELEVISION STATION'S HELICOPTER (K-P-N-X -- T-V).
    WACHTA, HIS 19-YEAR-OLD WIFE JANET AND THEIR 18-MONTH-OLD SON WERE
IN GOOD CONDITION.
    DEPUTIES SAY THE COUPLE'S VEHICLE WAS STUCK IN SAND.
    A SEARCH WAS LAUNCHED THIS MORNING AFTER THE FAMILY WAS REPORTED
OVERDUE FROM A WEEKEND OUTING.
    UPI 08-26-81 01:41 PHS
```

Chapter 62

Celebrities and Politicians

As a TV reporter, and while traveling with Senator Goldwater, I was fortunate to meet quite a few celebrities and form my own impression of them. Some, like Senators Goldwater and McCain, were great to know; others, not so much. The latter group does not need to be mentioned here. But it seems only fitting to acknowledge those who especially impressed me with their warmth and kindness.

One of these was Willard Scott, the NBC weatherman for *The Today Show*. He is someone I admired and tried to emulate. His personality draws people to him. When he did the weather, viewers knew they would get much more.

I tuned in *The Today Show* whenever I could to watch Willard and his interaction with people at events, as well as to get a briefing on national weather for our noon and 5 p.m. shows. Willard was the beginning of a new generation of TV weather guys. His beat was America and my beat was Arizona.

On one occasion I met him at the Grand Canyon and we did the weather together, but he did the Arizona forecast and I did the national report. I learned a lot from him about being a celebrity, both in public and on the tube. When the camera lights came on, Willard just rolled with the flow. A little weather, a little folksy humor, and a look at one of the many cities, towns, or communities he visited.

After doing the weather at the Grand Canyon that morning we packed up and headed for Phoenix, taking the scenic route. From the south rim we went straight to the bottom and flew low level up the Colorado River to the confluence of the Little Colorado River where the water turns a turquoise blue.

That flight up the canyon is one of the most beautiful I have ever done. There are places where you have to slow way down to make a sharp "S" turn because of the towering canyon walls rising thousands of feet on either side. The early morning sun shone red on the massive cliffs and glinted off the turquoise water, making it a flight neither of us would ever forget. It remained a perfect flight from the canyon back to the valley. When we landed at my Cave Creek ranch, Vicki served us lunch on the front porch.

Willard Scott was one of the few people who loved his job as much as I loved mine. In his book, *America is My Neighborhood*, Willard lays out his way of life and all the many incredible and exciting things he has done. I was impressed that he had really listened when we talked about being away from home so much while having a great time. There is always a price to pay. This excerpt from his book recaps some of our conversation that day.

"It absolutely does get in the way," Jerry admits with some pain in his voice. "That's what cost me my first marriage. It got to the point where my first[2] wife said to me, 'Jerry, which is more important, me or the helicopter?' That was a tough one. But flying is the love of my life, and I had no choice, not really." (Jerry's second wife of six years shares his passion for flying; they also share a love of scuba diving, and the two of them recover evidence and, sometimes, bodies from local lakes and rivers for the police department.) I can relate, a little bit, to what Jerry went through, it sometimes seems that my career pulls me away from my family too often, and for too long, and I know the push-and-pull he tells me he felt between the people he loved and the work he loved."

Willard Scott and I shared that tug of war between family and career. I'm honored I had the opportunity to get to know him.

Another of my favorite meetings took place when we did a story on Roy Rogers and Dale Evans. They were opening a new Happy Trails RV Park on the west side of the Phoenix valley. When the assignment desk offered us the story I didn't hesitate. Along with my sidekicks, Bryan and Susan, we flew to the site.

---

[2] This is an error, since Dianna was actually my second wife, and Vicki the third.

We arrived a little bit early, since I wanted to get a private interview. As we walked into the clubhouse it was just us and the staff setting things up for the grand opening, with Roy and Dale looking on.

Roy reached out to shake hands, but I held up both outstretched arms indicating an embrace. "Roy, you have been my hero since I was a little boy," I said.

When we separated, he told me, "That is the nicest thing you could have said."

I was still in awe that I was looking into the blue eyes I had seen so many times in movies and on TV, with his wife, Dale, always by his side. Everyone from my generation, before and after, all over the world, would know exactly who the couple in front of me was, by name and reputation.

After the heartfelt greeting we talked about their long career. Neither of them had to be prompted and many times one would playfully interrupt the other with a different version. It was obvious they truly enjoyed being with each other and doing what they were doing.

We got around to talking about horses, and when I told them about my beautiful black stallion, Roy told me that one of his life's tragedies was losing his golden palomino, Trigger, his steed and partner for so many years. Roy still insisted Trigger was the smartest horse on earth.

"I just couldn't imagine him buried in the ground so I had him preserved and put into our museum. Sometimes when I go in there and see him I get tears in my eyes," he said. "I loved that horse nearly as much as I love Dale," he kidded, as she poked him in the side.

"When Roy passes I may have *him* stuffed and sitting on Trigger," Dale joked back.

When we finished the interview, Roy and Dale walked out to Sky 12 with us to have a look. I offered to take them for an aerial tour of Phoenix, but they had to decline.

Roy Rogers and Dale Evans are gone now, but they left an amazing legacy of movies, TV shows … and memories.

For Bryan, Susan and me, this interview was another one of those surreal moments that will always be very special. We flew back to the station singing, "Happy trails to you, till we meet again." I hope so!

We once had the pleasure of interviewing country music outlaw Waylon Jennings backstage at the Veteran's Memorial Coliseum before his show. His compadre, a slightly stoned Willie Nelson, came in to ask us if he'd gone on stage yet. Yep, that was memorable!

As was the time the NBC show *Real People* sent Sarah Purcell out to Phoenix to interview Vicki and me at the Morning Star Ranch. She was a delight.

I also had the pleasure of meeting Jack Benny, George Gobel, Bill Cosby, Jonathan Winters, and Robert Mitchum, as well as Roger Waters, the lead singer and song writer of my favorite group—Pink Floyd. There were many others, and I was thrilled to be able to get photos with some of them.

In addition to Senator Goldwater, I also had the privilege of flying other politicians in Sky 12. Arizona Governors Jack Williams, Bruce Babbitt, Ev Mecham and Rose Mofford, and U.S. Congressman Sam Steiger all flew with me at one time or another. Sky 12 became the great equalizer for me and anyone who strapped in as a passenger.

I first met John McCain when he was a congressman. When he ran for the senate, I occasionally flew him around the state on his campaign trips. He was a great guy and became a good friend.

On one of the campaign trips —from chopper to train

A Few of My Favorite Celebrities

Red Skelton in the studio

Dale Evans & Roy Rogers

George Hamilton

James Coburn

Governor Jack Williams

Governor Bruce & Hattie Babbitt

Leslie Stahl

Pat Boone

Chapter 63

Another New Bird

 In the summer of 1984 our news director, Al Buch, landed a general manager job at a TV station in Florida. He was well-liked and had done a marvelous job at Channel 12. So good in fact, that he had his choice of several large markets. He would be missed by all of us. Al had been my mentor and friend. He assured me his replacement was just as dedicated to a "News Chopper" as he had been and nothing would change for me. He was right. The new guy was our ally in a growing storm.

Jim Willi is a giant of a man, who could pass for an NFL lineman. If he was smiling he looked like a big teddy bear, but if he wasn't happy, he could be intimidating. When Al Buch told me he was leaving and Jim was going to be my next news director, I sure didn't have a problem with it. Jim had been Al's assistant for the past few months and was well liked. If we had to change news directors, this was a good move.

Jim Willi: *"As the new managing editor, I knew one of my first jobs was to get to know and gain the confidence of Jerry Foster. There were mixed feelings about him in the newsroom; some felt that Jerry was spoiled, hard to get along with, a bully, and too brash for his own good. The truth is he was all of those things. From my perspective, Jerry was the heart and soul of this news operation. Each team member worked to create something new every single day and this gave Jerry the drive to be the best. He had little time for slackers who didn't want to work hard. I loved his approach, as it mirrored mine."*

Our first meeting after Jim took over was hilarious. I knew he was a kidder and a good sport, so when he walked into my office with a smile, I gave him a little test.

Jim Willi: *"The first time I had a one-to-one meeting with Jerry was in his office in the newsroom. His cowboy boots were up on his wooden desk and he was opening his mail with a big Bowie knife.*

"As we talked, Jerry said, 'You know, I get a lot of privileges around here,' and he flipped the Bowie knife toward me. It flipped over once in the air—and stuck in the desk in front of me. Boing! Jerry kind of glared at me for emphasis.

"I calmly pulled the knife out of the desk, and flipped it back at him, where it stuck in the desk in front of Jerry, and I said, 'And if you keep working hard you'll keep getting those privileges.'

"Jerry gave me that great smile of his, stuck out his hand for me to shake and from that point on we were fast friends. He could do pretty much anything he wanted, as long as he delivered results. Results included beating the snot out of the competition on every big, breaking news story that came along.

"Many people in the KPNX newsroom back in the day looked upon Jerry Foster as a spoiled brat who always got his way. There was some truth to that: Jerry was always a handful to manage. He could be a real pain in the ass at times—confrontational, feisty, pouty, angry—the list of adjectives went on and on. But I always worked my way past that because even though he could be all those things, Jerry was always my "go-to-guy" when the stuff was hitting the fan.

"If something needed to be covered, he was there 24/7. If I needed him to fill in on a weathercast anytime, he was there for me. That was the part of Jerry many people never saw, even though it was right there in front of their eyes. Some of it Jerry brought upon himself—because even though he would be there for me whenever I needed him—his demeanor often came across as angry while he was doing it. But I have said over and over, if I could have cloned Jerry and created 20 more of him, I would have. He truly cared about what we were doing.

"There was also a softer side of Jerry that many never noticed. His demeanor might have been feisty and gruff—but he was really a softy under all of that bluster. He cared about people. Jerry Foster didn't rescue

people because he wanted to be a hero. He rescued people because he genuinely cared and wanted to help. He didn't work 24/7 because he wanted to be on TV. Jerry worked 24/7 because he wanted us to be the best every day.

"The biggest illustration of the softer side of Jerry came when I was leaving KPNX to join a TV consulting firm in Dallas. My two young boys adored Jerry, and over the years—like many school kids during that time—they made drawings of Sky 12 and gave them to Jerry. Unknown to me, Jerry kept all the drawings from my guys and handed them back to me as a going-away gift. That was really special, and I've never forgotten it.

"Jerry and his very dedicated Sky 12 crew did it all, 24/7/365. I came to respect Jerry as one of the hardest working, most caring people I ever met in my long career."

The first order of business for Jim and me was the new helicopter we had purchased a couple of months before he became news director. We had updated from a Hughes 500D to a 500E. The only difference was a pointed nose, a new sound-proofing kit and a better air conditioner. The problem was that the soundproofing was so heavy that as we got into the hot summer months I could only fly with half-fuel plus Bryan and myself.

Hughes 500 E

Jim Willi: *"Jerry came to my office and asked me to join him on the roof. We climbed into the new ship, buckled up, and as Jerry made the takeoff I watched the turbine outlet temperature red line … it maxed out! Not a safe situation, and I was glad to get back on the ground."*

When our maintenance guys checked the power output of the engine, they found it was below normal. In the two months we had been operating the machine, we'd had some close calls as the engine temperature soared up to the red line, causing me to abort whatever we were doing. I talked it over with Bryan, who had agreed with me and our chief mechanic at Air Services International (ASI) that it was not safe for our kind of operation. That said, we put the new ship in the hangar, rented a JetRanger, and flew back to the station to deliver the bad news.

By the time I finished my explanation, Jim's eyes and mouth were open wide. What a load to drop on him his first day as news director. All I could do was shrug my shoulders and try to look sad. "You're kidding," he said, and with that he picked up the phone and called Pep Cooney. The conversation was very brief, and two minutes later we were sitting in Pep's office.

His hands were folded on his desk and he was ready to listen. This wouldn't be a new story for Pep because I had been complaining for the past two months about the low power. The previous day we had bumped into each other in the hall and I told him I was having a power check made the next day by our guys at ASI.

Pep was always upbeat, soft spoken, and a pleasure to be around. I have never known anyone who didn't like this white-haired, distinguished man. After we got ourselves seated Pep looked at me and said, "The helicopter is grounded?"

"Pep, I hate to tell you this, but that new soundproofing doesn't work; it weighs a ton. Add to that an engine that is making minimum power at best. The only way Bryan and I can safely fly that machine is with half fuel and no passengers. Even with a stronger engine we still have the same problem. The ship is just too heavy for the kind of work we do with it. This new machine has me spooked. Even the air conditioner doesn't cool like the 500D, and when we need it on a hot day we can't run it because it takes power we can't afford to lose. That ship is an accident waiting to happen."

There was another problem; Bryan and I both felt that something was just not right about the way it flew through the air.

Pep took it all in and hardly moved the entire time I was talking. With his hands still folded on his desk, he looked over at Jim and asked him for his thoughts. Jim shrugged his shoulders and backed up my decision to stop flying the machine until the problem was resolved. He agreed that to cover us for the short term we should rent a JetRanger and only fly it when needed. The cost was 250 dollars per flight hour plus fuel. At that point, Pep slumped back and slid down in his chair, put his hands to his head and said, "Why me, Lord?"

Pep said he would contact Hughes Aircraft again and tell them we were not flying the new helicopter because it was unsafe. "Keep the flight time down on the rental as much as you can, but don't miss a good story," he said.

As we got up to leave, Pep told Jim he would like to see him after lunch. And with that we were out the door and back to the newsroom. Battle lines had been drawn.

Jim Willi: *"Imagine it's your first day on the job as head of the news department at KPNX and you're in charge of managing the budget. It's 30 years ago. You decide you need to spend $60,000 dollars a month to rent a helicopter. And by the way, your company had just spent hundreds of thousands of dollars to buy your current, brand new helicopter. It was actually an easy decision for me. It was unsafe and if Hughes did not correct it, we would buy elsewhere."*

Talk about uncertainty. None of us in the newsroom really knew how to handle the new dilemma. The Bell JetRanger we rented didn't have a live capability and no police scanners or two-way radios. We had to carry a portable radio from the newsroom and another for the sheriff's office. It was sure better than no helicopter at all, but we were seriously compromised and our competition at Channel 10 was our big concern.

Bryan and our engineering department came up with a solution. They rigged up a portable microwave unit by taking a transmitter and antenna that was held by the engineer. Our signal was beamed to a satellite truck on the ground and relayed to the station. It was primitive but it worked.

We were now in the same position Channel 10 had been in for so long before they got their auto-tracker figured out. Now *we* were the underdogs until we had an airship equipped for television. It was not a position we were accustomed to.

At the same time, we were negotiating with Bell on a new machine. The Bell JetRanger was too small for our operation. If we had to go to a Bell, I felt the Model 206L-3 LongRanger was the only option. It was a stretched version of the JetRanger, but with a lot more power and capability. It would also carry two litters internally. That was my choice and down deep I figured Pep would only go for the JetRanger. But nothing ventured, nothing gained.

Jim Willi: *"To put it into perspective, not only were we grounding our brand new helicopter, but we wanted to go from what was the equivalent of a compact Kia to a Cadillac Escalade, both in cost and size. No one could ever accuse Jerry and me of making small plans. To his credit, Pep agreed to make it happen."*

We ordered a new Bell LongRanger with all the bells and whistles including the litter kit. It would be two months before we could pick up the new ship in Dallas. Pep worked out a rental agreement with Bell, in which they leased us a used LongRanger to use in the interim, at a reduced rate: only $2,000 a day plus fuel.

It was a long two months. The rental machine had a smaller engine than our new one, but it still had a lot of muscle. The only disadvantage was its size. No way were we going to land in small spaces like we had done in the Hughes. We also weren't going to go as fast, but we could carry what we needed or who we needed regardless of the temperature or density altitude. The baggage compartment was nearly as roomy as the back seat of the Hughes.

When the day finally arrived, Bryan and I flew to the Bell factory in Dallas. We both attended the three-day ground school in the morning, and I had flight training in the afternoon. When we first saw the new ship at the delivery center, it was a proud moment for me. I would never have believed just a few short years ago that I would fly a news machine that looked like a limousine.

It was red and silver with blue trim and a big blue 12 on its side. The Gannett logo and FAA number plus NBC logos were tastefully added to make it one beautiful helicopter. It carried a maximum of seven passengers, including the pilot, and it had lots of muscle from the 650 horsepower, Lycoming C-30, Turbine Engine.

The spacious interior was blue and white. The cockpit was separated from the passenger compartment by a bulkhead with a two-foot square window opening behind each of the two front seats. The instrument panel had dual radios, and two VOR receivers, plus transponders, ADF, and a good air conditioner.

What a treat. What a machine! And—get this—an autopilot. A three-axis autopilot which, up to this point, was something new in a small helicopter. We also had the instrument package that allowed us to fly IFR if we encountered bad weather, although I had my own rule that if I could not see the ground, I didn't fly.

Following a short ceremony, the president of Bell handed me the keys and paperwork for Sky 12 and I handed him a check for just over $450,000 dollars. It was one happy pilot and photographer who lifted off the Bell pad, took off on a heading of west, and landed at Scottsdale Airport six hours later. We had stopped in El Paso for fuel and at a couple of fast food joints along the interstate.

Cross country in a helicopter is a real hoot! I loved following roads, highways and interstates. Even those long stretches through Texas, New Mexico and Arizona that are so boring to motorists, are awesome from 500 feet. The ground slips beneath you fast at 150 mph, and you see anything that moves in the open expanses. The difference between being on the ground and in the air is amazing, as the perspective is totally different.

We got to Scottsdale Airport too soon for both of us. The flight had been perfect and I had been dreading landing at Air Services International. The maintenance crew was going to take this brand-spanking new helicopter apart to install the Electronic News Gathering (ENG) gear, such as company and police radios, scanners, and two small TV monitors that would be installed in a brand new instrument panel, including the microwave transmitter and antennas.

All that work was going to take about three weeks. In the meantime, we were still flying the leased LongRanger. In all the time since grounding the Hughes 500E we had not missed one major story, school visit, or community event. We kept the flight time down until the new ship was ready to fly.

The ASI crew did a fantastic job. The helicopter was now a showpiece for the TV industry and I couldn't wait to fly it. Everything worked on the first flight test, including a live broadcast on the noon news. The transition from Hughes to Bell was complete and I was one happy guy. Even happier were Jim and Pep, who had fought and won a tough battle with our new owners, Gannett Broadcasting. We were the flagship of the fleet and ready to rumble.

Bell LongRanger

Chapter 64

FAA Problems

 I had many "adventures" with the FAA over the years, but this one was unique. It began with a story about an elusive pair of bank robbers who got away. The irony is, I was the only person ever punished in this incident. After a court hearing that lasted four days and cost thousands of dollars to defend, I lost my pilot certificate for six months.

In December 1985 I was on a two-mile straight-in approach to runway eight-left at Sky Harbor Airport. It was late afternoon and the tower controllers had their hands full with two parallel runways. Behind me, a business jet was closing in, so the controller asked me to move to the left and land on the taxiway so he could get a departure off in plenty of time before the next arrival.

I was 400 feet above the ground when out of the corner of my eye I saw the airplane coming right at me from the north at my altitude. I pulled the nose up sharply and rolled to the right. Bryan and I both watched the airplane pass below us heading south.

In a stressed and panicky voice, I called the tower and asked if they saw our near miss. No one had seen a thing, but the controller said he had a low target three miles southwest that he "wasn't talking to." I told the tower we would depart the control zone to the west and the chase was on.

Bryan had been sitting in the front cockpit with me when we had the near miss. After we leveled off, he dove into the back seat through the little two-foot opening, powered up his camera and started rolling tape. From this point on we have video of everything that happened next, including sound from the law enforcement agencies involved.

The airplane was a single-engine, low-wing, red and white Piper Cherokee. By the time we caught up with him he was flying at 120 miles per hour, as low as 100 feet over a residential area. Bryan was shooting out the right side behind me. My heart was beating like a drum. "I think we have us a big one here," I told Bryan over the intercom. "Remember the bank robbery we were on last week? I think we are on it again."

The previous week, two men had walked into a bank in the rural community of Chino Valley, north of Prescott. They terrorized the bank employees, robbed them at gunpoint and fled in a dark van on the dirt roads through the hills of Yavapai County, with a Chino Valley police car in hot pursuit. A few miles later the van slid to a stop next to a partially hidden airplane in a large pasture.

The police officer pulled up just as the plane roared off down a bumpy dirt strip, leaving a frustrated cop on the ground. But in their haste, these professional robbers left most of the loot behind, scattered inside their getaway van.

An all-points-bulletin went out: "All units be on the lookout for a small red and white plane, occupied by two men, one of whom is wearing a baseball cap. These suspects are considered armed and dangerous."

The Department of Public Safety's Ranger helicopter in the Prescott area picked up the radio alert. Within minutes the crew spotted a small red and white plane with two men aboard. It was almost too good to be true. Guns drawn, the crew of Ranger 31 mentally prepared themselves for a showdown as the helicopter closed in on the plane. The DPS pilot signaled to the man behind the controls to set the plane down immediately.

It was at this time we picked up the chase on one of our KPNX newsroom scanners. The Sky 12 crew quickly rallied and we were off for Prescott.

Just before we arrived, the drama in the skies had moved to the ground as the red and white plane landed at the Prescott airport. It was like a scene from the Dirty Harry movie. Police from several agencies surrounded the plane with shotguns drawn. The startled men were ordered out of the aircraft, forced to spread-eagle on the pavement, and endured numerous guns pointed at their heads until the questions could be answered.

By the time we landed, the guns had been put away and an embarrassed DPS crew told us they had the wrong airplane: it was a serious case of mistaken identity. Luckily, the surprised and startled pilot took it all in stride, even praising the DPS for being on the job.

"We were just in the wrong place at the wrong time," said pilot Howard Glusha.

Now Bryan and I had another red and white airplane in our sights.

I called the Maricopa County Sheriff's Office on the radio: "Lincoln 30: Do you know if there is still an APB out on a red and white airplane used last week in a bank robbery in Chino Valley?"

Dispatcher: "That's 10-4, Lincoln 30, that aircraft has not been found."

Lincoln 30: "Be advised we are following a red and white aircraft that nearly ran us over a few minutes ago near downtown Phoenix, and is now at low level over a neighborhood, southbound 27th Avenue and Baseline Road at two or three hundred feet. What do you suggest?"

The dispatcher told me to stand by and stay with the aircraft. I gave her my location and told her we were still heading south. Our video shows that we followed about 300 feet right behind the plane so he couldn't see us.

We stayed behind the airplane for about 15 minutes. The sheriff's office dispatcher asked me to keep the plane in sight and said she would get back to me. I had nearly a full tank of fuel so I knew I could stick with this guy until he landed. It didn't take long for the dispatcher to call me back.

Sheriff's Radio: "Lincoln 30, we have DPS Ranger 30 northbound from Tucson and two drug enforcement airplanes that should join you in a few minutes. Are you able to tell how many passengers are in the airplane, and do you see any weapons?"

I told the dispatcher to stand by, as it would be a couple of minutes until I could catch up and have a look. With Bryan shooting over my shoulder, I moved left and positioned us above and a little behind so the pilot would have to turn around to see us. We could clearly see that only the pilot was in the cabin. He was nearly bald, heavy set and didn't look happy at all. He held up his fist, flipped me the bird and started a descent. I reported all this to dispatch.

Within a few minutes I was able to talk to Ranger 30 and the two DEA airplanes on an air-to-air frequency. All three were getting close.

By now the sun was setting. As the airplane descended toward the desert, I saw a small dirt strip about two miles straight ahead, next to a house and another small building. The other pilot lowered his flaps and we knew he was going to land. He was going straight in, even though the wind was from the northwest, creating a tail wind.

The pilot touched down, taxied to the back of the house, shut the engine down and was met by a woman and two small children. We stayed at 500 feet while circling and were soon joined by Ranger 30 and the two DEA airplanes. We were all talking on aircraft radios and monitoring the sheriff's chase frequency. The two airplanes maintained 1,000 feet above the ground and the helicopters were at 300 feet.

We could see units coming from the interstate two miles away, as well as cars converging into this rural neighborhood from nearly every direction. DPS, DEA, Air Rescue, two county sheriff's departments, and every cop in the area who heard the call, all showed up. Within a few minutes the place was surrounded, and it was just before dark when the posse moved in.

About that time, someone inside the house stepped out onto the porch and popped a flash bulb, prompting the lawmen to scatter and dive for cover. The order was given over a loudspeaker for everyone to come out of the house with their hands up.

486

A few minutes later the all clear was broadcast and we followed Ranger 30 into a dirt field next to the action. We both shut down our engines and walked over to the assembled officers to see what we had netted.

It was then I realized we had the wrong airplane. At first I felt sorry for the family because it was me who had started all this hubbub. Apologies were issued all around, but the man didn't want to hear it. He told officers that he was taking a short cut from Deer Valley north of Phoenix to his farm. I asked him why he flew through the high density airport control zone and he didn't explain.

He was loud, foul-mouthed and arrogant; he was also ordering everyone off his land. The old farmer was never charged by the FAA for any of the violations, which should have included "careless and reckless operation of an aircraft."

I, however, *was* charged. But before a hearing took place, another incident two months later sealed my fate.

It was one of those beautiful, clear-as-a-bell February days in Arizona, which is not unusual in the Valley of the Sun. From the downtown heli-pad I could see the Superstition Mountains 40 miles to the east, and the White Tank Mountains 30 miles to the west. The temperature was in the low 70s, with a gentle breeze out of the north. Just another day in paradise.

I was at the station, just back from lunch. Bryan and Susan were still out when I got a call from a very agitated friend in Carefree, just north of Phoenix and a few miles east of my ranch in neighboring Cave Creek. Woodson "Woody" Woods owned the local airport he had developed over the years. It was in an upper-class neighborhood where the homes were customized with aircraft hangars.

Woody asked me if I could come out to Carefree right away. He said a single-engine Cessna had been buzzing his neighborhood for about an hour, flying dangerously low. He had received numerous complaints from nearby neighbors who thought the Cessna might be from his airport, and he had already called the sheriff's office.

Nothing was scheduled for the afternoon and I had planned to go home anyway, so I told him I would be on the way within minutes. Woody and I would meet in the air on the Unicom frequency assigned to uncontrolled airports; he would be in his single engine Bonanza. I told news producer Bruce Taylor I would be on call at home, and checked out. The crew of Sky 12 was taking the afternoon off.

I lifted off the downtown pad and headed north. As soon as I cleared the airport control zone, I switched frequencies and called Woody as agreed. He had the airplane in sight north of Carefree airport and described the Cessna as flying "crazy." Woody was staying high and watching, in case the pilot left the area.

Before I could respond, a strange voice came on the radio asking, "Are you talking about a blue and white Cessna 150 just north of Carefree Airport?"

I thanked him for responding and then asked what he was doing. He said he was a photographer from Oklahoma City, taking aerial images of expensive homes for sale by his employer. Woody came on the frequency telling him that he had scared a number of homeowners and that a sheriff's deputy was waiting to talk to him at Scottsdale Airport. The pilot was polite and said he would see us there. I never got closer than a football field away and neither did Woody in his Bonanza.

I called the sheriff's radio and advised that we would be landing in a few minutes at Scottsdale Airport. The dispatcher responded that a deputy was on the way.

We all called Scottsdale tower at different intervals. I landed on the heli-pad, the Bonanza and the Cessna 150 parked in the transit area near me. By the time I called for a fuel truck and had shut down the engine, Woody and the pilot were standing on the ramp. I watched the two men shake hands and was surprised, because Woody had been real cranky about all of this. I was happy to see he had cooled off.

The Oklahoma pilot introduced himself and explained he was new to this job and to flying. He admitted to being a little low a time or two, but he always stayed over open ground because most of the big homes had clear zones and he thought he was being cautious. He wasn't arrogant or defensive; he was a nice young man who was learning the hard way about people, noise, and airplanes.

When I saw that the truck had refueled the helicopter, I said goodbye to Woody and the photographer, who were waiting for the deputy to show up. I had done what I had been asked to do by Woody and the sheriff's office. On the way home I beamed the video to the station and gave them the story for the evening news. The anchorman read the story over my video showing the Cessna making low passes around big homes.

That evening Woody called and said several people had complained to the local FAA and sheriff's office about the low and noisy airplane. Woody said he had filed a complaint with the deputy and had given him a list of people who had called to complain. He wanted to be sure residents of Carefree knew that it wasn't one of his airport locals. Carefree is a noise-sensitive area and the airport wasn't popular with a small, but powerful, group of residents in the area. Conservationists would use an incident like this to further their cause. That, as much as the safety aspect, was why Woody reacted so fast.

As soon as I landed at home I told Vicki the story, saying, "That young man is in a heap of trouble." But once again, it wasn't him, but I, who would be in a heap of trouble.

Three weeks later I received another one of those registered letters from the FAA's Western Region office in Los Angeles, advising me that I was under investigation for flying too close to another aircraft near Carefree, and for "careless and reckless operation of an aircraft."

Both the farmer and the photographer filed complaints against me and neither of them was ever charged with any violations. Both agreed to testify for the government. It seemed pretty obvious to me, Woody, and others that a deal had been

489

made between FAA prosecutors, and the farmer and photographer.

Both pilots were facing serious charges, and would very likely have had their certificates suspended. As in a criminal case, a defendant will tell prosecutors what they want to hear to save their own skin. I knew the farmer was vengeful, and the photographer was just trying to survive.

More than a year later, in June 1987, a revocation hearing was held at the old Phoenix downtown post office. It was a two-day hearing held in a cramped room on the second floor. Most of the local press was there and the place was packed. I was charged with flying too close to another aircraft in a manner that was "careless and reckless."

While I have a high regard for the FAA and their mandate to make flying safer for everyone; in this case, the hearing was extremely one-sided. I had great witnesses and my attorney did the very best he could with what he was allowed to present. But much of my case was deemed inadmissible.

The law enforcement community, including the two county sheriff departments involved, was solidly behind me. But the National Transportation Safety Board (NTSB) judge didn't allow testimony from any of my witnesses or experts.

The FAA was "unable to locate" the tower recording of the conversations that would have proved the pilot lied about his location. He also lied about the fact that he was alone in the airplane, saying that his son had been with him and was also endangered.

Bryan had shot footage of the entire chase, which showed the flight path of the farmer, and that he was clearly alone in the plane. It was submitted, but the NTSB judge refused to look at the footage or allow it to be shown. The only reason given was that the judge said he was concerned that we may have edited the tape, even though we had an expert witness who would testify there were no edits and the tape was not tampered with.

Without witnesses or the videotape to corroborate our story, we didn't have much of a case. All our witnesses, experts, film, and support were for naught. My license was suspended for six months.

I paid the price and served my time, so to speak. My attorney kept the suspension under appeal until I retired a couple of years later; and by then prosecutors had a couple more violations for me to answer. If you ever get on the wrong side of a large bureaucratic agency such as the FAA; you might as well be on the dark side of the moon.

I hated having such a bad reputation with the Feds. Throughout the first 15 years of my flying career, I had a good relationship with the FAA and participated in all their safety seminars and events. I was a pilot examiner for 10 years in airplanes and helicopters. I have a plaque from the FAA thanking me for my contribution to their safety programs and I am very proud to hang it on my wall with other treasures of my day.

I believe the tragic death of Karen Key and her mechanic triggered the FAA to step up their vigilance. The media attention from that crash put a lot of pressure on the FAA for not taking action, even though they knew she left Phoenix because of a drinking problem.

In addition to Karen's fatal accident, the safety record for TV helicopter operations was terrible all over the United States. This was a brand new industry which required a different flying style, and it had started off poorly. Nearly every accident was deemed "pilot error." The race to be number one in local and national news seemed to be a priority over flight safety and common sense.

The FAA felt the need to increase their focus on safety, and I presented a highly-visible target; someone they could make an example of. I could—and should—have paid more attention to the growing animosity between the FAA and myself. I also could and should have done a better job of keeping my mouth shut.

E.J. Montini, a columnist for the Arizona Republic, made this comment after the suspension: *"We teach our celebrities, our 'heroes,' to fly, sometimes literally. We get them to climb higher and higher, to take bigger and bigger chances until the height is so great that any fall to Earth would mean certain death. Then we try to shoot them down."*

Now, more than any time in the past, I could relate to the high climb and being shot down.

Ironically, just a couple of weeks after my hearing, the July 6 Newsweek magazine hit the stands with its "A Celebration of Heroes" issue. One person per state was selected as that state's hero of the year. In 1987, *I* was Arizona's hero.

Chapter 65

Comer Manhunt - February 1987

My involvement with the Maricopa County Sheriff's Office sometimes provided more excitement than I bargained for. One incident was the search for a depraved, homicidal maniac named Robert Comer.

In February 1987 Comer and his girlfriend, "June" had been camping near Apache Lake in the Tonto National Forest about 50 miles northeast of Phoenix. They also had June's two boys, ages five and seven, with them.

After striking up a conversation with nearby camper Larry Pritchard, Comer invited him to join them for dinner. Later Comer shot and killed Pritchard in his own tent and then stole his property, which included a high-powered rifle and scope.

Still not satisfied, around 11 p.m. Comer and June went to another campsite where a young couple was sleeping. Comer tied the man up, then, brutally raped his girlfriend in front of the terrified man. After tying the man to his own car bumper, Comer stole their belongings, then took the girl and left the campgrounds with June and the kids.

From there they drove to a place called Edward Park, which is not really a park, but a large desert area within the Four Peaks mountain range. When their truck became stuck in the sand, the hostage managed to escape. Though barefoot, she spent the next 23 hours trekking through desert and mountain terrain until she stumbled onto Highway 87, where—cold and exhausted—she was picked up by a passing motorist and taken to the hospital in Payson. She reported the kidnapping and relayed that her boyfriend had been left tied to the bumper of his car. At this point, neither she nor anyone else knew about the murder of Larry

Pritchard in the campground. Gila County authorities quickly called the Maricopa County Sheriff's Office for help and the manhunt for this maniac began.

Units from both counties and the Department of Public Safety sent every resource they could find, including DPS helicopter Ranger 27, horses, four-wheel-drive trucks, and off-road quads. I was on my way to Williams with Bryan when Deputy Larry Black contacted me and asked if I could help in the search. We immediately turned and headed for the campground. Road blocks were set up to seal off the area around the Four Peaks Recreational Park, and a command post was established near Pumpkin Center.

Deputy Larry Black: *"We knew Comer was extremely dangerous and armed, but we still didn't know about the homicide. We went straight to the campground and landed. The boyfriend was found, still tied to his front bumper. He told what he could remember of the past night and was able to give us descriptions of the vehicle. During a search, the shooting victim was found under some brush near his tent. Now we were looking for a desperate killer. When other units arrived, we got back in the helicopter and started looking for the truck."*

I was skimming the ground over a dirt road leading downward from the top of Four Peaks. We were only about three feet above ground when we spotted small barefoot tracks in the dirt, headed down the hill. Backtracking up the road, we found the place where the woman had come out of the brush. I landed on the road and sat there while Larry got out of the helicopter. He pushed his way into the brush with Bryan right behind him; camera on his shoulder, recording every step.

After about 10 minutes I began to worry. All those "What ifs" came to mind: *What if they were ambushed? I'm sitting here, engine running at idle, and wouldn't hear a thing. Comer could slip up behind me and I would be toast.*

I didn't realize it then, but even some of those back in the newsroom were concerned about our safety when they heard what was going on. Susan Sorg was one of those:

"We knew this guy was a bad dude, as he'd killed before and likely would again. And yes, I was worried about the guys out there. It was something that I knew Jerry couldn't fly his way out of, or Bryan couldn't talk his way out of, if they came up against Comer."

After another five minutes I knew either they had found something or something had found them. Now I was really nervous, and as the minutes ticked by I got spooked and shut down the engine. The silence was creepier than the engine noise. I remembered that Bryan kept a gun in his camera bag. After carefully scanning my surroundings, I jumped out, got into the back seat area, checked his bag, and ... nothing! *He must have it with him,* I thought. After a few more agonizing minutes, Larry and Bryan appeared from the brush. Before they could say a word, I was on them like a fly on a cow pie!

Larry remembers, *"We had found what we were looking for, but before I could tell Jerry anything, he was freaking out because we had left him without a gun. He said something like, 'The guy could have slipped up behind me and kidnapped me!'*

"I said, 'What are you making such a big deal for, he can't fly!' I remember he got all pissed off over that.

"We had found the truck and the amazing part was the way Comer had covered it with tree branches and brush. We would never have spotted it from the air or the road. We figured out which way they were headed, so I called for DPS to fly our SWAT team to the area in their Bell 212, which was big enough to bring in the whole team. Other units converged on the ground, bringing in dogs, ATVs, and trackers.

"Our plan was to get up in the air and try to keep Comer from moving; keep him pinned down while the SWAT team caught up with him. He still had June and her two kids, so we felt confident we had them surrounded. We never saw them, but we would later find out they saw us, and we were in Comer's 'sights' several times."

Sergeant Ralph Pendergast of the sheriff's office brought a tracking dog to the scene of the hidden truck. He was joined by a coon dog used for hunting, owned by the Payson Justice of the Peace, Ron McDaniel.

DPS Pilot Wayne McKinney came lumbering in with the recently acquired Bell 212 and the SWAT team, and landed up the road near an area where we thought Comer was hiding. Now began the intense manhunt for a very violent criminal. This was a chance for Bryan and me to see our law enforcement at their best.

In the cramped back seat, my partner had to sit knees-to-chin and shoot video. He really came to appreciate what my friend and first photographer, Howie Shepherd, had to put up with when he shot that incredible police chase in downtown Phoenix. Howie outweighed Bryan by more than 120 pounds. I never worried about Bryan though; he was always there with the shot we needed.

For more than an hour we circled over an area no more than a mile square, much of which consisted of thick pines and large boulders. I stayed low to the ground, at tree-top level. We knew Comer and his companions had to be hunkered down and hiding.

Eventually Deputy Pendergast radioed Larry asking us to move back, as they were close. That was good news. They were hoping to take them by surprise. The lawmen had to be very careful, since Comer was traveling with two young—and probably worn out—kids. No one knew how he would react when he was finally cornered. We felt that the net was getting very tight. Now the SWAT guys needed to stop, look, and listen.

Our job on the mountain was over and we were getting short on fuel. We landed at the command post right behind the DPS "Big Bird." On approach, I saw Channels 10 and 3 helicopters sitting on the ground, which made me smile.

When we touched down we put on quite a show for the other TV news folks. Bryan was quickly out the back door with his headset still on and attached to a long cord. He stood guard for the required two minute shutdown. We weren't gloating at all. We had just witnessed and participated in a mission that would have made a great TV episode up to this point.

Now if the hunters could catch the bad guy and his accomplice without hurting those innocent kids, it would be a good day for all of us.

We gave the news crews a friendly smile and wave. Bryan hollered that we needed to brief those in the command center and would join them later, and under his breath muttered,"Much later." Once inside the command post, we had a cup of coffee and listened for an update from the SWAT team. We had been on the ground less than an hour when Zebra 2 broke the silence on the radio: "Suspect is in custody and it's Code 4, no shots fired."

Susan Sorg: *"Late in the afternoon, we got word that Comer was caught. We didn't have details, just Jerry making a brief radio call back to the newsroom to say the suspect was in custody and everything was Code-4. Okay … we breathed huge sighs of relief, and got down to the business of getting a newscast ready. I wrote a short lead-in for the anchors to toss to Jerry, giving a little background and the few details I knew, while each newscast producer told me what they wanted from Jerry.*

It was over. The kids were safe and no one had been injured or killed. Lawmen brought the suspect and his girlfriend to the command center a little before 5 p.m., handcuffed and filthy dirty. All the cameras rolled as Comer and June were placed in the back of separate sheriff's cars. After getting their film, the news crews were off the ground within minutes. I was preparing to leave as well, when Larry asked us to wait, saying he needed a big favor from us.

Wait? *Wait!* I couldn't believe he was asking me to wait. I had a *deadline*. It was now 5:10 and our newscast only went until 5:30. I told him I was going to be scooped by everyone. Our next newscast was at 6:00 p.m. I had to go now!

Susan: *"At 4:45 our ENG coordinator Steve Widmann started calling for Jerry on the radio, asking him to power up and give us a signal so we could get tape or at least their live presence. No Jerry. At 4:50 and 4:55, same thing. I got on the two-way radio, saying we were about to go into the newscast. Still nothing. The producer got on and called for him; still silence. Then we watched the other stations going live with their reports, while our news anchor read the short report I had written.*

"The assistant news director and a few reporters stood under the monitors tuned to the other stations, while the rest of the newsroom was crowded around Steve and me at the live center. I did hear some sharp words from the back corner office where the news director was. 'We're getting our asses kicked! What the hell??? Where the %$#* is Jerry?'

"I knew my usual shrug wasn't going to cut it this time."

I was fuming over Larry's request for me to wait, when he looked at me and quietly said, "We need you to fly me and our prisoners back to Phoenix."

Okay! We could make up for missing the five o'clock newscast and be just in time for the 6 p.m. news that followed NBC's half hour. What a scoop! "Sure, Larry, we can do that," I said with a big smile. "Take your time."

The kids were driven back in patrol cars, and Comer and his girlfriend were put in the back of Sky 12. We took off about 5:45. As soon as I crossed over the backside of Four Peaks, I powered up the microwave and called the station. It was obvious from the way they answered that they were not pleased. "What happened to you guys at five?" my news director demanded.

B r y a n Neumeister: *"We missed the 5 p.m. news and Comer was the lead story on all the stations. NBC wanted it for a national newscast later that night. "Do you have anything?" they were asking.*

Comer (center) being led to helicopter by Deputy Larry Black

"The producer and news director were looking for an answer. Jerry just sat there grinning, with his front-mounted camera on. They were angrily carrying on about our missing the newscast, until Jerry switched to my rear camera, which showed the fugitives sitting there in Sky 12, wearing handcuffs and leg irons.

Comer, with long, greasy hair and filthy, ragged clothes, looked like Charles Manson. His girlfriend, now identified as Geneva Willis, didn't look much better. When the newsroom clicked their mic to acknowledge, we heard a loud cheer go up. We went from zero to hero in a flash!"

Jim Willi: *"Every TV station and all the newspapers in the area were calling—wanting to get a picture of the fugitive. I graciously invited them to our roof to get their video and pictures—being sure that we kept them far enough away from the landing pad that they would have to get the big silver and red Sky 12 helicopter in their shots. Jerry and I also instructed the deputy*

Deputy Black reporting on the capture from the helicopter

how to remove the fugitive from Sky 12 so the helicopter—and our big logo—would have to be visible in their video and still pictures."

Bryan Neumeister: *"Forty minutes later we landed on the Channel 12 roof pad to a swarm of photographers and reporters. What an unusual scoop that was. Sheriff's deputies were there to transport the pair to the downtown jail. It was a real circus.*

"As lawmen took the pair out of the helicopter and moved away, photographers were walking backward, all hoping for the best shot. Before Jerry could shut down the engine, our own shooter, Howie Shepherd, tripped backward over an air vent in the roof. His video camera flew up and he landed hard on his back, breaking a shoulder. He was hurting badly, so I signaled Jerry to keep the engine running.

"A few minutes later we had Howie in the back seat and were on the way to the hospital. Even while hurting, our gentle giant of a friend smiled when we mentioned, 'The Howie Factor.'"

After dropping Howie off, I left the hospital, fueled up at Sky Harbor, then headed down to the station and landed on the roof, since I was scheduled to fill in for the 10 p.m. weather. Susan had my lead story on the manhunt ready to go, as well as the weather script. I watched Stu Tracey do the weather at 9:30 on

Channel 5, while Bryan edited the video for my story and weather report. Everything went according to plan, and by 10:30 we were all ready for a good night's sleep.

A few days later Bryan and I had lunch with Larry Black at Saguaro Lake. When I landed on the sheriff's pad and shut down, Larry handed me a rifle case. Inside was a mini-14 assault rifle that Larry said was from his personal collection. It was a thank you to me, and I still have that rifle.

Comer went to court, was given the death penalty and executed at Florence prison in 2010. His girlfriend received a light sentence after testifying in court about the murder, rape and kidnapping. She had also told deputies that Comer had taken aim at Sky 12 several times while we were searching for him. The only reason he didn't fire was because he didn't want to give away his position. It wasn't until then that I realized just how much danger we had been in.

Chapter 66

The Black Jacket Affair – February 16, 1988

It was nearly two years after my hearing and suspension, but appeals were still going on, and I was still flying. Our schedule for the day was light enough that I stayed home until about 9 a.m. I then flew to the station to see how Bryan and Susan were doing with a half-hour special they were in the process of writing and editing. I was on my own, and unless there was an earthshaking news event, they would stay on their project until it was finished, which could be several days.

I had two things scheduled for the afternoon. The assignment desk needed video of the Saguaro Lake dam for a story later that evening, and I had a school visit at 2 p.m. in the suburb of Gilbert, just a few miles away.

Before taking off I did the noon weather in the studio with anchor Vince Leonard. Once a week had Marge from the Humane Society on our noon show with either a little puppy or a kitten that was up for adoption. On this day it was a cute little Labrador mix just full of life and very playful. When we finished the interview with Marge I asked her if I could hold the little dog while I did the weather.

As I stood in front of that imaginary weather board holding the little guy with my left hand and arm, and pointing at the map with my right, it all went well until I got to the forecast. The temperatures were on the screen and I was reading from the teleprompter as I walked to my seat off screen. I tripped on a cable and down I went, puppy and all. I held on to the little fella until I hit the floor, then I turned him loose.

The viewers at home saw none of this; they only heard me crashing, and the scared puppy yelping. The director held the forecast on the screen until I regained my composure and got back in my chair. Then the camera was back to a three-shot of me, Marge and Vince, but no puppy.

Vince explained what had just happened and assured everyone that the cute little dog was okay and we would show him right after the break. The telephone switchboard operator said the phones didn't stop ringing for an hour. We always had a good time with the animals and helped a lot of homeless pets find new homes with our viewers.

Shortly before 1 p.m. I took off from the roof to film aerial shots of the Saguaro Lake dam about 40 miles east of Phoenix. The story had to do with the dam being renovated and updated. I circled a couple of times, shooting about two minutes' worth of video.

That done, I started downriver to head for Gilbert. I decided to land and change tapes in the recorder so that I would have a separate tape to shoot aerials of the school activity. The kids were having a Flag Day and I had promised that if I could, I would circle overhead at 2:00 o'clock sharp and catch the action for the closing shot of our evening news.

It was a cool February day so the campgrounds along the river were deserted. I picked a spot right next to the water and landed next to an old camping site where a large circle of rocks outlined a previous campfire.

I was monitoring the time very closely and figured I had about 10 minutes to kill. The first thing I did was check my video of the dam. It looked good, so I changed the tape in the recorder, sat back, checked my watch and decided to go a few minutes early.

As I twisted the throttle and started back to flight rpm, I noticed something next to the campfire that looked shiny and out of place, so I went back to flight idle, frictioned the controls, and jumped out to have a look.

When I landed, my rotor wash had cleared away enough sand to partially expose a small, nickel-plated handgun. It was an old, rusted 32-caliber revolver. Close by was a fingernail clipper and several little papers folded into envelopes, typically used by drug users to hold a small quantity of cocaine or speed. A little black container, the type used to carry 35mm film, was lodged between two of the fire-pit rocks. It contained a small amount of marijuana seeds and stems.

I took what I had found back to the helicopter and put the drug paraphernalia in the pocket of a black jacket I kept in the back seat. I put the gun on the seat under the jacket. I would have liked to spend more time looking around, but I needed to get airborne and on the way.

As soon as I lifted off I tried to call the lake patrol lieutenant on the sheriff's car-to-car frequency, but received no answer. I then tried a blind call to any lake patrol unit and still got no answer, which is not unusual on a cold winter day. I would find someone later and turn in my find, but for now it could wait. The important thing was the pistol. It may have been stolen or used in a crime, and could even be the missing link in a homicide.

For now it was no big deal and by the time I got over Gilbert Elementary school I was in another mode. Below me, a large playground was full of several hundred kids in a formation that spelled out, "Sky 12" and depicted an American flag. I circled the playground several times and shot video of the formations. When I had the shots I needed I made a fast low pass, gave a big wave followed by a vertical climb, and I was out of there.

I always felt good after a school visit. It had taken a lot of work by the staff and kids to make up those formations. I had a big smile on my face and in my heart when I landed downtown to turn in the two tapes I had shot. It had been a good day and I was planning on heading for home shortly—maybe even ride that beautiful black horse down to the creek and splash around a bit.

When I walked into the newsroom everything changed. Al Macias, our assignment editor, was on the phone and when he saw me he started waving, so I walked over to him. As he hung up he said, "Jerry, that was the principal out at Gilbert Elementary school, he says you need to come back right away, your jacket blew out the window when you were circling the school."

On the way back to Gilbert I tried again to contact Lt. Paul or Sgt. Black. This time I was answered by a lake patrol deputy, Michael Iglielski, who told me the two supervisors were off that day. I asked Michael if he could meet me at the campground just below the Bluepoint Bridge in about 30 minutes to receive some found items. He gave me a 10-4, meaning he would be there.

As I landed in the same open area of the elementary school I saw the principal and a police officer at one end of the field and about 100 kids watching nearby. It never dawned on me until that very moment that I was suspected of any wrongdoing. I frictioned the controls and left the engine running at flight idle.

As I walked up to the men, the uniformed officer identified himself as Officer Fast of the Gilbert Police Department. He asked, "Mr. Foster, is this your jacket?"

"Yes, that's my jacket," I replied

"Do you know what is in the jacket pocket?"

"Yes sir, I sure do; items I found on the Verde River."

Officer Fast then held up a card, and over the noise of the idling helicopter, started reading the card: "You have the right to remain silent. Anything you say can and will be used against you in a court of law ... "

I had heard that read to so many suspects, that my mind turned to jelly as he read on.

When he finished, I explained how and where I had found the items. I didn't mention that the gun I found was still on the rear seat in plain sight. When asked if the sheriff's office knew about it, I told the officer they did: a lie.

Officer Fast told me he would keep the items in my jacket pocket and that I was free to go while he investigated the case. I thanked him, jumped in my helicopter and headed for the Verde River and a waiting deputy.

I intentionally landed away from the spot where I had previously landed, so the deputy could see the tracks I'd left and would know I had been there earlier. I shut the engine down and joined Deputy Iglieleski as he walked up to the helicopter.

I explained the whole story to him from start to finish. I also told him that in my panic I had told Officer Fast that I had already advised the sheriff's office of my discovery. I gave him the handgun and pointed to the campsite where I had found it. When I ran out of things to say, the deputy headed for the campsite. I heard him tell the radio dispatcher he needed a supervisor to join him at the campground.

By now it was late afternoon and starting to get dark. I wasn't scheduled to do the weather at 5 p.m., so I took off and headed for the ranch. I needed to think this out. The only thing I had done wrong was not tell Officer Fast the truth. I knew this was going to be a big deal, but I had no idea how big it would become.

At home I explained my day to Vicki and before I could finish, my news director was on the phone looking for some answers.

Jim Willi: *"I was in my office when I got a call from a parent in Gilbert, who told me a story that immediately received my full attention.*

The caller asked, 'What are you doing about your helicopter pilot?' I received calls like this at least once a week, usually because our helicopter had flown low over someone's house or blown pebbles on someone's car. But that wasn't the case this day.

"A couple of kids had seen the black jacket fly out of the helicopter and ran to retrieve it. When they discovered the marijuana and other paraphernalia inside a pocket, they took it to the school principal. He was not happy—to put it mildly—and called the Gilbert Police.

"This happened several hours before I received the phone call, and Jerry had apparently forgotten to tell me about it. He was not doing the weather and wasn't in the newscast that night. I called him at home and he explained the whole incident from start to finish.

"I went downstairs to tell my boss, General Manager Pep Cooney, what had happened. I loved working for Pep; one of the all-time great guys and an eternal optimist. After I told him the story, Pep said, 'Well, it probably won't even be in the newspaper.'

"I woke up early the next morning hoping Pep was right. Not so much. That morning the Arizona Republic had a large headline—above the masthead on the front page—that read, 'Marijuana falls out of Sky 12.'"

For the next four days I lived in a state of hell. I had received calls from every news publication in the state. I must have repeated my story at least a hundred times. When our rival TV stations called, I gave them the same response and cooperation I gave everyone else. The following Monday morning, on ABC's *Good Morning America*, the story was read and the anchors got a big laugh at my expense.

The Maricopa County Sheriff ordered a complete investigation at the request of Gilbert Police Chief Fred Dees. *"I had known Jerry would be visiting the school that day, and wished I could take my kids out to see him fly in. They were big fans. Later, an officer stuck his head in my office to report that Foster's jacket had fallen out of the helicopter and marijuana was found in the pocket. He said Foster was on his way back to retrieve the jacket. As much as I admired Jerry, I had to tell them to handle it like they would anyone else. We eventually referred it to the sheriff's office, since the drugs and gun had been found on their turf. I figured it would turn out to be much ado about nothing, and that's exactly what it was."*

The sheriff put Major John Coppock, chief of internal affairs, in charge. That Monday morning Major Coppock interviewed me for more than two hours. It was the toughest and most complete interview I have ever been exposed to. Every statement was gone over and over, and several times I had to clench my teeth and take his unmerciful demanding accusations.

In a press release the Major said, "We wanted to make sure he (Foster) was not using his affiliation with this agency to mask his possible possession of an illegal substance."

For the next two days I was interviewed three different times by Major Coppock, as well as by deputies I had worked for and with. The media kept up a relentless barrage of my past run-ins, which included the FAA, the Grand Canyon National Park Superintendent, and eagle watchers, just to name a few.

On Friday, February 19th, the Maricopa County Sheriff's Office released its findings to the press. The headline in the Phoenix Gazette read:

"INVESTIGATION SUBSTANTIATES FOSTER STORY"

In part, the article said, *"The investigation concluded that Foster was well-intentioned Tuesday when he took the marijuana and other items, including a revolver, from an abandoned campsite near the Salt River and Usury Pass Road, said Maj. John Coppock, who conducted the two-day investigation.*

"He said evidence indicated Foster, a pilot for KPNX TV (Channel 12) and a member of the sheriff's search and rescue posse, was going to turn his find over to deputies.

"However the report also found that Foster made a few mistakes, including lying to a Gilbert police officer who asked the pilot about the marijuana, Coppock said."

Most of the valley newspapers carried the story that I had been exonerated, although TV network stations didn't say a word about it, except the independent station, KPHO, Channel 5, which carried the whole story. It really didn't matter that much because

506

the damage had already been done. I knew I would hear about this one until the day I died.

I was more than a little relieved when it was finally over. But to really bury the incident, there was one more thing I needed to do. The following Monday I called Principal Quinby at Gilbert Elementary School to ask if I could make another visit and talk to the kids. He was very gracious and relieved that the investigation was over and I had been cleared.

Principal John Quinby: *"I felt he wanted to say something to set things right, in his mind and in the minds of the kids."*

Randy Reid, *Phoenix Gazette*

Helicopter pilot Jerry Foster chats with students Wednesday at Gilbert Elementary School.

Foster's toughest job: Apologizing

By Glen Creno
Phoenix Gazette

GILBERT — Television helicopter pilot Jerry Foster says he hasn't had to do anything tougher.

But his apology to youngsters who had idolized him, then learned that he had lied about a canister of marijuana, was eagerly accepted Wednesday at Gilbert Elementary School.

"I've had easier things to do," Foster said, "but I've never had anything tougher to do."

The pilot, who flies for KPNX-TV, Channel 12, spoke briefly to the students, saying it was wrong to lie. He said it was important to get an education and stay away from drugs and alcohol.

That was good enough. The students swarmed around Foster and his machine, asking questions and clamoring for autographs.

The controversy began Feb. 16, when Foster's jacket was sucked out of his chopper while he was taping a ceremony at the elementary school.

Chris Martin, 14, an eighth-grader from nearby Mesquite Junior High School, retrieved the jacket and noticed something funny inside. The jacket was taken to a teacher. The something funny was a film canister containing marijuana.

Mesquite was observing "Say No to Drugs and Alcohol Week" at the time.

Chris said he suspected what was in the container. "I knew it was something like that," he said.

Chris was among the horde of youngsters gathered in a field next to Gilbert Elementary to witness Foster's return.

After the jacket fell and Foster landed,

See ■ **Foster, B-3**

A few days later I landed on the Gilbert Elementary School playground. It was a very warm reception by the kids and staff, but it was bittersweet for me. I told the kids the truth: I had lied to the officer because I was afraid of being arrested. I was wrong and violated a proverb that my mother taught me as a youngster. "There is no right way to do a wrong thing." My mistake was forgiven by my little friends. To publicly admit to a lie was a very difficult thing to do, but it was the right thing, and I have never regretted it.

After the jacket blew out of the helicopter over a school yard, I knew my days in the business were coming to an end. The incident damaged my reputation as well as my attitude. I drew attention from all over the country, but it wasn't the kind of attention anyone would want. I was eventually found "innocent and well-intentioned," but that part wasn't worth mentioning at the time.

It was all part of my incredible adventure, and I would do it all over again if I could; but maybe a little differently.

Chapter 67

Lake Powell

Lake Powell is, in my opinion, the most beautiful place on this earth. From the first night I slept in this peaceful landscape in the late 1960s, as a young helicopter pilot just passing through, I had found a serene place that thrilled me deep in my soul. Lying under the tail boom of that Bell 'copter, I gazed at a brilliant sky— one I had never taken the time to really see before. The soft lighting of the moon reflecting off the water, the towering monuments and sandstone cliffs, made it one of the "life moments" I would never forget. My only demons were the ones I brought with me.

Throughout my career I would visit Lake Powell many times on stories, vacations, special projects, documentaries and family visits. I kept a boat there for many years and took advantage of any excuse I could find to visit. My crew and close circle of friends discovered the peace and beauty of the area, and we were able to pass that onto our viewers.

We traveled there several times a year looking for stories of all kinds. In addition to Lake Powell, we'd go to Monument Valley and the many small communities on the Navajo and Hopi reservations in Northern Arizona, which are still much as they were centuries ago. Bryan was an expert at capturing the moment and putting the scenes together with music that, many times, he created in his home studio. He not only filmed it skillfully, he was also gifted in the editing room and in the use of special effects.

Susan would gather all the facts, interviews, and video, and write a script for me to narrate. Then she and Bryan disappeared into a video editing booth and created half-hour specials and feature stories on a wide variety of subjects.

The filming could go on for days or until a big story broke. The news stories were our main responsibility, and breaking off one project to go to another happened even when we were out of town. The assignment editors at the station were always able to track us down. It was hard to go anywhere unnoticed in a noisy red, white and blue helicopter with a big 12 painted on the side. There was no place to hide, not that we were trying.

It's hard for anyone to imagine the splendor and magnitude of Lake Powell until they've been there and seen it for themselves. The lake resulted from the Glen Canyon dam, which was completed in 1969. But it would take another eleven years before the lake reached the high-water mark. This huge reservoir straddles the Utah-Arizona border, and stores over 24 million acre-feet of water. Natural features include Rainbow Bridge, many rock formations and plateaus, and scores of side canyons, some of which housed Indian ruins tucked into the canyon walls. Lake Powell became part of Glen Canyon National Recreation Area in 1972, and is managed by the National Park Service.

For me, a trip to Lake Powell was an opportunity to carry on a relationship with my dad's family, the Wards. Uncle Mack and Aunt Wanda, my dad's sister, always welcomed me and my family. I watched my little cousins, Steve, JoEllen, Janie and Phil, go through school, college, and on to raise families of their own.

Steve Ward worked on Lake Powell his whole life. Besides piloting tour boats, he drove fuel and supply tankers to marinas on this massive lake to places accessible only by water. During those years he turned himself into a professional photographer and tour guide, conducting whitewater trips down the mighty Colorado River on large rafts. Next to my job, I thought my rugged cousin had the

Steve Ward (right) with me 2011

best job in the world. Steve came to be known as "Mr. Lake Powell," and whenever I needed info on the lake, Grand Canyon or the Navajo country, he was my first call.

Sadly, Steve passed away in 2012, as we were working on this book. He contributed much of the information on Lake Powell and details of the following stories during my last visit with him in 2011. I miss my friend.

While we had many wonderful adventures at Lake Powell, we were also involved in several search and recovery operations in the area. One sad event took place in July 1985.

Danny Nasca was a friend of mine from Parker, Arizona. He owned a Bell JetRanger, which he used for various jobs. He didn't have a lot of flight time, but he was a good pilot. We often ran into each other at Scottsdale Airport when he came to ASI for maintenance on his bird. We had flown together in the mountains north of my ranch a couple of times to help him gain experience. He was eager to learn and do it right. All he needed was time. But a month after I flew with him, my friend was killed in a crash.

Danny had been hired to fly in the movie, *Hands of Steel*. The location was about 10 miles southwest of Lake Powell on the Colorado River at Marble Canyon.

My cousin Steve called me late in the afternoon to tell me about the crash. He didn't have any details, other than the pilot and an actor had been killed. I knew right away it was Danny, and told Steve that Bryan and I would pick him up at daylight the next morning at the Page airport. Vicki, Bryan and I landed at Page around 7 a.m. We met Steve and removed the doors and gear we didn't need, refueled and headed for Navajo Bridge.

Steve Ward: *"The bridge across the canyon is about 600 feet high. They were filming a movie at that spot, and actors were on the bridge shooting machine guns at the helicopter. The helicopter would duck back under the bridge and come back shooting some more.*

"Apparently, when Danny came out again a sudden wind draft lifted him up into the bottom of the steel bridge. The rotor blades disintegrated, causing the aircraft to plunge into the Colorado River, 540 feet below. A short way upstream the Paria River feeds into the Colorado, causing silt and mud to restrict visibility, so we couldn't see any signs of the wreckage near the bridge."

The cabin was visible more than 700 feet downstream from where it impacted. The water was too swift and muddy to tell much of anything else. Later that day the body of the actor, Claudio Cassinelli, was found still strapped in his seat.

This was the first search I had been on where I personally knew the victim, and there wasn't much conversation during our three-day search. The National Park Service Superintendent at the Grand Canyon was threatening me with a flight violation. Sheriff Joe Richards told them to leave me alone, because I was working for the Coconino County Sheriff's Office and it was their jurisdiction. That made me smile.

After three days we called the search off. We had to go home. Our friend Danny Nasca was never found.

Steve Ward: *"Two summers in a row we had helicopter fatalities in the same area while filming. The next summer, Larry Hagman was shooting a movie close to the same place. One day after filming, the director—also a low-time pilot—decided to fly some people through the Canyon. He hit a cable stretched across the river at Lee's Ferry, killing all four occupants of the helicopter."*

Prior to these two crashes I had been involved in two other searches on the Colorado River in the Grand Canyon National Park domain. On both occasions I was called in by Coconino County Sheriff Joe Richards to help.

In one instance a prominent citizen of Page had gone on a pleasure flight with his son into the canyon downriver from the dam at Lake Powell. Steve Ward knew this pilot very well.

Steve Ward: *"Don "Smedly" Safely, was the guy the NPS called on in those days to fly his plane and deliver emergency messages to rafters on the river. He would fly his acrobatic plane low over all the rafts on the river until he found the group he was looking for, then he dropped messages in vacuum canisters. On this particular trip he had come downriver to buzz his airplane over a group of 20-plus of his river-runner friends and family from Page, just to say 'Hi'. He turned around to make another pass and his plane lost power, crashing nearly in front of his friends.*

"It was late afternoon, about 19 miles from Lee's Ferry. In those days before cell phones, river crews were instructed to place a large X on the beach for emergencies. When Smedly didn't return, a search was started at first light the next morning."

Because it was in Coconino County, and they didn't have a dive team yet, the sheriff called Sgt. Larry Black at the Maricopa County Sheriff's Office requesting divers to help find the aircraft and bodies. He also requested Lincoln-30 (Sky 12) to assist in the search if available.

The scene was 50 miles downstream from Page on a rugged stretch of the mighty Colorado. The only way in was by raft or helicopter. It was an area of narrow canyons with white water and huge boulders.

That evening Larry and two deputies drove to Lee's Ferry with all the dive gear they could carry. Other divers would be flown up later in the day. The following morning Bryan and I flew the helicopter to Lee's Ferry to pick up the sheriff and show him the scene. Sgt. Black and the divers had left at daylight on a large commercial raft with a river crew.

Sheriff Richards told me the Park Service had reported me to the FAA for violating flight restrictions and landing in a wilderness area. He said he had been threatened with a citation if he permitted our news helicopter to land. Sheriff Richards had advised the Park Service to back off, because he was personally running this search.

This was as much a jurisdictional problem between the sheriff's office and the NPS, as it was with a news helicopter and me personally. When I started out there were few helicopters around and most of the rules were added as we went along. Sometimes I knew about them and sometimes I didn't ... that is, not until I violated one of them. That's what happened with the Park Service.

In July 1980 I had flown an 11-year-old boy and his dad into this same area we were now searching. Howie Shepherd was my photographer back then. We had landed on a sandbar, where we unloaded the boy's wheelchair and helped them both to the river's edge. We took pictures as the father and son each caught their first fish. An hour later we loaded up to head home. As we were leaving, a party of rafters floated by taking pictures, smiling and waving. It had been a great experience for us all.

Six weeks later, the little boy died of leukemia.

Two weeks after that fishing trip I got a call from the Park Superintendent's assistant. The first thing he said was that he was holding a picture of the Channel 12 helicopter buzzing a river rafting party and flying in a dangerous manner. Before I could say a word he told me he was forwarding a letter to my general manager, Pep Cooney, which the superintendent had written to the FAA.

I tried to tell him what had happened and why, but he wasn't interested. He had called to threaten me, and I took the bait and lost my temper. The last thing I said before slamming down the receiver was, "Kiss my tail rotor, pal!" After that things with the Grand Canyon National Park Service were never the same.

I have said this before and I believe it worth repeating. The one who loses his temper is the one who loses the confrontation. Had I taken the time to fly to the Grand Canyon and sit down and talk to the superintendent, apologize and tell him I would like to work with them, things would have been a lot better. And that goes for the FAA, the U.S. Forest Service, or Arizona Game and Fish. My problem was always me.

Now I was being reported again during this search for Smedly. We flew to the crash site to find a place for the divers to camp and recon the areas downstream from the impact point. Later in the day we flew to Page to pick up the other divers from Phoenix and drop off the sheriff.

Once on the ground, Sheriff Richards was advised by his dispatcher that the Park Service was insisting divers and equipment should be taken in and out by river boats or rafts. That didn't happen.

Lt. David Paul: *"Jerry liked to bend the rules a little bit. When we went down into the Grand Canyon, we took a dive team down there and asked Jerry to go along. Jerry didn't get along well with the Park Service, or the U.S. Forest Service. They realized they needed him, but wanted him on their terms only. The Park Service was going to arrest Jerry, and I don't know if it was me or Larry, but one of us said, 'If you're gonna arrest somebody, we're in charge, so arrest us. He's here because we want him here!' They relented, but weren't happy about it."*

When the search began, we would land a mile or so ahead of the divers and let them know what was around the bend. On one of the stops, Lt. David Paul slipped on a rock and broke several ribs. Had the helicopter not been available, the mission would have had to be called off or delayed. Later that day, using a metal detector, we found what we were looking for.

Sgt. Larry Black: *"We found the plane and the motor, but we couldn't get to it because it had lodged against a large boulder beneath the surface and the current was so strong that we had to leave it, knowing the bodies were just out of reach. It was heart-wrenching for all of us, especially the family."*

The little boy's body was found a couple of months later by hikers, a few miles downstream from the crash site. The father's body was later recovered from the plane, using special equipment we didn't have.

Another heartbreaker occurred just below the Glen Canyon Dam. Two firemen from Mesa were fishing along the shore, wearing wader boots. One of the men lost his footing and was swept into deep water by the current. The other fireman went after his friend, but his boots turned out to be anchors as well.

I got the call on a Thursday evening from Sgt. Larry Black who advised me of the drownings. Sheriff Richards wanted the Maricopa County dive squad and me as soon as possible.

I would head right up there and start looking for the men at daybreak. Larry figured if they were moving slowly I might be able to spot them farther down in clear water. He would call the Arizona National Guard and get them to fly the team and dive gear to Lee's Ferry, which was only a mile from the scene.

Bryan and I headed out. We refueled that night in Page, then spent the night on a sandy knoll overlooking the dam and the Colorado River. Through binoculars we could see a lot of activity at the boat ramp at Lee's Ferry. With all the Park Service trucks there, I figured it would be a good idea to wait until morning to make our entrance.

We carried everything in the LongRanger that we needed for a comfortable night. It would have been a very enjoyable night had it not been for the circumstances. Two strong, young firemen were dead in a tragic accident. Firemen were supposed to be the rescuers, the heroes we count on in times of need.

At daylight we were up and ready to go. The canyon below the dam was still dark and would be for at least another couple of hours. We would need good light and direct sun to spot a body. We flew back to the airport to drop our doors, grab breakfast and to check in with Susan. She said the station had sent a satellite truck up and it should arrive soon. That way we could cover the story live, on the ground or in the air.

Sgt. Black and the dive team would be landing later that afternoon in a National Guard helicopter. This was going to be a huge story and very expensive for the station. With a satellite truck *and* a news helicopter, we would be under a lot of pressure. NBC wanted a report for their national news.

We were in the air and over the scene around 8:30. I landed for a briefing by the deputy in charge who pointed out where the men had disappeared. A Park Service Ranger showed us on a map where the current was likely to carry a body, and noted the location of deep pools. The briefing was helpful, and by then we had good light.

We took off from the parking lot and went out over the middle of the river at about 50 feet. The visibility of the water was excellent. As we started slowly upriver we hadn't gone more than a quarter-mile when I spotted one of the bodies. The hip waders held him in almost the same place he had slipped under. It was surreal. You ask yourself why he didn't just get out of those boots and swim to shore.

But we all know how those things happen. A careless moment; all it takes is one gulp of water and no matter how strong a swimmer you are, you can drown.

Deputies and rangers were able to make the recovery very quickly. The body was in about 10 feet of water near the shore. A park service boat with a deputy and a ranger made the recovery. Bryan shot video and we continued to search for the second fireman.

We took a break shortly before noon to refuel and do a live report for our noon news, then continued our search. By early afternoon the Guard helicopter arrived with Larry and three deputies. They would be using a large raft and a smaller rubber boat. Even though it was a bright sunny day, the conditions were miserable.

Sgt. Larry Black: *"The water was coming out of the bottom of the dam from Lake Powell and it was 42 degrees and stinging cold. We had to wear dry suits, and even then we could still only dive 15 minutes at a time. The water was moving at eight-to-ten knots and was clear. But the current swirled us around, making it hard to stay balanced and watch where we were being taken. We crossed many dark, deep pools where we suspected the body might be hidden.*

"Jerry was our backup. He would land ahead of us on a rock formation or sand bar and tell us what was downstream, and we could warm up in the helicopter. If it was rough whitewater he would fly us over it. We kept that up for two days and covered miles of river, but never found a thing."

It was heartbreaking for everyone involved. We had to give it up and that was something we hardly ever did. For search and rescue people it's one of the worst outcomes you can experience. We all packed up and went home knowing we had given the mission our very best effort. Eventually, the second fireman was found nearly10 miles downstream.

Chapter 68

Final Goldwater Thoughts

Relaxing at Sedona airport

By the late 1980s, I had been flying around with Senator Goldwater for nearly 20 years, and we had become close friends. I respected him and never quite got over the awe of having him as a friend and mentor, yet I felt completely comfortable around him, and could give as good as I got in the teasing department. I guess I never thought of it as being a special relationship until his son Michael mentioned it to me years later. In my mind, we were just two guys who enjoyed flying together. And we did a lot of it!

There were few airports in Arizona where we hadn't landed. When Barry was in town and not busy, I would pick him up at his house and he would cruise around the city with me looking for news. I sensed it was a quiet time for him because we seldom talked. He liked listening to the radio traffic coming through our headsets, as well as the news I was reporting. There were other times when he never put a headset on until he was ready to go home. He enjoyed the solitude as much as the action.

Even when he didn't fly with me, if I knew he was home from Washington I would make it a point to fly by his home office w i n d o w .   T h e Goldwater home sat on a hill overlooking downtown Phoenix and

Barry's office window, which I would "buzz"

had a clear zone on the south side of the house. I could fly nearly up to his window, wave, and then be off again like a hummingbird. We both got a big kick out of it.

Early one morning I appeared in front of their window and caught Mrs. Goldwater in a housecoat. She stood there, hands on her hips, glaring at Barry and then at me. He didn't look up, but he waved and I got out of there. Later he said, "Peggy was giving me hell until you showed up, then she was giving *you* hell because the last time you landed here you blew her flowers everywhere."

It was always a joke between us because with each takeoff and landing the helicopter wreaked havoc on the finely manicured lawn. "Mrs. G, I am only the pilot," I say, and she would smile.

We actually had a good relationship. She had taken me under her wing right from the very beginning. I think she and I bonded even before Barry and I did. She always liked me, and I definitely thought the world of her.

When the two of them attended events, Barry was always busy talking to one person or another, and so he relied on me to look after Peggy, and make sure she had what she needed. And Peggy often relied on me to be her ears, as her hearing was failing. If Barry were on a dais speaking, and Peggy and I were at a table in the audience, she would ask me, "What did he say? What was that?" and I'd let her know what was being said.

The Goldwaters were fun to be around and I always looked forward to traveling with them. They could push each other's buttons in a heartbeat, but they were very close.

When Peggy died in December of 1985, Barry called to let me know. I said, "Let's go flying when you're feeling up to it."

Several weeks later I flew him up to Lake Powell. From there we flew to the foot of Navajo Mountain where his trading post and lodge had once stood. Peggy had bought Rainbow Lodge for Barry in 1946, intending it to be a hideaway where he could get away from politics for a while. He had always loved the Navajo land and people, and felt more at home there than anywhere else.

In the summer of 1951, the lodge had burned down, and there wasn't much left other than the foundation. We walked around in silence while he remembered the good times they had spent there. It was a special day, and one that I was humbled and happy to give him. It was also the last time we flew together.

When Barry retired from the Senate in 1987 he set about writing his memoirs, which were published in 1988. One day I received a call from him. "Are you busy?" he asked.

"No, I'm free for a while," I said. "What's up?"

"I'll be right over."

He arrived within an hour and presented me with a copy of his book, "*Goldwater*." I was touched to see that he had signed it to me. But when he opened it to the pages that described our friendship and travels over the years, I was stunned. I was incredibly moved by that gesture, and still am.

When he died on May 29, 1998, I was devastated. It was as heartbreaking as when I lost my dad. He had been that important in my life.

A million times I have thought, "Barry Goldwater ... Wow!"

Chapter 69

End of the Golden Years

Over the years I had worked myself into a corner. I had tried taking an occasional weekend off, going on vacation or taking a trip out of the country. But I worried so much about missing that "big story" that I couldn't really enjoy myself, and it was aggravating to Vicki. I think she, too, had had enough. I had been going strong for two decades, and when something big happened in Arizona, our viewers—even my competition—expected me to be first on the scene. When I missed a story I should have had, I was difficult to be around.

TV news was changing and I was now the "old guy" in the business. By the late 1980s there were five TV helicopters in the Phoenix market, meaning I had four other stations to beat. We seldom took a day off.

I had made a lot of friends over the years, but I also had my share of critics. The fights with the FAA, National Park Service, the US Forest Service and too many others, finally got to me. I still loved what I was doing, but I no longer loved how I was doing it.

With the advent of cable channels, the TV industry was booming. When we had only four channels in the Phoenix area, that's when we were in our prime. Now there were over 80 channels with more coming on all the time. KPNX was no longer owned by a hometown entrepreneur, and the other stations were also soon coming under ownership of the large broadcast conglomerates.

There was even talk that the helicopters were being put on a strict budget and flight time would be limited. The belt was starting to tighten. Even though my station was owned by Gannett, one of the industry giants, they had let me run my way for six years. Now the end of my era was nearly over.

As much as anything, the years of covering so many tragic events nearly had me talking to myself. I knew it was time to give it up and so did my crew.

Susan Sorg: *"Looking back, more than 20 years later, I can see now how conflicted Jerry was. On one hand he had his work with law enforcement and the friendships that developed out of that, while on the other hand there were the friendships born from his old life; his "other side of the street," as he calls it. Throw in the pressure of being on call 24/7, constantly in the public eye, and all the gruesome sights he saw, and his own post traumatic stress disorder intensified silently as the years went on.*

"His behavior became more erratic. Bryan and I started driving to events, knowing Jerry would fly in later. It wasn't that we were afraid to fly with him, it just became the best way to get the job done. It was also the best way to avoid Jerry's black moods, because we could only shrug it off for so long.

"It all spiraled downward beginning with the infamous jacket incident, followed by the FAA hearing. We knew Jerry wasn't going to last much longer with Sky 12, as he became his own worst enemy.

"You see it happening in relationships that start out with the best of intentions, until people grow apart, and no one wants to say anything about it. The three of us were headed in different directions. Bryan and I were growing up, maturing in our fields and feeling more comfortable and confident with our talents. I think Jerry saw that and was scared; scared of losing us, scared of losing what he'd achieved with Sky 12, scared of losing his reputation, and scared of himself and the image he felt he had to uphold. Because we all loved each other, (and still do) we didn't want to point out the obvious—that it was time to part ways. But Jerry,

taking the lead as always, did one of the bravest things ever. He announced he was walking away ... and he did."

August 15, 1988

I was up early that last morning. As the sun rose I was feeding the horses, playing with the dogs and stealing glances over at that beautiful red and silver Bell L-3 sitting on its pad and ready to go. I stood there a few minutes, looking and thinking. It had been a long and incredible career. Tomorrow when I fed the horses I would be unemployed. It would be my first day in 20 years without a helicopter, and my first day in many of those years without it right outside my bedroom.

The feeling was bittersweet as I lifted off, knowing it was my final take-off from the pad I had launched from thousands of times; on all kinds of missions, in good weather and bad.

When I reached one thousand feet I could clearly see San Francisco Peaks more than 100 miles to the north and the entire Valley of the Sun to the south. The early morning sun was shining off the downtown high-rise buildings. That day, during my flight to the station, I noticed so many things I had been taking for granted. I was seeing it all this morning as I had seen it on my first flight off that pad, when Vicki and I moved to Cave Creek years before.

As I landed at Channel 12, I looked over at the Channel 10 pad and saw it empty. For the first time, I didn't care. I even thought, *I hope nothing tragic happens.* The day was planned out for me and then I could go home (one of those bittersweet thoughts) and do whatever I wanted to do, which was nothing. I didn't have any job offers and had no interest in looking for one. I had been in this position before, but it had been a very long time ago.

My only meeting was with news director Jim Willi and general manager Pep Cooney, the two guys who had backed me, trusted me, and allowed me to do it my way—at least, most of the time. We all knew that now my time had come and gone. And we all agreed it was a time that made broadcast history and would likely never be repeated.

I roamed around to all the departments saying goodbye. Many of my co-workers had ridden with me at one time or another, and we laughs and hugs.

Following the last noon show with me doing the weather, I was joined by Bryan, Susan, Vicki and my mother for lunch. We all went to Jordan's for Mexican food, where my longtime friend, owner Joe Jordan, cooked us a special lunch served by his daughter, Devoney and her "Mother Mary."

At two o'clock we went to the Maricopa County Sheriff's Office for a sendoff. Years before I was made an honorary deputy because of the work I had done with them for so long.

Most of the friends I worked with were there, including my longtime friend and partner, Sgt. Larry Black. Sheriff Dick Godbehere presented me with the Sheriff's Distinguished Service Medal and a citation that read in part:

"The Sheriff of Maricopa County, Arizona is pleased to present the Sheriff's Distinguished Service Medal to Special Deputy Jerry Foster for his personal valor and outstanding record of assistance to the Maricopa County Sheriff's Office.

"For nearly two decades Mr. Foster willingly and enthusiastically dedicated his time and talent as a helicopter pilot, repeatedly risking his life to save others. His determination and ability have taken him on countless missions to remote places under hazardous conditions on search and rescue missions ..."

It was the most emotional moment of my departure. I held up as long as I could, but when the sheriff announced he had retired my radio call sign, "Lincoln 30," I looked over at my mother, whose eyes were full of tears. I had to put my hands over my face when I lost it.

I remembered the day in 1959 when, while standing outside the Marine Corps base at Camp Pendleton, California, I promised Mom that someday I would make her and my dad proud. I finally felt I had done it.

When we left the sheriff's office, I sideswiped the sheriff's car bumper while pulling out onto a one-way street the wrong way. A big crowd had come out to watch me leave, and did they get a show! But even after doing that, I still got a round of applause as I went by again, this time going the right way.

We all got back to the station in time for a farewell party with my co-workers in the newsroom. There was a cake with a helicopter on it, and well-wishes all around.

When the publisher of the Arizona Republic presented me with a huge portrait of my old pal, Sky 12, I had another burst of emotion. It was a tough day to get through, and I wasn't done yet.

When Mom, Vicki, and other guests had departed, I did my last weather report for the 5 p.m. newscast. When the time came, Bryan and Susan accompanied me to the roof for my final takeoff.

We had become very close over the years and this was the beginning of a huge change in my life as well as theirs. We had worked our way through a lot of ups and downs while sharing experiences that few people will ever have. Good friends are forever and that is true for us even as I write this.

I left the roof for the final time and headed for Scottsdale Airport to drop off the helicopter for the ex-Vietnam pilot who would take over for me.

After takeoff, I tried to power up the microwave for my final report. It was dead. *Just like the old days*, I thought. I shut off the system, called the station, told them the problem, and said adios. My old friend and anchorman, Vince Leonard, made some nice comments about working with me over the years. And I was TV history.

☰ CITATION ☙

The Sheriff of Maricopa County, Arizona is pleased to present the Sheriff's Distinguished Service Medal to Special Deputy Jerry Foster for his personal valor and outstanding record of assistance to the Maricopa County Sheriff's Office. For nearly two decades, Mr. Foster willingly and enthusiastically dedicated his time and talent as a helicopter pilot, repeatedly risking his life to save others. His determination and ability have taken him on countless occasions to remote places under hazardous conditions on search and rescue missions for the Maricopa County Sheriff's Office. Among the hundreds of missions Mr. Foster has flown, one especially calls for recognition. Mr. Foster volunteered on 18 March 1982 to search for a small plane with nine passengers that crashed in a violent snowstorm north of Phoenix. With little information, in fog, precipitation and high winds, Mr. Foster demonstrated exceptional courage and flying skill to locate the plane, in the mountains near Sunflower. He flew Deputies to the site, directed Department of Public Safety medical evacuation personnel, and helped coordinate the multi-agency effort that saw the rescue of three survivors. Exceptional performance has been the rule in Mr. Foster's service to the community. The scope of his contribution truly is beyond reckoning. Mr. Foster's conduct as a citizen, Special Deputy and Sheriff's Posseman is in keeping with the highest standards of the Maricopa County Sheriff's Office. Jerry Foster has earned the Sheriff's Distinguished Service Medal.

PART FIVE

Chapter 70

Back at the Ranch

After I retired the FAA enforced the nine-month suspension. I appreciated that it wasn't done before, and knew I was overdue for a break. I was completely worn out and stressed to the max. I can look back now and find closure in owning my part of the situation and the mistakes I made; but at the time it was devastating and very hard to endure.

After my suspension time ended I got a call at home from an old friend who had joined the local FAA office as a brand new inspector in the early '70s. He and I had attended many functions together and he was well-liked by the general aviation community. He was an excellent example of the FAA inspectors I had known early in my career.

I was very happy to hear from my long-ago friend, Gary Koch, and surprised to learn that he was the new head of the local FAA office. We talked a few minutes, laughed, joked and caught up on the past years. He said he would like to make a trip out to my ranch and see my heliport. I was delighted and gave directions to the ranch. I warned him that it was a rough road and he would have to travel through a canyon, across a wash, and up a steep hill, and that a four-wheel drive was a good idea. "No problem," he said, "the government has one with my name on it. I'm going to bring one of my new inspectors, who is one of us good guys."

I thought that odd, but it sounded like the old Gary I used to know. "How about tomorrow?" he asked, and we set it up for 2 p.m. When I told Vicki, she was concerned that there might be something else involved. "Not a chance," I told her, "this is one straight shooter." I looked forward to it.

The next afternoon we watched as a white Ford Bronco appeared on the dirt across the canyon from us, disappeared as it headed down toward the creek, then climbed the hill and rolled to a stop in front of the house.

It was the first time I remembered anyone showing up at the ranch in a business suit. Gary was all smiles, and after warm greetings we moved to the front porch where Vicki was waiting with refreshments. The new inspector was from the East and impressed with the view and privacy of our Morning Star ranch.

After a few minutes the conversation turned serious. Gary told me that his visit had nothing to do with wanting to see our helipad; that he was here on FAA business. Vicki and I froze, until Gary broke into a smile and handed me my pilot's certificate, saying "I'm here to return this and get you back in the air."

I was very touched by Gary Koch's gesture. It meant a lot to me and changed my thinking about the FAA once again. As I watched the white Bronco climb out of the ravine, I realized there were a lot of good people like Gary in the world.

I had been under a lot of stress while flying, but didn't realize it. I thought I was Superman. It didn't hit me until I was retired and away from it. I used to think Post Traumatic Stress Syndrome (PTSS) was a crock. I didn't understand how soldiers could have some kind of delayed reaction to what they had seen and experienced, because I had seen similar things regularly. I recovered bodies from floods, falls and desert heat, and just kept on going. But once I wasn't working anymore, those visions and memories returned often. I had a hard time dealing with it.

Now I realized that while I was working I compartmentalized what I saw. I just pushed it all into a corner of my brain and continued working around it. When I no longer had new projects, new experiences, new adventures to keep those visions pushed back, they began to come forward and haunt me. I finally understood PTSS.

The first few months of retirement were difficult. My only responsibility was taking care of the ranch and the horses and dogs. I seldom left home and I avoided friends. My mom and daughters stopped by often, but I never carried a phone and seldom answered the house phone. I never watched local news, but sometimes when a news helicopter circled overhead I would go out and wave. Occasionally an Air Rescue Ranger landed for coffee and brought me up to date on what was going on.

Vicki had been very good with our money and had put a nice pile away, but not enough to retire on. After six months or so Vicki went to work as a flight attendant for America West, and life took another turn. She loved her new job and was often gone on four-day trips. Her flights took her all over the country and as far away as Hawaii and Japan. She was in heaven, but I missed her and came to resent her job. Everything had changed, and not necessarily for the better. In addition to being jealous of her job, I felt guilty that I wasn't the breadwinner any more, and had little ambition or desire to do anything about it. The truth was, I was starting to like bumming around and having no responsibility.

About this time my old friend Buzz had split up with his sweet wife, Carole, who I just loved. I hated to see them break up. But can you imagine *me* giving advice on how to be happily married? So I considered it my duty to make sure he stayed amused and I began spending a lot of time with him.

We rode horses, ATVs, sand rails, dirt bikes, and Harleys. There was no shortage of toys in those days and we used them all. We would head out for days at a time to different playgrounds, depending on the activity. If we rode horses we could leave from the ranch or we might trailer to an area of interest that I knew from my past life.

Buzz was in the great position of owning a money-making business and having the good sense to let somebody else run it; someone he knew and trusted. All he had to do was show up on payday. To be fair, he had worked hard for years to build his business. The Wheel Shop, which catered to motorcyclists, sold parts and accessories and did repairs. His manager had two helpers and business was good.

If I wasn't with Buzz, sometimes I went alone to Lake Powell and drifted around for days, cruising slowly to spots I had flown into. This time it was different, yet just as surreal as when I had skimmed above these waters and canyons at 150 miles per hour.

On these trips I relished the quiet as I slowly idled through some narrow canyons, hardly making a sound. I had spent more than 23,000 hours of my life with a jet engine howling just three feet above my left ear. In this new silence, I savored the sound of a bird singing or a fish jumping.

Powell trips were always capped by a visit to see Uncle Mac and Aunt Wanda in Page. We always had a family dinner and some time to visit. Uncle Mac's chili was the best I have ever eaten. When I left their home I inevitably felt better. I felt that I had honored my dad by visiting his sister and her family. This was a place I could go and feel the comfort and love of family.

When Uncle Mac died, his two oldest kids, Jo Ellen and Steve, followed in his footsteps and filled a big pair of shoes by serving on the city council and being involved in countless other community events.

That was the quiet and peaceful side of my new life. When I wanted a little more action I started spending a lot of weekends at the Imperial sand dunes near Yuma, Arizona. That area was sand rail and ATV heaven in the winter months. There I became friendly with a group of Phoenix people who all parked their motor homes in a large circle, reminiscent of covered-wagon days, and built a big campfire in the middle of it at night. There were kids, dogs, and high-powered machines running across the sand dunes 24 hours a day. It was always deafening, but I would be so tired from running day and night that I had no trouble sleeping.

The motorcycle trips were probably the most bizarre adventures of all. Buzz and friends—sometimes a dozen of us, all riding Harleys—would make a weekend run somewhere in the state or over to San Diego, where we would spend the night and come home the next day. Like flying, that was a thrill you have to experience to understand. On one run, I was the only one wearing a white helmet. I woke up the next morning to find it had been painted black while I slept.

Riding in a large pack of chopped down Harleys is an experience all its own and can be just as dangerous as flying, depending on how you ride. Sometimes if a rider had too much to drink or got high on something, he would be taken off his bike until he got straight. The offending rider spent his penalty time in the pickup truck that usually followed us on the long runs. His bike was loaded into the truck bed, and if the cab was full he rode in the bed with it. I have always been impressed by the way bikers take care of each other, yet dole out justice and punishment when one of the "brothers" breaks the few rules they have.

I still occasionally ride as a senior citizen. When one of my biker friends died recently, I rode my son-in-law's Harley in the procession. Chris gets a little stressed out when I borrow it. That makes me smile!

One of my lifestyle changes included staying up late at night. I hadn't been able to do that since I had started flying for Channel 10. Most nights back then I would hit the sack early, knowing I could be called out at any time. And even though I might have worked all night on some kind of story or emergency, I still had news and weather to cover the next day. Now all I had to worry about were the horses and dogs. Vicki was gone half the time now, but she had been right about the job, and things between us were good—or at least better.

That was my life for nearly two years. We had family events at the ranch, and the kids were grown up and long gone on their trip through life's ups and downs. I had calmed down to the point that I was starting to feel normal. I even watched the local news and could see the changes taking place in the short time that I had been gone. There were five helicopters in the Phoenix market and two in Tucson, so the competition was still fierce. I flipped around to different stations if a big story was going on. Sometimes the big stories brought all of the news 'copters over a scene. In later years the inevitable tragedy occurred that I always feared would happen to me. Two TV helicopters collided in Phoenix, killing four journalists. That mid-air collision would spark a major change in TV aerial operations.

Chapter 71

Westcor Aviation

I still didn't have much enthusiasm about going back to work, but I was getting restless. One thing I knew for sure, I would not be going back to broadcasting. But the only skill I had was flying helicopters, so I set my sights on Westcor Aviation, mainly because I knew the owners.

Rusty Lyons was a major partner in Westcor Development, a very successful company that specialized in huge shopping centers and property around the country and Mexico. The aircraft side (Westcor Aviation) was owned solely by Rusty and his wife Rosie. Rusty was a flying enthusiast who started out as a fighter pilot in the Air Force. Now he used helicopters to get around the state, and business jets for the long runs.

I first became acquainted with Rusty when we moved to our Cave Creek ranch. The Lyons owned a beautiful home in nearby Carefree, that was built into the huge boulders and included a heli-pad on the roof. That was how Rusty commuted to work, which irked a zoning commissioner for the county, who filed a violation against him for not acquiring a landing permit. The commissioner also brought me into the action even though I lived in a remote area.

One evening while I was still flying for 12, Rusty called me at home to advise me of the action filed against us and asked if it would be alright if his attorneys represented me. He told me the county didn't even have an ordinance for helicopters and if it was alright with Vicki and me, he would like to offer his legal beagles to represent me as well. I was delighted and it worked out well. I got a letter a couple of months later from the county telling me the citation had been canceled.

In early March 1991, I met Rusty for breakfast at the Boulders, a huge resort in Scottsdale. I had grown a full beard and had never met Rusty in person so we both sat in the waiting area for nearly 15 minutes when someone walked in and said, "Hey Rusty, join me for breakfast?"

He started to answer when I jumped up and said "Rusty, it's me!" and we had a good laugh. He later told me I looked like Gabby Hayes.

Over ham and eggs I told him what I came for. I needed a job and would like to work for his company. He told me he had a chief pilot who was also president of the aviation company. He gave me a business card with the name and number I should call. Rusty said he would let his man know I would be calling, but the decision would be up to Bob Oliver, his good friend and the head of Westcor Aviation. I made the call and was invited to stop in the following day.

Westcor Aviation was located in the business park connected to Scottsdale's municipal airport, and had access to the runway by taxiways. The company owned two helicopters; an Aerospatiale A Star and a Twin Star. Both machines were operated for hire to do the jobs helicopters are best at doing. The Twin Star was primarily Rusty's personal machine, but was used for charter when it wa available.

In addition to the helicopters, they owned a Citation III that was used primarily by Rusty and Rosie for business and personal travel. For charter work, Westcor leased and operated a Beech Jet 400 and they supplied the crew. This was a first-class operation. The maintenance hangar was spotless and up to date, and three mechanics kept the Westcor fleet flying, while also performing maintenance for customer aircraft.

My first meeting with Bob Oliver went well. I liked the operation and I liked the man in charge. He would become a close friend and mentor. Bob explained that he was Rusty's personal pilot in the Citation and accompanied him on all flights. Rusty flew in the pilot's seat and was fully qualified in the airplane. Bob had the same arrangement with Rusty that I'd had with Senator

Goldwater all those years as a second pilot. Bob's wife, Linda, worked in the office at Westcor, and she and Rosie Lyon were also good friends.

There were three other pilots who flew full time for the company. Dave Welsh and Jeff Danitz were dual-rated and qualified in all the company aircraft, and another pilot I will call "Captain Groucho," was the lead pilot in the Beech Jet. I'll explain him later.

Bob didn't have an opening at the time, but he offered me a retainer of two thousand dollars a month to be on call. That was perfect for the time being, as I didn't really want to jump into anything full time. Business jets were a whole new world and I wasn't sure I could provide what it would take.

All the current electronic equipment would be new to me, as would the style of flying. Business jets have always fascinated me. I had my first ride in a Lear-25 with Senator Goldwater, by the jet's builder, Bill Lear himself. And let me tell you, he scared the hell out of both of us, but what a thrill! That one flight was my total experience, and that was from the back seat.

Paybacks are hell, by the way, because later that day I gave Mr. Lear a ride in my little Hughes 300. We had a good laugh and it sure showed me what those little "rockets" are capable of doing.

For the first couple of months I flew a few charters in the helicopters and customer airplanes. I got to know the other pilots and became familiar with company procedures. Linda Oliver did much of the paperwork for the company, and their son Chris also worked there. It was a good atmosphere to work in and I felt like I had found a home.

It didn't take long for Vicki and Linda Oliver to become friends. When Vicki was in town we often went out to dinner or lunch with the Olivers. With my new job came a new lifestyle. I put my toys in the barn and concentrated on my work. All company employees were on a random drug testing program and when the lab called we stopped what we were doing and went straight to testing. To my knowledge no employee ever failed a test.

536

Robert J. Oliver is a former United States Marine Captain who had flown fighters off a Navy carrier. He was cocky, well educated, and could recite the flight manual verbatim for every aircraft he flew. He stood about 5′ 9″, was stocky and nice looking, and always impeccably dressed. Bob relished being in charge and making decisions on nearly everything. He was definitely a hands-on kind of guy and just exactly what I needed. All I wanted was to be told when and where to fly, and how to dress for it. I was okay with that and enjoyed very much just being one of the pilots.

My first flight in a business jet came when everyone was tied up on other flights. I flew with Rusty, Rosie and Bob to Vail, Colorado in the Citation III, to drop off the Lyons at their winter condo for a ski trip. I still had to be qualified in the Citation, which required that I do three take-offs and landings. I did those at Vail and then Bob and I high-tailed it home.

What a thrill it was to look down—at that airspeed—which indicated a ground speed of more that 350 mph. As I scanned the instrument panel I knew it was way over my level of expertise. All the switches, gauges, bells and whistles were intimidating for a chopper pilot. The jet was not as simple as a helicopter and I never felt totally comfortable with it, even after considerable training with Bob and Captain Groucho.

Captain Groucho was the pilot for the Beech Jet 400. The airplane required two pilots as did the Citation. When trips came up, one of the Westcor pilots would fly with Groucho. It wasn't a preferred duty for any of us. After a two-week ground school with the Captain I was deemed qualified to be assigned. Being the junior man, I got the assignment more than I would have liked. Though I didn't care for him, I really enjoyed the airplane. It flew high and fast and handled very well.

The problem was that Captain Groucho was a know-it-all. No matter what the subject, he was the authority and loved to brag. I didn't like him, but I have to admit he was the best flight instructor I was ever teamed up with. He and Bob knew that airplane like no one else. The guy had a personality and disposition that only a mother could love, and there was no love lost between the two of us. We had our run-ins on the ground, but never in the air. My mother always said not to talk negatively about anyone, which is why I won't name him here. Sorry, Captain!

Finally qualified in the company aircraft, I settled into a routine of flying several times a week. I usually flew the helicopter, but had to serve my time in the Beech Jet when Dave and Jeff were unavailable. It was turning out to be a good job. Our customers were high-end business people who spent most of their air time on computers or sleeping. There was a snack box and hot and cold beverages in the jet, and passengers could help themselves. If they didn't like pouring their own coffee or drinks, then once we leveled off I would go back and do it for them.

My most memorable flight was in the Beech Jet over Houston, Texas at 45,000 feet on a moonless night. We had commercial jets passing far below us and easy-to-spot satellites above us. From that altitude we could see the entire state of Florida. Groucho pointed out the major cities along the gulf coast and the Atlantic Ocean. Descending toward Tampa, our destination, Groucho said we had visibility of more than 1000 miles. It was 980 ground miles from Houston to Tampa, so he was probably right. I was one high-flying helicopter pilot.

Westcor began doing maintenance work for three of the five TV stations' helicopters, so I was able to stay in touch with what was going on in broadcasting; but I can honestly say I was very happy where I was and with what I was doing. I didn't miss the TV rat-race at all.

What I liked most was knowing what I would be doing tomorrow, and if I was scheduled for time off, I could count on it. Life seemed to have come full circle for me. I was just another guy doing a job that was clearly defined. On the downside, I found out what a hassle it was to have to drive to work and home again at night; although Bob occasionally let me keep the helicopter at home if I had an early morning flight.

538

Bob Oliver was a stickler on the rules and came across as cocky, which he was. But that didn't bother me one bit. He and I hit it off and I deeply appreciated him taking such an interest in getting me back in the air and qualified again in some very expensive flying machines. In return for his help I followed all the rules, and if something did come up I felt comfortable talking about it with my peers.

I had a couple of minor incidents with the Air Route Traffic Control System, like missing a checkpoint report or failing to report when I left an assigned altitude. Each time, Bob used the occasion to give me and the other pilots a little refresher course on rules and procedures. He always referred to us as "The Black Sheep Squadron," but I always felt like part of a good team.

Chapter 72

Legal Scuffles

During my news career I was often served with notices to appear in court, because I was often at the scene of accidents; some with tragic results. Even after having been out of the news for a while I'd still get a summons when one of these cases got to court.

One day I was off work, watering the back courtyard at home when the telephone rang. When I answered, the caller hung up. I didn't think anything about it and went on about my business. A few minutes later I heard a car racing up the hill into my driveway. The driver jumped out and ran up to my patio gate holding out a roll of papers, loudly announcing, "I'm an officer of the court delivering a summons."

In the past, process servers would call me at the station, or if they came out to the ranch, they would call and I'd meet them on the other side of the creek. The road was a nightmare for city cars.

What this guy had done was call and hang up, then had driven his pretty little street car down the canyon, across a creek, up the canyon, and then jumped out of his car in my driveway as if I might suddenly run off or try to hide. The only thing he accomplished was to piss me off.

I walked up to the gate where he was holding a small ring of papers. He said, "I'm here to serve you," still waving the papers at me. Before he could say another word I snatched the papers out of his hand, turned around and walked away.

He went off like a firecracker, screaming, "You have all the papers; you have the original!" That made my day. I turned around, gave him a big smile and walked into the house. I could see that he had gone back to his car and was on his cell phone.

Taking my time, I went into the garage and got on my ATV. With the original papers in hand I rode up to his car to give them to him. He rolled up his window and locked the door. I put the papers under his windshield wiper and rode off to a neighbor's house for a visit. I came home an hour later and he was gone. End of story.

At least, it should have been the end of it, but the next day a deputy came out for a visit and to take a statement. I told him what happened, signed the report, and a few weeks later was notified by registered mail that a lawsuit had been filed for assaulting and injuring that "Officer of the Court." He claimed he had been injured when I knocked him down outside my patio.

The incident turned into a full blown trial. My homeowners insurance provided the lawyers and several months later we went to trial. The process server was claiming medical bills and unspecified damages for pain and suffering. The latter is what this was all about: money.

A little background on this process server: He played intramural sports and was active on several teams, he was 20 years younger than I, quite a bit heavier, and taller. According to him, his shoulder and neck were in so much pain that he had to stop participating in sports.

He had shown a freshly scraped elbow to the deputy who took his report, and swore under oath that I sucker-punched him when he wasn't looking. I never touched him.

During the trial, one hilarious scene cracked up the jury when my attorney asked me and the plaintiff to stand face to face. I stepped up real close and had to tilt my head up to see his face as he looked down at me. It was a David and Goliath moment. We stood there for a few moments, then began laughing, along with nearly everyone else, including the judge.

The jury didn't believe either one of us. They awarded him his medical expenses, but no damages. After the trial we spoke to the jurors, who all said they thought more happened than either of us said. There is one thing for sure: one of us committed perjury; and it wasn't me!

Chapter 73

Passing of an Angel

My mother was always there for me like no other human could be. We were close in heart because we were so close in age. She was barely 15 when I was born.

My Uncle Garlin had died in an ATV accident while out prospecting for gold several years earlier. Aunt Ceil died of cancer shortly afterward. I was going through the process of getting older and suffering the same sadness of losing those I loved, that all of us must one day face.

Right now things were good for me. I was back to a place in my life where I socialized and had a life that was more than just work. The ranch was a good place to be. I had all the privacy a person could ask for; plus toys, animals, and a beautiful wife. I was getting reacquainted with my family, who were full of love and willing to share it. I was even a grandfather now. It was a good time in my life.

During the Christmas holidays in 1992, I received a call from Mom asking me to stop by as soon as I could to help her move some furniture around. I went over early the next morning and joined her for coffee and a roll.

Observing the peaceful look on her lovely face, I had no clue what was coming, until she said, "Jerry, I have an untreatable form of clear cell cancer. The doctor has given me six months to live."

I was stunned and didn't know if I had heard her right. The word "untreatable" still rings in my ears. She had such a gentle way of telling me she had considered all the sources and treatments, but the bottom line was: "Doctors have diagnosed and agree there is nothing more they can do, and I do not want a life prolonged by drugs. Period!"

Mom showed me a small red lump that was growing on the side of her neck. She explained it had been growing rapidly over the last several months. All tests had come back positive for one of the fastest growing types of cancer.

I tried to convince Mom to move out to our place, but she wanted no part of that. She had been involved with a ladies club in Mesa that helped run the Senior Citizens Center. It was a large organization that held a raffle and auction every year—a huge event that included all the city movers and shakers. That was her world and Mesa was where she would die … end of discussion!

The next day Vicki and I started packing what we would need to live in Mesa. I had a caretaker living at the ranch, so our leaving wouldn't be a problem.

Mom knew exactly how she wanted to leave this earth and she wanted me to help her arrange it.

When she showed me the list I looked at her and sadly shook my head. "Mom I don't think I can do this; I really don't."

But I had to and I knew it. Our first stop was at the First National Bank downtown, where she legally turned over all of her assets to me. She was so thorough in her planning that by the time we were done, all that was left for me was to write a check for her burial when the time came.

The next day we were off to see her attorney and long-time friend. She made sure her will was up to date, taking nothing for granted. She told me a letter would be left with her attorney for me.

Her attitude made these final visits memories that I will always treasure, and will try to duplicate when my time comes.

The last visit was the toughest. We went to the funeral home to make final arrangements. I guess because I had briefly worked at a mortuary, I could not imagine my mother's body being in a cold preparation room. But I sucked it up and watched as she went through her list, telling the funeral director what scriptures would be read and which music should be played. Finally, we went into the casket selection room where she made her choice.

Our last stop was to a marble company that specialized in tombstones. Mom had a drawing of what she wanted: four roses on the left to represent her siblings; her name, date of death and a photo of her with "Mom" written below.

For the next few months the three of us lived a very happy life, going to movies, dinner, the zoo, or taking a drive somewhere. It could have been a heartbreaking time, but it wasn't. In fact, we lived every day as if it were her last day.

As the months passed, her condition worsened as the cancer spread throughout her body. I will always be thankful to Vicki for caring for Mom in ways I could not. She really stepped up and kept my dear mother medicated and comfortable.

On our final night, Vicki fixed a nice dinner and we ate it in Mom's room while watching the NBA Championships. When the game ended, Mom and I watched a late movie. I woke up about midnight, shut off the TV and tip-toed to bed.

Sometime early that morning she died peacefully in her sleep. It was almost six months to the day that she had been diagnosed with the fatal disease. Those months were some of the best times of our lives. Thankfully, she died with dignity and peace of mind.

Everything she insisted be done was taken care of per her wishes. Her service was just as she had planned and all that was left was for me to write a check for the funeral and burial. A few days later I went back to the funeral home to pay the bill, only to find out Uncle Phill had paid it the day of the services.

Mom was buried in a family plot next to her brother and sister. There was room for me, Uncle Phill, and two more. The only thing left for me to do was get the letter from her attorney and find out what she didn't feel comfortable talking about. I just couldn't imagine anything that she wouldn't tell me. Then I read it.

"Jerry, I asked Vicki to sign a 'Quit Claim Deed' to make sure that my house and personal belongings were left to you. I love her dearly, but many times things change. Also I have left you my little red Bible. Please keep it as a reminder that I will see you in heaven. And remember your promise to take care of Uncle Phill if he needs help. Love Mom."

Funny how all these years, I expected that when her end came I would grieve for the rest of my life. And while I miss her everyday and always keep her little red Bible by my bed, it was nothing like I expected. Mom had prepared me well. She had seen to the things that would have been pure hell for me to do, had she died suddenly.

Norma Ellen Foster was only 67 years old. Her sister Ciel died at 67, and so did her brother, Garlin. Her youngest brother, my Uncle Phil, was now 64. That was a worry—and ironic— because he was the wild and crazy one and the one we all thought would go first. That is, until I got into flying; then *I* was the odds-on favorite to go first. But I'm 72 as I write this, and have probably surprised a lot of people.

While staying with Mom, I'd had an opportunity to lease the ranch out to an Emu or Ostrich farmer. I gave him a two-year lease and sold all my horses except Rey de Reyes, who I boarded with a friend. That meant we would live in Mom's house for at least another 17 months. That was okay with Vicki and me, since the ranch had been a lot of work and was a long way out of town.

Living in Mesa the past six months had been a pleasant experience. We loved the old, historic neighborhood. Movies, restaurants and paved roads were such a luxury. To be able to go to a Circle K in just minutes without having to cross a flowing creek and climb out of a canyon was a welcome change.

I continued flying with Westcor and Vicki stayed with America West. Bob and Linda Oliver had been a big help and gave me all the time off I needed during Mom's last few months. Things would eventually get back to normal, but there was always that empty spot that comes from losing a dear mother.

Bob and Linda went to a charity auction one evening and came home with the cutest little puppy I had ever seen. It was a male brown Labrador retriever. The little guy was so small he fit in the palm of my hand. It was a gift to us, with the idea that when Vicki was out of town I would have some company. It worked out great and I named him "Oliver."

I filled in for a couple of TV stations when pilots needed time off, but I was never on the air and didn't have a problem at all with sitting back and being just a pilot. It made me smile when the reporter would stumble on words or look worried when we were in rough air.

When Channel 10 bought a new A-Star I traveled to Tennessee to pick it up and fly it back to Phoenix. Not only did this machine have all the bells and whistles, it had also been outfitted with all the TV gadgets, including a gyro-mounted camera. This was new generation electronics and it was impressive.

Descending into an Oklahoma City airport, I was passing through 3,000 feet when I spotted what I thought to be another aircraft. A few seconds later that dot turned into a large buzzard. In that brief instant, we were face to face. I only had time for a natural reflex—to close my eyes. *Whump!* I felt the impact. When I opened my eyes everything seemed normal. The windshield was still intact, and the warning light panel was dark. I had dodged a bullet! *Thank you, Lord.*

The impact was solid, however, so I knew there was damage. I could feel a vibration in the rotor system unlike anything I had ever encountered. When I landed at Will Rogers Airport, it didn't take long to see the strike.

The bird had impacted on the little round cover called the "Chinaman hat" that sits on top of the rotor blades and covers the hub at the center point where the three blades meet. It was nearly gone, but enough of the bird remained to tell the story. It was a turkey buzzard that was estimated to weigh 40 to 60 pounds. If he'd hit a few inches lower, it could have been fatal for *both* of us.

During my entire flying career I had never felt like I wasn't in control until this happened. I learned another lesson and from then on I paid a lot more attention to what was out there. The rest of the trip was without problems. There is nothing in my business quite so much fun as taking a long trip in a helicopter.

Chapter 74

KTVK - Channel 3

While at home one evening, I got a call from an old friend I had worked with at Channel 10. Phil Alvidrez was now vice president of news at Channel 3. We had a short conversation about how things were going with me and Westcor. I thought he might be calling me about us doing maintenance on their helicopter.

He told me there would soon be a big change in the local TV market; that the affiliation KTVK had with ABC was ending and going to an upstart station on Channel 15. That meant Channel 3 was going to be an independent station. The Delbert Lewis family owned the station and had big plans for the future.

There was a shuffle of network affiliations going on. Channel 5, the long-time independent station in Phoenix, was now with CBS and no longer family-owned. Big corporations were buying up local stations all over the country.

Channel 3 had big plans, Phil said, then asked me if I had considered getting back on the air. I had been afraid someone would eventually ask me that. I'll admit I had often thought about it. Whenever I went into our maintenance shop and a TV bird was there being worked on, yes, I thought about it. A lot.

I left it with Phil that I would get back to him in a few days; that I needed to talk to Bob Oliver and my family. It was a big step. I really enjoyed the company I was working for. Rusty and Rosie Lyon were great employers. The pay was good and anytime we flew them somewhere, the crew stayed wherever they did, and we often all had dinner together. The Lyons and Bob Oliver had slowed me down and cleaned me up and now I owed it to them to talk it over.

For the next several days I gave it a lot of thought. I didn't like myself when I left Channel 12. That had been several years ago, and during that time I'd had the chance to experience an entirely different lifestyle and live like everyone else.

I really loved that job at Westcor and job security was a lot better with Rusty and Rosie than it would be in a newsroom ... and a lot less stressful. The camaraderie with Bob and Linda had turned into a good life for all of us.

While at dinner that evening I told Vicki and the Olivers about my talk with Channel 3. Without exception, they agreed I should take the offer if I thought it would be good for me. Phil had also told me I wouldn't be expected to do all the side jobs I had done before, which made it more appealing.

The general manager of KTVK, Bill Miller, had also been at Channel 10 for years, as had news director Dennis Miller. *If you have to work for someone in broadcasting*, I told myself, *here is the "dream management team."* We were friends going in and I still knew many of the newsroom players.

It sounded like a challenge, and just considering it brought back some realities. My Uncle Phill's only concern was whether Channel 3 management knew about my felony and discharge from the Marines. I couldn't imagine that Bill Miller didn't already know from our Channel 10 days. Besides, he was a trusted friend of Homer Lane.

The more I thought about it, the more I wanted to go back. Bob assured me that if it didn't work out I could return to Westcor and pick up where I left off. So I let my new bosses know of my concern, and Miller told me he already knew. I was glad I spoke up. I still carried a fear that someone would find out ... perhaps a TV critic, and there were lots of those around.

I took the job and, in the long run, it turned out to have been a huge mistake. Not because of anything my co-workers or management did; this time it was all me.

I went back with a whole new attitude. I had to, because my reputation preceded me and once again I was stuck with the "hot dog," "cowboy," "jerk," "maniac," and many more labels I had inherited over the years.

I also replaced a well-liked pilot who had been in this market for years. Jerry Clifton was an ex-Vietnam war hero and a nice guy. He had moved to Channel 5, and a few years later he was replaced by his son, Scott, who is now one of those educated pilots replacing guys like me and his dad. I always envied their relationship and enjoyed watching their interactions.

The first six months back were tough. Some photographers refused to fly with me and others were leery. I did the best I could and was gradually seen in a better light, but it was never the same as before. Things had really changed.

The on-air personalities were led by Patti Kirkpatrick, a former Channel 12 teammate. I found a newsroom full of professionals who really had their act together. There wouldn't be any room for amateurs, and that put me under a lot of pressure.

Actually, everyone at the station was under pressure, because now they were an independent station taking on a brand new format for news and regular programming.

The news department underwent a complete change, starting with the early morning show. It was now called *Good Morning Arizona*, and ran from 6 to 9 a.m. Jodi Applegate, the anchor was "hot" in all respects. We were up against the network shows like *Good Morning America* on ABC, the *Today Show* on NBC, and the *Morning Show* on CBS. That was and still is some pretty stiff competition.

The noon news was half an hour and the evening show, ran from 4 to 6 p.m. Predictably, it was called *Good Evening Arizona* and was anchored by Patti Kirkpatrick. We had a good group and it didn't take long for the show to make its mark.

My assignment was to do traffic reports on the morning and evening shows. That would include any breaking stories or other events going on in the Phoenix valley. I would be flying five hours a day Monday through Friday, with weekends off, but I knew that wouldn't last.

I didn't at all mind the new hours except that early morning show. My first live would be at 6 a.m. I had become used to getting up at the crack of noon and really hollered loudly, to no avail, to push it back to seven o'clock.

I did it and after a while I started enjoying it, because I was reporting much more than traffic accidents. When the news was light and we had time to fool around, it got to be fun. The helicopter was like a second studio in the sky. The viewer never knew what we would come up with until Jodi or Patti introduced "News Chopper 3." More than once, out of habit, I signed off as "Sky 12," but I finally got it right.

The competition was fierce and many times we ended up with five helicopters over the same scene. I always had a photographer assigned to me. At the end of the evening show I would sometimes drop him or her off at the station, then head for Mesa and home, shooting the closing shot live with a camera hanging on a bungee cord. But my days of shooting the story myself were over. It was just too dangerous with so many of us in the air.

My favorite story was a low speed chase that lasted 45 minutes and was very entertaining. A homeless man jumped into an idling 18-wheeler and took the local law enforcement community on a comical tour that reminded me of the Keystone Cops. The driver circled the state capitol, drove through fences and over medians. It was hilarious. He finally ended up in a dead-end street and when he tried to back out, police cars were scattering to get out of the way. When he jackknifed the trailer he was taken down by half of the Phoenix Police Department.

During my stint at Channel 3 I met a young man who reminded me a lot of Bill Leverton from my Channel 10 days. Bruce Haffner was a combination reporter and photographer. He was working on his helicopter rating and wanted my job when I left. We got along well and I enjoyed teaching him the ins and outs of helicopter flying.

Bruce had a good feel for the helicopter and also had a good on-air presence. He was a well-educated and experienced newsman. The new generation would soon replace me.

Our ratings after the first year were great, bouncing between first and second place. Our closest competitor was Fox News on channel 10. The gamble by channel 3 had paid off and we had done what we set out to do. Channel 3 was still a player in the Phoenix market.

Chapter 75

The Indictment - May 20, 1996

It was a beautiful Sunday afternoon and perfect for a round of golf in Mesa. Bob Oliver and I were just teeing off on the ninth hole when my cell phone rang. It was Vicki, and the conversation went something like this:

"Jerry, a process server just handed me a summons from the Attorney General's office advising you that a Grand Jury has indicted you on four felony counts and you are ordered to go to the Maricopa County Sheriff's Office to be fingerprinted and photographed. You better come home. It's serious!"

I clearly remember looking at Bob, rolling my eyes like I was trying to hurry, and shrugging my shoulders like it was no big deal. And it wasn't to me, because if what she told me was true they wouldn't send a process server they would send the posse. We talked it over and I brushed it off, saying we would be home right after our game.

As it turned out, it was very serious. I called Phil Alvidrez, who came to my home right away to see for himself. The next day I landed at the station after our morning show where, following a meeting with Bill Miller, Phil Alvidrez and Dennis Miller, it was mutually decided that I should take a leave of absence until we got it cleared up. Phil then drove me back out to my home in Mesa, leaving the helicopter sitting on the pad. At this point we had no idea what the case was about.

It didn't take long to find out. Two days later I had a law firm and two days after that Vicki and I and my new lawyer started going through several boxes of copied documents about the case and its players.

A neighbor of mine, who I will refer to as "Charlie," shared some things in common with me. Our daughters had attended the same school; we both had Harleys, and we especially liked exploring the back country on ATVs. Charlie had a thriving car business going and whenever he was on an outing with me and my friends, we had a great time.

This all took place just before I made the move to Channel 3 and was flying part-time for Westcor. On a couple of occasions when we were exploring the desert, Charlie brought along a small tin of speed for those who needed a boost. I was one of them. I never, ever, drank or used any kind of drug while flying, but I was on my own time and having fun. It was no big deal at the time, but it came back to haunt me.

What I didn't know was that Charlie was being investigated by a drug task force headed by the DEA. Nor did I know that he was under surveillance and his phones were tapped. I later found out this surveillance had been going on for more than a year.

In my lawyer's office, it took us several days to sift through the mounds of evidence containing hundreds of surveillance photos of me and Charlie plus hours of taped conversations. We listened to every tape and read each document. I was relieved at what I saw and heard, and so was Jim. There was little, if anything, there to incriminate me.

The following week I entered a plea of Not Guilty at a preliminary hearing; trial was set for mid-October; several months away. There was nothing I could do but sit, wait, and see what else came up.

What worried me more than the indictment was my discharge and felony conviction when I was 18. So far nothing had been said. *Do they know?* I wondered. I never mentioned it to my attorney and I don't believe he ever knew.

I had been indicted as a co-conspirator to manufacture, distribute, sell and use methamphetamine. According to the Attorney General's office, twenty pounds a month was being manufactured in a secret location somewhere in New Mexico.

On two occasions when Charlie borrowed my dually pickup, he had been followed by agents who were keeping an eye on him. Even though I was never mentioned, I believe that's when my name came up and I was dragged into this mess.

To make matters worse, *Court TV* petitioned the court to cover my trial. The judge approved that request over my attorney's objection. That would mean more exposure, and on a national level. It was all adding up to be a real media event.

In addition, my FAA friends in Washington were also in on the event. I received a registered letter from them advising me they were taking action against my pilot's certificate to revoke all my flying privileges. Forever.

Then it got a little deeper. The prosecutor and her staff arranged a meeting through my attorney to discuss the case evidence against me. That turned out to be a waste of time for all of us. It was more posturing than anything. The prosecutor made a point of saying we could introduce all the good deeds and high-powered references we wanted. But she warned that she would have some surprises at trial.

My attorney, Jim Hart, let her know that we weren't one bit afraid of what they could dig up, and with that we were out the door. Now I didn't feel so confident. We talked about the case on the way home and I started several times to tell him about my past, but I just couldn't bring it up.

Jim had a different take on our meeting. He thought the tough talk by the prosecutor was a bluff. What could they have? We had seen all the evidence they had, he reasoned, however there were things he didn't know. I should have opened up and told him about my felony and discharge, but I never did. To this day, I'm not sure he ever knew.

For the next two months I had to make several court appearances as the case moved on. Each time I appeared, the courtroom was full of media. Radio, TV, newspapers and publications had a field day. My family, particularly my daughters, were heartbroken. All they saw and heard from the media was ugly and cruel.

In July my attorney attended a pre-trial meeting with the prosecutor and her staff. They offered me a quick way out. If I would admit I experimented with speed on a four-wheeling trip in the desert, all charges against me would be dropped.

I really knew nothing about some of the charges that had been brought against me. I had no clue that my friend Charlie was running an illegal business and sure as hell didn't know anything about what he was charged with. If the prosecutor had known about my discharge and felony as a young man, that could have been leaked, making it look to the public like I was guilty.

For me, it was a no-brainer: my broadcasting career was over, and going to trial on drug charges with *Court TV* digging, sensationalizing, analyzing and repeating it over and over every day would be a nightmare. I had to stop it now.

During my career I had never hidden my fascination for motorcycles and the people who ride them. When I was working on writing a book about an "outlaw" motorcycle club, I had been photographed by undercover officers and "snitches" over the years. Nothing incriminating ever came of it because I was working on a book. And to do that I had to stay straight with both sides.

The prosecutor wasn't about to pass that one up, and *Court TV* would go crazy with "FOSTER AND THE OUTLAWS" or some such teaser headlines. It would go on and on. I envisioned "hot tip" telephone lines, talk shows and editorials. And who would be sitting out there watching? My family and people in my life who really cared and were hurting, right along with me.

I know my attorney was very surprised when I instructed him to take the deal. Jim had been a great attorney and friend. The decision was painful, but my mind was made up and that was exactly the way it went.

That September it was settled with the court order that read, "All charges are dismissed in the interest of justice."

Good decision or bad, I will never know. I cannot describe the feeling after I walked out of the courtroom. It was a huge relief that I was finally past one of the hardest and longest falls of my life. And there was no one to blame but myself.

I couldn't blame the DEA task force, the prosecutor, or my friend Charlie. I had put myself in a position to be looked at and investigated. For me, it was no victory. I am fortunate that prosecutor Billie Rosen didn't bite me harder. Someday I hope to apologize in person to her, as well as to the then Attorney General of Arizona, Grant Woods. It was particularly embarrassing for me that his parents had been close friends of my mother and her husband Ray. They all worked hard each year on a charity for the Senior Center in Mesa, Arizona.

As for Charlie, I only know that his case was settled and according to court dockets he was placed on probation.

The career in which I had worked so long and hard was gone for good. And so were many of my friends and fans. I wished a million times that Mom was here. I longed for her comforting embrace, her soothing reassurance. This was my first fall from grace without her.

How prophetic it was that two of my mother's sayings all through my young life and career were, "Jerry, you are judged by the company you keep" and, "There is no right way to do a wrong thing." She was right on both counts.

I miss her everyday and wish she was here, but maybe it's a blessing she wasn't here for my last fall. She would have been hurt, and I would have been all the more devastated.

Chapter 76

Back to Westcor

Vicki was a huge help through all this and stuck with me, but it was hard on everyone around me. Family and friends didn't know what to say or do, and there was nothing *I* could do but suck it up and move on.

My flying license had not been revoked after all, so my friend Bob Oliver talked my future over with Rusty and Rosie Lyon. I was welcomed back to Westcor to pick up where I had left off. I had to put everything I'd been through out of my mind and try to settle back into the job. I had no problem with the helicopters, but instrument flights into bad weather were never the same for me. I had always been sharp at instrument flying and loved it in my pre-broadcasting days, and I had enjoyed IFR (Instrument Flight Rules) flying and instructing. But now I just didn't feel comfortable on instruments any more. My confidence level just wasn't what it had been.

I had good training from Bob and Captain Groucho, and as long as I was flying with one of them or another experienced captain, it all went smoothly. But on a couple of occasions while flying solo I scared the hell out of myself. To this day I cannot figure out what caused me to lose my confidence.

On two occasions I even went to Flight Safety Inc. in Wichita, Kansas. It's a top-notch aviation school that provides ground, air, and simulator training. It was excellent and I learned a lot.

Shortly after I returned to Westcor, Rusty and Rosie Lyon decided to upgrade to a newer and faster business jet: but not just any luxury jet, mind you. The Citation X was powered by two huge Rolls-Royce Turbo-Fan jet engines: a go-fast rocket that would cruise at 59,000 feet at a speed of mach .92, (just over 700 mph!), near the speed of sound, making it the fastest civilian aircraft in the world.

The first time I saw photos of the panel and read the specs I was completely intimidated and knew it was way over my head. When Bob told me I was going to be the third pilot I was thrilled. As long as someone well qualified was in the left seat, I would be comfortable. At least that was my plan.

Rusty's plan for the airplane was also good news. He and Rosie wanted to get out and enjoy the success they had worked so hard for. Rusty wanted to fly to places like Ireland and Hawaii, where the golf courses are among the best in the world. That would require long flights and Rusty liked to stretch out in the back. So I was going along as the third pilot. I could handle that.

When the airplane was almost completed, Rusty, Bob and I headed for the Cessna factory in Wichita Kansas. That was also the location of our two-week ground course at Flight Safety. The first week would be on systems, performance and emergency procedures. During the second week we would "fly" in the Citation X simulator.

It was much too technical for a helicopter pilot. I sat through the classes and learned a lot, but I sure didn't ask any questions.

What a thrill that simulator was! It had motion, sound, and a huge screen that was nearly as good as being there. The instructors could program the simulator to fly anywhere in the world; any kind of weather, any airport and every kind of emergency maneuver you could imagine.

It was so realistic that when we were taxiing out to the runway we could see and feel the bumps as the aircraft passed over them. In the air, there were similar effects with bumpy weather. After the course was completed, Rusty and Bob were qualified as Captains and I was qualified to fly as co-pilot. Since the Citation was still being built, we flew back home on a commercial plane and waited for the call.

Ten days later, the Citation was ready. Rusty was unable to get away, so Bob and I took a commercial flight back to Wichita to pick it up. What a sight it was: 71 feet long, swept wings, and a T-tail. The exterior was white with deep red stripes. A beautiful, single red rose had been painted at the top of the stairs, which Rusty had had done for his wife, Rosie. The interior was tan leather trimmed in a soft brown and dark wood. There was room for eight passengers and two pilots. It had all the creature comforts: sink, refrigerator, bar, and a small bathroom and closet.

The cockpit was all electronic, with five small computer screens that indicated everything the pilot could possibly want to know about how the airplane was performing. In addition there were scores of switches and circuit breakers on the overhead panels. It was state-of-the-art in every respect.

We looked it over, signed the delivery papers, filed a flight plan, and were finally ready to head home. Up to this point we had never actually flown a real Citation X; but when we strapped ourselves in, we were as comfortable with it as we had been in the simulator. We loaded the computer with our flight plan and went through the check lists, then it was time to fire off this rocket and see what we had learned.

Everything went smoothly for us on that first flight and we made it home in record time, even though we had to cut back our speed because of the busy skies. I truly enjoyed the  airplane—even flying in instrument conditions. With the navigation system in this bird, we could see on one of the screens exactly where we were, what our heading was, airspeed, route of flight, and the approach procedure diagram to our destination. From my perspective this was pure "rocket science."

Rusty loved the airplane and for the next year we did a lot of flying, and planned the future trips he and Rosie wanted to take. I flew some of the trips with Rusty and Bob to the east coast. Whenever Rusty and Rosie were going to stay more than a couple of days, Bob and I would bring the airplane home and then go back when called. When I didn't go on their trips, I spent my time flying the helicopter contracts. If I was the only pilot available, I'd also have to keep Captain Groucho company in the Beech Jet.

On several occasions Linda Oliver and Vicki accompanied us on pleasure trips. During one of my favorite trips Vicki and I went to Vail with Rusty, Rosie, Bob and Linda for three days. We all stayed in their top floor, five-bedroom condo at the bottom of a ski lift. On our first morning the Lyons had ski instructors work with me and two other friends, since we hadn't skied in a long time. In no time at all we were on the slopes.

Rosie cooked some delicious dinners in the evenings, and loved entertaining. Of the very rich people I have known in my career, she and Rusty were the most sharing and considerate of their employees; although Rosie was someone you didn't want to rile. Rusty, you *couldn't* rile.

Sometime during that year things began to change. Bob and Linda were having problems and it was obvious something was wrong between them. The four of us didn't go out as often, and the tension was noticeable in the office. I was flying a King Air for one of our customers, which kept me out of town a lot more than I liked. Between my trips and Vicki's regular out-of-town flights, it seemed we were also drifting apart, though I was confident we'd work it out.

Bob soon moved into an apartment and Linda stayed in their house. It was truly heartbreaking. They had been so close and seemed to have the perfect marriage. I did my best to console both Bob and Linda, but whatever the problem was, it seemed to be terminal. I was sorry to see it happening to a couple who had once been so happy.

Meanwhile Vicki and I had moved back to the ranch after our tenant's lease expired. It was good to be back and I swore I would never again live in the city. Our ranch life had been so good and I hoped it would improve. We no longer had a stable full of horses; just Rey, my best friend Oliver, (the chocolate Lab) and a little white cutie named Meeshka that I had given Vicki on her birthday.

Vicki and I had our problems, but I believed that moving back to the ranch, a place we both loved and had been happy, would help. Then Vicki came home from a four-day flight with America West and broke the news to me that she was going to move out and wanted a divorce. I was stunned! I had not realized our problems were that serious. I didn't want her to go and made every effort to change her mind, but to no avail. She wanted out.

She told me she had rented an apartment in Phoenix, but wouldn't say where. The only way I was able to reach her was through a post office box. She said she and another flight attendant, who was also going through a divorce, were splitting the rent. I felt a little better, knowing she had a roommate and wouldn't be lonely or afraid.

Bob came to my rescue. We ate out together after work, flew together and spent hours talking about our future. Bob told me he was looking elsewhere for another flying job. That was a big surprise; I always thought he would be with Rusty and Rosie until they all retired. I told him that if we could work together I'd like to go with him. He agreed, saying we made a good team.

A few weeks later Bob and Rusty flew to California, leaving Linda and I alone at the office. I was leaving for the night when Linda came into my office and sat down. She had been crying and I tried to console her. Then, with tears pouring down her cheeks like a waterfall, she said that I just didn't have a clue why she was so upset. When she told me, it all started to add up.

"Jerry, for the past year, Bob and Vicki have been having an affair behind your back. You're the only one around here who hasn't caught on, and I just can't stand it any longer."

I sat and stared at her. I could not—and would not—believe her at first. Then I demanded to know why she had let it go on. Her only defense was to wail, "Because I love him so much. Please don't hurt him," she sobbed, now nearly hysterical. I walked around my desk and embraced her for what seemed a long time.

My body had turned a "hot white" and I told her I had to get out of there. I turned around, left the building and started for home. As I crossed the creek I stopped, got out of my truck, sat on a rock, and sobbed like I had never done before.

Linda had been right. I'd had no clue that Vicki and Bob had been playing around behind my back. It would be a long and dark time before I looked back and saw the clues. My own children and friends later said they knew, but were afraid to say anything. How could this happen to me, and in this way?

Things started happening fast after that. I didn't hurt Bob—or worse—and we were both very fortunate that I didn't. Rusty and Rosie already knew from of a friend of theirs what was going on. I told Rusty I'd had enough: of flying; of everything. He was understanding and treated me more than fairly. The result was that Bob and I were both given a very fair severance package and we both moved on. It would be 15 years before I ever set foot on another airport, except to fly with airlines. I wanted nothing to do with helicopters, airplanes or people.

I filed for divorce and put the ranch up for sale. I was a dead man walking. Hurt, depressed, embarrassed, humiliated and totally alone within myself, I shunned everyone and everything. I felt that everyone knew what had happened and all I wanted to do was get away to where no one knew me. The only people I cared to be around were Buzz and Uncle Phill. The lines from a Pink Floyd song came to me:

"And far from flying high in clear blue skies,
I'm spiraling down to the hole in the ground,
Where I hide."

And hiding was exactly what I wanted to do.

PART SIX

Chapter 77

Building the Wall - June 2001

It was all gone now. I'd had enough and just gave up. I turned the ranch over to the new owner and left Rey de Reyes with a friend. I put everything I owned in a storage locker, loaded up my motor home with a few clothes and personal items and hit the road.

The hardest thing had been saying goodbye to my kids and my brown lab, Oliver. I wanted to take him with me, but we were both getting old, and it wasn't practical. I knew my pal Don would be his new best friend and love him as I had.

As I drove north up Interstate 17, every few miles brought back memories of my news days and events I had participated in: a search here, an accident there, or a plane crash over that hill. I went through Flagstaff and onto Highway 89 and the Navajo Reservation. I had traveled that highway so many times on the way to Lake Powell with my little girls, all of us giggling and laughing, every few minutes hearing, "Daddy, are we there yet?"

As hard as I tried, I could not keep those thoughts out of my head. When I came to the junction of highways 89 and 89a I had to make a choice. A right turn onto 89 would take me to Page and Lake Powell. I took 89a, even though it was longer and a much slower drive. Visiting my family in Page and driving by the lake was out of the question. I didn't even call my close friend and cousin, Steve Ward. I didn't want to see or talk to anyone.

By early morning I had made it to Interstate 80 and turned west toward Battle Mountain, Nevada. I was beat and in no hurry, so I pulled into a Flying J truck stop, parked in the lot, showered, cleaned house, had lunch and got some sleep.

While sitting at the lunch counter of the truck stop, I'd overheard two truckers talking about the severe shortage of drivers. According to them, it was a driver's market and the pay was good. Actually, the pay was lousy, but what really appealed to me was that it was something to do with myself; something to take my mind off all I'd been through.

Financially, I was okay, having sold my mom's house and my half of the ranch. What I was really looking for was to blend into a new life and start again. I needed to look around and see the country. I really didn't know what was out there.

After lunch I was back on the interstate with a three-hour drive to my Uncle Phill's place. An idea was beginning to take form. I was driving about 65 miles an hour on a 75-mph highway, and the big rigs were nearly blowing me off the road as they sailed by. I started noticing that many of the trailers had stickers offering driving jobs—no experience needed.

Truck drivers roamed all over the country in big, beautiful rigs, pulling 53-foot trailers. Forty years earlier I had been delivering freight around Phoenix, and I had always loved trucks. Drivers also had that big sleeper to live in while on the road. I needed to think through this idea.

Battle Mountain, Nevada is right on Interstate 80, halfway between Salt Lake City and Reno. Located in Lander County, said to contain the world's richest gold and silver trends, the little city of around 3500 residents has only one stop light, which flashes amber and red 24 hours a day.

The landscape is high desert, elevation 4500 feet, in a huge valley surrounded by mountains, some of which reach over 8000 feet. Outside the city are rural homes, ranches and farms, scattered around the huge valley.

Uncle Phill's property was about six miles outside of town, and a mile off the Interstate. It's easy to spot because his maintenance shop is the largest building in the area, standing nearly four stories, all white, and sprayed with a bright white foam to keep it warm in the winter and cool in the summer.

As I turned off the interstate access road I drove by the Battle Mountain airport, where I used to land when I'd fly in for a visit. Most of the homes in the area are manufactured, and very few outside of the city are landscaped: no trees or grass, just gravel they call "chirt."

The only small ranch in sight that had trees, shrubs, and a lawn, was just before the turnoff into my uncle's gate and property, a 26-acre parcel of land he called "the yard." The entire property was fenced, graded and covered with dark chirt, and it was all business.

Gigantic equipment storage shed

Besides the large white shop, I also noticed the heavy equipment, motor homes, camp trailers, and two huge drilling rigs mounted on triple-axel tractors. This was all part of Uncle Phill's mining operation. His mine, the Dee, was one of twelve deposits in the Carlin Trend, and he was doing quite well with it.

The most striking vehicle in the yard was his Cadillac Biarritz, with gold-plated hubcaps, grille, headlights, fenders and door locks. The hood ornament was adorned with diamonds, rubies and emeralds. It was a sight to behold!

There was a nice-looking prefab house on the property that Uncle Phill had had built several years ago. But he'd been in his old trailer for so long he hadn't quite been able to make the move into the house. The whole operation looked very impressive; but most importantly, it looked familiar. I was home.

I parked my motor home behind the shop and was immediately challenged by the security guard, but I paid no attention. I just smiled and turned around to see my grinning uncle. After a quick hug and small talk, we hooked up my home to the shop and the satellite TV.

There was no need to explain anything, since we had been talking nearly every day. Later that evening we sat outside my motor home and I fixed dinner: two cans of Chef Boyardee spaghetti and meatballs, followed by root beer floats.

The weeks and months became a blur. I only knew when weekends rolled around because of NASCAR and sports on TV. I became an avid reader and when I wasn't watching the tube, I was reading about submarines or first-person stories of Vietnam.

Occasionally I'd go into Battle Mountain, where I learned that Uncle Phill had a reputation as a recluse and a bit of a character. He was either thought to be eccentric, (maybe because he had purchased a 30-foot cruiser, though there was no water for miles around) or a good businessman, depending on who was telling the story. Some said he'd become weird and suspicious since he began getting regular payments for the gold mining on his property, to the tune of about $75,000 a month. Others said he had reason to be cautious after a girlfriend and some cowboys beat and robbed him of his first

Uncle Phill

month's payment, which he had insisted on taking in cash. I was glad to know he had since decided to trust banks. Some said he had turned mean since that incident, but others thought his orneriness was an act, citing the fact he gave a lot of money to charities and carried candy in his pockets to give to children. All I knew was that he was my uncle and right now, my best friend.

I made another trip to Phoenix to sign papers and collect my half of the divorce spoils. I was very pleased with the outcome and thought the judge got it right. When I got back to Uncle Phill's I was jacked up again about driving an 18-wheeler. I wouldn't be able to handle doing nothing for the rest of my life. I sure couldn't do anything about the past, but I needed to get through this phase of self-pity and humiliation I was struggling with.

Chapter 78

On the Road

Trucking School

By the end of summer I said goodbye to my uncle, packed up, and headed south to San Diego and truck-driving school. Two weeks later I had a commercial license and was fully qualified on paper. Now I needed to find a job, get some experience, and see some of those places I'd pointed out while doing the weather reports.

My first choice was the Phoenix based Swift Trucking. I figured since they knew me, and I had not been convicted of any crime and met all the requirements, it should be easy. I could leave my motor home and pickup in tow in the company lot.

After filling out the correct papers, I was accepted and assigned to the company training school the following Monday. Two days later I was called out of class by the security chief and told I had been fired by the management, who worried about bad publicity if I had a problem.

I applied to another company which turned out to be owned by Swift, though I didn't know it at the time. I got through the three-day familiarization course and was assigned to a truck and an experienced driver–trainer. We were delivering a load to Seattle when we were told to return as soon as we were empty.

The trainer thought that unusual, since we would normally have picked up another load in Seattle and taken it elsewhere. But

I knew immediately what was going on. The next day when we rolled into Phoenix, I was again let go for the same reason.

This confirmed in my mind that my fall from grace had not yet bottomed out. I hooked my pickup to the back of my motor home and headed back to California. This time I was pissed off at the world and determined to make it work if I had to call every trucking company in the country.

In San Diego I stopped by the United Truck Driving School, where I had graduated. I told my former instructor my story and he fixed me right up. "Call this guy at Werner, Jerry, they will snap you right up!" he said. I called the man and three days later I was in Fontana, California, reporting for duty.

The company was Werner Enterprises, based out of Omaha, Nebraska. It was one of the largest trucking firms in the country, and the only one using a "paperless log." That meant they could see where you were in real time, in addition to knowing everything the truck had done. On the plus side, the driver no longer had to keep a paper log like all the other companies.

The computer log was a new system being tested by the company and the Department of Transportation. A computer in a truck was the coming thing.

There was no cheating on the time, since the satellite "knows all." That was okay by me. After three weeks on the road with a trainer, I was given a final driving test in Omaha and assigned to truck #21942. I was now a long haul driver and ready to hit the road.

My first few months were trial and error, however. Pulling into a parking lot at night to a delivery point in Dallas, Texas, I cut the turn too short. This caused my right rear trailer wheels to fall into an irrigation ditch, bringing me to a complete stop and blocking the driveway. Talk about being embarrassed! Every driver in the lot came over to look, laugh, listen, and tell me about the mistakes *they* had made during their early days in the business.

I called the company and told them my problem. Surprisingly, I did not hear a word of criticism from my dispatcher, who called a heavy duty wrecker. Within 45 minutes I was out of the hole and backed into a freight door for unloading. I had a lot to learn about driving a nearly 70-foot-long truck and trailer. It's a bit more difficult than it looks.

Trucking is similar to aviation in that there are a ton of rules and regulations, from the federal, state, and even the local level.

I remembered a bit of philosophy from my instructor in San Diego. "There are so many ways to get into trouble, and you can be sure someone out there is likely watching and waiting for you to make a mistake. It could be a 'bear in the air,' or a 'snake in the grass.'"

I had written it down, because he could as easily have been talking about the FAA. There is no escaping the bureaucrats. They are everywhere and have complete control of the industry. I had been through it with flying and had tried to fight the system. I went into trucking to get away from everything and hide behind my wall, but there was no escaping the watchful eyes.

The best part of the driving job was the truck. Werner bought the best. I had a long-nose Freightliner Classic. It was blue with dark blue accent stripes, powered by a big 550 horsepower diesel engine. It had plenty of power, but company insurance regulations required a governor set at 65 mph.

That was the only negative about the job. In states like Arizona, where the speed limit is posted at 75, trucks with no speed restrictions sail by, making 65 mph feel like you're walking. Some other states, like California, limit the truck's speed to 55 mph. Since company drivers are paid by the mile, the lower speeds hurt them financially, not to mention all the hands that are held out looking for their part of the money.

The driver is responsible for the weight and balance of his or her trailer and load, just as a pilot is for his aircraft. Regulations also require the driver to do a daily inspection of his rig. If he's pulled over for a safety check, he had better have everything ship-shape to avoid a violation followed by a citation. It's all about money, and drivers can't afford too many mistakes or fines.

Drivers are watched closely by law enforcement. There are weigh stations in every state that trucks must pass through. The maximum gross weight is 80,000 pounds, and must be distributed evenly over each axle. Weight can be shifted by sliding the rear axles on the trailer forward or backward. It's easy enough to do, but it's also easy to make a mistake. Trucks found to be overweight can be held until the driver conforms to the regulations, which can mean a long wait until the driver figures out how to shed those pounds. Usually another company truck is sent to off-load the excess. As in any profession, if you do the job as you were trained, that and a little luck will keep you out of trouble.

The biggest surprise to me was how drivers are treated when they pick up or deliver a load. When assigned a load by the dispatcher, the driver is given a pick up time and a delivery time. Many times a driver would have to wait hours for his customer to load or unload his truck, which could cause a problem between the driver and the customer. Often tensions would flare. The worst situations were the large warehouses, where a dozen or more trucks were backed into loading docks while just as many more were waiting for a door. During those situations the tension was thick.

I never had a problem with a customer. For one thing, I was new and just wanting to stay busy and pass the time. If I encountered a long wait I spent the time in my truck, where I had a TV, refrigerator, microwave, stereo, laptop, lots of food and snacks, and a good selection of books.

Showers, meals, groceries, audio books, and everything I needed were available at truck stops. I didn't use the CB radio very often, but when a driver needed help all he or she had to do was call out on channel 19, and help or directions was readily available.

I was molded into the truck driver system and spent a lot of time zig-zagging all over the country. The coast-to-coast trips took several days, depending on weather and road conditions. In the six months I stayed with Werner, they sent me all over the country for 21 days out of every month. Then I was given two days off, and that became a problem. It just wasn't enough time.

Chapter 79

Linda

It was during my trucking days that I met Linda Smith online. She was a schoolteacher who graduated from ASU with a Master's Degree in Elementary Education and was getting close to retirement. We became good friends over the next couple of years, and helped each other through the heartbreaking aftermath of divorce, which we had both just experienced. She had lived in Phoenix since 1961 and had known me from my TV days, but we seldom talked about it. We both just took things one day at a time.

Like me, Linda was an only child. Her parents had both worked for NASA in California. After retiring, they moved to Sun City, just west of Phoenix. Linda's world was teaching and taking care of her parents and mine was being on the road. Before long, that two days off a month just wasn't working for me, so I told my dispatcher that I wanted more time at home. I was now over 60 years old and had learned just how tough truckers had it.

One day while on the road, I met a trucker who had retired as a pilot for Garrett-Air-Research in Arizona. He was now driving for Stewart Transport, a small company out of Phoenix. He told me it was easier to get time off with them, or even work part-time. It was just what I was looking for.

During my next trip to Phoenix I called Colin Stewart, who owned several trucks and trailers. He invited me to come on down that afternoon. I told him why I wanted to leave Werner, and that I didn't have a lot of experience, but I was accident-free and qualified. He offered me a part-time job and I accepted.

I still did a lot of driving, but the schedule allowed for several days off if it was at all possible. Colin was a good guy to work for and so were his dispatchers. I don't know whether they knew of my "infamous" side, but nothing was said and I never brought it up.

My inexperience finally caught up with me and I had two incidents right off the bat. In Illinois I backed into a stall at night and knocked a piece of the wall down. Then I side-swiped another tractor while pulling out of a stall in Arizona. They were both minor and didn't require an accident report, but still … I'd had 23,000 hours in all kinds of aircraft with no pilot-error accidents. Simply put, it was inexperience.

I remembered back to my starting days in aviation. I made some stupid mistakes that could have cost me my life. Every one of those mistakes was from inexperience. The longer I drove, the better I felt. It was the same story as when I was a young pilot.

Once in New Jersey I got lost and somehow ended up at the main gate of a prison. That caused a bit of a commotion because the main gate arch was two feet lower than my rig, and there was no place to turn around. Because I was blocking the road, the local police had to be called to help me back across a major intersection. I was a dumb-ass truck driver and that's exactly how I was treated. But I just smiled and showed them what they wanted to see and kept my mouth shut. Finally, with a little difficulty, I managed to back through the busy intersection with patrol cars on all sides. When I finally got in position to move forward, I smiled and waved, and without moving my lips, I yelled, "Jerks!"

The ten-hour days on the road gave me a lot of time to think. Try as I might, I could not get over the deceit that had ended my flying career. I could tell myself I didn't care, but I did. And try as I might to find someone to blame, I couldn't. Every problem I'd had, had been caused by me.

It was ironic that I was finally grounded by the actions of a former Marine Corps fighter pilot: Bob Oliver. So much for "Semper Fidelis," which translates to, "Always Faithful."

October 15, 2004 brought another big change in my life. Linda and I had become very close, and decided to get married. We flew to Buffalo, New York, planning to have the ceremony at Niagara Falls. We got a marriage license at the city clerk's office in Buffalo, and asked for directions to wedding chapels near the falls.

After seeing one, we looked at each other and decided it was too commercial. What we really wanted was a little white chapel in a scenic location. We drove through the countryside near the finger lakes until we found the Lighthouse Church, where the wonderful minister and his staff were happy to perform the ceremony.

For the next two days we drove the back roads of New York. It was the perfect time of year, with fall colors painting the countryside. The state took on a whole new meaning for us desert dwellers. We drove into New York City briefly, but after getting lost in Yonkers, we beat it out of town and back into the country. It was an incredible trip.

Back home, we settled in Sun City to be close to Linda's parents who were moving into an assisted-living complex. We began renovating our house; updating the bathrooms and the patio.

Now that I was a married man again, with a real home, I wanted a job that would allow me to be there and enjoy it. I had stumbled across a good driving job with the local Kenworth Truck dealer in Phoenix.

When a truck was purchased by a customer out of state, I would deliver it to other owners or dealers and bring back a used truck to be sold in Arizona. If there was no trade-in, I jumped on an airline and came home. It was exactly what I was looking for, and I was kept as busy as I wanted to be.

I was on a delivery in Illinois when Linda called to tell me her Dad had died peacefully, after having suffered terribly with Alzheimer's. In many ways it was a blessing, but losing a parent is heartbreaking under any circumstances. Linda was a "Daddy's Girl," and took his death very hard. She found a wonderful assisted-living home for her mother nearby, and we both visited regularly. I enjoyed helping Linda with her mother and wished so many times that I was caring for my own little mom.

By this time, Kari, Andryea and Barry were all married and doing fine. I was so proud of my daughters, and I was a very proud grandpa as well.

Life was so much better now, but I still kept to myself. When I was home I played tennis for two hours every morning to stay in shape. One good thing about a retirement area is that there is always someone to play with.

I hadn't seen Uncle Phill in nearly a year, though I had talked to him several times a week. He was in his 70s by this time and seemed to be doing alright. He had always been the wild and reckless one, and the one we figured would be the first to go. Yet he had already outlived everyone in his generation of the family. However, that was about to change.

Linda wrote a very touching account of my last adventure with my beloved Uncle Phill, which I've chosen to use here, just as she wrote it.

Chapter 80

The Summer of 2005
by Linda Foster

Give, and it shall be given unto you; good measure, pressed down, and shaken together, and running over. Luke 6:38

This is the verse that represents the summer of 2005. It was the summer of Uncle Phill and Battle Mountain. It was the summer of love, keeping a promise, giving, and going home.

When Jerry's mother was alive, she asked Jerry to take care of Uncle Phill and she asked Uncle Phill to take care of Jerry if either of them were in need. They both agreed to do this. She really didn't have to ask either of them to do so, because they would have done so anyway. But a promise was made, and a promise would be kept.

In May, Uncle Phill sent Jerry the doctor's reports of some tests he had taken. He wanted Jerry to read them and tell him what they meant. The news was not good. Uncle Phill had cancer of the colon and it had spread to his liver. Jerry didn't waste any time packing the motorhome and taking off for Battle Mountain to tell Uncle Phill the results of his tests, and to do whatever was necessary to help him through this illness.

Since Uncle Phill was such a private person and tended to be rather a recluse, Jerry was worried about him accepting help ... even from his nephew. But after a huff and a puff or two, Uncle Phill handed over all the keys and accepted Jerry's help. He realized that he needed Jerry to be his right hand, his strength, and his rowboat in the storm. So it began. Jerry lived in the motorhome and Uncle Phill lived in his trailer. It was where he had lived for many years and it was where he was comfortable.

For a while Jerry didn't know just what to do with himself. He began cooking for Uncle Phill and they visited on and off throughout the day ... but there were many unfilled hours. The place was a total mess.

The beautiful shop was in total disarray and every surface in the big mobile home had piles of paper from the businesses. There wasn't a single empty spot. After a while Jerry decided to dig in and the work began. He spent all of May and June organizing, rearranging, and going to the dump. He wondered if Uncle Phill would question him about the trips to the dump, but he never said a word. He just watched as Jerry left time and time again with the pickup filled to the brim. Uncle Phill quietly realized that Jerry was doing what needed to be done.

By the middle of July the double-wide mobile home finally looked like a home and Jerry moved in. At about the same time the bathrooms and patio reconstruction were finally complete in our Sun City home, and it was time for me to join Jerry and Uncle Phill in Battle Mountain. Barry and Jeff took me and our little dog, Rudy, to Las Vegas where Jerry met us. We went the rest of the way with him. It was a very long trip, but it was without incident and we were grateful to arrive safely. I was so surprised at how lovely the house was when I saw it for the first time. Jerry had worked so hard to make it clean and beautiful for me. It was so much more than I expected.

For the first three weeks I was there I didn't see Uncle Phill. We tried and tried to get him to move into the big house with us, but he would have none of it. He said that he had lived with little Edie (his dog) in his small trailer all those years, and he wouldn't think of living anywhere else. Uncle Phill and I talked on the phone during the day. He would call and tell me what he wanted to eat for breakfast, lunch, and dinner. From time to time we would just visit on the phone. He had become so thin that he didn't want to be seen by anyone except Jerry. So we did just what he wanted to do. Later, he didn't seem to mind if I saw him.

Uncle Phill went through several menu obsessions. Before I got there, Jerry was cooking rice by the pound for him. Then Phill decided that new potatoes were the way to go. After I got there he was really into french toast for breakfast. He would call it "omelet toast." He had to have it every morning for a while. Then he decided that he needed to have salmon. Of course there was no salmon in Battle Mountain, so Jerry and I went to Elko and bought several packages of it. After I fixed one of the salmon steaks for dinner, I gave him half of it. The next morning he was *beaming from ear to ear and told Jerry that the salmon had really done the job and that he had gained eight pounds! We had a good laugh about that one.*

The next jag was bananas and "avecadios." I am spelling it like that, because that is how he pronounced it...avecadios. We started saying it that way too, just to make us smile. Then he discovered my cream of chicken soup. He thought that was the best thing he had ever tasted. So from then on, he had "white soup" nearly every day. He would have white soup with fried eggs, with apple sauce, with spaghetti, and with anything else that we could get him to try.

While we were caring for Uncle Phill, Jerry and I made a new life in Battle Mountain. We had our own little routines. We went to the post office nearly every day. Two or three days a week we had lunch at the Senior Center. It had wonderful food, and it was only $1.25 each. We sure couldn't beat that. We also had lunch at the Mexican food restaurant, the Colt, the Owl, and McDonalds. But we always had dinner at home. We were never gone too long, because we wanted to keep an eye on Uncle Phill. Every couple of weeks or so we left early in the morning to go to Elko or Winnemucca to buy groceries and other things we needed. But we were always home by early afternoon. Jerry continued to work in the shop and I painted on flower pots and bird houses. Jerry fixed all the screens on the house and he even painted it. We kept busy and enjoyed the sunrises and sunsets. Even Rudy kept busy. He learned to wear little boots to keep his feet from getting stickers, and he took trip after trip to the studio and the shop.

We also met some very good friends. We had lovely neighbors and we found new friends at the Senior Center and at church. The people in this little town were very friendly and eager to help in any way they could. We felt very accepted and welcome in our new community.

Days turned into weeks and weeks turned into months. Toward the end of August Uncle Phill was not doing well. Jerry was becoming more and more uneasy about him. From the time I arrived, I would watch Jerry get up each morning and look out the window with his binoculars over to Uncle Phill's window to see if he was stirring. He had this dread of Uncle Phill passing in the night and him having to go over there and break the door down, and finding Phill dead. He worried about it all the time. Uncle Phill's stomach was becoming more and more bloated and distended. He was miserable. The doctor had told Jerry that when we thought Phill was too uncomfortable to stay in his home, that he could be brought to the hospital. So Jerry told Uncle Phill we thought he needed to go to the hospital so that he could feel more comfortable. He had gone a couple of times before to get blood transfusions and that did make him feel better, so he was willing to go. This time however, he needed to stay. We were both worried that Uncle Phill would put up a fuss and not be willing to submit to the treatments that were recommended for him. We were wrong. The Lord must have talked to him, because he did everything he was asked to do. He was gentle and had a sweet spirit in all that was asked of him. He had one little outburst when he was mistakenly told that he would have to leave due to a Medicare problem. When Jerry walked in he was sitting on the side of the bed and he said, "WE'RE OUT OF HERE!" But dear Dr. Peters came in and gently assured everyone that this was an error and that all was well. Outside the room, Dr. Peters told Jerry that Uncle Phill could stay there for the rest of his life. It was then that we knew that his journey was nearly over.

Uncle Phill certainly didn't know that his journey was nearly over. He totally believed that he would be healed. He wouldn't talk about death and he didn't want anyone else to talk about death. He would say, "I don't want to hear any of that negative talk!" He made certain that we kept giving his tithe to the different ministries that he supported, and he always had a positive attitude. Even after he was on morphine around the clock, his moments of clarity were moments of faith. Once when Jerry touched him, he opened his eyes and said, "I'm really doin' good." Another time he managed to raise his hand and give the OK sign. It always brought a smile to Jerry's face. And I think he was healed. Cancer took him from this earth, but the minute he left, he was healed when he was with the Father. It was the Father who sent Jesus to save him and prepare the way for him to be healed when he took his last breath here on this earth.

One day when I was sitting with Uncle Phill when he was first brought into the hospital, I asked him to tell me about when he was saved. He said that he was about 8 or 9 years old when he gave his heart to the Lord while he was in church. Since his dad was a minister he was *in church a lot when he was little. It was at that moment that I felt at ease for his future. I have always felt that if you can remember the time you gave your heart to the Lord, then you really did it. If you can't remember the experience then I wonder if it actually happened. There must be a time and a place that you actually say the words ... Lord Jesus, I accept you as my Lord and Savior. Come into my heart and save me from my sins.*

He gave millions of dollars to his ministries. He gave to the poor. He gave to hospitals and the needy. But only accepting Christ as his Savior opened the doors to heaven. The thing is ... when you love the Lord, you have a need to give back to Him in any way that you can. Uncle Phill lived his faith. Yes, he was healed from his cancer. Right now he is fully healed and praising the Lord.

During the days Uncle Phill was in the hospital, Jerry was with him from early in the morning until late at night. He would leave home about dawn and return after dark. I would go to see them in the middle of the day and take Jerry out for a bite of lunch. While there, I watched Jerry attend to Uncle Phill as only a loved one can do. He would cover him, uncover him, straighten his bedding, gently touch his arm, lift a fallen leg back into bed, and swab his dry mouth. He was so caring and vigilant in his watch. There had been a lot of love over the years. Jerry's memories of Uncle Phill were happy memories ... joyous memories. There had been love, even though it had been an unspoken love. I was so very pleased that during these past few months there was also spoken love. Uncle Phill told both of us over and over how much he appreciated all that we had done for him and that he loved us. Then ... in the hospital during these last days ... both Jerry and Uncle Phill told of their love, each to the other.

On September 6, 2005 just after Jerry had gotten home at the end of the day, the phone rang and it was the hospital. Uncle Phill had died. He waited until Jerry had gone, and then he took his last breath. He probably didn't want Jerry to have to live with hearing that last breath. We went to the hospital and spent some time with him. A couple of Phill's dearest friends came and we all sat quietly for a while and prayed. Then they left. It was just Uncle Phill, Jerry, and me. I left the room and it was Uncle Phill and Jerry. Jerry came out and joined me and we went home. It had all been so very peaceful. He didn't have great pain, he didn't die in his trailer, and Jerry didn't have to break in, as he was afraid he would have to do. There was no pain, there were loving words, and there was peace. Uncle Phill's journey was Jerry's journey, and it was my journey too.

After Uncle Phill died, we stayed in Battle Mountain a few more weeks. We continued to work on the place and we even had a lovely deck built onto the house. Jerry had asked Uncle Phill what he would like him to do with the place if the time came that he had to make decisions about it. Uncle Phill said that he would like for Jerry and me to enjoy it. So that is our plan. Until the perfect person comes along to buy the property and really enjoy the shop, Jerry and I will spend May to October in Battle Mountain and October to May in Sun City. We will become Sun Birds.

Since we have been back in Arizona I have heard Jerry tell our story about caring for Uncle Phill. Every time he tells it, he always ends it by saying what a wonderful experience it was. Jerry feels so blessed that he was able to be there for his uncle. Every memory is a blessing. Every job, every meal, every errand, and every trip to the dump turned out to be a string of blessings. The giving to this dear man turned out to be a package full of blessings. The Bible says ... Give, and it shall be given unto you; good measure, pressed down, and shaken together, and running over. This is truly the story of the Summer of 2005. We did everything we could for Uncle Phill. And in return, our blessings were pressed down, and shaken together and running over.

Chapter 81

Final Thoughts

Years ago, when my mother came up with the money for me to earn my pilot's certificate, she had said it was "pennies from heaven," and that's all she would say. While going through my uncle's things I found a receipt for $800.00 which had been paid to Saguaro Aviation for my lessons and supplies. Attached to the receipt was the bank loan, co-signed by Mom. The collateral was the same little trailer that Uncle Phill bought in 1958 and had lived in ever since.

When he hit the gold strike in 1985, he had the house built that he never lived in, and the new Cadillac El Dorado Biarritz that he seldom drove. The car sat in the shop at Uncle Phill's place for years, and is still showroom clean. All he wanted was to look at it. He felt more comfortable driving his little Toyota pickup, and living in his little trailer. He was still just a miner at heart.

I put his place up for sale and priced it high, figuring someone might come along who needed a large shop. Battle Mountain has a population of not quite 3,000 and I didn't expect there was much of a market for the place. But I was wrong.

Three months after we returned to Arizona, the realtor called and said she had sold the place. *Whoa*, I thought, and I tried to get out of it. Somehow, I wasn't ready to let it go. The realtor said "No way," because the buyer was paying the full price, and I no longer had a choice.

I returned to Battle Mountain for probably the last time. I collected the things I wanted to keep and left the rest for the new owner. I loaded it all into my new Ford dually, hooked the Cadillac up to the back and hauled it all to Arizona. Like my dear old uncle, I seldom drive the Caddy, but I look at it every day, smile, and remember. What a guy!

So there you have it. End of story? No, not really, because I still had my fame and shame back home. But one of my little daughters would come up with the solution that saved me, and I would once again be the man I had told all those school kids I was.

And that would be … "the happiest guy in this world."

EPILOGUE

My life with Linda had settled into a comfortable routine. We had our house in Sun City, and I played tennis for two hours every day with other retired guys. It was good exercise and not once was I asked about my time as a TV guy. We lived a very quiet life, with occasional visits from daughters Kari, Andy, and Barry.

We bought a place in Show Low, Arizona, where we spend the summers and enjoy watching nature. However, I still kept a low profile, not making an effort to see anyone except my kids and my friend Buzz. I still felt the shame of the indictment and the humiliation of Vicki and Bob's betrayal. I also had a sense that all those viewers who had enjoyed my exploits during my TV days now felt betrayed as well, and had written me off.

I couldn't have been more wrong.

In late 2009 my daughter Andryea encouraged me to get on Facebook. I was leery of putting myself out there again, and was sure I'd be setting myself up for another round of criticism. Andy convinced me to give it a try. "What's the worst that could happen?" she asked.

She set up my Facebook page and showed me how to use it. But it would be months before I could post anything on it. Every now and then I would comment on someone else's post, half hoping no one would notice, and certainly hoping no one would connect my name to the hot-shot helicopter pilot who'd had so much negative attention nearly a decade ago.

But I was soon pleasantly surprised to discover there were many who *did* recognize the name, and were happy to know I was still around! In addition to the "I thought you'd died," and "Where have you been hiding?" comments, others were positive, encouraging, and uplifting. Tears filled my eyes as I read ...

"Happy Birthday to the best pilot the valley ever knew!"

"I have many fond memories of you coming to my elementary school!!! You are awesome!"

" ... the high flying master. The man all others look up to (figuratively and literally) for achievement."

"You were a hero to our family, and you inspired my son to become a helicopter pilot."

... and many more similar comments. I still had fans out there; many of whom had been kids when I visited their schools, and many others who tuned into Channels 10 and 12 to see what I'd been up to that day.

I even heard from Bud Wilkinson, the TV critic who had been so disparaging of my poor grammar, among other things. He now commented that he may have been more negative than necessary in those days, and hoped there were no hard feelings.

The result of all this was the realization that I wasn't the pariah I had imagined myself to be; that those who had been fans during my flying days were still interested in my life; that those who wondered "whatever happened to..." were now happy to discover I was still around. I began to come out of my self-imposed exile, and post comments back to these friends.

Andryea encouraged me to write a book about my exploits: the good, the bad, and the ugly. I had my doubts about that. My first concern was that no one would want to read about my life. The second was that once my friends learned about my ghosts from the past, I'd lose the few friends I had reconnected with.

Once again, by putting on Facebook hints of what was to come if this book were to be published, I discovered just how many people *were* eager to read it. Nearly everyone encouraged me; reminding me we all had skeletons in our closets, we'd all made mistakes, and no one is perfect. With this reassurance, I moved forward with the project. I discovered that writing about it all has been cathartic, and has helped me realize that much of the time, I was my own worst critic.

In the way the world works, I also discovered on Facebook the person who would make this dream of a book come true. Dee Dees saw one of my comments to a post by a mutual friend, and wrote a very touching note, telling me her son had become a helicopter pilot after meeting and watching me as he grew up. When Andryea saw that Dee was a writer of life stories, we contacted her and knew she was the person who could make this happen. Over the two and a half years we've worked on this book, our families have become close friends.

Today I'm happier than I've ever been. My daughters and grandchildren are blessings in my life, along with Linda, who keeps me stable. I'm happy to say that Dianna—the mother of my two youngest girls—and I are still friends and can now joke about the rough times we had.

I'm thrilled to have reconnected with Bryan and Susan, my team at Channel 12, who have come back into my life. We're as close now as we ever were. I know now it wasn't they who left behind what we'd shared, it was I, when I walked away from life.

I'm also excited to have reconnected with so many others I had shut out of my life during my downward spiral: Larry Black, John Bass, Chuck Emmert, Jim Willi, Al Buch, Ed Mell, Tom Gerczynski and so many others.

I'm especially touched by all the Facebook friends I've come to know and love; people who remembered me from back in the day, and who let me know that I meant something to them, that they appreciated my efforts and even enjoyed my "folksy, chatty, way of speaking." My poor grammar didn't bother them a bit; they liked that I came across as human.

One of those new Facebook friends, Dave Boehmer, grew up watching me on TV. As I was finishing this book, Dave invited me to join him and others aboard a houseboat at Lake Powell. The houseboat was owned by the Norgrens, who built it as a legacy for their family. "Captain" Kerry Norgren had been one of the kids who watched me fly into his schoolyard years ago.

This trip impacted me in so many ways. It allowed me to reconnect with people I had once touched, as well as a place I've always loved; Lake Powell. The kids I entertained over 30 years ago were now adults entertaining me: on the boat, on Facebook, and with their stories of remembering me from years past. While sitting on the deck one day, reflecting on how my life had come full circle, another poignant irony struck me. My original intention in writing this book was simply to leave a legacy for my children and grandchildren. The name of the houseboat I was now enjoying ... the *Legacy*.

If there are lessons to be learned from any of this, here's what I came away with.

1) One stupid, thoughtless action *can* ruin your life, though it doesn't have to. But even if you overcome it and move on to better things, as I did, you'll always be looking over your shoulder wondering when "they" will find out about it. It's smarter to think about the future ramifications before acting on impulse and doing something you'll probably regret.

2) Nothing is so bad that you can't overcome it. If you've already made that stupid mistake, from this point on, do whatever it takes to make your life the best it can be, to be productive, and to help others. If you do so, those who learn of your past will often be able to overlook it; just as Barry Goldwater, Homer Lane, Tom Chauncey, Pep Cooney, Karl Eller and many others did for me.

3) Never assume others will turn their backs on you. All of us have made our own mistakes at some point or another, and everyone understands what we are going through. Those who can't or won't understand are judgmental and we don't need them in our lives anyway.

4) Let others help you—especially emotionally. When you most want to go into hiding, that's when you most need to have people around you. Let those who love you be there for you.

My only regret now is that I lost so many years hiding, feeling sorry for myself, and believing that no one wanted to be around me. But, as I've finally learned, it does no good to look back. The future can be whatever we choose—and I choose to see only the good things in life.

I choose to spend the rest of my years being thankful for the amazing career I had, the lessons learned along the way, and mostly for my wonderful, supportive family and friends. You all know who you are.

I did not write this book as a tell all. In fact I did *not* tell all. I still have secrets and very personal things in my life that I choose not to reveal, just like everyone else. My critics saw it one way, I saw it another. At this point in my life it doesn't matter.

I lived two lives during my broadcasting career. My roots were the mining and lumber camps. My elders and friends were rough and tough miners and lumberjacks. I was raised by an honest, hard-working family. In a manner of speaking, we came from and lived in the poor side of town and that's where I was most comfortable.

My "other life" as a celebrity was one that I slowly adapted to, but I never felt quite at home there.

I don't blame anything or anyone except myself for the mistakes I made. I learned many things the hard way and paid dearly. I will go to my grave apologizing to those I offended. Now that I have written this book, I have nothing to hide—and that truly is a good feeling.

So there you have it. It has taken me nearly three years to write this autobiography and I am happy and relieved to be back from the deep abyss I had created. I'm 73 years old as I complete this, and I'm back to living a wonderful life; very thankful for so many things I had previously taken for granted.

As I look back on my life, I know I was able to help and in some cases save the lives of those in need. I believe the good outweighs the bad and I'm satisfied with that. Could it be that God sent me here for that purpose? I choose to think He did and I am forever grateful.

There is a popular saying in flying circles that goes something like this:

"There are *old* pilots and there are *bold* pilots ... but there are *no* old, bold pilots!"

Really?

Shine on You Crazy Diamond

More
Photos

*Ready for a flight with
Senator Goldwater*

My friend Larry Black

*The Lake Patrol team - an amazing group of guys.
I was proud to be associated with them.*

The most peaceful place in the world; the bottom of the Grand Canyon, where I loved to sit and reflect on the surrounding beauty.

Ollie Carey - good friend of the Goldwaters and ours

Even with all my problems with the NPS, this ranger and I were able to laugh and share our stories of Goldwater.